D1159941

Southern Biography Series
Bertram Wyatt-Brown, Editor

Notorious Woman,

THE CELEBRATED CASE OF MYRA CLARK GAINES

Elizabeth Urban Alexander, 1947-
iii

 Louisiana State University Press   BATON ROUGE

Copyright © 2001 by Louisiana State University Press
All rights reserved
Manufactured in the United States of America
First printing
10 09 08 07 06 05 04 03 02 01
5   4   3   2   1

Designer: Barbara Neely Bourgoyne
Typeface: Sabon
Typesetter: Coghill Composition, Inc.
Printer and binder: Thomson-Shore, Inc.

Library of Congress Cataloging-in-Publication Data:

Alexander, Elizabeth Urban, 1947–
    Notorious woman : the celebrated case of Myra Clark Gaines /
Elizabeth Urban Alexander.
        p. cm.
    Includes bibliographical references and index.
    ISBN 0-8071-2698-5 (cloth : alk. paper)
    1. Clark, Daniel, 1766–1813—Wills. 2. Gaines, Myra Clark,
1805–1885—Trials, litigation, etc. I. Title.

KF759.C57 A43 2001
346.7305'2'0269—dc21   2001033449

for my daughters, Lauren and Elizabeth

Contents

Illustrations

Preface

On the second floor of the New Orleans Cabildo—an old government building now serving as a museum—stands a bust of a woman with a small card identifying her as "Myra Clark Gaines, plaintiff in more than three hundred lawsuits in the nineteenth century." No other memorial recognizes the woman who was once called the "scandal of New Orleans." No street in the city is named for her; no marker in the federal courthouse mentions her name. Yet for most of the century, residents of the Crescent City as well as citizens across the United States knew her as the heroine of the era's longest legal melodrama.

The appeal of the Gaines case lies in the mystery surrounding Myra Gaines's claim to be the heir to a fortune in New Orleans real estate. Was she the legitimate daughter of a prominent New Orleans merchant, or was she the "fruit of an adulterous union," as her opponents believed? The paucity of objective evidence for or against Gaines's birthright meant that the trial judges based their decisions on testimony from witnesses whose memory of events long past was often contradictory. As I read through the pages of depositions I found myself sympathizing with Justice Robert Grier, who resented the need to decide a case "established by the dim recollections, imaginations, or inventions of anile gossips!" Both Gaines and her opponents used the opposing testimony to construct courtroom narratives that would convince judges, juries, and spectators of the so-called truth of their versions, and more than one hundred years after her death, New Orleans citizens can still engage in heated arguments over the veracity of Gaines's claims. I have tried to present the case as it developed through its litigation, gradually unfolding testimony and evidence to allow the reader to arrive at his or her own evaluation of Gaines's claims.

My goal is to unravel the strands of Myra Gaines's story and place her struggle in the context of the development of family law during the nineteenth century. Historian David Hackett Fischer has described a literary technique he calls a "braided narrative," which intertwines elements of social history with a narrative of events. Michael Grossberg's *A Judgment for Solomon: The D'Hauteville Case and Legal Experience in Antebellum America,* which demonstrates the use of this technique in legal history, served as a model for my treatment of Gaines's story. In retelling her tale, I have tried to weave together an account of the emergence of domestic relations law, the popularity of sentimental fiction, and the transformation of judicial attitudes toward women with the twists and turns of the litigation that made Gaines famous. The result is, to borrow the favorite label of contemporary newspaper accounts, a "true-life romance" that has fascinated me as much as it enthralled the public and frustrated its lawyers over a century ago.

Legal scholars have paid very little attention to the Gaines proceedings; few modern lawyers outside of New Orleans are familiar with the case once termed "the most interesting . . . in the history of jurisprudence." The last published material appeared in the late 1940s, and no more recent mention of Myra Gaines appears outside of biographical dictionaries. I began my search in the records of the seventeen appearances of the Gaines case before the United States Supreme Court, records that reprinted much of the testimony and outlined the basis of the case. Other records are located in several repositories. The circuit court in New Orleans published three compilations of testimony and briefs for the Gaines case, in 1858, 1877, and 1883. The eight-volume 1883 record is the most extensive, but even its documentation is not complete. Myra Gaines ultimately filed more than eighty suits in the United States courts in Louisiana and more than two hundred in the Confederate courts during the period of Confederate control of New Orleans. In the 1930s, copies of many of the records from the Louisiana Court of Probates and the First Judicial District Court at New Orleans, as well as the original records from the United States Circuit Court and the Confederate courts, were removed to the National Archives, Southwest Region, in Fort Worth, Texas. Without the patient help of Fort Worth archivists Barbara Rust and Meg Hacker and their staff, this book would not exist.

Several problems arose as I began to write. The Gaines case created a legal labyrinth in which getting in was simpler than getting out. Knowing that there is much more to the case than the question of the plaintiff's legitimacy, I chose to focus on the issue of her parents' marriage. Questions concerning the value of the property Gaines claimed consumed much of the later litigation, but those problems appear more suited for lawyerly disputation than historical interest. Another quandary was the question of what name to use in reference to Myra Clark Gaines. She used several last names during the course of her life: Davis, Clark, Whitney, and Gaines. For simplicity, I have used her first name for the period before 1849, when she was widowed for the second time. Likewise, all testimony and legal documents refer to Gaines's mother, Zulime Carrière, as simply "Zulime." To select any one of her several surnames (Carrière, Des-Grange, Clark, or Gardette) would indicate acceptance or disbelief in her story. I have chosen to follow the nineteenth-century model, thus maintaining the mystery of her many marriages. Another puzzle concerns the last name of the Frenchman Zulime Carrière married in 1794. His name appears in the records variously as DesGrange, Desgranges, Degrange, and DeGrange. I have chosen to use the spelling DesGrange consistently since that is the spelling he used when signing the two existing letters written by his hand. Finally, I have avoided long quotations from the trial record, choosing instead to integrate quotations from the testimony into the story of Myra Gaines. Letting the characters speak for themselves allows them to express the impact of events on their lives.

I owe my thanks to many who have read and commented on portions of this manuscript. Dr. Gene Smith, Dr. Ben Procter, Dr. Don Worcester, and Dr. Julie Hardwick, all of Texas Christian University, have been gracious with time and encouragement. I alone am responsible for any errors that remain. Librarians at the Historic New Orleans Collection; the Department of Archives, City of New Orleans; the library of the United States Circuit Court of Appeals; the library of the Louisiana Supreme Court; the library of the Louisiana State Museum; and the Louisiana Collection at the New Orleans Public Library guided me to many sources on Gaines in New Orleans. The staff of the Louisiana Room at the Howard-Tilton Memorial Library at Tulane University helped me copy the printed records of the Gaines case. An archivist at Emory University searched the Nolan Harmon papers and found a copy of the litigation over Myra Gaines's own will, when the New York Surrogate's Court had assured me that it did not exist. Above all, for his unstinting help, enthusiasm, and support—and for rediscovering Myra Gaines—Dr. Ken Stevens of TCU has my many thanks. I could not have finished this book without his aid. Finally, I owe the completion of this manuscript to my husband, who gave me the motto that sits on my desk and was my constant inspiration when writer's block threatened: "Persistence prevails when all else fails." I think Myra Gaines would agree.

Notorious Woman

Introduction

The Celebrated Case of Myra Clark Gaines

On the morning of January 10, 1885, occupants of New Orleans breakfast tables put down their coffee and beignets, picked up their copies of the *Daily Picayune,* and read the obituary of Myra Clark Gaines. For years her wizened figure had been a familiar sight to residents of the Crescent City, always dressed in black silk, a black bonnet on her head with improbably red curls peeping from underneath its brim. The two-column, front-page notice chronicled a life spent in the "shadow of the law." Gaines had challenged the entrenched interests of the New Orleans business community, tied up land titles for more than fifty years, and threatened to bankrupt the city—becoming, in the process, a national celebrity as well as the most notorious and most hated woman in New Orleans.[1]

The lawsuit begun by Myra Clark Gaines in 1834 had all the trappings of classic melodrama—a lost heir, a missing will, an illicit relationship, a questionable marriage, a misplaced trust, and a murder. Lasting over half a century, this struggle by the daughter of Daniel Clark and Zulime Carrière to prove her legitimacy and justify her claim to her father's enormous

1. "Death of Mrs. Myra Clark Gaines," *New Orleans Daily Picayune,* Jan. 10, 1885, p. 1; Anna Clyde Plunkett, *Corridors by Candlelight: A Family Album with Words* (San Antonio, Tex.: Naylor, 1949), 155. The metaphor of the law's "shadow" represents Alexis de Tocqueville's insight into the authority given to "the courts of justice by the general opinion" of Americans. *Democracy in America,* trans. Henry Reeve (New York: Knopf, 1948), 1: 151–2. Michael Grossberg, *A Judgment for Solomon: The D'Hauteville Case and Legal Experience in Antebellum America* (New York: Cambridge University Press, 1996), also employs Tocqueville's metaphor.

fortune excited the interest of the nineteenth-century public, providing fodder for gossips and employment for lawyers. Today, the records of the longest continuous litigation in the history of the United States court system lie moldering in courthouses and libraries, unexamined for more than fifty years.[2]

Few modern lawyers have even heard of the famous lawsuit, but no nineteenth-century attorney could escape knowledge of the Gaines cases. Between 1834 and 1891 the Gaines litigation wound a tortuous path through the American legal system. At one time or another most of the distinguished members of the nineteenth-century American bar participated in the case as attorneys for either Myra Clark Gaines or her adversaries. Such legal luminaries as Reverdy Johnson, Caleb Cushing, Francis Scott Key, Jeremiah Black, and Daniel Webster left their mark on the case. On its main issues the lawsuit came before the United States Supreme Court ten times and before the Supreme Court of Louisiana twice. Counting appeals on collateral issues, the United States Supreme Court heard the Gaines case seventeen times and the Louisiana Court heard it five times. Besides its appearances in these upper chambers, the main lawsuits, or cases arising from them, occupied the probate or district courts of Louisiana and the district or circuit courts of the United States in New Orleans at least seventy times. At almost any moment during the fifty-seven-year lifetime of the litigation, a Gaines lawsuit was pending in one of these many courts. In 1861 Justice James Wayne of the United States Supreme Court, announcing what he hoped and expected to be a final decision,

2. The records of the New Orleans District Courts for the United States and the State of Louisiana that heard the various Gaines cases have been transferred to the National Archives, Southwest Region, in Fort Worth, Texas. During the 1940s, Nolan J. Harmon published *The Famous Case of Myra Clark Gaines* (Baton Rouge: Louisiana State University Press, 1946); Harnett Kane wrote a novel, *New Orleans Woman* (Garden City, N.J.: Sun Dial Press, 1948), based on the case; and Anna Clyde Plunkett published *Corridors by Candlelight* (1949), a memoir of her father Franklin Perin, one of Gaines's attorneys. These books are the most recent printed material on Myra Clark Gaines.

Records of the Gaines case appear in the archives of the Louisiana state court system, the United States federal courts, and the Confederate courts. Louisiana lower courts that heard the case include the court of probates, the Orleans Parish Court, the First Judicial District Court, the Second District Court (a continuation after 1853 of the court of probates), and the Third District Court. Records of all these courts are kept in the New Orleans Public Library. Copies of most proceedings are included in the records of the federal courts that heard the Gaines case. Federal and Confederate court records are preserved in the National Archives at Fort Worth.

termed the Gaines case the "most remarkable" in the history of that Court.[3]

The leading character in this protracted legal contest was Myra Clark Gaines. From 1834 to her death in 1885 at the age of eighty, she fought with energy, persistence, and courage for recognition as the legitimate child and legal heir of her father, Daniel Clark. After her death the administrator of her estate continued the suit six more years for the sole purpose of recovering enough property and damages to pay the expenses of the long litigation.

The events that formed the basis for the Gaines case began in 1787 when Daniel Clark arrived in New Orleans to join his uncle, Colonel Daniel Clark, in business. Ten years later Colonel Clark conveyed all of his extensive property in Louisiana to his nephew, and at the age of thirty Daniel Clark found himself one of the richest men in North America. Clark's many business ventures brought him large revenues that he invested primarily in New Orleans real estate. During the early years of the nineteenth century, as he established himself in New Orleans as "a man of much personal pride and social ambition," Clark became romantically involved with a young Frenchwoman. All accounts of Zulime Carrière emphasized her extraordinary beauty, vivacity, and charm, and both sides of the lawsuit admitted Clark's fascination with her. Myra, daughter of Clark and Carrière, later came to believe that her parents had contracted a legal, though secret, marriage, making her the true heir to Clark's fortune. As she grew up, however, she was raised by friends of Clark and kept in ignorance of her real parentage as well as of her father's death in 1813, when she was nine. Nearly twenty years afterward, Myra and her young husband arrived in New Orleans with a tale of a lost will and a claim that she was the true heir. Few believed her story. For the rest of her life, as a young wife and mother, as the third wife of a prominent general, and as a widow, Myra Clark Gaines pursued the vindication of her "rights."[4]

Estimates of the value of the property at stake in the Gaines case varied,

3. *Myra Clark Gaines v. Duncan N. Hennen*, 24 Howard 553 (1861). Justice Wayne's hope proved premature; the case continued for thirty more years, long after his death in 1867.

4. Deposition of Daniel Coxe, Aug. 25, 1849, in *E. P. Gaines and Wife v. Chew, Relf, Delacroix, et al.*, case no. 122, Circuit Court of the United States, Eastern District of Louisiana, General Case Files, Record Group 21, National Archives, Southwest Region, Fort Worth, Tex.

but in 1861, when the United States Supreme Court heard her suit against the city of New Orleans, amounts mentioned topped $35 million. When the Court decided in favor of Gaines, the newspapers proclaimed her the richest woman in America. The suit involved title to a vast amount of modern New Orleans, including much of Canal Street—then the principal commercial district of the city. Myra Gaines also claimed title to numerous plantations, hundreds of slaves, many bank deposits and shares of bank stock, and rents and profits from Clark's property for all the years since his death. When the Court later decided the main issues of the case, newspapers noted that the occupants of four hundred of the finest residential properties in the city suddenly awoke to the appalling fact that they were no longer the legal owners of their dwellings.[5]

No one knows exactly how much money Myra Clark Gaines received from her long legal battle, but she never recovered more than a tiny fraction of the rumored millions. Six years after her death, final settlement of the claim against the city of New Orleans required the city to pay $923,788. When it reluctantly complied, creditors filed with estate administrators for satisfaction of the loans made to Gaines over the years of her litigation, and lawyers who had never received their fees filed liens on the estate. Totaling more than $860,000, the claims left little for her heirs to divide.[6]

More than one hundred years after the last Gaines case disappeared from the courts, its transcripts do not offer a definitive verdict on Gaines's claims. But describing the case as a series of opposing narratives allows an interpretation of the conflict in terms of a conflict of interpretations. Myra and her supporters told one story; her opponents told another; the opinions of the judges who heard the case told still different stories. Each narrative reflected the backgrounds, prejudices, and preconceptions of its teller. Acknowledging these multiple viewpoints allows the reader to penetrate the layers of meaning intrinsic to this complicated litigation.

The Gaines case creates an intersection through which run many of the most important highways of American cultural history and also demonstrates how popular trials both reflect and shape the society they inhabit.

5. "Decision in the Famous Gaines Case," *New York Times,* Mar. 15, 1861, p. 1; "The Victory of Mrs. Gaines," ibid., p. 4; *New Orleans Daily Picayune,* Dec. 6, 1874, p. 2.

6. "The Gaines Case Settled," *New York Times,* July 27, 1892, p. 1.

During the litigation, the courtroom served as a public site for a contest over the meaning and application of law, translating a complex human dilemma into an adversarial story with which the public could identify. In the nineteenth century, American trial courts assumed what historian Michael Grossberg terms "hegemonic authority over dispute resolutions"; the public commonly accepted that disputes between individuals should be resolved in a court of law. Trial courts became the most visible manifestations of the new republican legal order. As the legal system penetrated deeper and deeper into American social consciousness, it gained a hold over individuals who expressed their desires in terms of rights, duties, and power. The shadow of the law caught Myra Gaines, both her husbands, and her opponents, holding them fast as they used the mechanisms of law to legitimize their versions of "what really happened."[7]

Much recent scholarship has emphasized the dark side of the law—how legal institutions and processes appear as tools of domination and disempowerment. Gaines's opponents used their preeminent position in the New Orleans power structure to delay, confuse, and overwhelm her. The Gaines case demonstrates that law upholds the ideology of the dominant class and reflects the interests of those who make the rules, determine which rules to enforce, and render the decisions. But Myra Gaines's lawsuit also demonstrates that those outside the power structure can use law to advance their own interests. As a place of contest, the courtroom holds the key to empowerment, and the outcome of the Gaines case revealed a deep republican obsession with the misuse of public power.[8]

By capturing the public mind, trials extended the law's hegemony and institutionalized the era's tendency to turn to the law as an arena for resolving conflicts and confronting change. The intense interest generated by the Gaines case indicated the popularity of trials as public entertainment in the cities and states of the new republic. Litigants engaged in nar-

7. Michael Grossberg, "Battling over Motherhood in Philadelphia: A Study of Antebellum American Trial Courts As Arenas of Conflict," in *Contested States,* ed. Mindie Lazarus-Black and Susan F. Hirsch (New York: Routledge, 1994), 154. Another important Louisiana case that began during this period is the Batture Case, which involved Daniel Clark's friend Edward Livingston. (The "batture" is the land between the river water level and the top of the levee.) Unlike the Gaines case, the issue of ownership and use of this property has never been settled and is very much alive in today's courts. The land in question is underneath Harrah's Casino on Canal Street.

8. John L. Comaroff, foreword to *Contested States,* ed. Lazarus-Black and Hirsch, ix; Sally Engle Merry, "Courts as Performances," ibid., 53.

rative competitions to tell their stories in ways designed to arouse public sympathy. The acceptance or rejection of arguments presented in the trials of the Gaines cases offers clues to what stories its audience counted as true or compelling. Myra Clark Gaines and her lawyers ultimately won by constructing a legal narrative that mirrored the accepted version of woman's role in society.[9]

As the New Social History of the 1960s and 70s located women in political organizations and at workplaces, it introduced new arenas and institutions as worthy of study. But this new historical viewpoint took "women" as "a fixed social category, a separate entity, a known phenomenon" and assumed the homogeneous character of women's experiences. The "identity politics" of the 1980s revised the scholarship of the two previous decades and challenged the white, middle-class, heterosexual hegemony of the term "women," arguing that fundamental differences of experience made it impossible to claim a single identity for all. What followed was the fragmentation of the universal notion of women by class, race, sexual identity, and ethnicity. The experiences of Myra Clark Gaines as she fought through the legal system demonstrate that, even within the subgroups, the experiences and expectations of women were not equal.[10]

Alexis de Tocqueville described the "inexorable opinion of the public" that relegates the American woman to a "narrow circle of domestic interests and duties and forbids her to step beyond it." The prevalent picture of a middle-class nineteenth-century white woman (like Myra Gaines) saw her as a lady of leisure, dedicated to a life of fashion "in whose service she distort[ed] her ribcage and internal organs with corsets." The mythology of the lady as the keeper of everything "chaste, unworldly, and moral" in American culture lodged securely in the popular imagination, bolstered by mass-circulation magazines such as *The Ladies' Friend, The Ladies' Magazine and Repository for Entertaining Knowledge,* and *The Weekly Visitor or Ladies' Miscellany.*[11]

9. Grossberg, "Battling over Motherhood in Philadelphia," 172; Lawrence M. Friedman, "Law, Lawyers, and Popular Culture," *Yale Law Journal* 98 (1989):1595.

10. Joan Scott, "Women's History," in *New Perspectives on Historical Writing,* ed. Peter Burke (University Park: Pennsylvania State University Press, 1991), 53 and passim.

11. Tocqueville, *Democracy in America,* 2: 201; Frances B. Cogan, *All-American Girl: The Ideal of Real Womanhood in Mid-Nineteenth Century America* (Athens: University of Georgia Press, 1989), 3. Historians of nineteenth-century culture have traditionally written of women in terms of conflicting dualities or "separate spheres." Jane H. Pease and William H. Pease, *Ladies, Women, and Wenches: Choice and Constraint in*

In any society the classification or labeling of a significant aspect of that society provides control over what is classified. Whatever cannot be classified appears dangerous or frightening. In the nineteenth century the "Cult of Domesticity" generally held that a woman's moral strength kept her home together. But if a woman came down from her pedestal to enter public life, she "would ruin her health, damage her family's well-being, and tarnish the image of womanhood." The woman who deviated from the accepted model of a "lady" risked constant peril; at any moment she might become one of the "threatening, dangerous, unsexed, monsters incarnate" so abhorred by the ladies' magazines.[12]

Historian Anne Douglas argues that women paid only lip service to this ideal, actually exerting considerable power within their homes and churches. But whether a woman played the role of a domesticated gentlewomen, a servant to her husband, a teacher to her children, a maiden aunt, a pious evangelical, a radical reformer, a rebellious millworker, a belle, or a lady bountiful (all categories used by historians to classify nineteenth-century middle-class women), she remained constrained by her gender. Women who ventured out of their homes and into any "public" space found their actions circumscribed by men's conceptions of women's roles. Even feminist leaders who did not accept the dominant social mythology still had to contend with the effects of the myth in their public and private lives. The most successful challenges to male domination in the nineteenth century came from women able to manipulate the classification system without violating it. As the protagonist of a genuine true-life romance, Myra Clark Gaines stepped outside of the traditional, nineteenth-century female role to dominate that most public of spaces—the courtroom—yet she carefully maintained the public persona of a conventional and submissive female when not in that arena. Her entry into the male preserve of the

---

Antebellum Charleston and Boston (Chapel Hill: University of North Carolina Press, 1990), 1. Barbara Welter, in "The Cult of True Womanhood: 1800–1860," *American Quarterly* 18 (summer 1966), found that domesticity, purity, piety, and submissiveness were the virtues most associated with women and the proper woman's sphere of home and family. Michelle Rosaldo's essay, "Women, Culture, and Society: A Theoretical Overview," in *Women, Culture, and Society,* ed. Michelle Z. Rosaldo and Louise Lamphere (Stanford, Calif.: Stanford University Press, 1974), 17–42, developed the concept of public and private space, with women consigned to the private space of the home.

12. Pease, *Ladies, Women, and Wenches,* 8; Sara DeLamont and Lorna Duffin, introduction to *The Nineteenth-Century Woman: Her Culture and Physical World* (London: Croom Helm, 1978), 13–6.

courtroom achieved success by articulating her goal in terms acceptable to the dominant male culture, thereby minimizing hostile response to her actions from both men and women. Public comment, except in the New Orleans newspapers, praised Gaines's devotion and courage. Her combative attitude and willingness to argue with virtually anyone regarding her case did not detract from her image as a loving daughter determined to remove the stigma of licentiousness from her mother's name and the stain of bastardy from her own—an action well within the accepted woman's sphere of family concerns.[13]

Apprehension about the well-being of the family was a special concern during the middle third of the nineteenth century. By 1840 a diverse group of family reformers began to speak of a "crisis in the family." By then Americans had formulated a new moral code based on three principles: the sanctity of marriage, the sacredness of the home, and the dependence of civilized life on the family. Since the family was viewed as the primary institution of American life, the law charged public authorities with maintaining its stability and using its structure to guarantee the peaceful use and future transmission of property. Anything that threatened the family structure—divorce, desertion, male licentiousness—appeared to menace the survival of republican principles. In determining whether the secret marriage of Clark and Carrière was a "true" marriage, the judges who heard the Gaines cases demonstrated how they could translate individual circumstances into legal rulings and how those rulings could shape popular debate. As these nineteenth-century judges assessed the place of one

13. Ann Douglas, *The Feminization of American Culture* (New York: Knopf, 1977); Pease, *Ladies, Women, and Wenches,* 160; Mary P. Ryan, *Women in Public: Between Banners and Ballots, 1825–1880* (Baltimore: Johns Hopkins University Press, 1990), 8; Katherine Fishburn, *Women in Popular Culture: A Reference Guide* (Westport, Conn.: Greenwood Press, 1981), 17; DeLamont, *Nineteenth-Century Woman,* 11–6. Ryan believes that searching for and finding women in public subverts the general assumptions of feminist scholarship, which hold that "social space is divided between the public and private and that men claim the former while women are confined to the latter." Ryan also notes the difficulty of defining "public" and suggests distinguishing between "domestic" and "social" (4–10). Michelle Rosaldo, writing six years after she originally proposed the terms, agreed that the division between public and private spheres was not as absolute as she first postulated; women were more often found acting in public arenas than had first been apparent. "The Use and Abuse of Anthropology: Reflections on Feminism and Cross-Cultural Understanding," in *Signs,* supp. 5 (1980): 389–417.

particular woman under the law, they began to see all women as "a dependent class with special claim on the conscience of the bench."[14]

The Gaines case aroused the attention of more than just courtroom observers; the mass reading public avidly followed the trial because it read like a novel but had the alluring advantage of being true. "Women's fiction" (the formulaic novels of contemporary life by and about American women published between 1820 and 1870) dominated the literary market during the case's heyday, with the most popular categories being melodrama and romance. These "sentimental novels" presented a confused mixture of plots and subplots filled with unlikely coincidences, mysterious characters, and tragicomic events. The typical heroine was a young woman "who has lost the emotional and financial support of her legal guardians—indeed who is often subject to their abuse and neglect—but who nevertheless goes on to win her own way in the world." The parallels between the popular novels and the events in the life of Myra Gaines escaped neither Gaines nor those who interviewed her. If aspects of her story did not completely fit the prescribed literary tradition, she did not hesitate to alter facts or rewrite her past. And writers on the Gaines case showed no compunction about slanting evidence and distorting testimony to conform to popular ideas of marriage and motherhood.[15]

Myra Gaines's many courtroom engagements provided copy for the newspapers, and the "commercialized publicity system" focused on the case's sensational revelations. The plaintiff and her attorneys staged the trials as media events, well aware of the value of publicity in the "culture of celebrity" that appeared during the Victorian era. Gaines recognized

14. Ronald Walters, "The Family and Antebellum Reform: An Interpretation," *Societies* 3 (1973): 87; Grossberg, "Battling over Motherhood in Philadelphia," 167; Michael Grossberg, *Governing the Hearth: Law and the Family in Nineteenth-Century America* (Chapel Hill: University of North Carolina Press, 1985), 3–38.

15. Nina Baym, *Women's Fiction: A Guide to Novels by and about Women in America, 1820–1870* (Urbana: University of Illinois Press, 1993), xi; Kathryn Weibel, *Mirror, Mirror: Images of Women Reflected in Popular Culture* (Garden City, N.Y.: Anchor Books, 1977), passim; and Ernest Earnest, *The American Eve in Fact and Fiction, 1775–1914* (Chicago: University of Chicago Press, 1974), 31. Another famous nineteenth-century trial aroused the same kind of interest; see Richard Wightman Fox, "Intimacy on Trial: Cultural Meanings of the Beecher-Tilton Affair," in *The Power of Culture: Critical Essays in American History,* ed. Richard Wightman Fox and T. J. Jackson Lears (Chicago: University of Chicago Press, 1993).

very early in the course of her legal proceedings the value of keeping her name in the public view and forced her opponents to fight battles on the pages of newspapers all over the country. By the end of her life Myra Clark Gaines had become one of the first true celebrities.[16]

The resolve of Myra Gaines in pursuing her rights in spite of defeat after defeat ultimately aroused the admiration of even the citizens of New Orleans affected by her final victory. The eulogy preached at her funeral concluded that "she was one of the historic characters of her time . . . whose name will go down in history, associated with ideas of courage and determination." By the turn of the century, however, new scandals had turned the public's attention away from Gaines and her famous litigation. Resurrecting the pages of testimony from the historical dustbin provides a look backward at a forgotten chapter in American legal history.[17]

16. Fox, "Intimacy on Trial," 121.

17. Rev. Dr. B. M. Palmer, "Funeral of Myra Clark Gaines," *New Orleans Daily Picayune,* Jan. 11, 1885, p. 1.

I

A Journey of Discovery

When William Wallace Whitney wed Myra Elizabeth Davis on September 13, 1832, he was not quite twenty-two, several years younger than his bride. According to the recollections of a bridesmaid many years later, their marriage began with a dramatic twist well suited to the pages of a romance that would later enthrall a nation. As the ceremony began, the minister discovered that no one had procured a marriage license. "The bridegroom was annoyed, the bride trembled, the bridesmaids fluttered with additional tremors of excitement," as the bride's family dispatched a messenger to ride "with all speed, upon the swiftest horse in the stables" to Wilmington for the necessary document. By the mistake of a "stupid servant" the messenger received, instead, "an old blind animal, who stumbled and blundered along in the rain and mud." Finding a magistrate with difficulty, the messenger returned to the waiting wedding guests after ten o'clock in the evening. Fate, however, smiled on the bridal couple as the ceremony ended. The bridesmaid remembered that "the storm . . . ceased. The wind fell, the night calmed, and from among the scattered clouds the moon shone with peaceful rays across the lawn." This theatrical beginning marked the start of the drama that for fifty years newspaper editors, columnists, and gossip-laden memoirs called the "Great Gaines Case."[1]

Stories written about her lawsuit in the latter half of the nineteenth century seldom mentioned Myra Clark Gaines's first husband. Editors pre-

1. "The Romance of the Great Gaines Case: A Lifetime Lawsuit," *Putnam's Magazine: Original Papers on Literature, Science, Art, and National Interests*, New Series 2 (Aug. 1868): 208.

ferred to concentrate on either Gaines herself or her more famous second husband, General Edmund Pendleton Gaines. Yet without William Whitney's support no Gaines case would have existed. Nineteenth-century married women had no legal standing before United States courts. Only in her husband's name could Myra fight for her inheritance. William Whitney enthusiastically aided and encouraged his wife's pursuit of her rights, and he instigated the first lawsuit. His early death at twenty-seven gave his young widow an additional reason to continue the suit, convinced as she was that only victory in the case he initiated could justify her first husband's untimely death, which she blamed on his incarceration for libel.[2]

Young Whitney grew up in Binghamton, New York, the scion of a prominent New York family. He still lived at home with his parents when he met Myra. His father, General Joshua Whitney, was a founding resident of the upstate community, serving as land agent for the holders of the original Bingham Patent and as the first postmaster for the town. An early proponent of internal improvements, General Whitney supported New York governor DeWitt Clinton's project to build a state road from the Hudson River to Lake Erie through Binghamton. He also backed the Chenango Canal and, in the 1830s, served as one of the local incorporators of the Erie Railroad. His varied business interests allowed him to amass a comfortable fortune, and he became known around the state as a man of wealth and influence. In 1806 he built Whitney Place, considered "the finest dwelling in [that] part of New York State." Located on Upper Court Street in Binghamton, the house stood on a terraced knoll overlooking the Susquehanna River. It cost four thousand dollars to construct—a considerable sum—and the family furnished it on a grand scale. Imported furniture by Sheraton and Chippendale and silver by Sheffield created an atmosphere of taste and luxury. Secure in his position as a member of a respected family, William Whitney read law in a local office and established a modest practice. He developed an especially strong relationship with his father. "No child could cherish a parent with greater affection

2. For legal restrictions on nineteenth-century women, see Michael Grossberg, *Governing the Hearth;* Peggy A. Rabkin, *Fathers to Daughters: The Legal Foundations of Female Emancipation* (Westport, Conn.: Greenwood Press, 1980); and John Proffatt, *Woman before the Law* (New York: G. Putnam's Sons, 1874). Louisiana law, based on the civil code of 1825, gave married women more leeway to control their own property than did the common law used in other parts of the country. The Gaines cases were fought, however, primarily in the United States District Court and Supreme Court, where Myra Gaines needed her husband's concurrence for her suits.

and gratitude," young Whitney assured the general. The assistance General Whitney gave his son and Myra and, after William's death, his special care for his son's widow demonstrated that the father returned his son's regard.[3]

Myra had a more equivocal relationship with the man whom she knew as her father for the first twenty-five years of her life. She lived in the household of Colonel Samuel B. Davis almost from birth, raised as a daughter by Davis and his wife, Marian. In various depositions given in the court cases, both Davises, as well as their son, Horatio, concurred that Myra knew nothing of her true parentage until shortly before her marriage.

That moment of discovery became the subject of great speculation and imaginative reconstruction in the later years of the Gaines case. One author recounted that young Myra, taunted by schoolmates as a bastard, searched Colonel Davis's papers while he attended church. Finding "unquestionable evidence" that she was not his daughter, she confronted Davis. In this vignette Colonel Davis assured Myra that, although she was not his true daughter, she was heiress to a considerable estate in New Orleans. Since, according to her brother's testimony, no one outside their family knew of Myra's real origins—and the family never discussed it— this dramatic scene seems contrived solely for its emotional impact on followers of the Gaines case.[4]

The colonel's own explanation can be pieced together from the four depositions he gave in the various lawsuits and a letter he wrote to the editor of the *New York Evening Star* soon after the litigation began. Several newspaper articles in New York and New Orleans papers had criticized Davis for failing to pursue Myra's claims against the Clark estate,

3. William Foote Seward, ed. *Binghamton and Broome County* (New York: Lewis Historical Publishing, 1924), 1: 44–9; "The Case of Relf, Whitney, and the Late Daniel Clark, of New Orleans," *New York Evening Star,* Nov. 11, 1835, reprinted in *Transcript of Record, Gaines v. City of New Orleans,* case no. 8825, United States Circuit Court, Fifth Judicial Circuit and District of Louisiana, on appeal to the Supreme Court of the United States (New Orleans: Clerk's Office, United States Circuit Court, Oct. 1883), 2: 2090; Frederick Clifton Pierce, *Whitney Genealogy* (Chicago: Conkey, 1895), 568–9.

4. Pennock Pusey, "History of Lewes, Delaware," *Papers of the Historical Society of Delaware* 38 (1903): 31; deposition of Horatio Davis, June 25, 1849, reprinted in *Transcript of Record, Gaines v. Relf, Chew, and Others,* case no.122, United States Circuit Court, Eastern District of Louisiana, prepared for Appeal to the Supreme Court of the United States (New Orleans: Clerk's Office, United States Circuit Court, 1858), 651.

and he replied in an effort to defend his reputation. The editors of the *Evening Star* encouraged the increasingly vituperative exchange because the case excited considerable attention from their readers and boosted their circulation. The public debate marked the first use of the press to promote a one-sided interpretation of events in the Gaines case.[5]

According to Colonel Davis, Myra learned the truth in 1830. Early in that year, while Davis served as a representative to the Pennsylvania legislature in Harrisburg, he asked the young woman to search his private papers left in Philadelphia for some documents he needed. Rummaging through the colonel's correspondence, Myra discovered letters in which Clark acknowledged her as his daughter. Davis testified that this revelation gave his adopted daughter much distress, and when he returned home he decided to reveal the circumstances of her birth.[6]

Davis's four trial depositions provide few details of Myra's early life. According to the colonel, she was the daughter of Daniel Clark, a New Orleans merchant who died in 1813, and Zulime Carrière DesGrange, a young Frenchwoman. In late June of 1804 or 1805 Clark asked Davis to find a house where Mme. DesGrange could give birth to their child privately. Davis induced his brother-in-law, Pierre Baron Boisfontaine, to loan a house near Esplanade for Zulime's "lying in." Their daughter was born on the last day of June; soon after the birth, the infant was put out to nurse with the wife of a coach maker, a Mrs. Gordon. But Myra remained with the woman less than two weeks. The wet nurse had a child of her own, and Myra appeared neglected. When Davis told his wife of his concern for the infant's welfare, Marian Davis went at once to see her. "Touched with compassion at her forlorn and desolate situation," Davis insisted on taking the little girl into her own household. A niece of Davis had a child at the breast and consented to nurse Myra, too. According to the colonel, his wife's actions sprang from "a prompt and feminine benevolence" that Clark appreciated. Since Clark refused to acknowledge Myra publicly as his own, the baby remained with the Davis family. Marian Davis had no daughter, and becoming attached to the infant, determined to keep her until she should be claimed by her parents.[7]

5. "The Case of Relf, Whitney, and the Late Daniel Clark, of New Orleans," *New York Evening Star*, Nov. 11, 1835.

6. Colonel Samuel B. Davis, letter to the editor of the *New York Evening Star*, Dec. 19, 1835, reprinted in *Transcript of Record, Gaines v. City of New Orleans*, 2: 2128.

7. Davis letter, *New York Evening Star*, Dec. 19, 1935; deposition of Samuel B. Davis, July 10, 1849, reprinted in *Transcript of Record, Gaines v. City of New Orleans*, 2: 1379.

Clark had requested help from Davis because of a business relationship and personal friendship developed over a six-year acquaintance. Davis led a checkered life up to the time he met Clark in 1799. Born in Lewes, Delaware, on Christmas Day 1765, he went to sea as a boy. By the early 1790s he owned a half interest in a schooner, the *Delaware*. For several years Davis captained the ship on trading ventures between American ports and the French West Indies. In 1793 a British "man-o-war schooner," the *Flying Fish,* returning from the burning of Cap-Français, captured the *Delaware* and took it to Jamaica. According to Davis the war between England and the revolutionary government in France made this a common fate for American ships trading with the French. Davis kept his entire fortune on board the *Delaware,* the "profit of many years' exertion and labor." This sum, thirty thousand dollars in specie, belonged to Davis and his Philadelphia partner John Brown. The British admiralty court awarded the *Delaware* and all its contents to the captain and crew of the *Flying Fish* as a prize of war, leaving Davis destitute.[8]

Davis's fortunes soon improved. An acquaintance from Philadelphia came to his aid with a considerable sum, which allowed Davis to buy back and refit his vessel. His encounter with the British courts convinced Davis to seek revenge as a member of the French navy. Under the assumed name of Lieutenant Vaisau, Davis acquired a valiant reputation as an officer, but he resigned his French commission in 1798 when his own country became engaged in an undeclared naval war with France. His naval experiences gained him a position as first officer on the *General Washington,* an armed merchant vessel owned by Daniel W. Coxe of Philadelphia but consigned to Coxe's partner, Daniel Clark of New Orleans. Again Davis's ship fell victim to the British navy. Two English men-of-war, the *Lynx* and the *Pheasant,* captured the *General Washington* and took it to Bermuda. Coxe journeyed to the island, redeemed his ship, and gave command to Davis. As captain, Davis sailed for several years between Liverpool and New Orleans. In 1802 or 1803 he ended his naval career and joined the growing number of Americans seeking their fortunes in New Orleans. Davis prospered as a merchant. He invested in a "rope-walk" owned by Clark on

8. William B. Marine, "The Bombardment of Lewes by the British, April 6 and 7, 1813," *Papers of the Historical Society of Delaware* 33 (1901): 8; deposition of Samuel B. Davis, Aug. 10, 1834, reprinted in *Transcript of Record, Gaines v. City of New Orleans,* 2: 1807; deposition of Samuel B. Davis, May 4, 1836, ibid., 2: 2055. Davis himself used the term "man-o-war schooner" in his deposition.

the riverfront at Canal Street and bought his own ship, the *Eliza*. In 1805 (just before the date Davis gave for Myra's birth) Daniel Clark financed a partnership Davis formed with his nephew, William Harper. As "Davis & Harper" the firm purchased a hardware and ship chandlery business, using Clark's credit as security. Gratitude for Clark's assistance, as well as Mrs. Davis's desire for a daughter, motivated Davis's willing acceptance of Clark's young child into his home.[9]

Davis could tell Myra little of her mother. She was "Madame Zulime DesGrange of New Orleans," and Davis understood that rumor accused her husband of bigamy at the time of their marriage. Many years later, in a deposition given in 1849 shortly before his death, Davis testified that Zulime frequently came to see her daughter while Myra lived with his family. After the Davis household moved north in 1812, Zulime never spoke to Myra again during her childhood. Davis described one short meeting that took place on the streets of Philadelphia when Zulime "looked very hard" at the child. Except for that incident, no contact occurred between Zulime and her daughter for more than twenty years.[10]

Although Clark refused to claim Myra openly as his daughter, Davis explained that her father often visited her as a child and seemed proud of her. Clark also appeared willing to accept financial responsibility for Myra. Before a voyage he undertook in 1811 from New Orleans to Philadelphia, Clark made some special provisions for her. Hostilities between England and the United States seemed imminent; fearing capture or death at sea, Clark left a small trunk presumably containing valuable property for her support at a bank in New Orleans. He also assigned several notes of hand from General Wade Hampton to Davis for Myra's benefit. Davis returned the receipt for the trunk and the assignment of the notes when Clark arrived safely back in New Orleans. On an earlier occasion Clark had transferred several lots in New Orleans by bill of sale to Davis, and Davis later transferred the lots to another friend of Clark, the chevalier Delacroix. Neither bill of sale mentioned Myra, but both men understood that they held the property in trust for Clark's child, and no money passed from either man to Clark for the lots.[11]

After war began between the United States and England in 1812 the Davis family left New Orleans for Philadelphia. Davis planned to join the

9. Samuel B. Davis, depositions of 1834 and 1836.
10. Samuel B. Davis, depositions of 1834, 1836, and 1849.
11. Ibid.

forces defending the East Coast ports. His leadership in the heroic defense of Lewes against British bombardment gained him a commission from President Madison as lieutenant colonel in the Thirty-Second Regiment, United States Infantry. One of Davis's contemporaries during the bombardment of Lewes described the colonel's "imposing stature, decidedly fine in appearance" with "prominent features, large cheek bones, heavy jaw, large nose and mouth, expressive of firmness." Over six feet tall, Davis "possess[ed] qualities of discipline and intellect for the management of men."[12]

After transferring to the Forty-Fourth Regiment, composed of fellow Louisianians, and reaching the rank of colonel, Davis commanded the defense of the entrance to New York harbor at Sandy Hook. Later that year (1813) he acted as one of the judges in the court martial of General William Hull, who had surrendered Detroit to the British in 1812. His next assignment found him leading his regiment to the defense of New Orleans. From Wilmington he marched his troops to Wheeling, West Virginia, where they embarked on flatboats for the trip down the Mississippi. The regiment arrived in New Orleans the day after Andrew Jackson's victory. Colonel Davis remained on active duty, stationed in Louisiana, until 1819. His family joined him, living on their plantation of Terre Boeuf north of the city; Myra, however, remained behind in Philadelphia at boarding school.

Upon his retirement the colonel sold Terre Boeuf and bought property outside of Wilmington on a hill where he and his men had camped on their march to New Orleans in 1814. The natural beauty of the site had impressed Davis, and now he obtained more than two hundred acres of riverfront property, on which he built Delamore Place as a home for his family. Years later a newspaper described Myra's childhood home: "Towering pillars ranged along the wide porch, reached by a flight of steps, [and] formed a pleasing example of the semi-colonial and Southern style of architecture." Myra lived at Delamore Place until her marriage to William Whitney in 1832.[13]

When the colonel moved his family north in 1812, Clark threatened to

12. Marine, "Bombardment of Lewes," 8.

13. "Historic Homes of Wilmington," *Wilmington (Delaware) Every-Evening*, Apr. 18, 1914, p. 22; "Delamore Place Passing: Home of Noted Delawareans," *Wilmington (Del.) Delmarva Star*, May 22, 1921, p. 19; "Myra Clark's Early Life: How She Married Mr. Whitney in Spite of Opposition," *New York Times*, July 25, 1881, p. 3.

take Myra from the Davises. The colonel refused to give up the child unless Clark took his daughter "under his protection or gave some other public and notorious evidence" of his paternity. Clark refused. Davis explained that his insistence and Clark's refusal caused a "coldness" to develop between the two friends that continued until Clark's death a year later. Despite Clark's denial of public recognition, Davis expected that he would provide for the child "as his ample fortune and generous disposition" warranted.[14]

But no such acknowledgment appeared when the announcement of Clark's death in 1813 reached them. The following spring Davis wrote Clark's executors, Richard Relf and Beverly Chew (Clark's New Orleans partners), asking if any provision had been made for Clark's daughter. They replied that Clark's will, made in 1811, left his entire fortune to his mother, Mary Clark of Germantown, Pennsylvania. Moreover, the executors insisted that the war with Britain had rendered the estate insolvent, and they requested immediate payment of $2,500 to redeem a debt contracted by Davis. That amount represented the principal of a note for $2,361.00 plus 10 percent interest since 1812.[15]

The demand for payment angered Davis. He wrote the two executors that Clark had forced the sum in question on him, and the entire amount was for the child's benefit. Davis explained that he and Clark had formally signed an agreement binding Clark to supply funds for Myra's education; Davis would invest Clark's money and use the interest for the child. Davis promised not to exceed the sum stipulated. The executors should find the agreement among Clark's papers. Davis concluded his letter with the hope that Clark's executors would "have too much respect" for his memory "to proceed further in this business to give trouble to one who for over ten years has never rec.d one cent for the support of [Clark's] child—except what is here mentioned."[16]

Unfortunately Davis's hopes were misplaced. Relf and Chew replied that no agreement could be found among Clark's papers; Clark himself had endorsed the note to them shortly before his death. On December 8,

14. Samuel B. Davis, depositions of 1834, 1836, and 1849.

15. Richard Relf and Beverly Chew to Samuel B. Davis, May 4, 1814, General Case Files no. 3393, Circuit Court of the United States, Eastern District of Louisiana, Record Group 21, National Archives, Southwest Region, Fort Worth, Tex.; "Application of Myra Clark Gaines for Proof of the Will of Daniel Clark," ibid; Relf and Chew to Davis, Mar. 20, 1814, ibid.

16. Samuel B. Davis to Richard Relf and Beverly Chew, Mar. 20, 1814.

1814, Richard Relf and Beverly Chew brought suit against Davis in the First Judicial District Court of Louisiana to collect the debt. The judgment by the court ordered Davis to pay the executors the full amount of $2,500. He paid reluctantly. The whole experience, he later told Myra, convinced him that no funds would come to her from the estate of her father, and she continued in her ignorance of her real identity for fifteen more years. Davis explained that he and his wife had often considered whether they should tell their adopted daughter of her true parentage but had decided that "it would be less for her happiness and [their] own to change in any manner the ties that existed" between Myra and the Davis family. Only her accidental discovery of her father's letters eventually convinced him to break the silence.[17]

Other evidence presented during the litigation questioned the accuracy of Colonel Davis's recollections. His letter in the *Evening Star* gave the source of the "coldness" that diminished his friendship with Clark as Davis's insistence in 1812 that Clark acknowledge Myra. On two other occasions, however, Davis explained that the coldness developed because of business differences that arose in 1807 or 1808 when Clark tried unsuccessfully to drive a wedge between Davis and his partner Harper. In this account Davis maintained that Clark's insistence that he accept money for Myra's education before he left New Orleans in 1811 was the first sign of their renewed friendship. More likely, Davis's plans to rejoin the military forces prompted Clark's concern for his daughter's future. Before Davis left New Orleans he conveyed the property he held in trust for Myra to Delacroix. Clark may have demanded this transfer to remove the property from Davis's estate should he be killed; for the same reason, Clark insisted he accept a sum of money whose interest would provide for Myra's upkeep if Davis died.[18]

Another discrepancy exists in Davis's rendition of Myra's discovery of her parentage. He stated positively that Myra learned of her history in 1830, two years before her marriage, during a time when Davis served in the Pennsylvania legislature. Yet Davis, although elected in 1830, served

17. Statement of Richard Relf, undated, General Case Files no. 3393, Circuit Court of the United States, Eastern District of Louisiana, Record Group 21, National Archives, Southwest Region, Fort Worth, Tex.; Samuel B. Davis, depositions of 1834, 1835, and 1849.

18. Davis letter, *New York Evening Star,* Dec. 19, 1835; Samuel B. Davis, depositions of 1834 and 1836.

his two terms between 1831 and 1833. Depositions by other family members agreed that Myra learned of her birth "shortly" before her marriage in 1832.[19]

One piece of evidence indicates that Colonel Davis did not tell Myra of her heritage in early 1830 as he testified. In May of that year the chevalier François Dusnau Delacroix conveyed to "Miss Myra Clark" property in the Faubourg St. John, land that Delacroix originally received from Samuel Davis in 1812. According to the record of sale filed with notary Philip Pedesclaux on May 16, 1830, Delacroix sold the property to Myra for $2,000, a sum furnished by Davis. The record also indicates that the purchase price received from Davis supposedly came from money provided by Clark before his death for his daughter's welfare. Since that amount given by Clark to Davis had already been reclaimed by the executors of Clark's will, Relf and Chew, the purchase money must actually have come from Davis's own pocket.[20]

The record of sale does not indicate whether the young woman knew anything about the sale. In an 1848 deposition Delacroix recalled meeting "Captain" Davis in the Exchange and asking him if Myra had accompanied him to New Orleans. Learning that she was indeed present in the city, the chevalier offered to transfer two portions of land Clark had placed in his possession for Myra. Davis replied that his adopted daughter would not be able to accept as she "was entirely ignorant that she is the . . . child of Clark." Several days later Davis accepted the transfer of property in Myra's name. Under Louisiana law the age of majority for a woman was twenty-five; if, as Davis avowed, Myra was born on June 30, 1805, this sale took place just before her twenty-fifth birthday.[21]

Whenever and however Myra learned the truth of her relationship with the Davis family, she showed no change in her attitude toward her adopted

19. "Historic Homes of Wilmington," *Wilmington (Delaware) Every-Evening*, Apr. 18, 1914, p. 22; deposition of Marian Rose Davis, Aug. 10, 1834, reprinted in *Transcript of Record, Gaines v. City of New Orleans*, 2: 1813; Horatio Davis, deposition of 1849.

20. Deposition of François D. Delacroix, June 11, 1848, *Myra Clark Gaines v. F. D. Delacroix*, General Case Files no. 2619, Circuit Court of the United States, Eastern District of Louisiana, Record Group 21, National Archives, Southwest Region, Fort Worth, Tex.; "Sale of Property by F. D. Delacroix to Myra Clark, May 16, 1830," Notarial Records of J. Pedesclaux, copy (and translation) reprinted in *Transcript of Record, Gaines v. City of New Orleans*, 2: 2135. In court documents Delacroix's middle name also appears as "Dusnan" and "Dusuau."

21. François D. Delacroix, deposition of 1848; Samuel B. Davis, deposition of 1849.

parents until after she met William Whitney. She made no demands that Davis seek money for her from the Clark estate, nor did she write directly to the executors or make plans to go to New Orleans. Davis told her she had no claims on her natural father's estate, and this statement apparently satisfied her. When she married William in 1832 the wedding took place at the Davis home in Wilmington and the newspaper announcement listed the bride as "Myra E. Davis."[22]

The brief announcement of the wedding of Myra and William in the *Philadelphia Gazette and Daily Advertiser* gave no indication of the family controversy that swirled about Myra's decision to marry. Yet the marriage apparently changed Myra's relationship with her adopted father. A letter from William to his father makes clear that Colonel Davis did not approve the match but provides no indication of the colonel's reasons. Years later, during the heyday of the Gaines case, the popular press sought to portray the colonel as the stereotypical wicked guardian who schemed to obtain Myra's fortune for himself. One account accused the colonel of hiding valuable property given him by Clark for Myra and then scheming to marry her to one of his own sons to keep the property in the family. Another suggested that Colonel Davis proposed to marry Myra to another man— unnamed—of wealth and worldly stature and refused Whitney because of his youth and supposed lack of prospects. A popular legend dramatized the public's identification of Myra with the heroines of current sentimental novels. In this tale Myra fled her home, thwarted by the colonel's refusal to sanction Whitney's suit, and only her near death convinced her foster father to relent.[23]

Colonel Davis's opposition to the marriage is difficult to explain. William Whitney, although younger than Myra, was a man of good, even excellent, family background, whose professional abilities earned him the respect of his community. Possibly the colonel believed Myra's marriage to a man trained in the law would reopen a subject he hoped would remain closed. Whitney did question Davis about Myra's background, and the answers indicated that Davis grew defensive about his acceptance of the executors' statements that the estate was bankrupt and no provision could

22. *Philadelphia Gazette and Daily Advertiser,* Sept. 17, 1832, p. 3.

23. W. W. Whitney to General Joshua Whitney, Oct. 2, 1832, Joshua Whitney Papers, Broome County Historical Society, Binghamton, N.Y.; "Myra Clark's Early Life: How She Married Mr. Whitney in Spite of Opposition," *New York Times,* July 25, 1881, p. 3; Laura C. Holloway, *Famous American Fortunes and the Men Who Have Made Them* (New York: J. A. Hill, 1889), 14–5.

be made for Myra. The forced repayment of Clark's advance humiliated the proud colonel, and he did what he could to discourage any further contact with the executors of the Clark estate. The property regained from Delacroix was another source of friction. Whitney demanded that Davis sign a statement indicating that he held that property in trust for Myra so that it would not become part of Davis's estate. Seeing the demand as an indication of a lack of faith, Davis refused, and the relationship between the two men worsened. William wrote his own father just after their wedding that Myra had suffered great anxiety over the past eight months, and that "the loss of sleep at night [made] her almost crazy." "Her Father's unkindness has very much distressed her," he continued, and "it will be better to have no further communication with him at the present time." In all her later letters, Myra called her father-in-law, General Whitney, "Father" but never referred to Davis as anything but "the Colonel."[24]

The answers the reluctant colonel provided Myra and William fired their imaginations. Although Davis swore that he never told the young couple that Clark had married Zulime, since he neither knew nor asked if the two were man and wife, Whitney nevertheless felt the possibility that Myra might be able to claim an inheritance from her wealthy father warranted further investigation. At some point in their interview with Colonel Davis, Myra and William gained access to a letter written to Davis many years earlier by a close friend of Clark, Josef Deville Degoutin Bellechasse. The Frenchman, then living in Cuba, wrote that Clark had entrusted property to him for his daughter Myra. How, Bellechasse asked, should he place the property in her hands? This was another source of friction between the couple and Davis. Whitney later charged that Davis had tried to gain control of this property also without telling Myra—a charge Davis explained by his concern for Myra's emotional state should she learn he was not her true parent. When Bellechasse refused to convey any property to Davis, the correspondence between the two ceased.[25]

Upon discovering Bellechasse's letter to Colonel Davis, Whitney immediately wrote to him. The letter he received in return, just after his marriage,

24. Samuel B. Davis, deposition of 1836; W. W. Whitney to General Joshua Whitney, Oct. 2, 1832.

25. Samuel B. Davis, deposition of 1849; Samuel B. Davis to Josef Deville Degoutin Bellechasse, June 14, 1820, copy included in the 58th cross-interrogatory of Samuel B. Davis, deposition of 1836.

convinced him that the bridal trip planned for New Orleans should include a stop in Cuba to see the old man. Clark's old friend had important
information that he was willing to impart only to Myra. When the newlyweds reached the Spanish island in the early spring of 1833, they found
Bellechasse living on his sugar plantation near Matanzas. The seventy-
year-old Creole still held the rank of lieutenant colonel in the Spanish militia. Born in Louisiana in 1760, M. Bellechasse had followed his profession
of arms until the transfer of the province to the United States in 1803. His
friendship with Daniel Clark had formed during the decade prior to the
cession, their "liking for each other . . . cemented and made permanent by
. . . business and political connexion." In November of 1803 the French
colonial prefect, Pierre Laussat, requested that Bellechasse accept command of the provincial militia; Clark encouraged him to take the post, and
Bellechasse proved a popular choice. His intimacy with Clark continued
through the next decade. Clark headed the political faction to which Bellechasse belonged, although they disagreed over the annexation of West
Florida (with its mainly American population) to Louisiana before statehood—a controversial issue for most Louisiana residents. Bellechasse
served on the Legislative Council of the Territory of Orleans and on the
1812 convention that framed the state constitution. In spite of some political differences, Bellechasse's friendship with Clark endured until Clark's
death.[26]

Statehood and the war with England meant misfortune for Bellechasse.
On June 13, 1814, not quite a year after his friend's death, Bellechasse left
Louisiana to visit family in Cuba. Business matters sent him first to St.
Augustine in Florida, where news reached him through Richard Relf (one
of the executors of Clark's will) that he was accused of complicity with
British plans to capture New Orleans. A report circulated in the city that
Bellechasse "had been seen in [the British] camp almost with a torch in
[his] hand to burn [his] country and fellow citizens." This report, wrote
Bellechasse to Clark's Philadelphia partner, "obliged General Jackson to
put a price on [his] head." Arriving in Cuba with this calumny following
him, he learned that his family had hurriedly left New Orleans for Havana.
Bellechasse blamed the disgrace of his accusation and the poverty that fol-

26. Deposition of Josef Deville Degoutin Bellechasse, 1837, reprinted in *Transcript of Record, Gaines v. City of New Orleans*, 2: 1332; Lewis W. Newton, *The Americanization of French Louisiana: A Study of the Process of Adjustment between the French and the Anglo-American Populations of Louisiana, 1803–1860* (New York: Arno, 1980), 13.

lowed it for the death of his wife and eldest son. The double tragedy convinced him to abandon Louisiana and make a new life in Cuba. He was now delighted to meet the daughter of his old friend, whom he remembered as a little girl. The depositions Bellechasse gave in the Gaines cases contain the amazing story he recounted to Myra and her husband.[27]

"Few men," declared Bellechasse, "were equal to Clark in talents and intelligence." As a gentleman and "the proprietor of vast possessions," Clark was a proud man whose coat of arms proclaimed his descent from "the ancient kings of Ireland." Bellechasse assured Myra that "the future happiness, fortune, and standing of his child was the object dearest to [Clark's] heart." Daniel Clark had taken Bellechasse to see Myra on many occasions, during which the father had demonstrated "the most ardent love" for his child. She, Clark disclosed, "would be the heiress of his fortune."[28]

According to Bellechasse's testimony, Clark made his initial plans for his daughter's future in 1811. Called north by a business emergency, he had made a provisional will naming his New Orleans business partners as executors and his mother, Mary Clark, as his heir. This will did not name Myra because, Bellechasse explained, her father had provided for her in other ways. By formal deed before a notary Clark sold Bellechasse "some lots, perhaps fifty." On the face of the deed it appeared that Bellechasse paid for the property, although "in truth, nothing had been paid." Clark "sold" the property "under the confidential understanding" that Bellechasse would hold the lots for Myra in case Clark died on his journey. In the same fashion Bellechasse understood that Clark had deposited property with M. Delacroix and Colonel Davis for Myra. The sudden emergency that drew Clark north prevented him from making a detailed will, and "with or without cause," Bellechasse claimed that Clark doubted the integrity of his partners, Relf and Chew. Questioning their good faith, Clark "placed out of reach of those persons . . . the interests of his daugh-

27. Josef Bellechasse to Daniel W. Coxe, Dec. 10, 1819, reprinted in *Transcript of Record, Gaines v. Hennen,* comprising cases Nos. 2619, 2695, 2715, and 2734, in the Circuit Court of the United States, Eastern District of Louisiana, entered in the Appeal of *Gaines v. P. H. Monseaux,* case no. 3663, in the United States Circuit Court, Fifth Judicial Circuit and District of Louisiana, to the Supreme Court of the United States (New Orleans: Clerk's Office, United States Circuit Court, Nov. 28, 1877), 896.

28. Deposition of Josef Bellechasse, 1837.

ter." But, Bellechasse admitted, Clark did place the 1811 will in the hands of Richard Relf.[29]

Myra and William were delighted to learn that Bellechasse still held the lots despite repeated efforts by the executors to obtain possession of the property. Although Bellechasse had offered to give the property back to Clark on his return, Clark refused to accept, "such was the full confidence he had in [Bellechasse's] honor and integrity." The old gentleman fully merited Clark's confidence; he immediately offered to convey the lots to William and Myra, and the three made plans for the transfer when the Whitneys arrived in New Orleans.[30]

These fifty lots, located along the Bayou St. John, represented a significant inheritance. But Bellechasse insisted that they did not comprise the total of Clark's bequest to his daughter. Two years after his journey north Clark had made a second will. In order "not to . . . risk the standing and fortune of his child" any further, he determined to declare Myra "his legitimate child and heiress of all his estate." He requested Bellechasse, the chevalier Delacroix, and James Pitot, presiding judge of the Court of Probates in New Orleans, to serve as his executors, ignoring any claims Relf and Chew might have to the position.[31]

Clark completed his second will shortly before his last illness. Bellechasse indicated that both he and Judge Pitot saw the will, wholly in Clark's handwriting, and read its provisions. As Clark pledged, the will named Myra as his legitimate daughter and the heiress of all his estate. A few days later when Bellechasse called to see Clark he learned from Relf that Clark was too sick to be seen by anyone. Indignant, Bellechasse pushed his way into Clark's room where his old friend chided him for failing to visit since he fell ill. Relf, Clark mentioned, had been told to send for him. He had received no message, Bellechasse assured Clark, but would not abandon his friend. At this, Bellechasse told Myra and William, Clark "looked at me and squeezed my hand." Fearing to tire his friend, Bellechasse left the room but advised Relf he would remain to care for

29. Deposition of Josef Bellechasse, Aug. 24, 1834, reprinted in *Transcript of Record, Gaines v. City of New Orleans*, 2: 1832; Josef Bellechasse, deposition of 1837.

30. Daniel W. Coxe to Josef Bellechasse, Nov. 24, 1819, reprinted (with translation) in *Transcript of Record, E. P. Gaines and Wife v. Relf, Chew, Delacroix, and Others*, 602; Richard Relf to Josef Bellechasse, Aug. 21, 1820, reprinted (with translation) ibid., 603; Josef Bellechasse, deposition of 1834.

31. Josef Bellechasse, deposition of 1834.

Clark. Relf replied that the doctors had ordered that Clark be kept as quiet as possible with no visitors. Relf insisted that Clark's illness was not serious and urged Bellechasse to go home, promising to call him if Clark appeared worse. Still trusting Relf, Bellechasse departed. Upon his return the next day, having received no message, he found his friend dead. Leaving Clark's house Bellechasse hurried to the nearby home of Judge Pitot. The judge was equally indignant at Relf's conduct. None of Clark's friends had been notified of his illness, and none were present at his deathbed. If they had been, Bellechasse and Pitot believed, they might have prevented the "fraudulent suppression" of Clark's last will. Pitot told Bellechasse that the case in which Clark placed the will after showing it to them was empty; Relf had brought forward the succinct and provisional will of a dozen lines, which Clark had previously made before sailing for Philadelphia in 1811, and which he had delivered to Relf. Pitot and Bellechasse attributed the disappearance of the 1813 will to "interested villainy."[32]

The tale told by the old Creole fascinated Myra and William Whitney. But Bellechasse's claim that Clark declared Myra legitimate puzzled the couple. If Myra's mother was a Mme. DesGrange, how could she have married Clark? Because, Bellechasse answered, DesGrange had been prosecuted and condemned for bigamy several years before Myra's birth. Near the close of the Spanish domination in Louisiana the "first and lawful wife" of DesGrange came to New Orleans in pursuit of her wayward husband; DesGrange had practiced an "infamous deception" by marrying Myra's mother when all New Orleans had believed him a bachelor. Their marriage was therefore void. Bellechasse would not swear that Clark had subsequently married Zulime, since Clark had never spoken of a marriage. But rumors about their marriage filled New Orleans, and, Bellechasse reminded the Whitneys, Clark had declared Myra legitimate in his will.[33]

The old man had further news. The woman who nursed Myra, the niece of Mrs. Davis, now lived in Cuba, and she could confirm his story. Harriet Harper Smythe was happy to meet the Whitneys. Her first husband, William Harper, had been Colonel Davis's partner and had felt indebted to Clark, whose credit had backed their firm. After Myra's birth Marian Davis brought the child to the house the Davis and Harper families shared. Since Harriet Smythe (then Mrs. Harper) was nursing an infant of her own, she consented to feed Myra, too, after Davis told her the child was

32. Josef Bellechasse, deposition of 1837.
33. Josef Bellechasse, depositions of 1834 and 1837.

Daniel Clark's. Harriet Harper Smythe maintained that Clark considered her care for his daughter "constituted a powerful claim on his gratitude and friendship," which he rewarded by continuing to consult Smythe about Myra's upbringing.[34]

Harriet Smythe affirmed the story Bellechasse told in every particular. Clark was a concerned and attentive parent, "caressing [Myra] and calling her his dear little daughter." She remembered his extravagant provisions for the child's clothing and the "costly" slave he purchased for her care. Myra was Clark's only child, she agreed, and "destined to inherit his splendid fortune." His "paternal solicitude" only increased as Myra grew older and did not cease when the Davises took the child north.[35]

Smythe informed Myra and William that not only had she seen and read the contents of Clark's second will, but she recalled its provisions exactly. The peculiar circumstances of its disappearance, she claimed, "contributed to fix in [her] mind the recollection of its contents." About four months before his death Clark informed her of his intention to make his "last will." He felt impelled, she testified, to secure his child's inheritance. In doing so he "dwelt on the moral benefit to her in society from being acknowledged by him in his last will as his legitimate daughter," and expressed his pleasure that his oldest and most trusted friends had agreed to serve as executors of his wishes. He had appointed Delacroix as Myra's "tutor," the guardian responsible for her upbringing. The chevalier, Clark told Smythe, "would be a parent to her."[36]

The will itself was a simple document, although Clark spent considerable time in its preparation. Smythe explained that in addition to the testamentary provisions Clark compiled a "complete inventory of all his estate, and explanations of all his business . . . as a safeguard . . . in case he should not live long enough to dissolve and adjust all his pecuniary relations with others." Four weeks before his death Clark showed Smythe the completed will. "Now my will is finished," he proclaimed, "now if I die tomorrow she will go forth to society, to my relations, to my mother, acknowledged by me in my last will as my legitimate daughter, and will be educated according to my minutest wishes under the supervision of the chevalier Dela-

34. Deposition of Harriet Harper Smythe, Jan. 10, 1835, reprinted in *Transcript of Record, Gaines v. City of New Orleans,* 2: 1818; deposition of Harriet Harper Smythe, Apr. 12, 1838, ibid., 1318; deposition of Harriet Harper Smythe, May 14, 1846, reprinted in *Transcript of Record, Gaines v. Hennen,* 155.

35. Harriet Harper Smythe, depositions of 1835, 1838, and 1846.

36. Ibid.

croix." Clark's will left his entire estate to Myra, less several minor legacies: an annuity of $2,000 to his mother during her lifetime; an annuity of $500 to Caroline DesGrange, paid until she reached the age of majority, when the annuity would cease and she would receive a legacy of $5,000; $5,000 to the son of Judge Pitot; another $5,000 to the son of a Mr. DuBuys of New Orleans; and freedom for Clark's slave Lubin with a provision made for his future maintenance. Clark appointed Judge Pitot, Delacroix, and M. Bellechasse as his executors and designated Delacroix as Myra's tutor. According to Smythe the will was completely in Clark's handwriting—an "olographic" will—dated in July 1813, and signed by him.[37]

The provisions of the will contained several surprises for Myra and William Whitney. The failure to include Colonel Davis as an executor or to appoint him as Myra's legal guardian confirmed the colonel's story of a rupture in his friendship with Clark. Apparently Myra's father did not expect his daughter to continue in the Davis household. Clark's determination to acknowledge Myra's legitimate status conflicted with his failure to recognize her publicly during his lifetime, and neither Bellechasse nor Mrs. Smythe could explain the discrepancy. Perhaps the most surprising item was the legacy to another child, "Caroline DesGrange," whom Bellechasse and Smythe disclosed was the child of Myra's mother Zulime and her first husband, DesGrange—Myra's half-sister. Both positively asserted that Caroline was not Clark's child, although he had paid for her maintenance in a Philadelphia boarding school since her infancy.[38]

Bellechasse and Smythe could add little to the information the Whitneys already knew about Myra's mother, Zulime Carrière. Neither would swear to a marriage between Clark and Zulime. Myra's mother bore "an unblemished character" whose "intimacy with Mrs. Relf, first wife of Richard Relf" marked her as "a lady of respectable standing." As such, the impossibility that "she could form any connexion except under the sanction of marriage" presumed the existence of a marital bond, but neither Bellechasse nor Smythe witnessed such a ceremony. Bellechasse believed that Clark's excessive pride caused him to conceal his marriage to

37. Ibid. A handwritten or "olographic" will was legal in Louisiana, provided it was dated, written, and signed by the testator. Such a will did not require the services of an attorney or notary.

38. Josef Bellechasse, deposition of 1834; Harriet Harper Smythe, depositions of 1835, 1838, and 1846.

Zulime. The "deception practiced upon her by DesGrange" through their bigamous union, created too much scandal for one who "carried his pedigree up to the ancient kings of Ireland."[39]

Harriet Smythe was able to acquaint Myra with the rumored reason for the breach that ended the relationship between Clark and Zulime. When Clark, chosen by the territorial legislature to represent Louisiana in the United States Congress, departed New Orleans for Washington, he left Zulime in the care of the wife of his slave Lubin. Unnamed persons who "had, or supposed they had, a great interest in dissolving his connexion with the mother of his child" wrote to Clark accusing Zulime of infidelity. They succeeded in so poisoning his mind against her that a serious quarrel erupted when he returned to New Orleans. Immediately afterward Zulime fled the city.[40]

The information Myra and William secured in Matanzas reinforced their decision to pursue the inheritance in the New Orleans courts. Although the Whitneys never returned to Cuba nor spoke again with Bellechasse and Smythe, they kept in contact through letters. The gallant old Creole gentleman and Myra's former wet nurse gave five depositions supporting Myra's claims, and their testimony provided the foundation for the challenge Whitney filed to the probate of Daniel Clark's will of 1811.

39. Harriet Harper Smythe, deposition of 1838; Josef Bellechasse, deposition of 1837.
40. Harriet Harper Smythe, deposition of 1838.

II

The City by the River

In the spring of 1833 a ship carrying Myra and William Whitney entered the mouth of the Mississippi River at Balize Point. For William, it was his first view of Louisiana. Myra had returned to her birthplace at least twice with her adoptive parents, but never with such a sense of anticipation, nervousness, and excitement. She and her new husband believed their journey was the beginning of a quest for fortune and honor; almost certainly, they did not expect it to be the start of a lifelong battle for justice.[1]

Travelers like the Whitneys who journeyed to New Orleans in the early 1830s had a choice of three approaches to the city. Those who came downriver on steamboats passed stately homes and slave cabins, with unending rows of cotton and sugar cane lying just behind the levee. For 120 miles above New Orleans, orange trees and oleander blossoms perfumed the air and live oaks hung with Spanish moss arched over the river. Other visitors to New Orleans arrived by steamboat from Mobile along a coastal waterway protected by a chain of low, sandy barrier islands. From the decks, these travelers could watch seagulls and pelicans on the beaches. Their steamboats stopped at Lake Pontchartrain where the passengers boarded a canal boat or railroad train for the six-mile journey through alligator-filled swamps into the city. Coming from Cuba, Myra and William used a third approach to New Orleans, through the South Pass of the Mississippi River where the muddy water of the river met the blue Gulf. Nineteenth-

1. W. W. Whitney to General Joshua Whitney, Oct. 2, 1832, Joshua Whitney Papers, Broome County Historical Society, Binghamton, N.Y.

century travelers described the entry point at Balize as a "sandy, boggy, loggy, grassy, and snaggy strip of land," the most "desolate and lonely spot on earth." Only a small cluster of shacks huddled at the base of the lighthouse marked any human presence, and for miles no vegetation marred the landscape.[2]

"Passing the bar" at Balize Point represented a challenge that could only be handled by experienced bar pilots. Every ship entering the river took on one of these navigators who were responsible for guiding the ship over the mud bar deposited by the river as it entered the Gulf of Mexico. For most of the distance from river mouth to New Orleans a channel fifty feet deep allowed oceangoing ships to reach the port, but at the entrance to the river the average depth was only twelve feet. Late winter and early spring—when Myra and William traveled—was the most treacherous time to approach New Orleans from the south. As floodwaters from the Mississippi poured soil-choked waters into its channel, the bars blocking the entrance might enlarge almost overnight, shutting off the river and its port from all major foreign commerce. Ships caught inside the river might be delayed for months, while ships outside also had to wait patiently for the waters to subside and the entrance to deepen.[3]

The one-hundred-mile journey upriver from Balize to New Orleans took an average of two weeks during most of the year. Swift currents could make the trip much longer. One ship from Hamburg took sixty-five days to cross the Atlantic and seventy-six days to sail from Balize to New Or-

2. Newton, *Americanization of French Louisiana,* 155; A. Oakey Hall, *The Manhattaner in New Orleans; or, Phases of "Crescent City" Life* (New York: J. S. Redfield, 1851), 2; Joseph G. Tregle, *Louisiana in the Age of Jackson: A Clash of Cultures and Personalities* (Baton Rouge: Louisiana State University Press, 1999), 1. Numerous travel accounts describe the approaches to New Orleans. See Henry Tudor, *Narrative of a Tour in North America, . . . with an Excursion to the Island of Cuba,* 2 (London: J. Duncan, 1834); Thomas Hamilton, *Men and Manners in America,* 2 (Philadelphia: Carey, Lea, & Blanchard, 1833); and James Stuart, *Three Years in North America,* 2 (New York: J. & J. Harper, 1833).

3. James P. Baughman, "Gateway to the Americas," in *The Past As Prelude: New Orleans, 1718–1968,* ed. Hodding Carter (New Orleans: Tulane University, 1968), 260. The French recognized the problem of sedimentation at the mouth of the river soon after the founding of New Orleans. In 1722, the duc d'Orleans offered 10,000 *livres* to anyone who could achieve and maintain fifteen to sixteen feet over the bars. No one succeeded in winning the prize. In 1725 royal pilots were stationed at the passes; later both Spanish and American governments also supplied pilots who tried to "outguess the river." Ibid.

leans. The first third of the journey presented a monotonous landscape to the travelers' eyes. An Englishman wrote in his journal that as his ship entered the river in early afternoon, "as long as daylight would permit us a view, nothing appeared but a dull, uniform marsh covered with reeds, no cheering prospect to refresh the eye. All around is one dead level."[4]

Physically, Louisiana seemed a foreign land to visitors from other parts of the United States. The state's geographic diversity rivaled that of its population. Swamps, snakes, pelicans, cypress trees, "pendant, melancholy moss and . . . logs and snags, where numberless alligators" slumbered—all made Louisiana seem an exotic place to a young man like William Whitney. The shores along the river were quiet and mysterious, empty except for large white seagulls and the ever-present alligators sunning on logs. Closer to the city, signs of human habitation appeared. Earthen embankments protected the lands beyond from flooding and the roofs of plantation houses, set back about two hundred yards, were barely visible over the levees. Below New Orleans the houses typically sat on great brick columns that raised them to allow air circulation and to give protection from floods. Hammocks hung on wide verandas protected by venetian blinds and lattices so that the occupants might enjoy the breezes from the river. As the ship carrying Myra and William moved upriver, the couple could watch small communities with romantic names pass by on either side: Pilottown (where the bar and river pilots exchanged responsibilities); Quarantine; the Jump; Venice; Forts Philip and Jackson; Jesuit Bend; the English Turn; and finally the Crescent City itself, "bustling and charming, dirty and delightful, disease-ridden and joyous, and above all, growing and prosperous."[5]

In the early 1830s New Orleans was the most exciting, diverse, and unique city in America. Its physical appearance, architecture, ethnic makeup, and frontier-boomtown atmosphere encouraged its citizens to claim that there

4. George Dargo, *Jefferson's Louisiana: Politics and the Clash of Legal Traditions* (Cambridge, Mass.: Harvard University Press, 1975), 3; Joseph Holt Ingraham, *The Southwest, By a Yankee* (New York: Harper, 1835), 2: 72; Christian Schultz, *Travels on an Inland Voyage . . . Performed in the Years 1807 and 1808* (New York: Isaac Riley, 1810), 2: 209.

5. David C. Dennis, "The Image of Louisiana in America, 1800–1890" (master's thesis, University of Southwestern Louisiana, 1995), 5; A. Hall, *Manhattaner in New Orleans*, 4; Tregle, *Louisiana in the Age of Jackson*, 1–3, 31; Ingraham, *The Southwest, By a Yankee*, 1: 74; Baughman, "Gateway to the Americas," 259.

was "no place like New Orleans." The variety of vessels docked at the wharves astounded observers. "Dirty and uncouth backwoods flatboats" laden with hams, ears of corn, apples, and whisky barrels jostled for room with the "rather more decent keelboats" carrying cotton, furs, whisky, and flour. Elegant steamboats, whose "hissing and repeated sounds announced their arrival," spouted columns of black smoke that hung in great clouds over the city. Farther out in the river the sloops and schooners from Havana, Tampico, and Vera Cruz, and the larger ocean-sailing ships formed a forest of tall masts seen from the docks. The busy season for the port of New Orleans lasted from November to mid-June. During those months work never ceased on the wharves, "each hour . . . grudged if not devoted to toil." At night, fires provided light for the crowds of sailors, bargemen, and slaves laboring to unload cargo.[6]

The noise and confusion of the docks assaulted the visitor. Architect Benjamin Latrobe, visiting the city in 1819, reported that the "incessant, loud, rapid, and various gabble of tongues of all tones," comparable to the sounds of "a million or two of frogs," filled his ears; and the sight of businessmen, merchants, slaves, Indians, and sailors of all countries mingling together widened his eyes. This "congregation of all kinds of people from every stratum of society," of every nationality and color, formed a panorama seen nowhere else. For Richard Bache, a son-in-law of Benjamin Franklin who visited the city in 1834, New Orleans was "one of the most wonderful places in the world."[7]

Geographically and economically the Mississippi River dominated New Orleans. The great curve described by the river gave the community its "Crescent City" designation. The site of New Orleans is the flattest, lowest, and geologically youngest of any city in the United States. Built on

6. Dennis, "Image of Louisiana," 91; Tregle, *Louisiana in the Age of Jackson,* 16; Thomas Low Nichols, *Forty Years of American Life* (London: Longmans & Green, 1874), 238; Albert A. Fossier, *New Orleans: The Glamour Period, 1800–1840* (New Orleans: Pelican, 1957), quoting Josiah Condon, a Londoner, describing the port of New Orleans in 1830, 26; ibid., quoting Tyrone Power, Esq., a visitor to New Orleans in 1834, 27; "Commercial Cities and Towns of the United States: New Orleans and Its Trade and Commerce," *Merchant's Magazine and Commercial Review,* 1844: 503.

7. Benjamin H. Latrobe, *The Journals of Benjamin Henry Latrobe, 1799–1820: From Philadelphia to New Orleans,* ed. Edward C. Carter II, John C. Van Horne, and Lee W. Formwalt (New Haven, Conn.: Published for the Maryland Historical Society by the Yale University Press, 1980), 3: 166; Fossier, *New Orleans,* 23; ibid., quoting Richard Bache in 1834, 26–7.

mud deposited by the river in the eleventh century between Lake Pontchartrain and the Mississippi's main channel, the elevation of the city is below the normal water level of the river, and New Orleans could not have existed without its system of protective levees. These dikes served both the commercial and security needs of the port. Never less than six feet high and fifteen feet wide (and often much higher and wider) the earthen levees sloped gradually down to the river and provided the city with a wharf several miles long. On the city side the nearest houses were about 150 to 200 feet away and about five feet below the top of the levee.[8]

The levee was the city's marketplace. There "commission men, speculators, and dealers" argued feverishly amid the piled-up cargo. Rows of hucksters, most with their wares spread on palmetto leaves on the ground, urged each new arrival to purchase food, trinkets, jewelry, clothes, or shoes with annoying insistence. Each afternoon, residents of New Orleans promenaded on the levees, "a long and pleasant walk" where one could socialize with neighbors and encounter sights that amazed visitors. Richard Bache saw "crowds of Negresses and quadroons carrying on their bandananed heads, and with solemn pace, a whole table—or platform as large as a table—crowned with goodies, such as cakes and apples and oranges, figs, bananas, pine apples, and cocoanuts." With crowds of slaves, free people of color, and whites, the turmoil of the levee captured the essence of New Orleans—a "bewildering variety of goods and people; a confusion of races and nationalities; and the determined pursuit of money."[9]

In addition to the bustling wharves and exotic sights, Myra and William Whitney were sure to notice that New Orleans had a distinctly European ambiance, "less American than any other city," reported one visitor. Its French and Spanish heritage remained obvious in the language heard on the streets, in the architecture of the houses, and in the cuisine served in the restaurants and cafés. The old colonial town—today called the French Quarter or Vieux Carré—was known in the 1830s as "The City." It followed the curve of the river, twelve blocks wide from Canal Street to Esplanade, and six deep from the levee to Rampart Street (where palisades once walled in the original site). Named after Catholic saints and the no-

8. Dennis, "Image of Louisiana," 92; Latrobe, *Journals*, 3: 171 and 223, note 2; Henry Bertram Hill and Larry Gara, "A French Traveler's View of Ante-Bellum New Orleans," *Louisiana History* 1 (1960): 337–8.

9. A. Hall, *Manhattaner in New Orleans*, 5; Hill, "French Traveler's View," 338; Latrobe, *Journals*, 3: 171; Bache, quoted in Fossier, *New Orleans*, 26–7; Tregle, *Louisiana in the Age of Jackson*, 12.

bles of France, the narrow, straight streets of the City intersected at right angles: Chartres, Bourbon, Royal, Conti, St. Peter, St. Ann, Conde. The Place des Armes (known in 1833 by its new name, Jackson Square) faced the levee at the center of the old section. The imposing St. Louis Cathedral, flanked by the Cabildo and the Presbytere (or courthouse) dominated the square, which served as the center of city life. Across the street the old Indian market still served residents, and along the sides of the square grog shops and dry goods stores crowded together.[10]

Myra and William almost certainly boarded in the old quarter. In the early 1830s New Orleans had many small hotels and boarding houses, but the vast number of immigrants who visited during the winter months caught the city unprepared. Lodging was at a premium, and the cost of living during the winter was exorbitant. The two largest hotels were the Strangers and the Orleans, both located on Chartres Street. The Strangers, built in 1818, held seventy guests, the Orleans, one hundred. Either of these hotels would have provided Myra and William with a central point from which to explore the city.[11]

The first object of their explorations was the former home of Myra's father, now fallen into disrepair. Situated at the fork of two roads, one leading to the Bayou St. John and the other to the Gentilly Road, the old Clark house stood vacant and dilapidated. Once a "fine building with . . . beautifully laid gardens, orchards, flower parterres, kiosks, statues, and fountains," the home had been empty for many years. Reports of ghosts stalking its corridors at night frightened prospective tenants, and the house tumbled into decay.[12]

New Orleans also showed a changed face to its visitors. As they wan-

10. Dennis, "Image of Louisiana," 93; Henry C. Knight, *Letters from the South and West* (Boston: Richardson and Lord, 1824), 117; Hill, "French Traveler's View," 336; Tregle, *Louisiana in the Age of Jackson,* 13. Although most visitors reported the polyglot composition of the New Orleans population, economic historian John Clark believes this diversity is overstated. As a seaport, New Orleans attracted many nationalities, but, he argues, "no more so than New York and probably much less so than a cosmopolitan center such as Marseilles." John G. Clark, *New Orleans, 1718–1812: An Economic History* (Baton Rouge: Louisiana State University Press, 1970), 254.

11. Fossier, *New Orleans,* 13.

12. Henry C. Castellanos, *New Orleans As It Was: Episodes of Louisiana Life* (1895; reprint, Baton Rouge: Louisiana State University Press, 1978), 339; Edna Freiberg, *Bayou St. John in Colonial Louisiana, 1699–1803* (New Orleans: Harvey, 1980), 337; John Sibley, "The Journal of Dr. Sibley," *Louisiana Historical Quarterly* 10 (1927): 478–81; deposition of Charles Gayarré, Nov. 27, 1880, General Case Files no. 8825, Circuit Court

dered the cramped streets, Myra and William could see that close to the square French influences predominated. The shops, confectionaries, perfumeries, and millineries all had signs in French. Chartres Street was the commercial center of New Orleans in 1833. Dry goods stores, jewelers, and booksellers sold clothing, notions, and imported fabrics and furniture. Locations between St. Louis and Canal commanded the highest rents. Many visitors pronounced New Orleans the "Paris of America" in recognition of its magnificent stores whose wares proclaimed the sophistication of their clientele. Latest styles of ladies' apparel, talented modistes, and imported tableware and glassware allowed New Orleans women to present an appearance equal to those in any European capital. Isidore Lowenstern of Leipzig observed in 1837 that New Orleans stores sold the "most beautiful and precious merchandise from France and Great Britain," and "their beauty and elegance surpassed in elegance those of any other city in America."[13]

The elegance of the residential areas reflected the style of the retail district. Spanish architecture allowed buildings in the old city to adapt to the region's hot, humid climate. Cool patios, high ceilings, shady walks, and breezy balconies characterized the most elegant New Orleans homes, found between Royal and St. Louis Streets. Close to the river the houses were two or three stories; shops facing the street occupied the lowest floor. From the street, residents and visitors entered through a porte-cochère into a courtyard holding a decorative fountain and tropical plants. A broad exterior staircase led to the upper apartments. Wide, arched windows opened onto the patio, their sills covered with aromatic plants such as rosemary. From Royal to Rampart picturesque one-story houses with high-pitched roofs lined the streets. No uniformity of color united these houses; pink and white plaster stood next to red brick or drab unpainted wood, giving the city a "mottled and dappled appearance" that travelers found charming.[14]

of the United States, Eastern District of Louisiana, Record Group 21, National Archives, Southwest Region, Fort Worth, Tex.

13. Tregle, *Louisiana in the Age of Jackson,* 13–4; John S. Kendall, *History of New Orleans* (Chicago: Lewis Publishing, 1922), 1: 139; Fossier, *New Orleans,* quoting Lowenstern, 56–7.

14. Latrobe, *Journals,* 3: 175; Castellanos, *New Orleans As It Was,* 152; Nathaniel Curtis, *New Orleans, Its Old Houses, Shops, and Public Buildings* (Philadelphia: J. B. Lippincott, 1938), 94; François-Xavier Martin, *The History of Louisiana from the Earliest Period* (New Orleans: J. A. Gresham, 1882), 10–1; Tregle, *Louisiana in the Age of Jack-*

The Whitneys encountered more familiar styles of architecture in the section of New Orleans favored by American residents. After the cession of Louisiana by the French in 1803, Americans flooded into New Orleans. As the city grew, faubourgs (or suburbs) extended along the levee, following the course of the river. A "kind of Philadelphia suburb in the tropics," the Faubourg St. Mary, located upriver of the Creole-dominated old city, became home to many Americans. During the 1830s its growth outstripped that of the older section. A foreign visitor to New Orleans in 1833 remarked that "few towns in the United States increase with greater rapidity. Within the last three years, a thousand houses have been added to its buildings, principally fronting along the river in the Faubourg St. Mary, most of them massive and commodious." A new faubourg, created by the city in the 1820s from land owned by Myra's father—the Faubourg St. John—added to the American section's commercial and residential growth. By 1830 much of the river trade came to the levee protecting the upper faubourgs. The main commercial district along Magazine and Camp Streets became filled with never-idle commission and wholesale trading houses. The commercial and residential potential of these suburbs held special interest for the Whitneys. A sizeable portion had been part of Daniel Clark's estate, and Myra and William believed that this valuable property rightfully belonged to her and had been sold unlawfully to its present occupants by her father's business partners.[15]

American visitors often commented that the Faubourg St. Mary resembled other United States cities; its red-brick houses reminded Benjamin Latrobe of the "dull, dingy character of Market Street in Philadelphia." Another northern visitor approved of the "new city" that contained "a little of Boston . . . a trifle of New York, and some of Philadelphia." Beside the prosperous Faubourg St. Mary, the original city's European-style architecture and crowded streets appeared "narrow, dark, and dirty." But an English visitor who admired the Spanish-French architecture of the older section insisted that the Faubourg St. Mary had "no attractions of any

son, 14. New Orleans historian Robert Tallant locates the townhome of Daniel Clark at 823 Royal Street. *The Romantic New Orleanians* (New York; E. P. Dutton, 1950), 338.

15. James M. Fitch, "Creole Architecture, 1718–1860: The Rise and Fall of a Great Tradition," in *Past As Prelude,* ed. Carter, 84; Newton, *Americanization of French Louisiana,* 159–61; Tregle, *Louisiana in the Age of Jackson,* 14. The Faubourg St. Mary (or *Ste. Marie)* was named after Marie Josephe Delondes Gravier who once owned the great tract of land stretching back from the river upstream of the original boundary of the city. Tregle, *Louisiana in the Age of Jackson,* 15.

kind; the streets are wider, but unpaved; the houses larger, but bare and unseemly, and their internal superiority of comfort gained at the expense of external effect." Most observers concluded that if the American section was cleaner and more energetic and ambitious, it lacked the mellowed quality of age so notable in the older section.[16]

The physical separation of the sections mirrored the ethnic divisions found in New Orleans society. New Orleans contained many French immigrants (refugees from the Reign of Terror, victims of Napoleon, or émigrés escaping the Bourbon restoration), but native-born descendants of French and Spanish colonists—the *ancienne population,* usually known as "the Creoles"—still formed a majority of the white population. Immigrants from other parts of the United States made up another quarter of the white society. Native residents referred to newcomers such as the Whitneys as "Americans," and this designation reinforced the unique character of each group.[17]

Despite differences in education and experience, foreign French residents and native Louisianians joined in opposing the encroachers from the Atlantic coast. Historian George Dargo calls the ethnic division that developed a *kulturkampf.* "Ethnic identity," he writes, "supplied the most meaningful orientation to political life" in New Orleans. After visiting the city in 1825, the duke of Saxe-Weimar gave evidence in his travel diary of

16. Tregle, *Louisiana in the Age of Jackson,* 16; Latrobe, *Journals,* 3: 187; A. Hall, *Manhattaner in New Orleans,* 35; Newton, *Americanization of French Louisiana,* 159.

17. The definition of "Creole" is confusing and controversial. The term is used to identify those in the population who could trace their roots to the original settlers of the French and Spanish colonial era, and many early-nineteenth-century visitors to Louisiana incorrectly limited "Creole" to the white population. See as example, James Silk Buckingham, *Travels through the Slave States of America,* 2 vols. (London: Fisher, 1842). Examining the contemporary records, Joseph Tregle makes clear that "in the 1820s and 1830s Louisianians used the term *creole* to designate any person native to the state, whether white, black, or colored, French, Spanish, or Anglo-American, rich or poor, eminent or lowly." Nevertheless, Tregle notes that "convenience dictated the acceptance of the phrase 'the creoles' in place of the more cumbersome *ancienne population*" to refer to those persons descended from French or Spanish settlers, though that did not prevent any native-born individual from claiming classification as a creole (Tregle, *Louisiana in the Age of Jackson,* 25). The "Creoles of color," defined as having African as well as French or Spanish ancestry, formed a distinct socioeconomic class, largely composed of merchants and artisans, many of whom owned shops in the Old Quarter.

the political implications of this clashing of cultures. "Creoles," the duke reported, "appear . . . to wish their country should be a French colony rather than annexed to the Union." Conversations with the native-born residents of the old quarter convinced him that the Creoles "do not regard Americans as their countrymen." A British writer concurred: Americans and Creoles did not "mingle much together." The difference between old and new became so pronounced that by 1830 New Orleans seemed to be two separate cities divided by Canal Street, the transition as marked "as between Calais and Dover."[18]

The steadfast attachment of the Louisiana Creoles to European customs and their refusal to become "Americanized" frustrated residents and visitors from the rest of the United States. Most Creoles spoke French and did not bother to learn English, or at best, spoke it poorly. Local politics and social events dominated their conversation; to one visitor, the Creoles appeared "to have a total disregard of the outside world." New York and Washington seemed so remote that a "limitless ocean" might separate them from the residents of the Crescent City. The social differences between Creoles and Americans grew so intense that even the famous ballrooms felt the effect. Northern writer Joseph Holt Ingraham reported that at dances Americans commandeered "one half of the hall . . . the other to the French."[19]

By simply walking through the streets of New Orleans as William and Myra Whitney did, a traveler could experience the contrast of cultures. The American side of Canal Street bustled with constant activity, while in the old city, Creoles socialized. Americans worked late at their counting houses, while Creoles went off to the theater or mingled with friends in

18. Dargo, *Jefferson's Louisiana*, 11; Tregle, *Louisiana in the Age of Jackson*, 32–3; Newton, *Americanization of French Louisiana*, 160–1; Charles A. Murray, *Travels in North America*, 2: 129–30, and the duke of Saxe-Weimar, *Travels through North America*, 2: 72, quoted in Mattie Wood Dugdale, "Travelers' Views of Louisiana before 1860" (master's thesis, University of Texas, 1938), 35; Timothy Flint, *History and Geography of the Mississippi Valley* (Cincinnati: E. H. Flint & L. R. Lincoln, 1833), 1: 267; Tyrone Power, *Impressions of America during the Years 1833, 1834, 1835* (London: R. Bentley, 1836), 2: 147–8. Until the early 1830s Canal Street formed a real barrier between the First and Second Municipalities. The canal or drainage ditch that gave that street its name prevented the streets in the two sections from connecting. Newton, *Americanization of French Louisiana*, 160–1.

19. Albert Rhodes, "Louisiana Creoles," *Galaxy* 10 (1873): 255; Harriet Martineau, *Retrospect of Western Travel* (New York: Harper & Brothers, 1838), 271; Dennis, "Image of Louisiana," 37–40; Ingraham, *The Southwest, By a Yankee*, 123.

one of the many cafés. If the Creole rejected American values, the American averred that the Creole was "neither practical, energetic, nor able; that he [was] a stumbling-block in the way of progress." Yankee observers reared under the precepts of the protestant work ethic charged that young Creole men lacked the inclination or necessity for productive work, a desire, one visitor wrote, that represented "the fundamental difference between the savage and the civilized man." Another American mused that "the loss of time is never considered an evil [by the Creole] because if it were not spent in this way, it would be wasted in some other, perhaps equally injurious, and more prejudicial to health." Such indolence, Amos Stoddard concluded, "often induces them to seek repose on the sofa or mattress." English sojourners could be equally critical of both lifestyles. Londoner Thomas Ashe observed that the Creole did not look to the future and progress but rather "linger[ed] in the past, dallying with the flowers of love and sentiment." The American, in contrast, "hurries forward with unhappy haste to pluck the thorns of ambition and self." The cultural difference between the two largest population groups in New Orleans drew in Myra and William Whitney as they sought evidence to sustain Myra's claims. Since members of both groups had bought land from the Clark estate, Creoles and resident Americans united as never before in opposing the interlopers from New York.[20]

Even though the Creoles resolutely refused to be Americanized, many visitors noticed that northern immigrants enthusiastically adopted local customs, an interesting observation considering the disdain Americans demonstrated for Creole culture. Benjamin Latrobe remarked that "to Americans the most offensive feature of French habits [was] the manner in which they spend Sunday." Although resident Creoles in New Orleans were diligent in attendance at Mass, they did not recognize Sunday as a "day of rest." No shops in the Old Quarter closed, the theaters and ballrooms remained open, and visiting, sports, and gambling continued as on any other day. Americans who began by criticizing the lack of Sunday observance rarely withstood the lure of New Orleans. Thomas Low Nichols, an Englishman who first came to the city in the 1830s, noticed that the French "desecration" of the Sabbath shocked many at first, but soon the Americans "did not fail to imitate it and exceed it." The American side of

20. Dennis, "Image of Louisiana," 69–70; Rhodes, "Louisiana Creoles," 255; Major Amos Stoddard, *Sketches Historical and Descriptive of Louisiana* (Philadelphia: Matthew Carey, 1812), 322; Dugdale, "Travelers' Views of Louisiana," 33–8.

New Orleans eventually became "far noisier on Sunday than the French." When the Americans did break the Sabbath, Nichols wrote, they "[broke] it into very small pieces." An American commentator concurred. Visiting New Orleans twenty years after Nichols, Frederick Law Olmsted found that Americans adopted the worst of local customs: living beyond one's means, borrowing heavily, and gambling. Travelers often accused Creole males of making a profession out of games of chance. Gambling was illegal and the subject of considerable legislation and occasional raids, but New Orleans gaming parlors attracted both residents and visitors, as long as they had cash in their pockets. A "spirit of speculation, swindling, and fraud" prevailed among both Creole and American residents.[21]

Myra and William Whitney encountered New Orleans at a particularly exciting time. The city's unique, exotic, even bizarre quality peaked in the 1830s and 40s. Its location made it a point of transshipment for the produce of the Mississippi River, and only a small portion of the goods that passed through the port were actually consumed in New Orleans. Downriver trade more than doubled between 1830 and 1840, growing from $20 million to $50 million. Other river cities such as St. Louis, Memphis, and Nashville lacked rail connections to the East until the late 1840s; these cities sent wheat, cotton, and tobacco to New Orleans for export. In 1836 New Orleans passed New York City as the greatest export center of the United States. Fifteen years earlier, in 1821, Lloyd's of London had forecast that New Orleans would become the world's greatest port, and its residents believed the prediction. Louisiana newspapers promised their readers that New Orleans was well on its way to "the maximum of all human grandeur." Nothing could "prevent her taking the very first stand among the celebrated cities of the world, whether for population or wealth." Its citizens would yet "see their city without a parallel both in the old and new worlds."[22]

Growth in New Orleans, as in other nineteenth-century cities in the United States, was hindered by sanitation problems that encouraged the spread

21. Kendall, *History of New Orleans,* 1: 199; Latrobe, *Journals,* 3: 186; Nichols, *Forty Years of American Life,* 130; Frederick Law Olmsted, *A Journey through the Seaboard Slave States* (New York: Mason Brothers, 1858), 236.
22. Tregle, *Louisiana in the Age of Jackson,* 16–7; Harold Sinclair, *The Port of New Orleans* (New York: Doubleday, Doran, 1942), 167; New Orleans *Mercantile Advertiser* as quoted in the *Alexandria Louisiana Messenger,* Dec. 15, 1826, quoted by Tregle, *Louisiana in the Age of Jackson,* 19.

of disease. The city's location and climate compounded such problems. Particularly during the summer months, New Orleans was not a pleasant place to live. The city sweltered in the heat as the sun dried the streets and turned them into swirling avenues of dust. To lessen the suffocating dust, the city splashed the streets with water from gutters that doubled as public sewers; the stench from the drying streets overwhelmed pedestrians. Standing water meant mosquitoes. Appearing early in March, the mosquitoes by April had "completely colonized bedrooms, drawing rooms, and saloons"; only mosquito netting at night brought any relief from their buzzing and biting. Summer also meant yellow fever epidemics or fear of epidemics; this mosquito-borne disease terrified newcomers and aroused apprehension among even the oldest residents. Since no one knew its cause or how to treat it most residents deserted the city during the summer months.[23]

Lack of adequate sewage disposal multiplied the city's sanitation problems. Residents used streets and empty lots for garbage dumps and, during the day, as public latrines. Bodies of dead animals, crabs, oysters, turtle shells, palmetto leaves wrapped around catfish heads and entrails rotting in the sun added to the fetid atmosphere. New Orleans newspapers estimated that nine-tenths of city yards and undeveloped lots were constantly covered with decomposing solid and semifluid matter. When the rains came, conditions only worsened. The city became a quagmire with mud so deep in the streets that carts had to carry pedestrians from one side to another. Breezes brought other smells of decay from poorly sealed tombs in the cemetery at the rear of the old town and from the waterfront, polluted by waste dumped along the riverside levee. Long-standing custom allowed New Orleans residents to throw garbage, refuse, and privy contents into the river. If the water level rose to near the top of the levee—as it did in early spring—this material quickly floated away. But for most of the year the level of the river left a strip of ground twenty-five to fifty feet wide (called the batture) between the water and the levee. In summer the city's air reeked with garbage.[24]

Beginning in the mid-1820s these sanitary problems prompted city

23. Tregle, *Louisiana in the Age of Jackson*, 19–20; A. Hall, *Manhattaner in New Orleans*, 56; Max Berger, *The British Traveler in America, 1836–1860* (New York: Columbia University Press, 1943), 44; John Duffy, "Pestilence in New Orleans," in *Past As Prelude*, ed. Carter, 98; *Louisiana Courier*, July 21, 1824, p. 2.

24. Tregle, *Louisiana in the Age of Jackson*, 20; Duffy, "Pestilence," 101–2.

fathers to undertake an extensive program of municipal improvements. Street paving began, but by 1835 only two streets were paved for their entire length. Paving required the use of imported stone from Europe or the northern states and represented a considerable expense. The *Louisiana Gazette* reported that "large stones would cost $4.00 per ton and small ones, $2.00." Curb stones at fifty cents per square yard added to the price. Despite the difficulty of raising tax revenue to pay for paving of new and existing streets, by 1835 thirty-four streets had been paved for at least part of their length. The heavy clay soil and high water table in New Orleans increased the problems faced by paving contractors, and the editors of the *New Orleans Bee* criticized public officials for the quality of the work done. "Paving now being done," the paper editorialized, "is disgraceful to the contractors. Not the slightest care is taken to prepare a bed for the stones, which are hammered down at random." The *Bee*'s editors feared that "these pavements as laid cannot endure more than a few weeks."[25]

To expand the use of the newly paved streets, the city erected lighting posts at diagonal corners of the principal thoroughfares; twelve large lamps with reflectors swinging on ropes between the posts were in place by 1821, and more followed as the city grew. Prior to the installation of these lamps, anyone venturing outdoors at night carried his own lantern. This custom continued through most of the 1830s until the city chartered the Gaslight Company and granted it the exclusive privilege of lighting the city. Placards bearing the names of streets appeared at intersections; visitors appreciated this convenience, which one stated was "unequaled by any other city in the nation."[26]

Bricked sidewalks made pedestrian traffic more secure. A report by city surveyor Joseph Pilié to the city council concluded that "dirty footways and cross bridges which were indeed receptacles for filth, had disappeared throughout the whole of the incorporated limits, to make way for proper and elegant trottoirs to cover sewers and paved ways offering all conveniences." New streets in the Faubourg St. Mary; repaired, enlarged, and newly whitewashed marketplaces; better fire protection provided by new engines and a "complete assortment of ladders"; new wharves that expanded the port facilities; and a new cemetery with a railroad to transport corpses to the burial ground completed the expansion detailed in Pilié's

25. *Louisiana Gazette,* May 19, 1823, and June 16, 1823; *New Orleans Bee,* Apr. 23, 1835, and Apr. 29, 1835; Fossier, *New Orleans,* 10–2.

26. Kendall, *History of New Orleans,* 1: 116; Fossier, *New Orleans,* 12–3.

report. One street in particular showed the effect of these public works projects. Lined with shanties in the 1820s, Bourbon Street in the 1830s became a street of elegant residences, housing many of the socially prominent and distinguished members of the community.[27]

Nor did the city neglect its landscaping. Trees were planted in the newly named Jackson Square, which until then had been a bare, unsightly expanse of untrimmed grass. The municipal government also planted trees on the levee and along Canal, Rampart, and Esplanade Streets, encircling the Old City. Widening and cleaning the canal that split Canal Street improved the appearance of a street that was fast becoming a major commercial district. An ornamental fence enclosed the "neutral ground" between the older section and the Faubourg St. Mary, which jointly developed the area into a park. In 1833 the French traveler Theodore Pavie exclaimed over the amenities appearing in the city. "What is most ravishing and most appreciable," he enthused, "is to find shade at every step, and especially ice, which is brought in by sea from Boston, Philadelphia, Providence, in fact from everywhere."[28]

All of these improvements increased the opinion of New Orleans citizens that their city would soon equal New York City in size and importance. Business expansion meant a need for capital funding. Several banks had been established in New Orleans after the United States acquired the territory in 1803. During the 1830s their number grew as trade increased and land speculation generated huge profits. Imposing bank buildings arose in the City and then spilled over into the American faubourg: the Bank of Louisiana and the Louisiana State Bank on the corners of Royal and Conti Streets; the Planters' Bank at the corner of Royal and Toulouse; the Merchants' Bank of New Orleans on Bienville and Royal; the Improvement Bank at 153 Chartres; the Bank of New Orleans on Canal and Exchange Place; the City Bank at 13 Camp Street; the Commercial Bank of New Orleans at Magazine and Natchez; and the Union Bank at the corner of Custom House (Iberville) and Royal. This proliferation of bank buildings indicated that a principal occupation of New Orleans residents was increasing their fortunes. New Yorker Alexander Hall called New Orleans the "Calcutta of America" because "except among the Creoles . . . a man of leisure is a wonder. . . . On street corners, at the dinner-table, between

27. Pilié's *Report* quoted in Fossier, *New Orleans*, 20, 56.
28. Kendall, *History of New Orleans*, 1: 116; Theodore Pavie, quoted in Fossier, *New Orleans*, 17.

acts at the opera and theater, in the drawing room, at the ball or soiree . . . money [is] the liveliest topic." Land speculation formed the basis of many fortunes. One lot between Custom House and Canal with a fifty-foot frontage on Canal sold for $50,000 in 1835 and sold again a year later for $500,000. Editors of the *Bee* concluded in 1835 that "there were few states in the Union where capital embarked, can produce more profitable dividends."[29]

Myra and William Whitney represented a threat to the booming economy of the Crescent City. Should they succeed in attacking Daniel Clark's will and estate, the resulting confusion in land titles would halt expansion and development in the most commercially important areas. William Whitney's only surviving letter from this early period of his marriage demonstrates his determination to "secure to [Myra] the possession of her property." He would, he wrote to his father, "refuse no responsibility or difficulty in the discharge" of this duty. He evinced no concern for what turmoil their actions might cause landowners in New Orleans nor any apprehension about what their opponents might do in response. Instead, he "contemplat[ed] with pleasure a life of industry and usefulness" spent with Myra in pursuit of their mutual goal.[30]

At the beginning of the slow season in New Orleans (in midsummer when the threat of yellow fever began) Myra and William Whitney returned to his family's home in Binghamton, New York. They had spent about five months in New Orleans investigating the story they had heard from Bellechasse and Harriet Smythe and searching for other old residents who remembered Myra's father. Just before they left the city they took possession of the lots held for Myra by Bellechasse, a legacy they could use to finance future legal expenses. Significantly, legal documents signed by Myra indicate that she began to use Daniel Clark's name during this visit. When they returned to the city on the river six months later, she and her husband began their challenge to Clark's estate, the first blow of the Great Gaines Case.[31]

29. *New Orleans Bee*, Apr. 7, 1835; Fossier, *History of New Orleans*, 12–3; Tregle, *Louisiana in the Age of Jackson*, 18; A. Hall, *Manhattaner in New Orleans*, 23; Kendall, *History of New Orleans*, 1: 142.

30. W. W. Whitney to General Joshua Whitney, Oct. 2, 1832.

31. Registration of Sale of Property by Josef Bellechasse to Myra Clark Whitney and William Wallace Whitney before Notary Louis T. Caire, June 4, 1833, Notarial Records of New Orleans, reprinted in *Transcript of Record, Gaines v. City of New Orleans*, 2: 1638.

III

"A Pair of Unscrupulous Adventurers"

Returning to New York in early summer 1833, Myra and William spent the next six months with Whitney's family in New York. General and Mrs. Whitney welcomed Myra wholeheartedly. The family held a ball to introduce their son's wife to Binghamton society—"the greatest social event that had ever been held in Broome County"—and among the guests was Governor Clinton. Other family members also entertained the newlyweds during their stay. Myra never forgot the warmth of her welcome into William's family. Long after his death she remained close to his parents, and as her case grew in notoriety, she tried to advance the interests of his brothers.[1]

Myra's welcome at Delamore Place did not match that offered in Binghamton. Colonel Davis angrily denied knowing anything about the second will made by Clark. In testimony given in court three years later, Davis recalled that he expressed doubts about the success of any legal action to obtain a legacy for Myra. Her husband remembered more specific objections. Colonel Davis, William believed, actively opposed Myra's lawsuits, even writing their opponents with an offer to testify against her.[2]

When Whitney accused the colonel of conspiring with Myra's opponents, he was referring to the executors of Clark's 1811 will, Richard Relf

1. Seward, *Binghamton and Broome County,* 44–50.
2. Samuel B. Davis, deposition of May 4, 1836, cross-interrogatories 40 and 43, *Richard Relf v. W. W. Whitney,* case no. 3452, United States District Court, reprinted in *Transcript of Record, Gaines v. City of New Orleans,* 2: 2055.

and Beverly Chew. Ultimately the Gaines case comprised more than eighty legal actions in United States courts, and hundreds of defendants demurred, answered, or made other pleadings in response to the various lawsuits. But these two men stand out among all the other defendants. Their activities as executors and attorneys for the heirs of Daniel Clark under the 1811 will provided the basis for all the litigation.

Richard Relf left Philadelphia for New Orleans in 1789 at the age of fourteen. He boarded in the household of William Hulings, United States vice-consul for Louisiana. Hulings's friendship with Daniel Clark brought Relf to Clark's notice, and Clark prevailed on his friend to allow young Richard to assist in his business. Relf served as Clark's confidential clerk for several years, and according to one longtime New Orleans resident, "gained [Clark's] esteem and confidence."[3]

Merchants such as Daniel Clark occupied an important position in the New Orleans economy. They sold staple crops for planters, accepting cash, bills, or goods in remittance. They purchased, stored, carted, or shipped goods on consignment, earning a commission on their services. Incoming products ordered by Louisiana planters required similar services. Merchants also procured insurance, collected debts, provided credit, and drew, endorsed, and negotiated bills of exchange. With specie in short supply and banking services nonexistent before 1803, Clark and his fellow merchant-traders furnished the means by which New Orleans became the trading center of the Mississippi Valley.[4]

In 1801 Richard Relf formed a partnership with a new arrival to the city, Beverly Chew. Born in Virginia to a family that held several influential positions in state politics, Chew came to Louisiana in 1797 with the same intention as most American immigrants—to make his fortune. Backed by Daniel Clark, the firm of Chew & Relf soon became the leading merchant house in New Orleans. Advertisements indicating the extent of their ventures filled the front pages of New Orleans newspapers. The firm operated its own general store located on St. Louis Street, between Royal and Chartres. Clark, though a silent partner in the firm, could be found in the store virtually every day. The shop sold a wide variety of merchandise: wine, cloth, tableware, furniture, and other consumer items. Staple products—

3. Daniel W. Coxe, deposition of Aug. 25, 1849, ibid., 2: 1502; Hubert Remy, deposition of Apr. 24, 1834, ibid., 2: 1674.
4. J. Clark, *New Orleans,* 306.

tobacco, cotton, and foodstuffs (especially flour)—also traded in the shop, either for the account of Chew & Relf or on consignment.[5]

As planters' agents Chew & Relf kept accounts balanced between overseas importers and Mississippi Valley planters—shipping staples to the former and manufactured goods to the latter. They corresponded with the Philadelphia firm of Reed & Forde, and the Liverpool firm of Green & Wainwright retained Chew & Relf as their New Orleans representatives. The link with the English firm originated in a family connection—Clark's sister Jane was married to George Green, the principal partner in the Liverpool house. Such business arrangements allowed the New Orleans firm to weather fluctuations in staple prices caused by crop successes or failures. Advances made on consignment goods equaled between two-thirds and three-quarters of the expected net proceeds but required payment of a 5 percent commission to the Philadelphia firm and 6 percent to the London merchants. The ability of Chew & Relf to obtain advances on prospective sales meant that Louisiana planters eagerly sought their services.[6]

Chew & Relf also engaged in the slave trade. The articles establishing the Territory of Orleans prohibited the importation of slaves, but smuggling slaves into New Orleans became a profitable venture for many merchants since slaves in the territory were in short supply. In 1803 the city council stopped Chew & Relf from landing a cargo of West Indian slaves, but the firm merely sent the slaves up the Bayou Lafourche out of the council's jurisdiction, and held their sale. A year later, Chew & Relf advertised 108 slaves, legally imported from other slave states, for sale and offered to accept payment in either notes or cotton. In another transaction, William Dunbar forwarded three thousand pounds sterling in notes on London, endorsed by Chew & Relf, to a Charleston slave trader. The firm handled all details of the trade. As the war between England and the United States approached, such transactions became more difficult. In 1811 John Palfrey bought twenty slaves from the firm for $7,750, paying $4,000 down with the balance due in one year. Chew & Relf held a mortgage on Palfrey's plantation as security for the debt. In 1812 Palfrey was unable to pay his debt, and the firm extended the time for repayment. The War of 1812

5. Ibid.; Latrobe, *Journals*, 3: 285, note 12; Henry W. Palfrey, deposition of May 25, 1849, reprinted in *Transcript of Record, Gaines v. Hennen*, 605; for advertisements placed by Chew & Relf, see page one of issues of the *New Orleans Bee* or *Louisiana Gazette* between 1804 and 1810.

6. J. Clark, *New Orleans*, 308.

meant a further delay in collection, and the debt was not paid until April of 1816.[7]

Richard Relf and Beverly Chew formed part of the inner core of the New Orleans business community that ran the town politically, set its social tone, and controlled its economic development. They and a few other successful merchants established a "virtual monopoly of corporate enterprise" in the city. As members of this business elite, Relf and Chew participated in the organization and operation of most of the new capitalistic ventures receiving charters after 1803. Soon after France transferred the province of Louisiana to the United States, American merchants in New Orleans petitioned the governor of the territory to charter a bank. Banking services meant a new source of credit for both merchant and planter. Banks served as places of deposit, authorizing drafts, issuing letters of exchange, and discounting notes. The firm of Chew & Relf bought stock in the new Bank of Louisiana, and Relf sat on its board of directors from 1807 to 1813. From 1818 to 1847 he served as cashier of another financial institution, the Louisiana State Bank. Chew was equally active, serving on the board of directors of the First Bank of the United States until its charter ran out in 1811. When Congress chartered a Second Bank of the United States in 1816, Chew accepted another appointment to its board, and in 1831 held the office of president of the board. In that year he resigned from the Second Bank of the United States and joined the Canal and Banking Company of Louisiana as cashier, becoming its president in 1832.[8]

Relf and Chew also exercised their leadership in the community by beginning the first insurance business in New Orleans. Relf was a founder of the New Orleans Insurance Company, chartered in 1805 to insure vessels, cargoes, and money in port and in transit. The firm of Chew & Relf subscribed to the first offering of the company stock, and each partner served at different times on the company's board of directors. In the same year Chew & Relf announced its appointment as exclusive agents of the Phoenix Fire Assurance Company of London; the firm held this appointment until 1818.[9]

The careers of Relf and Chew demonstrated a "deep and durable involvement in the economic life of New Orleans," according to one historian of economic life in the city. The two men personally filled 6 percent

---

7. Ibid.; *Louisiana Gazette,* advertisement, Mar. 25, 1804, p. 1.
8. J. Clark, *New Orleans,* 330–2.
9. Ibid., 332.

of all available corporate directorships between 1803 and 1812. All four corporations existing in New Orleans in 1808–1810 had a member of the firm on their boards. Richard Relf alone served on the boards of the Louisiana Bank, the Orleans Navigation Company, and the New Orleans Insurance Company.[10]

Nor did either man neglect political or social involvement. Relf served as secretary of the New Orleans Chamber of Commerce in 1806 and was elected to the city council in 1810. During the Battle of New Orleans in 1815, he participated as a member of the New Orleans volunteer fire brigade. In the next decade his name appeared as a contributor on the rolls of the New Orleans Thespian Benevolent Society and as a member of the board of administrators of Charity Hospital. When an Episcopal church formed in New Orleans Relf was a charter member and served as church warden. Christ Episcopal Church selected him in 1838 as their delegate to the convention to form the Diocese of Louisiana.[11]

Territorial Governor William Claiborne appointed Beverly Chew as a justice of the Territorial Court of Common Pleas and then as territorial postmaster. In 1806 he became a captain of the city militia, and during the Battle of New Orleans he fought in a company of volunteer riflemen. From 1816 to 1829, successive United States presidents selected Chew as collector of customs for the port of New Orleans. Architect Benjamin Latrobe credited Chew with securing a lighthouse on the Mississippi River at Balize Point and wrote that "a more meritorious officer of Government does not exist." Most of New Orleans agreed that Chew was "a popular man and a good officer," but he lost his appointment as collector when Andrew Jackson assumed the presidency in 1829. "So virulent" was Chew in his opposition to Jackson, wrote one political opponent, that he even refused "permission . . . to hoist a flag on the church [of which he was a vestryman] or to have the bells rung on the 8th of January in honor" of Jackson's great victory.[12]

*   *   *

10. Ibid., 290–1, 331.

11. Charles Gayarré, *History of Louisiana* (New York: William J. Widdleton, Publisher, 1866), 3: 165; J. Clark, *New Orleans*, 331; Latrobe, *Journals*, 3: 285, note 12; Georgia Fairbanks Taylor, "The Early History of the Episcopal Church in New Orleans, 1805–1840," *Louisiana Historical Quarterly* 22 (Apr. 1939): 435, 453.

12. Georgia Taylor, "Early History of the Episcopal Church," 449; Latrobe, *Journals*, 3: 285; and Tregle, *Louisiana in the Age of Jackson*, quoting David C. Ker, 232.

In the contest over Daniel Clark's will, Relf and Chew represented the New Orleans business establishment; Myra and William Whitney were the outsiders threatening to overset long-established commercial relationships. The firm of Chew & Relf successfully weathered the tumultuous years prior to the War of 1812, rode out the war years without damage, survived the postwar boom and bust, and was still operating in the 1830s. The Whitneys charged that Richard Relf and Beverly Chew had used Daniel Clark's fortune as a cushion to prevent their business from failing during the war and afterwards. Specifically, Relf and Chew allowed the Orleans Navigation Company to develop the Canal Carondelet–Bayou St. John waterway between New Orleans and Lake Pontchartrain along land owned by the Clark estate. The two men were major stockholders and directors of the company, and much of their postwar fortunes derived from the monopoly held by the Navigation Company over the canal's traffic. The need to protect their fortunes, as well as their reputations as honest businessmen and prominent members of the New Orleans community, required Relf and Chew to vigorously defend their actions from the Whitneys' accusations.[13]

The young couple learned just how vigorously Relf and Chew planned to defend their reputations when the Whitneys filed a preliminary lawsuit in February 1834 in the United States District Court in New Orleans. Alleging fraud in the management of estate assets, the petition sought the recovery of the $2,361 plus interest that Colonel Davis had unwillingly returned to the executors in 1814. The Whitneys contended that Clark demonstrated his "entire trust and confidence" in Davis by entrusting him with funds for his daughter's care. At Davis's suggestion, the two men had prepared a memorandum containing "an explicit declaration" that Davis held the money for Myra and that he should use the interest it earned for her education. That memorandum had inexplicably disappeared. The Whitneys charged that the two executors "fraudulently pretended" that Clark had assigned Davis's note to them and asked the court to order Relf and Chew to repay the sum with interest for twenty years.[14]

13. Tregle, *Louisiana in the Age of Jackson,* 196.

14. Petition of William W. Whitney and Myra Clark Whitney, Feb. 26, 1834, in *Whitney et ux v. Richard Relf and Beverly Chew,* District Court of the United States, Eastern District of Louisiana, General Case Files no. 3393, Record Group 21, National Archives, Southwest Region, Fort Worth, Tex. This suit was decided in favor of Richard Relf and Beverly Chew on December 20, 1834, by Judge Samuel Harper.

Through their attorneys, Relf and Chew denied all the allegations in the Whitneys' petition, especially the "base, gratuitous" charge that they had "acted falsely and fraudulently." However, their answer contained an important change. Relf and Chew, having claimed in 1814 that Clark had endorsed the note to them and that they had collected the money in their own names, now acknowledged that Davis's note really belonged to Clark's estate. As executors they had used the money from Davis to pay off a debt by the estate to Samuel Elkins, a New Orleans merchant. Concluding their answer, Relf and Chew attacked Myra directly, denying that she was anything more than the "pretended daughter" of Daniel Clark.[15]

This first case served only to draw the executors into the realm of the courtroom where they would have to defend their actions. Once the Whitneys had questioned the conduct of the executors, other suits attacking Relf and Chew's administration of Clark's estate came trickling into the New Orleans courts. On March 17, 1834, a creditor of the Clark estate, Charles W. Shaumburg, claimed that Relf and Chew failed to file the proper documentation for the administration of the estate, leaving it "vacant, abandoned, unclaimed, and unadministered." Shaumburg asked the state probate court to appoint him as the new administrator of Daniel Clark's property. Whitney's investigations the previous year had alarmed Shaumburg and made him fear for the eventual satisfaction of his claim on the estate, and Whitney had urged the action. As a creditor, Shaumburg could ask the court to reopen the probate of the estate, something the Whitneys could not do because Clark's will of 1811 had not mentioned Myra. But once the probate court began to consider the Shaumburg petition, Whitney could petition the court in Myra's name to revoke probate of the 1811 will.[16]

Relf and Chew viewed Shaumburg's petition as a serious challenge. The New Orleans business community knew Shaumburg; he was not merely a young outsider whose wife pretended to be the true heir to an estate Relf and Chew had managed for twenty years. Moreover, they were vulnerable, having failed to conform to the probate court's rules in their conduct as

15. Answer of Relf and Chew, ibid.

16. Shaumburg's petition for Letters of Curatorship has disappeared from the General Case Files held by the National Archives, Southwest Region. The reply of Relf and Chew contains a restatement of Shaumburg's request. Opposition of Relf and Chew to the Application of Charles W. Shaumburg for Letters of Curatorship, Mar. 17, 1834, Court of Probates of New Orleans, General Case Files no. 2715, Record Group 21, National Archives, Southwest Region, Fort Worth, Tex.

executors. The investigations Whitney had conducted in the court records the year before disclosed that Relf and Chew had never presented an accounting of their administration to the court, nor had they closed their executorship within a year after Clark's death—both actions required by Louisiana law. Neither had they filed a request with the court for an extension of their powers as executors. Seemingly, judicial oversight of their administration had lapsed in the confusion surrounding the war with England, and Relf and Chew continued to sell the estate assets long after their authority as executors should have ended.[17]

In their defense, Relf and Chew explained that "much litigation and embarrassment owing to defects in Titles to land" owned by Clark complicated their management of his estate. Clark, "never having been married and leaving no legitimate Descendants," left his entire estate to his mother, Mary Clark, of Philadelphia. Mrs. Clark gave Relf and Chew power of attorney to act for her "in all things touching the Estate." After her death in 1823, her executors, William Hulings and Joseph Reed, conferred the same power on the two men in New Orleans. Relf and Chew declared that they had managed and conducted the Clark estate "in conformity with law" and in the manner "best calculated to promote the interests of the Heirs . . . and of all persons having any just and legal claim to it." Even if, "under the peculiar circumstances of this Estate," the probate court did decide to reopen the administration of the estate, Relf and Chew asked that control of the estate be given not to Shaumburg but back to them, since they were creditors of the estate, friends of Clark during his lifetime, and still the "Agents of the Heirs of the Estate."[18]

Shaumburg's attorney, Richard R. Keene, was an old friend of Daniel Clark. In 1807 he served as Clark's second in a duel fought with the governor of the Orleans Territory, William Claiborne. Keene may have known of Myra's existence before the Whitneys arrived in New Orleans, since he readily accepted the evidence William unveiled in a letter written soon after the first exchange in the Shaumburg suit.[19]

In that letter, Whitney denounced the executors as "unworthy" and op-

17. W. W. Whitney to Richard R. Keene, Apr. 1834, Court of Probates of New Orleans, General Case Files no. 3452, Record Group 21, National Archives, Southwest Region, Fort Worth, Tex.

18. Opposition of Relf and Chew to the Application of Charles W. Shaumburg for Letters of Curatorship.

19. *Louisiana Gazette,* June 12, 1807, p. 3; W. W. Whitney to Richard Keene, Apr. 1834.

posed their continued control over the estate. Repeating his contention that Relf and Chew had defied the probate court by failing to comply with Louisiana law in the administration of Clark's estate, Whitney concluded that their management represented a "solemn and flagrant fraud" on the Louisiana court. Whitney's letter claimed that a serious disagreement over the dissolution of the partnership between Clark and the firm of Chew & Relf occurred several months before Clark's death. Because Clark suspected his business partners of dishonesty, he "withdrew his confidence from them." In his last will, Clark "carefully excluded them from any management of his Succession" and replaced them with Bellechasse, Delacroix, and Pitot as his executors. Whitney charged that this last will disappeared in an "extraordinary manner" and that Relf and Chew had defrauded his wife of her rights as the true heir of Daniel Clark.[20]

Publication of this letter by Keene alerted all New Orleans to the Whitneys' claim that Clark had made a second will naming Myra as heir. Although Shaumburg's request to reopen the probate of the 1811 will had not mentioned Myra Whitney, testimony during the hearing centered on her claim to be the missing heir. Several witnesses came forward to bolster Myra's story. Pierre Baron Boisfontaine, plantation agent for Daniel Clark and brother-in-law of Colonel Davis (and owner of the house in which Myra was born), gave a detailed picture of Clark's last hours. According to Boisfontaine, Clark made a will naming Myra as his heir shortly before his last illness. Together with other valuable papers, Clark locked the will in a "small black trunk" in a room used as an office on the ground floor of his home. Clark instructed his personal slave, Lubin, to take the trunk to the chevalier Delacroix upon his death. Boisfontaine remained at Clark's bedside and, shortly after Clark died, he saw Richard Relf take Clark's keys from an armoire and leave the room, first sending Lubin on an errand. Boisfontaine never saw Clark's will again, and he was "astonished" when it did not appear.[21]

A neighbor of Clark, Jean Canon, reinforced Boisfontaine's statement that Clark considered Myra his daughter and "manifested great affection for her." As an example of Clark's parental devotion, Canon testified that he had purchased a small Choctaw horse and saddle for Myra at Clark's

20. W. W. Whitney to Richard Keene, Apr. 1834.
21. Testimony of Pierre Baron Boisfontaine, Apr. 24, 1834, *Shaumburg v. Relf and Chew*, Court of Probates of New Orleans, reprinted in *Transcript of Record, Gaines v. City of New Orleans*, 2; 1673.

request and delivered the gift to the Davis household. But Canon also acknowledged that Clark "reposed entire confidence in Relf and Chew" and treated Relf "like a son." Relf, Canon asserted, was not capable of destroying Clark's will. Even if he had seen such an act, Canon declared, "he would not believe his eyes."[22]

Chevalier François Dusnau Delacroix confirmed only a portion of Boisfontaine's testimony. Clark had asked him to be the guardian of his daughter Myra. Delacroix, however, was certain that Myra was illegitimate; Clark, he remembered, intended to leave her "a sufficient fortune to do away with the stain of her birth." A few days before Clark's death, Delacroix visited and found his friend sealing a small packet. The words on its cover read *"Pour être ouvert en cas de mort"* ("To be opened in case of death"). Clark said the packet held his will and other important papers. He did not name Relf or Chew as his executors and asked Delacroix to say nothing to either man about the new will. Delacroix gave no explanation for the disappearance of the second will, and he, too, was convinced of Relf's honesty. The chevalier served as president of the Louisiana State Bank where Relf held the office of cashier, and he had never heard "anything against the integrity and correctness of Mr. Relf."[23]

Richard Relf responded to the implication in Whitney's letter and Boisfontaine's testimony that he had somehow destroyed a second will by filing civil suits for libel against Whitney and Shaumburg's attorney, Richard Keene. The treatment each suit received from the New Orleans courts demonstrates that local bias often complicated litigation. The District Court for the State of Louisiana quickly brought the suit against Keene to trial, and the attorney vigorously defended his publication of Whitney's letter. Several witnesses provided depositions supporting the allegations made in the letter, but the trial judge did not allow the jury to consider their testimony. Instead he dismissed the suit against Keene, refusing to allow the jury to consider whether the offending letter was libelous.[24]

In the second libel suit, Relf attempted to intimidate Whitney by swearing that the young lawyer was "indebted to him for $20,000" for the damage to his reputation caused by the publication of the offending letter. Judge Watts of the district court immediately issued a warrant for Whitney's arrest for debt, and on May 10, 1834, William Whitney entered the

22. Testimony of Jean Canon, Apr. 24, 1834, ibid., 2: 1675.
23. Testimony of F. D. Delacroix, Apr. 29, 1834, ibid., 2: 1671.
24. *New Orleans Bee*, Oct. 6, 1835, p. 2.

Orleans Parish Prison. The judge set bail at $35,000—an unprecedented sum that aroused much sympathy for the young man. Despite several offers from leading citizens to post a bond for his court appearance the judge refused to release Whitney. He remained in jail for three weeks as Myra frantically wrote General Whitney for help.[25]

The Orleans Parish Prison dated from the Spanish era. Located on St. Peter Street between Chartres and Royal, the old prison faced demolition upon completion of the new jail already under construction. Conditions at the "Old Calaboose" shocked a grand jury appointed by the district court in 1834 to investigate. Describing the jail as a "horrible den," they reported that "filth and odors of the most abominable kind" covered the floors. Overcrowding threw all culprits together "without the distinction of age, crime, or even color." The investigators found eight prisoners confined in a single wooden room, ten feet square and eight feet high; a single opening in the door, twelve by fifteen inches, admitted light and air. At one point, "as many as seventeen had been shut up in that Hell when the temperature out of doors was 90 to 95 degrees." The loathsome state of the prison incensed members of the grand jury who noted in their report that many of the inmates remained imprisoned "for no other fault than their inability to pay their debts." Technically, because of Relf's testimony, Whitney fit this category.[26]

Only intervention by a federal court achieved Whitney's release from the Old Calaboose. Since Whitney resided in New York, his attorney successfully petitioned the United States District Court to take over the libel suit (from the Louisiana District Court) and reduce Whitney's bail to $5,000. His health, never strong, was greatly injured by his twenty-one-day incarceration, but the experience did not lessen his combative spirit. Released in mid-June, he responded with a counterclaim for damages, charging Relf with "falsely and maliciously" accusing him of libel and causing his imprisonment. Relf's "malice" had influenced Judge Watts to refuse "the security of good and solvent men," and Whitney asked $20,000 in reparation for this "illegal oppression."[27]

At the same time, the Whitneys returned to the state probate court,

25. Answer of William Whitney, June 23, 1834, *Richard Relf v. William Whitney,* Louisiana District Court, General Case Files no. 3452, Record Group 21, National Archives, Southwest Region, Fort Worth, Tex.; William Whitney, Letter to the Editor, *New Orleans Bee,* Oct. 2, 1835, p. 1.

26. Fossier, *New Orleans,* 168–72; Castellanos, *New Orleans As It Was,* 102.

27. Answer of William Whitney, *Relf v. Whitney.*

which was still considering Shaumburg's request to take over the administration of the Clark estate. On June 18, 1834, the Whitneys instituted the
Great Gaines Case by asking the court to annul Clark's will of 1811, declare Myra the true heir, and order Relf and Chew to deliver all property
belonging to Daniel Clark to her. Defendants named in this suit included
all the heirs of Clark's mother, Mary Clark (who inherited under the 1811
will), Richard Relf, and Beverly Chew. To support their petition, the Whitneys paid the costs required to obtain depositions from Colonel Bellechasse, Harriet Harper Smythe, and Colonel Davis, thus placing the stories
they had told Myra and William in the court record.[28]

Gradually the citizens of New Orleans realized that the young couple
from New York presented a real threat, not just to the reputation of two
leading businessmen, but to property ownership in many sections of the
city. For over twenty years Relf and Chew had sold land from the Clark
estate; many of the most prominent citizens of New Orleans had purchased land from them or from someone else who had done so. Now
Myra's claim of fraud by the executors clouded all those titles. Most of
New Orleans thought the Whitneys a "pair of unscrupulous adventurers"
who threatened the welfare of the entire community. Louis Janin, an attorney who represented the city of New Orleans against Myra, later recalled
that New Orleans citizens considered her case "a rank fraud attempted
upon the courts. . . . It is impossible," he added, "to imagine, away from
New Orleans, the disturbance which the Gaines suits made."[29]

After filing their petitions with the United States District Court (for the
still-active libel case) and the Probate Court of New Orleans (for the challenge to the probate of the 1811 will), Myra and William left New Orleans. They returned to New York to spend the fall and winter with
William's family. Myra was pregnant with their first child, and William
needed rest and quiet to recover his health.[30]

While they were absent, the city of New Orleans completed an important land purchase from Évariste Blanc, buying land that Blanc had pur-

28. Petition of William W. Whitney and Myra Clark Whitney, *W. W. Whitney v. Eleanor O'Bearn, et al.*, June 18, 1834, Court of Probates of New Orleans, General Case Files
no. 843, Record Group 21, National Archives, Southwest Region, Fort Worth, Tex.

29. John S. Kendall, "The Strange Case of Myra Clark Gaines," *Louisiana Historical
Quarterly* 20 (Jan. 1937): 19, quoting Louis Janin.

30. Myra and William Whitney had three children: William W. Whitney Jr. and
Rhoda, born in Binghamton in 1834 and 1835, and Julia, born in New Orleans in 1837.
Pierce, *Whitney Genealogy*, 568–9.

chased from the Clark estate through Relf and Chew in 1821. The city intended the property to serve as a new cemetery. On June 28, 1834, the *Conseil de Ville* authorized the mayor to acquire sufficient property for three cemeteries, one to be located in each suburb of the city. On September 26, the city council approved the purchase of the Blanc property, comprising about 240 "superficial arpents" and bordered by the Bayou St. John, the Carondelet Canal (now Lafitte Avenue), the Bayou Road, and D'Argenois Street, for $50,000. Early in 1835 the city closed the existing cemeteries to new burials except in tombs or vaults already standing. All persons dying in the city were to be buried "in the cemetery established on the land purchased from M. Évariste Blanc at the Bayou St. John." The 1835 ordinance called for the new cemetery to be divided between Roman Catholics and Protestants, and each half should separate the burial grounds for white persons, free persons of color, and slaves. Since the city did not require all the Blanc tract for the cemetery, it subdivided and sold the remainder. Oak and magnolia groves wooded the well-drained property that had a view to the south of the city, and many wealthy New Orleans residents purchased lots along the graceful curve of the Bayou St. John. When the sales from the Blanc tract came under scrutiny thirty years later, the legality of the city's title to the property became a central issue in the Gaines case.[31]

When Myra, William, and their new baby returned to New Orleans in the spring of 1835 they learned that their opponents had not been idle in their absence. The answers filed by Relf and Chew and the court-appointed attorney for the heirs of Mary Clark denied all claims made in the Whitneys' petitions. Their answer established the defense that every defendant in the Gaines cases would eventually use: Daniel Clark had never been legally married; he had no legitimate children; he had made only one will, the will of 1811; if he had contemplated another will—or even actually signed one—he had destroyed it himself. Neither "by Law or Testament," her opponents argued, should Myra Whitney be entitled to any part of the Clark estate.[32]

31. Sale of Land, Évariste Blanc to the City of New Orleans, Sept. 26, 1834, reprinted in *Transcript of Record, Gaines v. City of New Orleans,* 2: 2168; Bayou St. John Cemetery Records, 1835–1844, online access on Sept. 29, 1997, http://home.gnofn.org/~nopl/inv/neh/nehff.htm#ff1; Curtis, *New Orleans, Its Old Houses,* 213–4. An arpent was a measurement of land equaling slightly less than a modern acre.

32. Answer of Relf and Chew, Jan. 15, 1835, *William W. Whitney and Myra Clark Whitney v. Eleanor O'Bearn et al.,* Court of Probates of New Orleans, case no. 843, reprinted in *Transcript of Record, Gaines v. Relf, Chew, and Others,* 1084; Answer of the

* * *

While they continued their exchanges within the legal arena of the court-room, the Whitneys and Richard Relf pursued their dispute on the pages of newspapers in and outside of New Orleans. A Philadelphia paper broke the news of Relf's suit for libel in the summer of 1835 in the northern press. The brief report described a "singular case" in which Daniel Clark willed "a large estate in New Orleans" to his daughter, Myra. The paper accused the executors of the estate, Relf and Chew, of withholding the daughter's inheritance and causing her to be "brought up and educated under another name until her marriage." Although Colonel Davis no longer served in the Pennsylvania legislature, the Philadelphia public knew the name, and the newspaper expected to catch its readers' interest by publishing a story about the colonel's family. The publication slanted the presentation of the case to favor Myra's version.[33]

Following the lead of the Philadelphia paper, editors in New York City and New Orleans began to publicize Myra Whitney's claims. Her story, "so extraordinary, so romantic, so deeply interesting," excited considerable attention. Relf's immediate response, published in both New York and New Orleans, denied all of the Whitneys' charges. Myra was not the daughter of Clark, "who was never married," Relf declared, but "the offspring of an adulterous bed." She had been placed in the family of Colonel Davis by Clark, and raised as a daughter in the Davis household. Never, asserted Relf, did Colonel Davis "set up any claim for her upon Mr. Clark's estate." Relf concluded his letter to the editors by lamenting the supposed "millions" left by Daniel Clark: "had [they] never existed, they might have spared me the years of toil and anguish I have gone through, and saved me from which I consider infinitely more injurious, the opprobrium with which it is attempted to tarnish my reputation."[34]

The *New Orleans Bee* welcomed Relf's "triumphant reply," which sustained his "public and private character" so well-known to his fellow Louisianians. The editor of the *Bee* applauded Relf's "determination to be above even suspicion" and prominently displayed his reply to the "sinister publication" from Philadelphia. The *New York Evening Star* was less en-

---

Heirs of Daniel Clark, through their Attorney, Lucius C. Duncan, Jan 15, 1835, ibid., 1083.

33. *New York Evening Star,* Nov. 11, 1835, reprinted in *Transcript of Record, Gaines v. City of New Orleans,* 2: 2090. The New York paper quoted an unnamed Philadelphia paper as the source of its story.

34. *New Orleans Bee,* Oct. 6, 1835, p. 2, datelined Sept. 14, 1835, and published in the *New York Evening Star,* Sept. 30, 1835.

thusiastic. Through General Whitney, William Whitney provided the paper with copies of the depositions received from Colonel Bellechasse, Pierre Baron Boisfontaine, and Harriet Harper Smythe. Relying on the testimony of such witnesses, the *Evening Star* printed a long article summarizing the evidence and criticizing the conduct of the executors. The newspaper employed "one of the most eminent jurists in the United States"—unnamed—whose published opinion was "highly favorable to Mrs. Whitney's claim."[35]

The New York coverage delighted the Whitneys. The interest shown by the editors in "the cause of the injured orphan" demonstrated the universal appeal of Myra's grievance. The *Evening Star* assured its readers that the case was one "in which the whole country is interested—every citizen who makes a will, every husband, every father whose last thoughts and words and wishes and desires on this side of the grave are for the protection of those beloved objects from whom he must part forever." With the New Orleans papers adamantly behind Relf and Chew, Myra and her husband continued to seek support from the northern press. In the later years of the Gaines case, Myra remembered the editors' interest in the romantic elements of her story and made further use of its drama to keep her case on the front pages of newspapers all over the country.[36]

New Orleans courts proved less fascinated than the northern newspapers with Myra's story. To fight the allegations of Relf and Chew in court, the Whitneys retained one of New Orleans's most colorful lawyers to represent them. John R. Grymes, a Virginian like Beverly Chew, had immigrated to New Orleans early in the nineteenth century. His "remarkable skill, tact, and judgment" earned him the respect of the New Orleans bar, while his extravagant lifestyle kept him in the public eye. An enthusiastic gambler—on horse racing, cockfighting, or cards—Grymes was an equally eager duelist, quick to avenge a point of honor. Shortly before he took the Whitneys' case, Grymes was involved in an incident in the Louisiana legislature that produced a sensation in New Orleans. Early one morning Grymes had entered the chamber of the Louisiana House of Representatives, advanced on house speaker Alcée Labranch, raised his cane, and struck him on the forehead. Labranch responded by drawing a pistol and firing at Grymes, and the ball passed through Grymes's overcoat. Grymes dropped his cane, drew his own pistol, and returned fire, wounding his

35. *New Orleans Bee,* Oct. 6, 1835, p. 2; *New York Evening Star,* Nov. 11, 1835.
36. *New York Evening Star,* Nov. 11, 1835.

opponent. Since the wound was not reported to be serious, the house merely reprimanded the attorney.[37]

A contemporary description stigmatized Grymes as a "dandy" who "changed his colors as often and as rapidly as the chameleon." One day he appeared "in full black, apparently in mourning; tomorrow he [would] surprise the public with a green cockney coat with foxhead buttons, buff pants, white hat, red neckerchief; the next day he [would] appear in full spotless white, and so on through all the colors of the tailor's calendar." His sartorial magnificence contrasted sharply with his "equitable and dispassionate" oratorical style. "Dignified, didactic, statesmanlike," he was regarded by his contemporaries as a "master lawyer."[38]

Grymes knew Clark during the early part of the century when the lawyer represented the notorious Lafitte brothers. Although they pretended to be privateers sailing with authorization from France to prey on Spanish commerce, the brothers led a band of smugglers who attacked ships of all nations, including those of the United States. Rumors circulated in New Orleans accusing Daniel Clark of arranging the sale of their ill-gotten gains. For whatever reason he took their case, Grymes's willingness to accept the Whitneys as clients caused some members of the New Orleans community to question the certainty with which they had rejected Myra's claims.[39]

But in spite of a few cracks, the wall erected by the New Orleans community to halt the Whitneys' pretensions held firm, and not even John R. Grymes's reputation could break it down. Transferred to federal court, the libel suit filed the year before by Relf came before Judge Samuel Harper, who, on December 20, 1834, had decided the first case (to recover the funds given to Davis) against Myra and William. Now he seemed equally convinced that William Whitney's published letter had libeled Richard Relf. When the case finally came to trial, Judge Harper carefully instructed the jury that Whitney's letter did not support his claims with evidence. The jury obligingly returned a guilty verdict, but demonstrated some degree of sympathy for the young husband by assessing a fine of only one dollar. Court costs raised the judgment to over seven hundred dollars, and, threatened with another jail term, Whitney paid.[40]

37. Fossier, *New Orleans,* 156; *Niles' Weekly Register (Baltimore),* Feb. 26, 1835.
38. Fossier, *New Orleans,* 155.
39. Gayarré, *History of Louisiana,* 3: 303–4; Fossier, *New Orleans,* 155.
40. Bill of Exceptions, Dec. 29, 1834; Demand for Payment of Costs, Dec. 24, 1836; Order for Arrest, May 16, 1837; Receipt for Payment, May 20, 1837, in *Relf v. Whitney,* Louisiana District Court, General Case Files no. 3452, Record Group 21, National Archives, Southwest Region, Fort Worth, Tex.

The state probate court case held a little more hope for a favorable outcome. In late 1835 the Whitneys decided to concentrate on Myra's status as Daniel Clark's legitimate daughter. Since Louisiana law prevented a father from disinheriting a legitimate child, if Myra could prove that Clark had married Zulime Carrière, she could inherit as his "forced heir" even under the will of 1811. By Louisiana law she would be entitled to four-fifths of his estate. Over the next year the Whitneys sought friends and family who had known Clark and Zulime; gradually, from their testimony, a composite portrait emerged of Myra's parents—confusing and often contradictory, but always "extraordinary . . . romantic . . . [and] deeply interesting."[41]

41. Dargo, *Jefferson's Louisiana*, 13; *New York Evening Star*, Nov. 11, 1835.

IV

A Man of "Energy, Intelligence, and Pliability"

As the testimony unfolded in the early courtroom appearances of the Gaines case, the relationship between Myra's parents became the center of the controversy. Daniel Clark and Zulime Carrière's love affair took place amid the turbulent atmosphere surrounding the acquisition of Louisiana by the United States. For both, politics complicated intimacy.

Modern-day historians portray Daniel Clark as a contradictory and enigmatic figure whose precise role in the purchase of Louisiana remains difficult to determine. His biographer, Michael Wohl, calls him "a man in the shadow" with a natural tendency to intrigue that led him to dissemble and keep hidden the effects of his actions. Wohl's comments reflect those of historian Arthur Whitaker, who described Clark as "a molelike individual, who burrowed his way through the life of his generation in the Southwest, leaving many surface indications of his activity, but seldom giving any signs of what that activity was all about." Nor were Clark's contemporaries any more certain about his character. His enemies believed him "a congenial spirit . . . distinguished for political depravity and moral turpitude," possessed of "a slanderous tongue" and "a craving for domination and distinction." His friends called him "an honest man . . . of good reputation" and "high-minded, honorable, [and] chivalrous." Unraveling the mystery of this apparently contradictory man requires an understanding of the intersection of Clark's public and private lives. Neither Machiavellian conspirator nor dedicated public servant, Clark juggled political, economic, and romantic involvements as he sought above all to build his fortune. His attempt to keep the various parts of his life in separate compartments provides an explanation for the "confused picture" Daniel Clark presented to his contemporaries and his biographer.[1]

Clark was born in 1766 in Sligo, Ireland. The maritime county of Sligo, in the province of Connaught, fronts on the Atlantic Ocean. Its namesake town is a seaport, the only port of any consequence on Ireland's west coast between Londonderry and Galway. The county abounds in picturesque mountains, lakes, and fertile valleys. In the eighteenth century the town contained a vigorous Protestant faction that apparently coexisted peacefully with the Catholic majority. Little is known of Clark's family, but letters from his mother mention considerable property in town belonging to Clark's father. Colonel Bellechasse remembered that Daniel Clark took pride in his descent from "the ancient Kings of Ireland."[2]

Daniel Clark's parents named their eldest son after his uncle, the most successful member of the Clark family. Daniel Clark Sr. immigrated to Louisiana in the 1770s and established a thriving mercantile house in New Orleans. This uncle paid for Daniel's schooling in England—possibly at Eton—and then invited his nephew to follow him to Louisiana. In 1786, at the age of twenty, Daniel Clark left Ireland for New Orleans, much to the dismay of his parents. For several years afterward Mary Clark "gently chided" her son for his failure to return home and seek his fortune in Ireland.[3]

---

1. Michael Wohl, "A Man in the Shadow: The Life of Daniel Clark" (Ph.D. diss., Tulane University, 1984); Arthur Preston Whitaker, *The Mississippi Question, 1795–1803: A Study in Trade, Politics, and Diplomacy* (Gloucester, Mass.: Peter Smith, 1962 [1934]), 92; Michael Wohl, "Not Yet Saint nor Sinner: A Further Note on Daniel Clark," *Louisiana History* 24 (1983): 204–5; James Wilkinson, *Memoirs of My Own Time* (Philadelphia: Abraham Small, 1816), 2: 6–7; George Mather, deposition, in Wilkinson, *Memoirs*, 2: appendix, 103; Pierre-Clément de Laussat, *Memoirs of My Life . . .*, trans. Agnes-Josephine Pastiva, ed. Robert D. Bush (Baton Rouge: Louisiana State University Press, 1978), 94; deposition of Zenon Cavallier, May 30, 1849, reprinted in *Transcript of Record, Gaines v. City of New Orleans*, 2: 1464; deposition of W. W. Montgomery, June 18, 1849, ibid., 2: 1489.

2. Mr. and Mrs. S. C. Hall, *Ireland, Its Scenery, Character, and History* (Boston: Francis A. Niccolls, 1911), 6: 41–2; Charles Duff, *Ireland and the Irish* (New York: Putnam's Sons, 1954), 181–3; Frank Wright, *Two Lands on One Soil: Ulster Politics before Home Rule* (New York: St. Martin's, 1996), 9; Mary Clark to Daniel Clark, Aug. 7, 1794, *E. P. Gaines and Wife v. Relf, Chew, and Others*, General Case Files no. 1765, Record Group 21, National Archives, Southwest Region, Fort Worth, Tex.

3. Daniel Clark, *Proofs of the Corruption of General James Wilkinson, and of His Connexion with Aaron Burr* (1809; reprint, Freeport, N.Y.: Books for Libraries Press, 1970), 66; Mary Clark to Daniel Clark, Aug. 7, 1794. The evidence of Clark's matriculation at Eton comes from the *New York Evening Star* article published in 1835 and based

*   *   *

Fortunes were much more easily made in Louisiana. For an ambitious young man, "possessed of unusual energy, intelligence, and pliability," New Orleans in 1786 offered great opportunities. Founded by the French in 1718, New Orleans became a Spanish city in 1763 when the Treaty of Paris transferred the "Isle of New Orleans" and the province of Louisiana west of the Mississippi River to Spain. Located at the edge of one of the vital trade areas of the world, the city lay within easy sailing distance of Tampico, Vera Cruz, Havana, and the Antilles. A combination of frontier marketplace, seaport, military garrison, and provincial capital, New Orleans occupied the center of economic and political life in the Spanish borderlands.[4]

Early Spanish governors of the province endeavored to bring the colony's trade into compliance with Spanish mercantile regulations, but their attempts failed when Louisiana exports—furs, lumber, indigo, and tobacco—could find no market in Spain. Other sources within the empire could supply the same merchandise at lower cost and higher quality. Spanish officials could either ignore the trade developing between Louisiana and the French and British colonies in North America or apply Spanish trade laws rigidly and see the colony destroyed.[5]

Trade in flour established ties between New Orleans and the cities of

on material provided by William Whitney. Neither Clark's autobiographical statement in his *Proofs* nor any of the depositions from friends who knew him mentions his schooling. Later nineteenth- and twentieth-century commentators on the Gaines case used the information from the New York paper to claim an upper-class education for Myra's father. New York Evening Star, Nov. 11, 1835, reprinted in *Transcript of Record, Gaines v. City of New Orleans*, 2: 2090.

4. Whitaker, *Mississippi Question*, 93; J. Clark, *New Orleans*, 51, 126; Carmelo R. Arena, "Philadelphia–Spanish New Orleans Trade: 1789–1805" (Ph.D. diss., University of Pennsylvania, 1959), 40. The Treaty of Fontainebleau, November 3, 1762, transferred Louisiana west of the Mississippi River from France to Spain, possibly in anticipation of the expected Spanish loss of Florida in the projected peace treaty. That treaty forced France to give up its claims to Canada and all North American territory south of the Great Lakes. In exchange for the captured French Caribbean islands of Guadeloupe and Martinique, Great Britain received all French territory east of the Mississippi River except the "Isle of New Orleans"—a parcel of land bounded by the Bayou Manchac, the Amite River, and Lakes Maurepas, Pontchartrain, and Borgne. England had coveted lower Louisiana and especially New Orleans as the key to control of the Mississippi River. Fearing attack on its Mexican provinces, Spain insisted that the Treaty of Paris provide for Spanish control of New Orleans. Joe Gray Taylor, *Louisiana: A Bicentennial History* (New York: W. W. Norton, 1976), 18–9.

5. J. Clark, *New Orleans*, 161–4, 174–8, 221; Whitaker, *Mississippi Question*, 81–2.

Philadelphia, Baltimore, and New York. The colony had a chronic food shortage since most plantations grew staple crops and relied on imported foodstuffs. Experiments in growing wheat ended when the plants failed to mature in the hot summers of the lower Mississippi Valley. A clandestine trade developed during the Seven Years' War. After the war, the growing traffic in flour and provisions encouraged many British (and later American) merchants to move to New Orleans where they acted as agents for merchant houses on the East Coast. Anglo-American merchants such as Daniel Clark Sr., Oliver Pollock, and Evan Jones became Spanish subjects to facilitate their trading ventures. During the American Revolution, the elder Clark and his fellow traders handled shipments of ammunition for the Continental Congress while trading, when conditions allowed, with their contacts in Philadelphia, Baltimore, and New York.[6]

The American Revolution forced Spain to alter its mercantile system in Louisiana. In 1778 the Spanish crown officially moderated the strict enforcement of trade restrictions in order to relieve the "distresses" from which Louisiana suffered. In 1782 the relaxation of trade restraints became permanent when the king issued a cedula permitting a direct but limited trade between New Orleans and France and the French West Indies. Since France also allowed American merchants to trade with its West Indian colonies, Philadelphia and New York merchants could participate in the New Orleans trade indirectly through French St. Domingue. That island quickly became center of transshipment for goods, disguised as French property, from the United States to New Orleans. Although techni-

6. J. Clark, *New Orleans,* 152. Oliver Pollock established his commercial house in New Orleans in 1769 after bringing into the city a desperately needed shipload of flour and selling it to Governor O'Reilly for $15 a barrel when the going price was $30. His generous action so impressed O'Reilly that the governor announced that "as long as he was in command [Pollock] would have free trade" in New Orleans. O'Reilly's successors, Unzaga and Gálvez, continued the policy and extended it to include Clark, Jones, and other Anglo-American merchants. During the American Revolution Oliver Pollock became the representative of the United Colonies at New Orleans. When Spain declared war on England in 1779, Governor Gálvez gave Pollock $75,000 to be forwarded to the colonies to purchase ammunition and other supplies. Daniel Clark Sr. placed his entire fortune at Pollock's disposal to cover bills incurred by the Continental Congress. Raymond J. Martinez, *Pierre Georges Rousseau, Commanding General of the Galleys of the Mississippi with Sketches of the Spanish Governors of Louisiana (1777–1803) and Glimpses of Social Life in New Orleans* (New Orleans: Hope Publications, 1965), 36. See also Light Townsend Cummins, *Spanish Observers and the American Revolution, 1775–1783* (Baton Rouge: Louisiana State University Press, 1991).

cally the cedula limited trade to Spanish shipping, crown officials over-looked the violations because Spanish shippers could not carry the volume of trade necessary. The Spanish governor in New Orleans wrote Madrid that this mutually beneficial, if illegal, trade was "considerable."[7]

The cedula of 1782 also raised the question of American navigation of the Mississippi River. After the American Revolution Spain preferred to encourage Louisiana trade with France (an ally) rather than with the United States (a neutral) or Great Britain (an enemy). To stop the importation of flour and other provisions from settlements on the upper Mississippi, Spain closed the river to American traffic in 1784, ending a profitable three-cornered trade that had developed among the western settlements, New Orleans, and Philadelphia.[8]

Spanish officials considered the right to navigate the Mississippi a lever that might pry the western territories of the United States away from their new political affiliations. To encourage American acceptance of the closure of the river, Spanish minister Diego Gardoqui offered trading concessions for American shippers in Spanish ports. The enthusiastic reception of Gardoqui's proposals by East Coast merchants drew angry responses

7. Gayarré, *History of Louisiana*, 3: 115; J. Clark, *New Orleans*, 223; Arthur P. Whitaker, "Reed and Forde, Merchant Adventurers of Philadelphia," *Pennsylvania Magazine of History and Biography* 61 (1937): 234. St. Domingue (or Santo Domingo) was the western portion of the island Columbus called Hispaniola. The main towns in the northern province included Cape Françoise (*Le Cap*), Fort Dauphine, Port le Paix, and Cape St. Nicholas. The leading town in the western province was Port-au-Prince. After 1791 slave insurrections left the island with an unstable government, and its value to trade lessened. Arena, "Philadelphia–Spanish New Orleans Trade" (Ph.D. diss.), 42, 64.

8. Arthur P. Whitaker, *The Spanish Frontier, 1783–1795* (Gloucester, Mass.: Peter Smith, 1962), 69–74; J. Clark, *New Orleans*, 224. As British subjects, Americans had enjoyed the use of New Orleans as a port of deposit. The seventh article of the Treaty of Paris in 1763 provided that "the navigation of the river Mississippi shall be equally free, as well to the subjects of Great Britain as to those of France, in its whole length and breadth from its source to the sea." William McDonald, *Select Charters and Other Documents Illustrative of American History, 1660–1775* (Ann Arbor, Mich.: University Microfilms, 1964), 264. A clause in the treaty of 1783 also declared that the navigation of the Mississippi from its source to the ocean was forever free to the subjects of England and the citizens of the United States, but Spain denied the validity of this clause. By virtue of the victories of Bernardo Gálvez over the British during the American Revolution, Spain claimed land on both sides of the river and claimed the right to control the navigation of all rivers within Spanish boundaries. Gayarré, *History of Louisiana* 3: 157; Caroline Burson, *The Stewardship of Don Esteban Miró* (New Orleans: American Printing, 1940), 144.

from western settlers whose only outlet for their produce was New Orleans. "If Congress refuses us effectual protection," they wrote in a 1785
memorial, "if it forsakes us, we will adopt the measures which our safety
requires, even if they endanger the peace of the Union and our connection
with the United States. No protection, no allegiance."⁹

The acquisition of the right of deposit at New Orleans became a principal diplomatic goal of the United States. In 1790 President Washington
stated his determination to secure the right of free deposit, "which we
must have and as certainly shall have as we remain a Nation." Secretary
of State Thomas Jefferson assured Judge Harry Innes of Kentucky that the
government "was not inattentive to the interests of your navigation" and
promised that Congress would take all possible action "short of actual
rupture" to redress their grievances. But in 1793 Jefferson had to acknowledge that the United States had made no progress. In a circular letter
to the foreign ministers of the United States, Jefferson complained that
"*Spain and Portugal* refuse, to those parts of America which they govern,
all direct intercourse with any people but themselves."¹⁰

While the United States government pursued ineffectual negotiations
with the Spanish crown for the restoration of the deposit, westerners used
the recurrent food shortage in New Orleans as their own lever to pry open
the port. In 1787 General James Wilkinson demanded permission from
Spanish governor Esteban Rodríguez Miró to ship, duty free, "a cargo
consisting of negroes, cattle, tobacco, flour, bacon, lard, and apples to the
amount of 50,000 or 60,000 pesos" from Kentucky to New Orleans. Wilkinson's contact in the city was "Colonel" Daniel Clark Sr., "a merchant
. . . who had considerable influence there." The elder Clark persuaded
Miró that offending Wilkinson would anger the Kentuckians and might
precipitate an invasion of Louisiana by outraged westerners. Perhaps, Colonel Clark told Miró, Wilkinson expected the cargo to be seized; the
whole attempt might be a trick to provide the Kentuckians with an excuse
to fight—"a snare laid for the government." Convinced by these arguments, Miró agreed to relax the confiscation policy as a favor to the gen-

9. Whitaker, *Mississippi Question*, 79–80; memorial from western settlers quoted
in Gayarré, *History of Louisiana* 3: 457.

10. George Washington to the marquis de Lafayette, Aug. 11, 1790, *The Writings of
George Washington*, ed. John C. Fitzpatrick (Washington, D.C., United States Government Printing Office, 1931–44), 31: 85–8; Thomas Jefferson to Harry Innis, Mar. 7,
1791, Paul Leicester Ford, ed., *The Writings of Thomas Jefferson* (New York: George
Putnam & Sons, 1892–99), 5: 294–5; Circular Letter, ibid., 5: 179–83 (italics in original).

eral. Wilkinson successfully completed his first voyage downriver in July 1787, a summer more noted by the citizens of New Orleans for "fevers," "an epidemic catarrh," and an epidemic of smallpox than for the general's successful experiment. Some residents did wonder at the apparent collusion between Miró and the general, and "sly hints and insinuations were thrown out as to its nature and tendency."[11]

In return for permission to trade in New Orleans, General Wilkinson drew a picture of western unrest colored to appeal to Spanish policy. In a letter to Miró he urged the Spanish crown to consider navigation of the Mississippi as "one of [its] most precious jewels, . . . for, whatever power shall command that navigation, will control all the country which is watered by that river and those streams which fall into it." Removing American shipping from the Mississippi "would immediately disrupt the Union, and separate for ever the West from the East," while relinquishing control of the river "would strengthen the Union, and would deprive Spain of all its influence" in Kentucky. Wilkinson's "First Memorial" stressed the indifference of the eastern states to the needs of the West and emphasized the extent of secessionist spirit in Kentucky. Alarmed that disgruntled Americans might ally with British troops still in the northwest and attack Louisiana, Miró agreed to grant the privilege of downriver trade to a favored few merchants recommended by Wilkinson and Daniel Clark Sr. The two men confidently predicted that this trade would become the source of "a rapid and large fortune."[12]

Other considerations may have contributed to the success of Wilkinson and the elder Clark's plans. The two men offered Miró a way to supplement his meager salary of $4,000 a year: the governor became a silent

11. "Extract from a Memoir Submitted to the Honorable Timothy Pickering, when Secretary of State, by the Honorable Daniel Clark," Daniel Clark, *Proofs,* 6–9; Gayarré, *History of Louisiana* 3: 190, 195.

12. Gayarré, *History of Louisiana* 3: 194, 231; Wilkinson, *Memoirs,* 2: appendix no. 6; James Ripley Jacobs, *Tarnished Warrior: Major-General James Wilkinson* (New York: Macmillan, 1938), 79–81. Governor Miró had several reasons for expecting that the western territories might be willing to join the Spanish Empire. Historian Arthur Whitaker notes that the distance separating the Atlantic states from the Ohio Valley (and "the intervening barrier of a wilderness and high mountains") caused the westerners to feel "less than any other portion of the United States the force of ties which bound them together and the necessity of that union." The settlers had complained to the weak central government established by the Articles of Confederation and obtained no relief. As a result, "the sturdy yeomen of the West determined to take their case into their own hands." *Mississippi Question,* 33.

partner in their plan to buy Kentucky tobacco at $2 per hundredweight and sell it to the king's warehouses in New Orleans at $9. Miró advanced Wilkinson and Colonel Clark $6,000 to finance their tobacco purchases, and funds earned in such exchanges were deposited with the firm of Clark & Reese in New Orleans. By the end of July 1787, Wilkinson's account with the firm held $9,835.50.[13]

The activities of Daniel Clark Sr.'s nephew and namesake also enhanced his ability to persuade Governor Miró to violate Spanish mercantile policy. Young Daniel exhibited a facility with languages that enabled him to obtain a position in the governor's office, where he translated documents from Spanish and French into English. His employment also gave him inside knowledge of Spanish policy. No hard evidence exists for the younger Clark's participation in Wilkinson's intrigues, but the activities of the two conspirators began soon after the nephew's arrival.

Profits generated by their trading ventures fulfilled Wilkinson and Colonel Clark's expectations. In August 1788 Wilkinson, Clark Sr., and Isaac Dunn signed "Articles of Agreement" to foster a three-way trade involving merchandise imported from Philadelphia, western raw materials, and Louisiana specie—all completely illegal according to Spanish policy. In a letter written two months earlier, Colonel Clark had carefully explained the methods (judicious bribery, loopholes in mercantile policy) by which these products could be smuggled into and out of New Orleans. He also reminded Wilkinson and Dunn that his nephew's position in the governor's office enabled young Clark to assist their undertaking. In return, Colonel Clark hoped Wilkinson and Dunn would make the firm of Clark & Reese rich "by introducing them to your respectable neighbors, and influencing them to address this house whenever they may have business to transact in this place [New Orleans]."[14]

Soon after Wilkinson's first successful trip down the Mississippi, Governor Miró persuaded the Spanish court to tolerate American commerce on the river under certain restrictions. On December 1, 1788, a royal order announced that Americans could bring raw materials and merchandise into New Orleans subject to an import duty of 15 percent; after further payment of an export duty of 6 percent, the products could be shipped to any of the ports with which Spanish law allowed New Orleans to trade. An article in the *Pittsburgh Gazette* of April 18, 1789, demonstrated the

13. Daniel Clark, "Memoir Submitted to Timothy Pickering," *Proofs*, 6–9.
14. Wilkinson, *Memoirs*, 2: appendix no. 13.

success of this measure: "A general and uninterrupted trade has taken place between the inhabitants of this country and those of the Spanish settlements at New-Orleans. Several boats loaded with goods to a very considerable amount have arrived here, and in return they took large quantities of tobacco, beef, [and] corn." Opening the river to American commerce upon payment of duties in New Orleans did not end western demands for free access to the port, nor did it further the separatist cause in the western territories by demonstrating the importance of New Orleans to western trade. But it did attract more Americans to New Orleans and increased their economic domination of its business community.[15]

The partnership among Clark, Wilkinson, and Dunn lasted only one year, but it provided the basis for the successful mercantile house that Colonel Clark turned over to his nephew a few years later. Daniel made important contacts among Spanish officials during his months in the governor's office, and he learned invaluable lessons about negotiating the labyrinthine Spanish customs regulations. His fluent Spanish, gracious manners, and "generally pleasing personality" made a favorable impression on the New Orleans business community and opened the doors of the Creole aristocracy as well.[16]

In the early 1790s the younger Daniel Clark took over his uncle's business and began to act as the New Orleans agent for the large Philadelphia firm of Reed & Forde. The Philadelphia merchants sent cargoes of flour, brandy, sherry, pepper, cloth, and furniture to Clark on consignment; in exchange he returned cargoes of "furs, seegars, [and] Indigo." Clark's connections in the Spanish governor's office and with the local city government (the Cabildo) enabled him to circumvent colonial trade regulations for his employers. Judicious bribery, if necessary, could persuade Spanish officials to wink at evasions of the commercial restrictions and allow Clark to obtain permits for Reed & Forde ships to trade in New Orleans.[17]

15. Whitaker, *Mississippi Question*, 83; *Pittsburgh Gazette*, Apr. 18, 1789, from a letter datelined Kentucky, Mar. 2, 1789, quoted in Arena, "Philadelphia–Spanish New Orleans Trade" (Ph.D. diss.), 178.

16. The partnership of Wilkinson, Clark Sr., and Dunn was dissolved by mutual consent on September 8, 1789. Daniel Clark, *Proofs*, 8–9; Arena, "Philadelphia–Spanish New Orleans Trade" (Ph.D. diss.), 13.

17. Daniel Clark, *Proofs*, 84; Reed & Forde to Coxe & Clark, May 26, 1793, Reed and Forde Letter Book, 1793–94, Reed and Forde Collection, Historical Society of Pennsylvania, Philadelphia.

Clark's clients also valued his shrewd advice on the best way to smuggle prohibited exports—especially specie (gold and silver currency)—out of New Orleans. Regulations required American merchants to pay an extra duty (above the normal 6 percent export duty) on all specie sent out of the province; the only exception was specie exported in payment for slaves. Clark could "persuade" Customs House officials to enter specie exports on their books as payment for slaves "while in reality it is the return made for merchandise shipped from the United States and for the account of some American House." Specie was in short supply in the United States after the Revolution, and New Orleans trade offered an opportunity to gain hard currency in return for trade goods from United States producers. Philadelphia property owners often advertised their willingness to accept Spanish coins in payment, and newspapers advertised prices in Spanish pesos as well as in American dollars. The prevalence of such ads indicates the extent of specie transfers between Philadelphia and New Orleans.[18]

In 1793 Clark formed a partnership with an active and influential Philadelphia merchant, Daniel W. Coxe. Coxe's contacts within the United States government complemented Clark's influence in New Orleans. Trading for themselves and acting as agents for other Philadelphia merchants, Coxe & Clark developed a "triangle trade" that sent cargoes of Louisiana sugar (after 1795) to Havana, exchanged them there for coffee, refined sugar, or cocoa, which was sent to Philadelphia and traded for flour sent back to New Orleans. Another complex trade route delivered merchandise from Philadelphia over the mountains into Pittsburgh by wagon or pack-horse. There the goods were traded for the bulky farm products of the West, which then floated down the interior waterways of the Ohio and Mississippi Rivers to New Orleans where Coxe & Clark sold the produce for specie or sent export goods on to Philadelphia by way of the French West Indies. Western farmers, anxious to reach New Orleans and sell their produce at the "fancy prices" produced by winter's scarcity, engaged in a mad scramble to be the first to reach New Orleans with the spring floods. But the unfamiliar language and laws of New Orleans hampered the

18. Memorandum, undated, Gilpin Family Papers, *Wilkinson v. Clark* Collection, Historical Society of Pennsylvania, Philadelphia; Carmelo Richard Arena, "Philadelphia–Spanish New Orleans Trade in the 1790s," *Louisiana History* 2 (1961): 435–6. In 1790 a peso equaled one dollar in American currency. See the *Philadelphia Directory, 1793,* appendix, quoted in Arena, "Philadelphia–Spanish New Orleans Trade" (Ph.D. diss.), 3.

"farmer, turned boatman, turned trader" and ensured that he would look to a mercantile house such as Coxe & Clark for storage and assistance. Without the services of a knowledgeable New Orleans agent such as Daniel Clark and a few others, the Philadelphia–New Orleans trade could not exist.[19]

The lack of a "deposit" at New Orleans remained a persistent problem for American merchants. By allowing produce intended for export to be placed in bond at the port, such a deposit would enable merchants to avoid Spanish export taxes. Involvement in the general European conflict with France encouraged Spain to end the dispute with the United States regarding this issue. In 1795 the Treaty of San Lorenzo granted Americans a place of deposit at New Orleans and recognized their right of free navigation of the Mississippi River throughout its course. The deposit did not actually open until 1798; when it did the first entry in the books kept by customs officials was for seventy bags of cotton placed in deposit by Daniel Clark. Four months later Clark withdrew the cotton and shipped it to Virginia. He was the single most frequent user of the deposit in 1798; of the fifty-two entries in the records, fifteen are in his name. His shipments sent cotton from Natchez and Nashville, flour from the Ohio Valley, and tobacco from Kentucky to Atlantic coast ports; other entries listed occa-

19. Arena, "Philadelphia–Spanish New Orleans Trade," 436; John Clark, *New Orleans*, 234–5; Whitaker, *Mississippi Question*, 142–3. Daniel Coxe's brother Tench Coxe became assistant secretary of the treasury under Alexander Hamilton on May 10, 1790. Upon his appointment, Tench Coxe transferred all his business holdings to his brother Daniel to avoid the conflict-of-interest charges that had forced the resignation of the previous assistant treasurer, William Duer. The outbreak of war between Spain and France in 1793 resulted in great profits for the firm of Coxe & Clark but also in increased risk for their ships. Cancellation of Spanish commercial concessions to France left the United States as the only major neutral carrier and the only available source of supply for Louisiana. Coxe & Clark ships usually sailed with two sets of papers—American and Spanish—and assumed the guise of Spanish ships when entering the port of New Orleans. The Spanish governor must have been aware of the deception, but the province's need for food and other supplies prevented any vigorous investigation of ownership. Clark may have found that his dual role as a planters' agent and commission broker for foreign firms represented a conflict of interest. As an agent he sought the highest prices for his client's crops; as a commission broker he tried to buy at the lowest possible price. Clark solved this problem by dividing his business ventures, using the firm of Chew & Relf as planters' agents and his partnership with Daniel Coxe to represent United States and British merchants. J. Clark, *New Orleans*, 238, 272.

sional exports of furs and skins, lead, iron, hams and bacon, salt pork and beef, and specie.[20]

Although he used the deposit at New Orleans, Clark believed that Spanish taxes on goods imported into the province in American ships—a duty of 21 percent—largely negated any advantage earned through the deposit. In practice the treaty provided only one-way trade: the export of American products through the deposit. For American ships to arrive in New Orleans "in ballast" to take on cargo from the deposit meant total freight charges high enough to deprive the merchants of all profit. Should the ships carry spurious Spanish papers, they would forfeit the right to take American goods from the deposit duty-free, forcing them to pay the tax of 12 percent charged Spanish shippers.[21]

Soon after the deposit opened Clark presented a memorial to Spanish intendant Juan Morales proposing equal taxation of American and Spanish exports through the New Orleans port. American ships would be allowed to carry Louisiana products from New Orleans to ports in the United States or other foreign nations after paying the export duty charged

20. Whitaker, *Mississippi Question*, 91; J. Clark, *New Orleans*, 210. Declaration of peace between Spain and France in 1795 changed Spanish policy. Fearing that the United States might join Great Britain in an assault on Spanish possessions in the Americas, Spain agreed to the Treaty of San Lorenzo (Pinckney's Treaty) to induce the United States to cling to its neutral status. J. Clark, *New Orleans*, 240, and Gayarré, *History of Louisiana* 3: 357–8. By the terms of the second article of the treaty, dated October 20, 1795, the future boundary between the United States and Florida was settled as the 31st parallel from the Mississippi River eastward to the Chattahoochee River, then along a line running due east from the mouth of the Flint River to the head of St. Mary's River, then down the middle of that river to the Atlantic Ocean. The fourth article declared that the middle of the Mississippi River should be the western boundary of the United States, from its source to the intersection of the line of demarcation designated in the second article. The king of Spain also stipulated that the whole width of the Mississippi River, from its source to the sea, should be free to the people of the United States and agreed "to permit the people of the United States, for the term of three years, to use the port of New Orleans as a place of deposit for their produce and merchandise, and to export the same free from all duty or charge, except a reasonable consideration to be paid for storage and other incidental expenses; that the term of three years may by subsequent negotiation be extended; or, instead of that town, some other point in the island of New Orleans shall be designated as a place of deposit for the American trade." Gayarré, *History of Louisiana* 3: 356–7. The Senate ratified the Treaty of San Lorenzo in March 1796. See Samuel Flagg Bemis, *Pinckney's Treaty: America's Advantage from Europe's Distress, 1783–1800*, rev. ed. (New Haven, Conn.: Yale University Press, 1960).

21. Whitaker, *Mississippi Question*, 93–4.

Spanish ships. In return, Spanish ships could take cargoes from the American deposit, without payment of export duties, to all ports except those of Spain and her colonies. Clark reminded Morales that Spain's maritime war with Great Britain had deprived the province of necessary shipping, but American shippers were reluctant to export Louisiana products because of the high 21 percent tariff. A precedent existed—American ships could export Louisiana sugar freely—and Clark asked that the principle be extended to all cargoes.[22]

Daniel Clark's wealth and official connections ensured that his proposal received a sympathetic hearing from the intendant. Regardless of the desires of the Spanish court, the colonial government in Louisiana wished to encourage American trade. After other New Orleans merchants enthusiastically endorsed Clark's memorial and Governor Gayoso gave his approval, a formal meeting of the *Junta de Real Hacienda* (the colonial treasury) not only adopted Clark's recommendations but expanded them. All neutral vessels could trade with New Orleans on the same terms as Spanish ships (payment of a 6 percent duty on both imports and exports); goods exported from New Orleans to the territory of the United States bordering the Mississippi River bore no duty at all.[23]

In Clark's May 1, 1798, memorial, he labeled himself the American vice-consul in New Orleans. This was not entirely accurate. Fearing that foreign consuls might loosen Spain's grip on its lucrative colonial possessions, the crown refused to recognize formal representatives of foreign governments in its colonies. Both Presidents Washington and Adams tried to persuade Madrid to change its policy since they believed that consuls were necessary for the protection of American trade and seamen. American merchants in New Orleans agreed, and the steady increase of commerce between the United States and Louisiana after the Treaty of San Lorenzo in 1795 prompted them to request that the federal government appoint an official agent to represent the United States and their commercial interests in New Orleans. Daniel Clark had already demonstrated his ability to negotiate with Spanish officials. In 1794, when a Spanish ship captured four American vessels and brought three of them into New Or-

22. Whitaker, *Mississippi Question,* 94; Daniel Clark, *Proofs,* 106; J. Clark, *New Orleans,* 242–3.

23. Whitaker, *Mississippi Question,* 93–6; John Clark, *New Orleans,* 242–4; Arena, "Philadelphia–Spanish New Orleans Trade" (Ph.D. diss.), 116–7; Daniel Clark, *Proofs,* 106.

leans for sale, a protest by Clark had succeeded when the government in Washington had failed to move the colonial officials. Using his political and commercial influence Clark obtained the release of two of the ships to their legitimate owners, and an armed merchantman owned by Coxe & Clark recaptured the third. Clark's success in representing the interests of American merchants convinced Captain Isaac Guion, commander of the United States troops at Natchez, and Andrew Ellicott, a member of the commission to establish the boundary between East and West Florida, to request that Clark assume quasi-official status as United States consul until one should be selected by the president. Clark's reputation and influence in the merchant community was such that Governor Gayoso acquiesced in this recommendation, and with this authority, Clark negotiated the reduction in duties paid by American shippers.[24]

Clark hoped to receive a permanent appointment as United States Consul. In March 1798, he wrote Secretary of State Timothy Pickering, enclosing a copy of Ellicott and Guion's letter and explaining his negotiations with Morales. To support his nephew's desire for official recognition, Colonel Clark wrote his old friend Wilkinson, asking the general to use his influence with President Adams to secure the consular position for Daniel Clark. However, Daniel Clark was not Adams's choice to represent the United States. The president appointed two vice-consuls—William Emperson Hulings, a Philadelphia physician who had made a fortune as a merchant in New Orleans, and Evan Jones, originally from New York but also a wealthy member of the merchant community in Louisiana. Neither Hulings nor Jones was acceptable to the Spanish crown. Governor Gayoso permitted Hulings to act "informally" as a consul for eighteen months, but he threatened Jones with arrest for accepting Adams's appointment. Jones had become a Spanish citizen and served as a captain in the Louisiana militia. When selected by President Adams, he was the commandant

24. Gayarré, *History of Louisiana* 3: 397; "Documents: Despatches from the United States Consul in New Orleans, 1801–1803, Part I," *American Historical Review* 32 (1927): 801; Arena, "Philadelphia–Spanish New Orleans Trade" (Ph.D. diss.), 101–2, 118; J. Clark, *New Orleans*, 244; Captain Isaac Guion and Commissioner Andrew Ellicott to Daniel Clark, Mar. 2, 1798, and Daniel Clark to Guion and Ellicott, Mar. 14, 1798, State Department Consular Despatches, New Orleans, in "Documents, Part I," *American Historical Review* 32 (1927): 803; Whitaker, *Mississippi Question*, 93; Daniel Clark, *Proofs*, 106.

of the district of Lafourche, and Spanish law did not allow a subject of the king to act as a representative of a foreign government.[25]

Although Daniel Clark had been more successful as a representative of American interests than either of the two official appointees, he, too, was not an American citizen in 1798. His uncle, who had a year earlier relinquished all his business holdings to his nephew, wrote from his Natchez plantation to urge Clark to join his future to the United States. Following his uncle's advice, Clark journeyed to the Mississippi Territory, where late in December he took an oath of allegiance to his new country.[26]

Two years later Clark received an official appointment as vice-consul to New Orleans from President Jefferson. The New Orleans merchant community, knowing the value of a recognized representative, had petitioned Jefferson to select a consul that the Spanish government would accept. On July 16, 1801, the president appointed Clark, and the Senate confirmed his nomination the following January. Some opposition to Clark's appointment arose among members of the Jefferson administration who questioned his loyalty to the United States. The commission nominating Clark indicated that he was a Spanish subject, but Clark insisted that he had "never been a Spanish subject, but had been naturalized, as an American citizen, in the latter part of the year 1798 in Natchez." The most compelling evidence that Clark remained a British subject until his naturalization came from the attitude of the colonial government in New Orleans. The Spanish governor, the marquis de Casa Calvo (although prohibited from officially recognizing Clark's position), tacitly accepted his role as United States representative without the friction that hampered Evan Jones's selection. Nevertheless, the taint of intrigue still clung to Clark after his explanation to Jefferson; one of the most common charges against him insinuated that he switched countries too easily. He

25. "Documents, Part I," *American Historical Review* 32 (1927): 803, 805–6; Colonel Daniel Clark Sr. to General James Wilkinson, Mar. 28, 1798, in Wilkinson, *Memoirs,* 2: appendix no. 8; Newton, *Americanization of French Louisiana,* 51–2 (note 5). President Washington made the first consular appointment to New Orleans when he nominated Procopio Jacinto Pollock of Pennsylvania, son of the New Orleans merchant Oliver Pollock, who had been so useful as the financial agent of the Continental Congress in New Orleans. Procopio Pollock never left Philadelphia and eventually resigned the office. "Documents, Part I," 802.

26. Colonel Daniel Clark Sr. to Daniel Clark, Nov. 2, 1798, Daniel Clark Papers, Pennsylvania Historical Society, Philadelphia.

was, one political opponent claimed, "a renegade, who had four times changed his allegiance."[27]

Despite lingering doubts of his loyalty, Clark proved to be the United States's most successful appointee to the post in New Orleans. His ability to untangle Spanish trade regulations allowed him to perform essential services for American merchants and to represent the United States government in negotiations with the colonial government. The "swarms of their unruly countrymen" who infested New Orleans between 1798 and 1803 enabled Clark and William Hulings (the other vice-consul) to wring some degree of cooperation out of the colonial government. Governor Casa Calvo permitted Clark (and, to a lesser extent, Hulings) to fulfill most of a consul's traditional responsibilities: granting certificates of ownership for cargoes and ships; providing some protection for injured sailors; forcing French privateers to comply with all legal formalities before American ships could be condemned as prizes of war; and furnishing the American government with its only reliable and detailed information on the commerce of the lower Mississippi Valley.[28]

Clark's business and political aspirations were soon complicated by a romantic liaison that developed between Clark and Zulime Carrière, a young Frenchwoman born in Louisiana in 1781 and christened Marie Julie but known to her family and friends by the *petit nom* "Zulime." The relationship between the two engendered much speculation and gossip in New Orleans, still very much a small and insular community at the end of the eighteenth century, and, of course, lay at the heart of the Gaines case.

Marriage records kept by the Cathedral of St. Louis in New Orleans provide what little is known about Zulime's parents. Her father, Jean Carrière, a native of the city of Libourne in Gascony, and her mother, Marie Chaufer, born in Bordeaux, joined the influx of émigrés into Louisiana after 1750. Like the Carrières, most of these immigrants came from the south and west of France. The family had four daughters, each of whose marriage was recorded in the cathedral Marriage Book. Though born in Louisiana, all four married French immigrants. Their intermarriage with

27. "Documents, Part I," *American Historical Review* 32 (1927): 807–8; Daniel Clark, *Proofs*, 142–3; Arena, "Philadelphia–Spanish New Orleans Trade" (Ph.D. diss.), 118–21; J. Clark, *New Orleans*, 106; Wohl, "Not Yet Saint nor Sinner," 200; Wilkinson, *Memoirs*, 2: 9, 103–4.

28. Whitaker, *Mississippi Question*, 97; J. Clark, *New Orleans*, 242; Arena, "Philadelphia–Spanish New Orleans Trade" (Ph.D. diss.), 26, 119.

"foreign French" husbands (i.e., not Creole or Louisiana-born French) confirms the observations of Louisiana historian Paul Lachance: at least half of Louisiana-born white women married "foreign" (and usually French) husbands. Creole families hoped to profit by such marriages; matching their daughters with wealthy foreigners was a strategy designed to improve the family's economic and social status.[29]

Betterment of the family fortunes appears to have been the motive for Zulime's marriage to Jerome DesGrange. A native of Clermont, France, DesGrange arrived in New Orleans in 1793. He described himself as "the youngest son of a wealthy nobleman" who had fled the revolutionary forces of republican France. Exact descriptions of DesGrange varied considerably, but most who knew him in Louisiana remembered an unattractive—even ugly—man. The widow of one of DesGrange's attendants at his wedding recalled a man six feet tall, stoutly built, with a light complexion and blue eyes. A friend of Daniel Clark described DesGrange as a "very common-looking man . . . about five feet, six or seven inches tall, and stout." Another witness remembered a man of medium height and "rather thinly inclined" with a "pox-marked" face, light hair, and a "very common look." A final witness swore that DesGrange was a "short, thickset man, with a round face [and] auburn hair." Despite his unprepossessing appearance, this "accomplished gentleman" impressed Zulime's fam-

29. Alice Forsyth, ed. *Louisiana Marriages: II, A Collection of Marriage Records from the St. Louis Cathedral in New Orleans during the Spanish Regime and the Early American Period, 1784–1806* (New Orleans: Polyanthos, 1977) provides marriage records for the Carrière family. Forsyth notes in her preface that the orthographical variations in the family names, common in the eighteenth and nineteenth centuries, were compounded in Louisiana by differences in national origin and language between writers and recorders. Paul F. Lachance, "Intermarriage and French Cultural Persistence in Late Spanish and Early American New Orleans," *Histoire-Sociale/Social History* 15 (1982): 52.

Louisiana historian Mary Gehman has suggested in a letter to the author that Zulime was the product of an interracial union and that her mulatto status was the reason for Clark's refusal to acknowledge their child. Gehman's research into family names in New Orleans found that "Carrière" was a common surname for mulatto families. Forsyth's investigations into the marriage records, however, provide considerable evidence to refute Gehman's belief. Each marriage of a Carrière daughter is documented, and in each case, the birthplaces of the parents in France are the same. No testimony in any of the Gaines cases ever mentions a mixed-race background for Zulime. Given the attitude toward miscegenation in the United States in the early nineteenth century, such an explanation for Clark's attitude would never have been omitted, had there been any evidence to support it.

ily with his tales of European travels, and they accepted his self-described status as an aristocratic—and bachelor—refugee. On December 2, 1794, he wed the youngest Carrière daughter.[30]

When Zulime married Jerome DesGrange he was about forty years old, and she was only thirteen. American residents of New Orleans noted that early marriage was common among Louisiana Creoles, but Zulime was younger than her sisters when she wed. Many witnesses in the Gaines case testified to her beauty and vivacity, although no specific description appears in any deposition and no picture exists. Visitors to Louisiana admired the attractive appearance of Creole women whose "dark, but clear and transparent" complexions and "black eyes fringed with long eyelashes and finely penciled eyebrows" made them "more beautiful than American women." Their graceful manners and "piquant and alluring charm" made Creole women "universal favorites in society." Even among the lovely Creole ladies, Zulime stood out in the memories of those who knew her.[31]

No matter how wealthy or aristocratic their positions in prerevolutionary France, most French émigrés could not expect to replicate their elevated status in Louisiana. Lachance's analysis of marriage records indicates that foreign French bridegrooms could be found in all economic ranks, from the richest, whose marriage contract declared assets of $327,000 and debts of $253,000 for a net worth of $74,000, to a more modest shopkeeper, whose net worth of $7,000 represented a house built on a half-lot near the river and the merchandise in his store. At the bottom of the economic scale was a carpenter, who declared that his net worth of 200 *piastres* included the "tools of his trade and other household effects."

30. Deposition of Sophia Despau, June 28, 1839, reprinted in *Transcript of Record, Gaines v. City of New Orleans*, 2: 1741; deposition of Rose Caillavet, Oct. 16, 1845, ibid., 2: 1748; deposition of Louise Benguerel, May 27, 1836, ibid., 2: 1876; deposition of Zenon Cavallier, May 30, 1849, ibid., 2: 1464; deposition of Jacob Hart, June 28, 1849, reprinted in *Transcript of Record, Gaines v. Relf, Chew, and Others*, 658; and deposition of Jean Canon, June 28, 1849, ibid., 660.

31. Extract from the Second Register of the Instruments of Marriage of the Parish Church of St. Louis, New Orleans, Geronimo DesGrange to Marie Julie Carrière, no. 434, Nov.–Dec. 1794, reprinted in *Transcript of Record, Gaines v. City of New Orleans*, 2: 2141; Timothy Flint, *Recollections of the Last Ten Years* (New York: Knopf, 1826), 325; Charles A. Murray, *Travels through North America*, 2: 130–1, quoted in Dugdale, "Travelers' Views of Louisiana," 36; Dennis, "Image of Louisiana in America," 50. For descriptions of Zulime by those who knew her, see deposition of Jean Canon, June 28, 1849, reprinted in *Transcript of Record, Gaines v. Relf, Chew, and Others*, 660; and deposition of Eulalie Watkins, July 6, 1849, ibid., 686.

Like the majority of his countrymen, Jerome DesGrange fell in the lower half of this occupational graph; in New Orleans he became the proprietor of a wine and confectionery shop at the corner of Royal and St. Ann Streets.[32]

An attractive wife was an asset to the proprietor of a café that drew its clientele from the American and Creole merchants who gathered each day to argue politics or discuss commercial affairs over apéritifs or after-dinner cordials. DesGrange claimed the necessity of Zulime's presence behind the counter of his wineshop as an excuse to hurry their marriage. Under normal circumstances, proper Catholic marriages in Louisiana were not hastily arranged. By signing a contract of marriage on November 11, 1794, Jerome DesGrange swore before a notary public that he was a resident of the Parish of St. Louis, a practicing Catholic, and a bachelor with no "impediment to contract matrimony." Two friends served as witnesses to the truth of his statements. The ecclesiastical judge of the parish then granted a license for the marriage, subject to the publication of three notices of the approaching nuptials. The parish priest announced two of the three banns, but DesGrange requested that the church dispense with the third notice since the coming Advent season would prevent the solemnizing of marriages. The church authorities accepted his need for his future wife's help in his business as a sufficient reason for eliminating the final notice of banns, and the parish curate performed the ceremony on December 2, 1794.[33]

Daniel Clark first met Zulime as she served liqueurs in the St. Ann Street café. Not only was the wineshop a popular meeting place for New Orleans merchants, but DesGrange and Clark had a business relationship that often brought Clark into the establishment. No banks existed in New Orleans before 1804, and merchants like DesGrange relied on merchant-

32. Lachance, "Intermarriage and French Cultural Persistence," 121–3; deposition of Zenon Cavallier, May 30, 1849, reprinted in *Transcript of Record, Gaines v. City of New Orleans,* 2: 1464; deposition of Etienne Carraby, June 4, 1849, ibid., 1473. George W. Cable's romances of early New Orleans mention a *Café des Exiles* on the corner of Royal and St. Ann Streets. George W. Cable, *Old Creole Days: A Story of Creole Life* (New York: Charles Scribner's Sons, 1921).

33. Herbert Asbury, *The French Quarter: An Informal History of the New Orleans Underworld* (New York: Knopf, 1936), 135; Freiberg, *Bayou St. John,* 334; Extract from the Second Register of the Instruments of Marriage of the Parish Church of St. Louis in New Orleans, Geronimo DesGrange to Marie Julie Carrière, no. 434, Nov.–Dec. 1794, reprinted in *Transcript of Record, Gaines v. City of New Orleans,* 2: 2141.

traders for credit with suppliers. Records of the Gaines cases include several letters exchanged by Clark, his Philadelphia business partner Daniel Coxe, and DesGrange in 1798 describing debts and methods of repayment among the three men. The letters are friendly in tone and refer to numerous mutual acquaintances, including Beverly Chew and Richard Relf.[34]

Just when Clark's friendship with Zulime DesGrange deepened into intimacy is uncertain. In March of 1801 Jerome DesGrange returned to France for an extended visit. The death of his wife's parents had left an estate to Zulime and her sisters. The sisters-in-law gave DesGrange authority to settle the legacy for them, and, in preparation for the journey, DesGrange gave Zulime a power of attorney (in which she is described as his "legitimate wife") over his business affairs in New Orleans. Perhaps the increased contact required by their business dealings led to a closer relationship between Clark and Zulime. One witness claimed that Zulime became Clark's mistress as early as 1800, with the knowledge of her husband. But a letter Clark received from DesGrange in the summer of 1801 makes this supposition unlikely. DesGrange opened this letter with a wish for Clark's continued good health, saying that with "such a friend as you we cannot feel too deep an interest." Enclosed with the letter, DesGrange sent a package to Zulime and requested that Clark give it to her. He thanked his "dear friend" Clark for an offer to look after Zulime: "should my wife find herself embarrassed in any respect, you will truly oblige me by aiding her with your kind advice." DesGrange indicated that he would not return to New Orleans for several months as the recovery of the Carrière estate proved more difficult than expected, and he hoped to spend some additional time visiting family in Provence. DesGrange's extended absence provided an opportunity for Clark and Zulime to begin their sexual liaison.[35]

At some point in the last half of 1801 Zulime found herself pregnant. An earlier son by DesGrange had died in infancy, but this new pregnancy

34. Daniel Clark to Daniel Coxe, two letters dated July 25, 1798; Jerome DesGrange to Daniel Coxe, Aug. 20, 1798, and Memoranda from Jerome DesGrange, Sept. 15 and 29; Daniel Coxe Papers, Historical Society of Pennsylvania, Philadelphia.

35. Deposition of Louis Bouligny, June 4, 1849, reprinted in *Transcript of Record, Gaines v. Relf, Chew, and Others*, 638; Jerome DesGrange (from Bordeaux) to Daniel Clark, July 1801, reprinted in *Transcript of Record, Gaines v. City of New Orleans*, 2: 2158; Power of Attorney, Carrière Sisters to DesGrange, Mar. 26, 1801, ibid., 2: 2137; Power of Attorney, DesGrange to his "legitimate wife," Mar. 26, 1801, ibid., 2: 2138.

was almost certainly not the result of her marital relationship. In late October and early November, while Clark traveled to the East Coast, Zulime sold several slaves using the power of attorney left by her husband. She then transferred that power of attorney to the husband of her sister Rose Caillavet; the next indication of the use of that power of attorney in the notarial records showed Sinforiano Caillavet accepting a final payment for one of the slaves Zulime sold. The need to escape scandal and leave New Orleans quickly presents a plausible explanation for her actions. If Zulime was pregnant by Clark, then the sale of slaves could raise needed money for a trip to join her lover in Philadelphia where she could have her child in secrecy.[36]

During the course of the Gaines case witnesses provided several versions of what happened next. Daniel Coxe, Clark's Philadelphia partner, testified for Myra's opponents. He declared that Zulime brought him a letter of introduction from Clark requesting that he find a residence for Zulime and her sister Sophia and engage a doctor for the delivery of the child. Coxe swore that he asked Dr. William Shippen, a well-known Philadelphia accoucheur (dead by the time the Gaines case began), to attend Zulime. According to Coxe, the baby, Caroline, was born in Philadelphia early in 1801. Clark was not present at the birth but acknowledged his paternity and accepted financial responsibility for the child. Coxe removed Caroline from her mother soon after the birth and placed the baby in the care of a nurse under his supervision. Coxe's choice of a caregiver for the baby did not please Clark, and when the child was two or three years old her father removed her to the care of Mr. and Mrs. James Alexander of Trenton, New Jersey, and asked an old friend from Ireland, identified in the records of the Gaines case only as "Kingston," to oversee her welfare.[37]

Coxe testified that Clark visited Caroline every time he came to Philadelphia and "treated her with the tenderness of a parent." Her expenses were paid by drafts on his account with Coxe or by direct remittances

36. Sales of Slaves by Zulime Carrière, Oct. 29, 1801, Nov. 3, 1801, and Nov. 6, 1801, reprinted in *Transcript of Record, Gaines v. City of New Orleans,* 2: 2147 2: 2139, and ibid., 2: 2146; Substitute Power of Attorney to Sinforiano Caillavet, Nov. 9, 1801, ibid., 2: 2148; Acceptance of Payment by Sinforiano Caillavet, Jan. 13, 1802, ibid., 2: 2148.

37. Deposition of Daniel Coxe, May 21, 1835, *W. W. Whitney and Wife v. Eleanor O'Bearn, et al.,* case no. 843, Probate Court of New Orleans, reprinted in *Transcript of Record, Gaines v. City of New Orleans,* 2: 1878; deposition of Daniel Coxe, Jan. 6–9, 1841, ibid., 2, 2004.

from New Orleans. After Clark's death in 1813, Coxe and Dr. William Hulings arranged for Caroline to enter "Mrs. Baizely's boarding school in Philadelphia" and teach the younger children in return for her board and education. At some point after Clark's death Coxe introduced Caroline to her grandmother as Clark's "natural daughter." Mrs. Mary Clark gave her granddaughter a small allowance while she attended Mrs. Baizely's, and Caroline was named as one of Mrs. Clark's heirs at her death in 1823. A few years before her grandmother's death Caroline left the boarding school to marry a Philadelphia doctor, John Barnes. During all of this time she was known as Caroline Clark.[38]

A different story of the events of 1801 and 1802 appeared in the testimony provide by Myra's aunts. Zulime's sisters Sophia and Rose claimed that Caroline was the child of DesGrange, and that became Myra's position during all of the trials. According to Sophia Carrière Despau her sister was pregnant before DesGrange left for France, and Zulime bore the child Caroline in New Orleans in 1801 before they left on their journey to the north. The sisters never explained why Zulime had no contact with the child, why she was reared in Philadelphia, or why Daniel Clark supported the little girl, if Caroline was the daughter of Jerome DesGrange.[39]

Letters found in the files of the Gaines cases indicate that Clark was in Philadelphia in the spring of 1802, just at the time Zulime would have delivered had she become pregnant by him in the summer of 1801 during the absence of her husband. In February, Clark wrote Relf and Chew to arrange a source of money in Philadelphia independent of Daniel Coxe—a "business kept to yourselves." Something quite important kept him in Philadelphia. During that spring Clark's parents left Ireland and journeyed to New Orleans, expecting to see their son for the first time in sixteen years. Clark, however, was in Philadelphia, and instead of immediately returning south, he remained in Philadelphia, leaving Relf and Chew to see to his parents' comfort.[40]

Myra and her two aunts claimed that the urgent business that kept Clark in Philadelphia while his parents waited in New Orleans was not the

---

38. Daniel W. Coxe, depositions of May 21, 1835, and Jan. 6–9, 1841.

39. Sophia Despau, deposition of June 28, 1839.

40. Daniel Clark to Richard Relf and Beverly Chew, Feb. 18, 1802, reprinted in *Transcript of Record, Gaines v. Hennen*, 894; Clark to Relf and Chew, Mar. 29, 1802, in *Gaines v. Cities of New Orleans and Baltimore*, General Case Files no. 2715, Record Group 21, National Archives, Southwest Region, Fort Worth, Tex.

birth of his illegitimate child, but his marriage to Zulime. Sophia Carrière Despau testified that the Carrière family knew of the attachment between Clark and Zulime but would sanction no relationship without marriage. Zulime's hurried trip north in the fall of 1801 resulted not from a need to conceal an adulterous pregnancy, but to prove rumors circulating in New Orleans of a previous marriage by DesGrange, a prior attachment that would invalidate her marriage and leave her free to marry Daniel Clark.[41]

Zulime and her sister Sophia claimed that they left New Orleans for New York where, according to the gossip, DesGrange had been married several years before he came to Louisiana. Sophia's testimony explained that in New York the sisters discovered that the church where DesGrange's first marriage supposedly took place had burned several years before and all its records were lost. Learning of the existence of a witness to the marriage living now in Philadelphia, Zulime and Sophia traveled to that city where they were joined by Daniel Clark. When they successfully traced the missing witness, a Dr. James Gardette, he confirmed that Jerome DesGrange had married a woman in New York who had subsequently left him and sailed for France. Sophia testified that upon hearing this story, Clark exclaimed that Zulime no longer had any reason "to refuse being married to me." A ceremony quickly followed, performed by a Catholic priest (whose name Sophia could never recall) with two witnesses present beside herself: a "Mr. Dosier of New Orleans" and an unnamed Irish friend of Clark's. This marriage, Clark insisted, must be kept secret until a New Orleans court could convict DesGrange of bigamy.[42]

Daniel Clark returned to New Orleans in the late spring of 1802 without Zulime. Depending on whose version of events is true, he was either a new father who had finished arrangements for his illegitimate child's upbringing, or a newly—and secretly—married man. In either case, discretion was necessary. Traveler's accounts usually describe the morals of Creole women as above question. They were faithful wives, devoted mothers, and devout Catholics. The social stigma attached to divorce and the religious convictions of the Catholic population made ending a marriage almost unknown. To publicly acknowledge seducing and impregnating the wife of a business associate might destroy Clark's reputation, especially

41. Sophia Despau, deposition of June 28, 1839.

42. Sophia Despau, deposition of Oct. 16, 1845, reprinted in *Transcript of Record, Gaines v. City of New Orleans*, 2: 1619; Sophia Despau, deposition of Mar. 19, 1849, ibid., 2: 1348.

among the Creole community. Alternatively, to announce a marriage to a woman who all assumed was married to another might result in charges of bigamy against Clark.[43]

In the late summer of 1802 events in Europe began to influence the fate of colonial Louisiana, the fortunes of Clark and his business associates, and the future of his relationship with Zulime. France had originally ceded Louisiana to Spain in 1763 as compensation for the Spanish loss of the Floridas to the British, incurred while fighting as an ally of the French in the Seven Years' War. Both the French Directoire and, later, Napoleon put heavy pressure on Spain to give back the province. Hints of a secret agreement to return Louisiana to France reached Thomas Jefferson who responded by sending Robert Livingston to France to negotiate for the purchase of the "island of New Orleans." French ownership of the port of New Orleans, Jefferson wrote to Livingston, meant that the United States must "marry itself to the British navy." Livingston should make sure that Napoleon understood the consequences for France if it refused to sell the colony.[44]

Daniel Clark returned from Philadelphia to find New Orleans seething with whispered rumors of a transfer of ownership of the province. In the middle of February 1802, while still in Philadelphia, Clark had written Relf and Chew that "there seems to be no doubt that France is to have Louisiana." By March he seemed less certain that the transfer would ever take place. A French informant mentioned the "improbability of France ever taking possession for some time, perhaps never," since Spain "did not like the sacrifice," England would "not look quietly on the measure," and the United States opposed any change in ownership. But by early summer Daniel Coxe informed Clark that business interests in Philadelphia confidently expected to hear confirmation of the cession of Louisiana to France—and American newspapers "from north to south, teem with op-

43. Fossier, *New Orleans,* 276; Dennis, "Image of Louisiana," 48.

44. By the secret treaty of San Ildefonso, signed on October 1, 1800, Napoleon offered to support the claims of the duke of Parma (the husband of the daughter of Charles IV of Spain) to the duchy of Tuscany in return for the retrocession of Louisiana and the Floridas. A second treaty, proposed on March 1, 1801 (but left unsigned until the Spanish king was certain of his son-in-law's kingdom), did not include the Floridas. The second treaty was finally signed on October 15, 1802, but the boundaries of the vast territory of Louisiana were not defined. Kendall, *History of New Orleans,* 1: 39–40; Joseph T. Hatfield, "The Public Career of William C. C. Claiborne," Brandeis University (Ph.D. diss, 1979), 155–6, 168; J. Clark, *New Orleans,* 215.

position to the event." Coxe, no supporter of Jefferson, thought that the transfer of Louisiana would unfavorably affect Jefferson's political future.[45]

Spanish reluctance to part with Louisiana delayed the transfer of the province to France. The crown made one last attempt to integrate Louisiana into the Spanish commercial system in 1802. In June Daniel Clark warned Secretary of State James Madison that Spanish intendant Morales would close the American deposit in response to the signing of the Peace of Amiens by France and Britain.[46]

Clark's prediction proved remarkably accurate. In October 1802, in response to a secret order received from the Spanish treasury, Morales announced the suspension of the American right of deposit. So well did Morales keep secret the source of his order that even his colleagues in the Louisiana government did not know that he acted under the authority of Madrid. After protests by the United States government, both Captain-General Someruelos in Cuba and Spanish minister Irujo in Washington ordered the intendant to restore the deposit or assign another to the Americans. Morales did not respond to their demands. Daniel Clark's private knowledge of Morales's character and the inner workings of the provincial government convinced him that the intendant had not acted on his own authority, as Madison and Jefferson originally believed. On March 8, 1803, Clark advised Madison that "informed people" in New Orleans were convinced that Morales "merely executes the order received from his Government." Morales, Clark assured the secretary of state, was "too rich, too sensible, and too cautious" to take such an important step without direct orders from the Spanish court.[47]

45. Daniel Clark to Richard Relf and Beverly Chew, Feb. 18, 1802, reprinted in *Transcript of Record, Gaines v. Hennen*, 894; Clark to Relf and Chew, Mar. 16, 1802, in *Gaines v. Cities of New Orleans and Baltimore*, General Case Files no. 2715, Record Group 21, National Archives, Southwest Region, Fort Worth, Tex.; Daniel W. Coxe to Clark, July 1, 1802, reprinted in *Transcript of Record, Gaines v. Relf, Chew, and Others*, 564.

46. Daniel Clark to Secretary of State Madison, July 22, 1802, "Documents, Part I," *American Historical Review* 32 (1927): 815-6.

47. Daniel Clark to Secretary of State Madison, Mar. 8, 1803, "Documents: Despatches from the United States Consul in New Orleans, 1801–1803, Part II," *American Historical Review* 33 (1927): 332; Gayarré, *History of Louisiana*, 3: 471–3; Hatfield, "Public Career," 158; J. Clark, *New Orleans*, 216. For the text of the Morales decree of Oct. 16, 1802, closing New Orleans as a port of deposit under the Treaty of 1795, see *American State Papers, Foreign Relations* (Washington, D.C.: Gales and Seaton, 1832), 2,

Closure of the deposit created financial hardship for American commercial houses in New Orleans and Philadelphia. A letter from Louisiana quoted in a Philadelphia newspaper reported "great consternation among the American merchants" in New Orleans. Business activity halted as merchants waited to see what would happen.[48]

Daniel Clark took immediate steps to ensure that Clark & Coxe did not suffer from any transfer of ownership or the closure of the deposit. Until a changeover actually occurred, he planned that the firm's ships should continue to enter New Orleans harbor, disguised as Spanish vessels, and to carry cargoes to Philadelphia. By October Clark's network of informants convinced him that the French government did expect to take immediate possession of Louisiana. "The moment is big with important events," he wrote to Chew and Relf, "and the political horizon is more than usually gloomy." His letter instructed his partners to sell property, slaves, and ships, "if you can possibly do it," and to call in all debts, including one owed by the Governor Casa Calvo.[49]

Clark's concern that a transfer of Louisiana to France would end his privileged position in New Orleans led him to attempt to ingratiate himself with the new French authorities. Having created for Zulime a "very handsome establishment" in New Orleans, Clark left for England in August 1802, and by November he was in Paris. Clark met with French prefect Pierre Laussat, appointed by Napoleon to accept the transfer of Louisiana from Spain, and with General Claud Victor, selected as captain-general of Louisiana. During separate meetings with the two, Clark concealed his American citizenship and position as United States vice-consul in New Orleans and presented himself only as a merchant concerned about future French policy in Louisiana. Clark may have hoped to gain assurances that France would restore the American deposit; if so, he was quickly disappointed. General Victor informed Clark that France regarded the Treaty of San Lorenzo and the American right of deposit in New Orleans as "waste paper." Laussat confirmed that the French government would immediately

---

470. Morales took extraordinary care to keep secret the orders of the Spanish government because Daniel Clark often obtained important information from minor Spanish officials in New Orleans. Whitaker, *Mississippi Question,* 309 (note 8).

48. *Frankfurt (Ky.) Palladium,* Jan. 20, 1803, item dated Philadelphia, Dec. 28, 1802, quoted in Whitaker, *Mississippi Question,* 196; Arena, "Philadelphia–Spanish New Orleans Trade" (Ph.D. diss.), 141–3.

49. Daniel Clark to Richard Relf and Beverly Chew, Oct. 22, 1802, reprinted in *Transcript of Record, Gaines v. City of New Orleans,* 2: 1786.

end that agreement; New Orleans merchants could not expect France to continue the Spanish custom of disregarding violations of trade policies. The meetings with the French officials convinced Clark that France would be even less likely than the Spanish to condone American use of the port of New Orleans and ended any thoughts he might have had about cooperation with the French. His confidential report of the conversations to friends in Louisiana concluded that "[s]hould the French continue in possession of Orleans, such of us here as have fortunes, must become beggars."[50]

Clark's visits with Victor and Laussat had the approval of the American minister to France, Robert Livingston, and the information Clark obtained contradicted the stated policy of the French government. Talleyrand, the French foreign minister, had verbally assured Livingston that France would honor the American right of deposit but declined to put the promise in writing. Livingston reported both conversations to President Jefferson, urging the president to "draw your own inferences." The American merchant community in New Orleans credited Clark's information with convincing Jefferson that only the purchase of New Orleans would ensure American use of the port. "The United States owed the acquisition of Louisiana to Daniel Clark," concluded his friend Colonel Bellechasse.[51]

Clark continued to provide confidential information to Jefferson and to use that information for the benefit of his business interests. The first public notice of the purchase of Louisiana appeared in the *New England Palladium*, published in Boston on June 28, 1803. A letter from Rufus King in Paris reached Jefferson on July 3, confirming the cession but mentioning no purchase price. On July 4, 1803, the *National Intelligencer* made the first public announcement of the purchase in Washington, D.C. On July 6, Secretary of State Madison formally informed Clark of the transfer. Clark, however, had advance knowledge of the agreement. On April 30, the day the treaty was signed in Paris, an informant wrote Clark urging him to buy New Orleans property before the cession became public knowledge. Such information allowed Clark to reverse his earlier decision

50. Gayarré, *History of Louisiana*, 3: 471; Daniel Clark to Secretary of State Madison, Apr. 27, 1803, in "Documents, Part II," *American Historical Review* 33 (1927): 339; Whitaker, *Mississippi Question*, 92, 237–8, 245; Wilkinson, *Memoirs*, 2: appendix no. 16. Clark's interviews with General Victor and Prefect Laussat are recorded in Robert Livingston's letter to Secretary of State Madison, *American State Papers: Foreign Relations*, 2: 526–7.

51. Livingston quoted in Gayarré, 3: 471; Josef Bellechasse, deposition of 1837.

to sell out and to buy land and slaves at depressed prices. He emerged from a turbulent year richer than ever.[52]

The year 1802 had been equally turbulent for Zulime. Left in New Orleans when Clark visited the continent, Zulime occupied an equivocal position in New Orleans society. If she did marry Clark in Philadelphia, no one outside her family knew it. Gossip linked her name with Clark's, but publicly she was still the wife of Jerome DesGrange. DesGrange, too, was back in New Orleans by the summer of 1802, but with rumors of bigamy swirling about him. The arrival of a visitor from New York heightened the controversy when "it was publicly stated" that Barbara Jeanbelle D'Orsi was DesGrange's first wife, come to New Orleans to reclaim her husband. By the end of the summer, scandal charged that DesGrange had been married three times, and both wives prior to Zulime had turned up in New Orleans. In September he was charged before an ecclesiastical court with falsely swearing to bachelor status when he married Zulime. Fearing that DesGrange "was about to leave with the last of these three wives," the court ordered him jailed while conducting its investigation.[53]

A partial record of the church investigation of the bigamy charge against Jerome DesGrange surfaced in 1849 and appeared as evidence in the later Gaines cases. According to Zulime's sister, Sophia, the ecclesiastical court condemned DesGrange for bigamy; he was "cast into prison, from which he secretly escaped by connivance, and was taken down the Mississippi River by Mr. Le Breton D'Orgenois, where he got to a vessel . . . [and] escaped from the country." The existing records of that inquiry do not substantiate Sophia's story. When the investigating officer, Thomas Hazlett (canon of the Cathedral of St. Louis) asked Barbara Jeanbelle D'Orsi if she had married DesGrange, she denied it. She had known him for sixteen years; "eleven and a half years ago" (about 1790) she had planned to marry DesGrange but had changed her mind when she learned that he planned to leave New York City. She admitted that she had seen him during the previous year in Bordeaux but insisted that "she did not

52. *Territorial Papers of the United States,* 9: 4 (note 4); Secretary of State Madison to Daniel Clark, July 6, 1803, reprinted in *Transcript of Record, Gaines v. City of New Orleans,* 2: 1705–06; Fulwar Skipwith to Clark, Apr. 30, 1803, ibid., 2: 2024; Daniel Coxe to Clark, Aug. 26, 1803, ibid., 2: 1943.
53. "Ecclesiastical Record of the Accusation of Bigamy Against Geronimo Des-Grange," Sept. 4, 1802, reprinted in *Transcript of Record, Gaines v. City of New Orleans,* 2: 1603.

again speak to him of the marriage because they were both of them married."[54]

Zulime was also called as a witness before the ecclesiastical court, and her testimony deepened the mystery of her relationship with Daniel Clark. She told the churchmen that she had heard the rumors of DesGrange's prior marriages and that she and her sister had gone north to find substantiating evidence. They had "learned only that he had courted a woman, whose father not consenting to the match, it did not take place, and she married another man shortly afterwards." Asked if she believed that her husband was married to three women, Zulime replied that she had "heard so in public [but] not believed it, and the report [had] caused her no uneasiness, as she is satisfied that it is not true."[55]

It is difficult to reconcile Zulime's statement to the ecclesiastical court with her desire to find evidence to annul her marriage to DesGrange so that the subsequent marriage to Clark could be openly acknowledged. With so little objective evidence and so much testimony resting on the memories of events occurring thirty or more years in the past, reconstructing a plausible (or even possible) version of what did happen is a challenging task. When the bigamy investigation took place, Daniel Clark was in England making business arrangements and preparing to visit Paris. Zulime was alone in New Orleans. Perhaps when Barbara Jeanbelle denied that she had married DesGrange, Zulime believed that she could not convince the court of her husband's guilt. If so, she may have thought it better to pretend a belief in her husband (DesGrange) than to announce that she had married again (Clark) and risk a bigamy accusation herself. Clark's absence certainly made it difficult for her as a young woman (she was twenty years old) to claim to be married to the richest man in New Orleans.

DesGrange was not actually acquitted of bigamy. The court "suspended" its inquiry, "not being able to prove the public report," but kept open the possibility of reopening the investigation if further evidence appeared. Released from prison, DesGrange left New Orleans. No additional records of a further inquiry could be discovered among the old Spanish records, despite diligent searching by both sides of the Gaines cases. In the notarial records, however, there is a certificate issued on May

54. Sophia Despau, deposition of June 28, 1839; testimony of Barbara D'Orsi, "Ecclesiastical Record."

55. Testimony of Zulime DesGrange, "Ecclesiastical Record."

27, 1803, reporting the absence of DesGrange from the city. His absence supported Sophia's testimony that he fled New Orleans to escape further prosecution.[56]

When Clark returned from Europe in February 1803, he resumed his relationship with Zulime. He never openly proclaimed a marriage between them existed, nor did he ever publicly refer to Zulime as his wife. Neither did he boast of her as his mistress. Instead, he kept their association as private as possible. Colonel Bellechasse believed that if Clark had married Zulime, his pride kept him from acknowledging it. Most of Clark's friends, however, remembered Zulime as a *femme galante* ("playful woman," an idiom for lover); the more charitable described her as the Widow DesGrange. None believed that their friend, a man of great "delicacy of feeling," had married his paramour.[57]

56. "Notarial Certificate of the Absence of DesGrange," Nar'zo Broutin, Notary Public, May 27, 1803, reprinted in *Transcript of Record, Gaines v. City of New Orleans,* 2: 6476.

57. Josef Bellechasse, deposition of 1837; Zenon Cavallier, deposition of May 30, 1849; Pierre Baron Boisfontaine, deposition of Nov. 18, 1840.

Engraving of Myra Clark Gaines at about age forty
Nolan B. Harmon Papers, MSS 134, Archives and Manuscript Dept.,
Pitts Theology Library, Emory University

Colonel Samuel Boyer Davis
Courtesy Delaware State Museums, Dover

Engraving of Myra Clark Gaines circa 1845, from a
photograph by Mathew Brady
Courtesy Historical Society of Pennsylvania, Philadelphia

Brigadier General (Brevet Major General) Edmund Pendleton Gaines
Courtesy Dept. of the Army, U.S. Military History Institute, Carlisle, Pa.

Justice James M. Wayne, perhaps Myra Clark Gaines's
staunchest supporter on the U.S. Supreme Court
Courtesy National Archives, College Park, Md.

Justice John Catron of the U.S., Myra Gaines's
nemesis on the Supreme Court
Courtesy Tennessee State Library and Archives, Nashville

MYRA MEETING HER MOTHER.

Illustration used as frontispiece for Ann S. Stephen's dime novel *Myra: The Child of Adoption,*
A Romance of Real Life (1860)

Courtesy Center for American History, University of Texas at Austin, CN Number 10850

Myra at seventy
Courtesy Linton Gaines Robertson

V

A Life of Intrigue

The existence of a legal marriage between Daniel Clark and Zulime Car- rière was the central focus of the fifty-seven years of litigation by their daughter. Letters, testimony, and notarial records reveal that in the years after the Louisiana Purchase the intersection of Daniel Clark's political, business, and romantic lives continued to circumscribe his actions. Both sides of the lawsuit tried to peel back these layers of complex interrelation- ships to unravel the mystery of Myra's parentage.

Before the transfer of Louisiana to the United States, Clark expected to be selected governor of the new territory, a question that engaged the attention of both government officials in Washington and Americans liv- ing in New Orleans. One resident wrote secretary of the treasury Albert Gallatin with specific recommendations. The new governor should speak French fluently, since "an interpreter will render his situation extremely awkward and irksome." Wealth was another requirement, as "the recipro- cation of hospitalities, in a very hospitable country, will be expensive." Clark fit these requirements, and he apparently believed that he deserved the post as a reward for his service as consul and his aid in the Paris negoti- ations.[1]

Acknowledgment of a clandestine marriage to Zulime would doom Clark's hopes of political office. Another office seeker's marital transgres-

1. John Pintard to Albert Gallatin, Sept. 14, 1803, quoted in Walter Pritchard, "Se- lecting a Governor for the Territory of Orleans," *Louisiana Historical Quarterly* 31 (1948): 279.

sions had hurt his own chances for further advancement and "lessened his standing in society" when he attempted to marry again after separating from his wife. Branded an adulterer, Army Surgeon Dr. John Sibley, a candidate for the Legislative Council of Louisiana, lost the respect of the New Orleans community after an "investigation of his character" revealed his unhappy domestic life. A letter to President Jefferson opposing his appointment concluded that his "conduct in life has been such as to render him unworthy of Confidence." Jefferson agreed with this "charge of weight," although he was willing to measure the accusation against other expressions of support for the doctor. But when the president announced the candidates for the council, Dr. Sibley's name was not on the list. Zulime's sisters testified that, with this example before him, Clark insisted that the marriage remain secret until after the confusion surrounding the change of government subsided and the ecclesiastical court ruled on the validity of Zulime's marriage to DesGrange.[2]

Jefferson's continued reliance on Clark's knowledge of Louisiana bolstered the merchant's belief that the post of territorial governor would be his. In August the president requested that Clark provide answers to a list of forty-three detailed questions about Louisiana. Clark diligently obtained responses from many sources, copying and translating the information himself so that none of the answers could leak out. Both President Jefferson and Secretary of State Madison praised Clark's work, citing "the pains you have taken to collect this information and the extent of the details composing it." A letter from a Washington acquaintance, Jonathan Dayton, provided further encouragement. Dayton assured Clark that he had gained the attention of "influential men" that would lead to his "active and honorable employment" in completing "so valuable and so important" an acquisition. Clark thought the praise of his "most acceptable services" meant an early appointment to the governorship. A letter from his sister mentioned her pleasure at learning that Clark "is in a fair way of being titled your Excellency"; a similar communication from Clark's brother indicated that his family, at least, expected Clark to be named governor of Louisiana.[3]

2. William Claiborne to Thomas Jefferson, Jan. 10, 1805, *Territorial Papers of the United States,* ed. Clarence E. Carter (Washington, D.C.: United States Government Printing Office, 1940), vol. 9, *The Territory of Orleans, 1803–1812,* 367; Claiborne to Jefferson, Jan. 29, 1805, ibid., 385.

3. Thomas Jefferson to Daniel Clark, July 17, 1803, and Clark's reply, Sept. 8, 1803, *Territorial Papers of the United States,* 9: 28; James Madison to Clark, Oct. 12, 1803, ibid., 79; Jonathan Dayton to Clark, Oct. 15, 1803, *Transcript of Record, Gaines v. City*

But although they praised Clark for his "knowledge of local circumstances, . . . acquaintance with the disposition of the people, and with the principal characters and their views," when Jefferson and Madison drew up a list of possible candidates for the Louisiana governorship they did not include the name of Daniel Clark. Jefferson's prejudice against Britain played a part in his reluctance to consider Clark. The president was willing to consider the marquis de Lafayette for the post but would not offer the governorship to a former British subject who still maintained active commercial links to British shipping firms. Even more important were Clark's ties to prominent Federalist merchants such as Daniel Coxe of Philadelphia. The president might state a wish to abolish all political distinctions, but concluded that "while the [Federalist] party throughout the U.S. retain and even increase their bitterness they must not be nourished by office." Jefferson's determination not to give a public forum to his political opponents received assistance from Clark's business rivals in New Orleans who reinforced the president's reluctance to appoint the former vice-consul. Benjamin Morgan, a fellow merchant, believed that Clark expected and wanted to be named governor, but he considered Clark "deficient in dignity of character and sterling veracity to fill the office of governor." Few Americans in New Orleans, Morgan assured his Washington correspondent, except "those dependent on him," truly liked Daniel Clark.[4]

---

of New Orleans, 2: 1888; Jane Green to Clark, Oct. 26, 1803, in Gaines v. City of New Orleans, General Case Files no. 2695, Record Group 21, National Archives, Southwest Region, Fort Worth, Tex.; Richard Clark to Daniel Clark, Oct. 27, 1803, E. P. Gaines and Wife v. Richard Relf, et al., General Case Files no. 1785, Record Group 21, National Archives, Southwest Region, Fort Worth, Tex.

4. Pritchard, "Selecting a Governor," 316; Thomas Jefferson to William Claiborne, July 7, 1804, Jefferson Papers, Library of Congress; Benjamin Morgan to Chandler Price, Aug. 18, 1803, Territorial Papers of the United States, 9: 9. Governor William Claiborne fanned Jefferson's fears of Louisiana political opposition by reporting the establishment of a strong Federalist Party in New Orleans. "Nearly all of the Gentlemen of the Bar and many of the Merchants are of that Sect," he warned the president. Claiborne to Jefferson, Dec. 21, 1804, Territorial Papers of the United States, 9: 357–8. Historian George Dargo, however, comments on the tendency of Jefferson to "look to Federalism as a breeding ground of political trouble in the remoteness of Orleans." The president's apprehensions proved groundless when the Federalist Party failed to gain a foothold in the territory, and Jeffersonian Republicanism dominated. Dargo notes that, in Louisiana, political affiliations "tended to be transitory, factional, and personal." Party labels might be used as a temporary designation, but political parties "as such did not exist." Jefferson's Louisiana, 34.

Unable to decide on a permanent choice, Jefferson selected as temporary governor William Charles Cole Claiborne, the twenty-seven-year-old governor of the Mississippi Territory. Claiborne and his co-commissioner, General James Wilkinson (Colonel Clark's old business partner), prepared to receive the new territory from the French. Negotiations set the transfer of Louisiana from Spain to France for November 30, 1803, followed by cession to the United States on December 20th. Even though he was unwilling to trust Louisiana to Clark's governorship, Jefferson urged Claiborne to make use of the merchant's connections and abilities. Clark's "worth and influence" could "powerfully" aid the United States in dealings with Spanish and French officials in New Orleans.[5]

Accepting Jefferson's advice, Claiborne wrote Clark, praising his "zeal in promoting the interests of the country"; Clark's information would "greatly influence [his] conduct," Claiborne assured Clark. But the new governor's willingness to defer to Clark's knowledge of Louisiana did little to mollify the disgruntled merchant. Bitter at being passed over for the governorship, he momentarily contemplated quitting New Orleans prior to the American takeover and becoming a "passive spectator" of events. His love of intrigue drew him back into the plots and counterplots that gyrated about the transfer of the territory, but he confessed to a friend that

5. Hatfield, "Public Career,"173; Pritchard, "Selecting a Governor," 274–5; Jefferson to Claiborne, July 3, 1803, Ford, *Thomas Jefferson*, 8: 71–2. Commissions were granted on Oct. 31, 1803, to General James Wilkinson and Governor William Claiborne to take possession of Louisiana as agents of the United States. Claiborne alone was initially considered for the assignment, but Wilkinson was added after rumors of possible Spanish opposition reached Jefferson through Daniel Clark. Hatfield, "Public Career," 173–4.

Claiborne knew that Jefferson intended his position as governor of Louisiana to be temporary. President Jefferson had requested that he serve until Congress acted on the status of the new territory. Claiborne's earlier selection as governor of the Mississippi Territory had been a reward for his loyal support of Jefferson during the 1800 presidential election. As a congressman from Tennessee, Claiborne had repulsed the blandishments of the Federalists who sought to deny Jefferson the presidency in 1800; instead, when a tie in the Electoral College between Jefferson and Burr threw the election to the House, Claiborne delivered the Tennessee delegation's vote for Jefferson. Claiborne accepted the temporary position of Louisiana governor because he hoped it would become permanent, or at least provide him with a more impressive position that would attract national attention and aid his future political ambitions. Jefferson had many applicants for the Louisiana governorship, but few had the qualifications the president sought. When his first two choices, General Lafayette and James Monroe, declined to serve, Jefferson decided to make Claiborne's appointment permanent. Hatfield, "Public Career," 71–2, 191–4; Pritchard, "Selecting a Governor," 273–4, 280.

he was hurt that Madison and Jefferson seemed to have ignored his service in Louisiana. Not even a "complimentary epistle on the expiration of [his] consulship" had arrived from Washington. Clark's friend relayed the message of his acrimony, and at last a letter did arrive from Madison thanking Clark for his aid. Clark, however, interpreted Madison's appreciation as a hint that President Jefferson contemplated a change that would place him in the governor's seat. "I flatter myself," Clark replied, "that the Inhabitants of Louisiana would be rendered happy by the change."[6]

In the months before the actual transfer of Louisiana to the United States, Daniel Clark demonstrated the extent of his connections in the Spanish government. Between July and December of 1803 Clark served as Jefferson's "man on the spot" in Louisiana. Requested to ascertain the intentions of Spanish officials, Clark warned that they might try to postpone the delivery of the province to France. Such delaying tactics might allow "numberless unforeseen and favorable circumstances [to] occur of which they would take advantage." A few days later Clark had changed his mind. Now he believed that Spanish commissioner Casa Calvo had given up "all idea of opposition" and that "no other delay or difficulty will be put in the way of delivery than what may arise from Etiquette or from personal pique between the French and Spanish Commissioners." Only one circumstance threatened—the protest lodged by the Spanish minister in Washington against the French sale of Louisiana. Carlos Martinez de Irujo, the Spanish minister, resented Madison's blunt declaration that the Spaniards would have to decide for themselves whether they wanted "a garden of peace or a field of war." Irujo retorted that Louisiana might cost far more than $15 million if the Americans "undertook a quarrel." Clark worried that if "news of the Protest by Spain reaches us," the Spanish governor might decide to oppose the transfer of the province to the United States. Clark had persuaded Governor Salcedo and Commissioner Casa Calvo that silence on the part of Spain was "the greatest possible proof she can give of her acquiescence to the Cession made [to] the United States," and he assured Claiborne, "they begin to place belief in the assertion." To guard against any knowledge of Spanish opposition, Clark

6. William Claiborne to Daniel Clark, Nov. 18, 1803, *Transcript of Record, Gaines v. City of New Orleans*, 2: 1775; Clark to James Wilkinson, Apr. 13, 1804, Wilkinson, *Memoirs*, 2: appendix 12; Clark to Madison, May 10, 1804, *Territorial Papers of the United States*, 9: 15.

bribed local officials to suppress the delivery of all newspapers by post, allowing only those that contained no mention of the Spanish minister's protest to circulate. Likewise, he intercepted all dispatches directed to the Spanish government. "I shall endeavor to learn their contents before they are delivered," he promised Claiborne, "and either suppress or deliver them as the circumstances may require."[7]

Clark's optimism about the possibility of a peaceful transfer for the territory evaporated as problems of "Etiquette" did create friction between the French and Spanish commissioners. When Spanish governor Salcedo failed to attend a fête held by Madame Laussat, wife of the French prefect, she denounced the Spaniards as "Souls of Filth," and her husband's explosive temper exacerbated the tense situation. Clark implored Claiborne and Wilkinson to "for God's Sake lose no time in marching this way to put an End to the horrid situation we are in. . . . [Y]our presence alone can calm the effervescence which the slightest Accident may cause to shew itself in the worst of Forms."[8]

The letters Clark wrote between November 23 and December 19 depict a steadily worsening situation. He constantly urged Claiborne and Wilkinson to make haste to reach New Orleans. Warning that "every delay is a day of fear and suspense," Clark cautioned the American commissioners that New Orleans was "placed over a Mine that may explode from one moment to another [with an] effect . . . dreadful beyond conception." Clark did not explain just what kind of opposition he anticipated. He warned of vague threats to "fire the town," and predicted that Prefect Laussat would "give the lower Classes a hankering for a French government," and rouse in his fellow countrymen a revolutionary spirit that Clark had "long attempted to subdue."[9]

George Dargo credits Clark's recommendation for a show of force at

7. Daniel Clark to William Claiborne, Nov. 11, 1803, *Territorial Papers of the United States*, 9: 103; Clark to Claiborne, Nov. 21, 1803, ibid., 115; Clark to Claiborne, Nov. 22, 1803, ibid., 117; Dumas Malone, *Jefferson the President, First Term: 1801–1805* (Boston: Little, Brown, 1970), 4: 322; Daniel Clark to William Claiborne, Nov. 11, 1803, *Territorial Papers of the United States*, 9: 102–3; Clark to Claiborne, Nov. 22, 1803, ibid., 117; Clark to Claiborne, Nov. 23, 1803, ibid., 121.

8. Daniel Clark to William Claiborne, Nov. 23, 1803, *Territorial Papers of the United States*, 9: 119; Clark to Claiborne, Nov. 29, 1803, ibid., 125.

9. Daniel Clark to William Claiborne, Nov. 29, 1803, *Territorial Papers of the United States*, 9: 125; and Daniel Clark to Claiborne and James Wilkinson, Dec. 12, 1803, ibid., 9: 137; James Wilkinson to the secretary of war, Dec. 20, 1803, ibid., 9: 138.

the time of the transfer for the smooth delivery of the territory. But Clark's own letters to Claiborne and Wilkinson indicate the futility of resistance to the American takeover. The total Spanish and French forces in New Orleans amounted to only three hundred men, of whom seventy-five were in the hospital suffering from dysentery and "nearly as many in arrest or in Prison." Debris clogged the guns placed on the ramparts around the town, and the forts at each corner of the walls were "very slightly and negligently guarded." Nor could any hostile force close the city gates against the American commissioners, since the gates were "incapable of turning on their hinges."[10]

Daniel Clark exaggerated tensions among Spanish, French, and Americans in New Orleans for reasons of his own. If he could not be governor of Louisiana, he intended to continue the same degree of influence over the American government that he had exercised over the Spanish. Using the uncertain situation in New Orleans to bolster his own position as the only American representative trusted by all sides, he promised Claiborne and Wilkinson to "do all my Endeavors to keep all Parties quiet, as I enjoy the Confidence of all, until you arrive and [I] shall be prepared to give you all possible Assistance." One such "endeavor" organized by Clark consisted of the formation of a militia unit "under American colours to preserve and guard the Town." One hundred volunteers from the merchant community elected Clark as their captain and offered their services to Prefect Laussat to keep order in the community during the three weeks between the two transfers.[11]

In spite of Clark's fears—or perhaps because of his preparations—the transfer of Louisiana to the United States proceeded peacefully. Descriptions of the town's reaction to the transfer ceremony vary with the nationality of the viewer. Prefect Laussat described for the French court a sullen populace who by their silence manifested their palpable disappointment at losing their newly regained French citizenship. Daniel Clark described a very different reception for Secretary of State Madison and President Jef-

10. Dargo, *Louisiana*, 31; Daniel Clark to James Madison, Nov. 29, 1803, *Territorial Papers of the United States,* 9: 123–4; Clark to William Claiborne, Nov. 22, 1803, ibid., 119.

11. Daniel Clark to William Claiborne and James Wilkinson, Nov. 29, 1803, *Territorial Papers of the United States,* 9: 125; Clark to Claiborne and Wilkinson, Nov. 30, 1803, ibid.; James A. Robertson, *Louisiana under Spain, France, and the United States, 1785–1807: Social, Economic, and Political Conditions of the Territory* (Cleveland, Ohio: Arthur H. Clark, 1911), 2: 219.

ferson. He emphasized the cheers (from the gathered Americans) that greeted the raising of the American flag. In his opinion, the French populace would support the American government as a welcome alternative to Spanish control, and he anticipated that his connections in the Creole community would make his aid invaluable to the new governor.[12]

Clark's expectations of honor and influence did not materialize. Letters exchanged by Claiborne and Clark prior to the transfer of the province indicate that the two established a respectful working relationship, but in the years after the Louisiana Purchase they became implacable enemies. In part this occurred because of Clark's constantly proffered advice, which Claiborne often refused to follow. Clark exhibited little tact in his suggestions to the younger man who occupied the position he felt was properly his own. Claiborne responded by treating Clark's expressions of the genuine grievances of the New Orleans community as a subversive attempt by a jealous rival to destroy his standing with President Jefferson, who still openly sought a more qualified candidate for the permanent position of Louisiana governor.[13]

One particularly divisive issue was the immediate admission of the state of Louisiana to the Union. Clark's support for Louisiana statehood reflected the desires of the Creole community, whom Claiborne distrusted, believing that "the principles of a popular Government are utterly beyond their comprehension." When Claiborne wrote Jefferson opposing statehood for the territory he described the citizens of Louisiana as "uninformed, indolent, luxurious, [and] illy fitted to be useful citizens of a Republic." The "old inhabitants" lacked political information and—a great concern to the new governor who spoke no French or Spanish—"not one in fifty . . . appear[ed] to understand the English language." The Creoles responded by characterizing the governor as "a stranger here, a stranger as far as the soil itself is concerned, its local interests, the customs,

12. Newton, *Americanization of French Louisiana*, 1–3. Robertson, *Louisiana*, 2: 77–8, 81–2.

13. William Claiborne to James Madison, Nov. 5, 1804, *Territorial Papers of the United States*, 9: 320; Claiborne to Madison, June 3, 1804, ibid., 242–3. Clark biographer Michael Wohl believes that the "ill-will" between Clark and the Louisiana governor is apparent in Claiborne's correspondence "almost from the beginning." Wohl, "Not Yet Saint nor Sinner," 197. But letters from Claiborne to Clark sent between Nov. 14 and 18, 1803, demonstrate the governor's gratitude for the merchant's advice. *Territorial Papers of the United States*, 9: 104–5.

habits and even the language of the inhabitants, and who is therefore without even the most absolutely necessary knowledge."[14]

American residents of New Orleans also expressed dismay over policies adopted by the governor. Fifty-five merchants, led by Daniel Clark, Richard Relf, Beverly Chew, Evan Jones, and William Hulings, presented a memorial to Congress claiming that the promised "Rights and Privileges" of statehood had not been granted, thus "greatly impeding the Commercial and Agricultural Interests of the Province." The problems detailed in the memorial demonstrate that Clark's political opposition to Claiborne had more behind it than mere jealousy of his position. Louisiana's uncertain status jeopardized Clark's commercial activities. With their ships unauthorized to "hoist any Flag whatever" and provided with no proper documentation, with their goods still subject to the Spanish tariffs that had penalized American shippers, Clark and his fellow merchants felt themselves victimized. Other American ports, they complained, carried on "a free, and untaxed Intercourse, and their exports are subject to no Duties whatever."[15]

Claiborne's reaction to this criticism indicated that he took such opposition personally. Knowing that Jefferson still sought another governor for the territory, Claiborne feared that those who frustrated his policies "have endeavored to render me personally unpopular." He believed that the efforts of "a few base individuals" had influenced the populace to "think against, and act against their interests." A supporter of the governor wrote to Washington that "these men, some of them desperate in their fortunes . . . segregated themselves from their own countrymen" and joined the Creoles, "flatter[ing] their vanity and pride by promising them a government in which they should have the preponderance of power." Claiborne placed Daniel Clark at the head of his political opposition. The governor believed that Clark protested the policies of the government because he thought his services had not received their deserved reward. As a result,

14. William Claiborne to James Madison, Jan. 2, 1804, Robertson, *Louisiana* 2: 233; Claiborne to Thomas Jefferson, Jan. 16, 1804, *Territorial Papers of the United States,* 9: 161–2; Étienne Boré, Feb. 10, 1804, and Alexandre Baudin, Feb. 14, 1804, to Jefferson, *Territorial Papers of the United States,* 9: 182–8; Martin, *History of Louisiana from the Earliest Period,* 322–3; Gayarré, *History of Louisiana,* 4: 2; Joseph Dubreuil de Villars, quoted by Dargo, *Jefferson's Louisiana,* 29.

15. "Memorial to Congress from the Merchants of New Orleans," Jan. 9, 1804, *Territorial Papers of the United States,* 9: 157–8; Daniel Clark to James Madison, Jan. 23, 1804, Daniel Clark Papers, Historical Society of Pennsylvania, Philadelphia.

Claiborne considered that "from the first period of my arrival here to the present day, Mr. Clark (in conjunction with one or perhaps two other persons) have made great exertions to injure me here, and I believe at the Seat of Government."[16]

The source of the violent antagonism between Clark and Claiborne lay not only in their political differences but also in their temperaments. Clark was impetuous, daring, and proud. Claiborne, equally proud, was more cautious and less quixotic. Offered a position by Jefferson on the first legislative council, Clark refused to serve under Claiborne, a position taken, according to the governor, out of a "sincere desire to embarrass the Government." Honest, efficient, and well-intentioned, Governor Claiborne saw himself as an administrator rather than an instigator of national policy. Clark, however, encouraged the governor to intervene actively in local conflicts. Prefect Laussat heard rumors that Clark had advised Claiborne that "until two or three Frenchmen have been hanged, we will not rule over this country." An opponent of Clark suggested that the merchant concocted a "diabolical plan" to ruin the governor: Claiborne should arrest a leading citizen (Clark supposedly volunteered) and then release him in a "shew of liberality and clemency." Only after the governor "refused to listen to a proposition so tyrannical" did Clark "throw off the mask and put himself at the head of the mal-contents." George Mather's dislike of Clark may have led him to exaggerate, but such a scheme surely appealed to Clark, who was thoroughly disgusted with the governor's "want of energy and decision."[17]

By the summer of 1804 the personal feud between Clark and Claiborne erupted into open political war. The governor blamed Clark when several of Jefferson's appointees to the first legislative council declined to serve. Later, when a mass meeting of New Orleans merchants and planters protested the proposed provisions of the Territorial Act, Claiborne named Clark as the host and instigator. That meeting led to another, more detailed (and, in Claiborne's opinion, "highly inflammatory"), memorial in

16. William Claiborne to Thomas Jefferson, Feb. 25, 1804, *Territorial Papers of the United States*, 9: 190–1; Claiborne to James Madison, Jan. 10, 1804, Robertson, *Louisiana*, 2: 233, note 114; John W. Gurley to the postmaster general, July 14, 1804, *Territorial Papers of the United States*, 9: 262; Claiborne to Madison, June 3, 1804, ibid., 242–3.

17. Thomas Jefferson to William Claiborne, Aug. 30, 1804, *Territorial Papers of the United States*, 9: 281; Claiborne to Jefferson, Nov. 19, 1804, ibid., 334; deposition of George Mather in Wilkinson, *Memoirs*, 2: 80–1; Newton, *Americanization of French Louisiana*, 47–8. Laussat, *Memoirs*, entry for Jan. 24, 1804, 96.

which the French and American opponents of the territorial government stated their grievances for presentation to Congress. Chief among the remonstrances was the congressional prohibition of further importation of slaves into the territory. Such an embargo, they contended, rendered Louisiana plantations "of little or no value." Neither sugar, rice, cotton, nor indigo could be cultivated, nor could the levee be kept in repair without a continued, "uninterrupted Trade to Africa," at least until 1808 (when Congress could end the importation of slaves into the rest of the United States). The memorial also charged that Jefferson and the congressmen who created the provisional government for Louisiana had based their impression of the unfitness of Louisiana for representative government on "illiberal and unfair representations, relative to the learning, information, and habits of the people of [Louisiana]" received from Governor Claiborne. The governor, who "does not speak the language of this country," became "less respected every day."[18]

Claiborne acknowledged the general belief that the colony could not prosper "without a great increase of Negro's." Although personally opposed to slavery, he urged Jefferson to moderate the prohibition for the Louisiana Territory. He also tried to reconcile the locals to the end of slave imports, but without success. Even "the most respectable characters," he reported to Jefferson, "cou'd not, *even in my presence,* suppress the Agitation of their Tempers, when a check to that Trade, was suggested." Failing to convince the citizens of the correctness of the government's position, Claiborne tried to discredit the memorialists by linking them to Bonaparte

18. William Claiborne to James Madison, Mar. 16, 1804, *Official Letter Books of William Claiborne,* ed. Rowland Dunbar (1917; reprint, Jackson, Miss.: State Department of Archives and History, 1983), 2: 42–8; Claiborne to Madison, July 13, 1804, *Territorial Papers of the United States,* 9: 261; "Louisiana Memorial," *Louisiana Gazette,* July 24, 1804, p. 2; Hatch Dent to James H. McCulloch, July 14, 1804, *Territorial Papers of the United States,* 9: 266. The Louisiana Territorial Act of March 26, 1804, divided Louisiana into two governmental divisions with the 33rd parallel west from the Mississippi River as the dividing line. The southern section was the Territory of Orleans, with executive power vested in a governor and legislative power given to a council of thirteen residents appointed by the president, whose actions were subject to the governor's veto. Louisiana residents who had wished for immediate statehood turned to Daniel Clark and Edward Livingston for leadership. Livingston wrote the Louisiana Remonstrance and Clark took it around the territory to gather signatures. When it came time for presentation of the memorial to Congress, however, three Creoles—Pierre Sauvé, Pierre Derbigny, and Jean Noel Destrehan—took the protest to Washington. Pritchard, "Selecting a Governor," 282–6; Robertson, *Louisiana,* 2: 278, note 139; Gayarré, *History of Louisiana,* 4: 5–6.

(if French) or to the Federalist party (if American). The "ill-will" of Clark and his closest associates Claiborne attributed to "a knowledge which they have of my *dislike to them and all their measures.* . . . They are great Intrigu'ers, and will probably do me injury (by their writings) in the United States."[19]

Claiborne failed to see that the hostility of Clark and his fellow merchant-planters arose more from a threat to their economic security than from personal differences with the governor. The slave trade was a source of considerable income to Clark, and many of the profits of that trade and his other mercantile interests had been invested in land. In the previous year Clark had been unusually active as a purchaser of land for himself, jointly with Daniel Coxe and as a commission agent for others. Limitations on the importation of slaves into Louisiana would decrease his income and the value of his plantation property.

Certain other provisions of the Territorial Act seemed to threaten the legal titles to Clark's property, thus providing an additional reason for his opposition. The Treaty of 1803 vested the United States government with ownership of all land in the Louisiana Purchase not legitimately held by private title. Congressional legislation required that holders of Louisiana land register their titles with a "Register and Recorder of Land Titles," appointed by President Jefferson. Territorial landowners feared this was "a complicated machinery to dispossess them of all their broad and fertile acres," and the beginning of endless litigation and arbitrary decision making by agents with no local background or with ties to one political faction or another.[20]

The turmoil surrounding the acquisition of Louisiana occupied Clark's

---

19. William Claiborne to Thomas Jefferson, Apr. 15, 1804, *Territorial Papers of the United States,* 9: 222; Claiborne to Jefferson, Nov. 25, 1804, ibid., 340; Claiborne to Jefferson, Dec. 21, 1804, ibid., 357–8; Claiborne to James Madison, Oct. 3, 1804, ibid., 304–5. Emphasis in all letters appears in the originals.

20. J. Clark, *New Orleans,* 273; Gayarré, *History of Louisiana,* 4: 6–7; William B. Hatcher, *Edward Livingston: Jeffersonian Republican and Jacksonian Democrat* (Baton Rouge: Louisiana State University Press, 1940), 103. Some claims were questioned. The U.S. government refused to recognize a grant of hundreds of thousands of acres, known as the Maison Rouge grant, by the Spanish government to the baron de Bastrop. Clark purchased a large portion of this grant; it ultimately became part of his estate and was sold by the executors (Relf and Chew) to Daniel Coxe, who vigorously defended his title for several decades. Tregle, *Louisiana in the Age of Jackson,* 140.

attention through 1803 and 1804 but did not prevent his continued involvement with Zulime Carrière DesGrange. As the richest citizen of New Orleans and the leading opponent of Governor Claiborne, Clark's relationship with the Creole beauty was the subject of considerable gossip. Colonel Bellechasse heard "no little talk of [Clark's] marriage with Madame DesGrange." Another close friend and the manager of several of Clark's plantations, Pierre Baron Boisfontaine, believed that Zulime was the wife of Daniel Clark. The memories of other friends differed. Clark, they recalled, kept a "bachelor's house" in New Orleans, and all knew that he and Zulime lived together in "an amorous and illicit connexion." According to the testimony of Zulime's sisters, Clark's political preoccupation prevented any publication of their marriage. An "honorable and high-spirited gentleman"—especially one who still harbored political ambitions—could not reveal a marriage that the civil courts might consider bigamous, since officially Zulime was still married to DesGrange.[21]

In 1805 gossip and rumor intensified when Zulime challenged the validity of her marriage to the Frenchman. As she did, the feud between Clark and Claiborne spilled over into a dispute that rocked the Catholic Church in New Orleans, paralyzing the church courts and complicating Zulime's action against DesGrange. The rupture in the Catholic community began when Father Patrick Walsh, the vicar-general of Louisiana who had granted the license for DesGrange's marriage to Zulime in 1794, suspended a popular parish priest, Father Antoine de Sedella, who had performed their marriage ceremony. Père Antoine first appeared in New Orleans in 1781, joined the staff of St. Louis Church, and was appointed pastor in 1785. In late spring 1789, the priest requested Governor Miró to provide him with soldiers to arrest and punish heretics. Fearing that emigration into Louisiana, which he encouraged, would end with the appearance of the Inquisition, Miró responded by arresting Sedella and deporting him to Cadiz. A few years later Père Antoine returned to New Orleans as a simple monk and served as curé of St. Louis Cathedral. For over forty years he was a familiar sight in the Old City, a gaunt figure clothed in a loose habit of coarse brown cloth, girded with a hempen rope and shod with wooden sandals. Although he was constantly at odds with

21. Deposition of Louis Bouligny, June 4, 1849, reprinted in *Transcript of Record, Gaines v. Relf, Chew, and Others*, 638; deposition of Etienne Carraby, June 4, 1849, reprinted in *Transcript of Record, Gaines v. City of New Orleans*, 2: 1473.

his ecclesiastical superiors and even the civil government, Père Antoine was "a great favorite of the Louisiana ladies . . . [having] married many of them and christened their children."[22]

Although the confrontation between Père Antoine and the vicar-general appeared confined to church matters, the alacrity with which the French- and English-speaking communities took sides reflected the tensions that divided Creoles and Anglo-Americans. Clark's position in the quarrel is uncertain; his previous alignment with the Creole community makes it likely that his sympathies lay with the parish priest. His closest friend among the Creoles, Colonel Bellechasse, led the opposition to Father Walsh. Governor Claiborne, whose customary caution kept him from openly supporting Walsh, considered Sedella a "seditious Priest." When Zulime filed against DesGrange in civil court, Père Antoine led a concurrent investigation for the church into the true nature of the ceremony he had conducted eleven years earlier. Sedella's trouble with Walsh put any action against DesGrange in limbo.[23]

No records of the religious investigation undertaken by Père Antoine remain in the archives of St. Louis Cathedral, and the incomplete transcripts of the civil actions brought by Zulime in 1805 and 1806 raise more questions than they answer. On November 30, 1805, while Daniel Clark was absent from New Orleans, "Zulime Carrière DesGrange" filed suit in the county court of New Orleans for "alimony" from her husband Jerome DesGrange, who, she charged, had deserted her. The Frenchman had apparently returned to New Orleans—a citation for his appearance in court is marked "served on defendant" on December 6. DesGrange made no answer to Zulime's petition and the court entered a default judgment against him on December 24, 1805. No money was forthcoming from

22. Père Antoine became one of the best-loved men in New Orleans. When he died in 1829 (at the age of eighty-one) the entire city closed its businesses to attend his funeral, and members of the city council wore black armbands for thirty days. Père Antoine was buried at the cathedral, but a few years later his body was removed to the "priest's tomb" in St. Louis Cemetery No. 1. Claiborne to Secretary of War, n.d., quoted in Asbury, *French Quarter*, 54–9; *A Dictionary of Louisiana Biography*, ed. Glenn R. Conrad (Lafayette: University of Southwestern Louisiana, 1989), 726–7; Clarence W. Bispham, "Fray Antonio de Sedella," *Louisiana Historical Quarterly* 2 (1919): 24–8; Tregle, *Louisiana in the Age of Jackson*, 47–8; and Grace King, *New Orleans: The Place and the People* (New York: Macmillan, 1895), 176–7.

23. William Claiborne to Thomas Jefferson, June 17, 1807, *Territorial Papers of the United States*, 9: 356; Robertson, *Louisiana*, 2: 284 (note 142).

DesGrange, however, and six months later, on June 24, 1806, Zulime filed for "damages" against him. This time, her husband replied (through his attorney) that no damages could be assessed for nonsupport until the "validity of the marriage" between the two could be assessed. The Church investigation led by Père Antoine may have ruled on the existence of a legal marriage, but no records of the ecclesiastical trial exist. Most of the records from the civil trial are also missing, but a brief summary of the results remains in the records of the Third District Court of New Orleans. The trial date was June 24, 1806; several witnesses testified, including Zulime's sister Rose. The judgment of the court awarded one hundred dollars in damages to Zulime. The records seem to indicate that this trial ended with a declaration nullifying the marriage of DesGrange and Zulime.[24]

Zulime's legal actions may have had their origin in her frustration at Clark's persistent refusal to acknowledge their marriage and their child. Although several different birth dates for Myra appear in the testimony, the most likely date is June 30, 1804. Pierre Baron Boisfontaine, the brother-in-law of Colonel Davis who had lent his house for Zulime's delivery, marked Myra's birth by remembering that it occurred a few months after his arrival in the territory in the spring of 1804, and his wife confirmed his memory. This date places Myra's birth at the height of the controversy over the Louisiana memorial. Clark's decision to request Davis to procure a house in which Zulime could give birth secretly indicates his unwillingness to publicly acknowledge any legal relationship. If, as Harriet Harper Smythe testified, Zulime was ill after Myra's birth, the seventeen months between June 30, 1804, and November 30, 1805, allowed enough time for her to recover and decide that she needed to act decisively to force her lover to recognize her and their child. Her petition for support from DesGrange may have been designed to push the Frenchman into an admission that their marriage was void and clear the way for Clark to announce that Zulime was his wife.[25]

24. Petition by Zulime Carrière DesGrange for support from her husband, Jerome DesGrange, filed Nov. 30, 1805, case no. 178, County Court of New Orleans; citation, Dec. 6, 1805, judgment by default, Dec. 19, 1805, reprinted in *Transcript of Record, Gaines v. City of New Orleans,* 2: 1651; petition for damages by Zulime Carrière v. Jerome DesGrange, filed June 24, 1806, case no. 356, County Court of New Orleans; answer of DesGrange, July 24, 1806; summary of judgment, July 24, 1806, reprinted in *Transcript of Record, Gaines v. City of New Orleans,* 2: 1652.

25. Several birth dates are given in the testimony of the Gaines cases ranging from 1804 to 1806. Colonel Davis placed Myra's birth on June 30, 1805, but Boisfontaine

Equally plausible, however, is the interpretation of Zulime's actions presented by Myra's opponents in the Gaines case. Relf, Chew, and the other defendants claimed that by the end of 1805 the relationship between Clark and Zulime was deteriorating. Zulime's petition for support from her absent husband represented nothing more than a scorned mistress seeking to return to an abandoned husband. The incomplete record of the civil and religious actions allowed both sides to interpret the scanty evidence in their own interests.

Daniel Clark might have acknowledged Zulime as his wife in 1805 had not a political scandal of national proportions enmeshed him in charges and countercharges of treason. On the afternoon of June 25, 1805, in "an elegant Barge" with "sails, colors, and oars" manned by "a sergeant and ten able, faithful hands," Aaron Burr arrived in New Orleans. The ostracized vice-president bore letters of introduction from General James Wilkinson to Governor Claiborne and Daniel Clark. Both men entertained Burr, their rivalry prompting them to try to outdo each other. Clark evidently liked Burr; "pleased with his society," Clark remembered later, "[I] shewed him the civilities usual on such occasions." This meant a banquet that gathered together all the prominent men of the community, including former Spanish intendant Morales, to meet Burr. Later, Clark lent Burr horses to take the vice-president to Natchez and sent along a servant to bring them back.[26]

The extent of Clark's involvement in Burr's schemes is a matter of conjecture. Claiborne reported to Secretary of State Madison that "during Colonel Burr's continuance in this City he was . . . in habits of intimacy with [Edward] Livingston, Clark, and [Evan] Jones." Wilkinson's letter of introduction to Clark contained the cryptic comment that Burr "would communicate to him many things improper" to write and that "he would not say to any other." Wilkinson's prior history of intrigue with Spanish governors Miró and Carondelet convinced Clark, at least, that Wilkinson

---

provided better evidence for 1804. Clark's letters place him in New Orleans in the fall of 1803. During the following year, however, he spent the fall traveling the territory seeking signatures for the Louisiana Memorial. Since Zulime did not travel with him, he could not have fathered her child born in June 1805. Deposition of Pierre Baron Boisfontaine, Nov. 18, 1840, *Transcript of Record, Gaines v. City of New Orleans,* 2: 2032; and deposition of Aimée Baron Boisfontaine, Nov. 18, 1840, ibid., 2: 2035.

26. Kendall, *History of New Orleans,* 1: 78–9; Gayarré, *History of Louisiana,* 4: 80–1; Jacobs, *Tarnished Warrior,* 221; Daniel Clark, *Proofs,* 94.

did know of Burr's plans and hoped to draw him into the plot. Whether from Wilkinson, Burr, or some other conspirator, Clark heard "absurd and wild reports" of a conspiracy between Burr and Wilkinson to separate the western states from the Union using "the Plunder of Spanish countries west of us." Writing to Wilkinson, Clark demanded to know "how the devil I have been lugged into the conspiracy or what assistance I can be of in it; . . . *vous qui savez tout* can best explain this riddle." Clark suggested that the general amuse Burr with an account of the plot but admonished Wilkinson not to let his schemes distract him from their business of land acquisition. "Recollect that you great men, if you expect to become kings and emperors, must have us little men for vassals," Clark wrote, and "if we have nothing to clothe ourselves with . . . if Congress takes [our] lands for want of formalities, we shall then have no produce [and] we shall make a very shabby figure at your courts."[27]

Eventually, Clark learned that what had lugged him into the conspiracy was Burr's freely pledging Clark's credit and naming him the chief financial backer of the venture. The former vice-president had apparently told his supporters that Clark had provided a letter of credit on the house of Chew & Relf in the amount of $200,000. Clark explained that Burr often claimed friendship and support from persons who were unconnected to his designs in order to impress his hearers "with a high idea of his resources." When Burr insinuated that he could draw on Clark for a substantial sum, he did so, Clark wrote, because "my credit there [in Kentucky], he knew, stood high, and that nothing would impress the public with a better idea of his fiscal operations than a persuasion that I was his banker." When Jefferson's investigator, John Graham, visited New Orleans, Richard Relf convinced him that the firm "never had any funds in their Hands liable to the order of Col. Burr," and Graham reported to Jefferson that rumor had greatly exaggerated Clark's involvement.[28]

27. General James Wilkinson to Daniel Clark, June 9, 1805, Wilkinson, *Memoirs*, 2: appendix no. 13; William Claiborne to Clark, Aug. 6, 1805, *Territorial Papers of the United States*, 9: 489; Clark to Wilkinson, Sept. 7, 1805, Wilkinson, *Memoirs*, 2: appendix no. 14. Clark's letter has been called "a masterpiece of dissembling" by those who link the merchant to Burr's plans. It may be, however, just what it purports to be, a warning to Wilkinson not to let Burr draw him into any foolish schemes.

28. Daniel Clark, *Proofs*, 98; John Graham to Daniel Clark, May 13, 1807, Daniel Clark Papers, Historical Society of Pennsylvania, Philadelphia. Historian George Dargo believes that Graham's investigation was too superficial and that Burr's suggestion of financial backing from Clark may have been true. Dargo, *Jefferson's Louisiana*, 63–4.

Some evidence of Clark's collusion with Burr comes from British archives. Through an intermediary, the former vice-president proposed to the British minister to the United States, Sir Anthony Merry, that British aid would allow Burr to place Louisiana and other southwestern territory into English hands. Merry, convinced that the western states and the Louisiana Territory actually were close to secession, wrote the British Foreign Office suggesting that several British frigates be sent to patrol Gulf waters until "Daniel Clark of New Orleans" should send word that "the revolution had taken place." When this missive reached England it fell into the hands of the new prime minister, Charles James Fox, who had better things for English frigates to do than wait for Clark to "deliver" Louisiana. Merry was promptly recalled.[29]

If Burr and Wilkinson did contemplate a Mexican conquest (or any separation of the western states from the rest of the Union) they failed to keep their plans secret. The whispers of conspiracy that amused Clark appeared in the *National Intelligencer* soon after Burr left New Orleans. Quoting a Kentucky newspaper, the *Western World,* which had "attract[ed] very great attention here [Washington, D.C.]," the editor of the *National Intelligencer* asserted that "Judge Prévost [a son-in-law of Burr and a judge of the Louisiana district court], Edward Livingston, General Wilkinson, Mr. Burr, and Mr. John Brown of Kentucky are charged as concerned in a *new conspiracy* against the peace of the whole Union, and with mediating a separation of this section from the eastern parts of the Union." Although Clark was not mentioned directly, his ties with Livingston, Wilkinson, and Prévost were sufficient to link his name in the minds of most Louisianians with that of the disgraced vice-president.[30]

Clark's actions following Burr's visit to New Orleans only increased suspicions about his involvement in the supposed plot. On September 11, 1805, two months after Burr left New Orleans, Clark set out on an extended journey that took him to several Mexican ports, including Vera Cruz. He returned to New Orleans in late December but left again for

29. Sir Anthony Merry to Lord Mulgrave, Nov. 25, 1805, MS in British Archives, quoted in Henry Adams, *History of the United States of America during the Second Administration of Thomas Jefferson* (1893; reprint, New York: Charles Scribner's Sons, 1921), 1: 230; Thomas R. Hay, "Charles Williamson and the Burr Conspiracy," *Journal of Southern History* 2 (1936): 185–7.

30. *National Intelligencer and Washington Advertiser,* n.d., quoted in Walter F. McCaleb, *The Aaron Burr Conspiracy* (New York: Dodd, Mead, 1903), 181; Hatcher, *Edward Livingston,* 126.

Mexico in February 1806. The reports circulating about Burr's intentions made these trips risky. On his return Clark wrote General Wilkinson that, surprisingly, he had returned safely from Vera Cruz even though his enemies had told the viceroy that he was "a person dangerous to the Spanish government and who had visited that country with no other view than that of acquiring information of its strength & how & when it might be assailed with the greatest probability of success."[31]

The Spanish fears had foundation. United States relations with Spain had grown steadily more hostile during 1805, and "the prospect of a Spanish war [was] a prominent subject of conversation among citizens of the United States." Many recent immigrants to New Orleans clamored for the conquest of Mexico and the other Spanish territories in North America. A group of three hundred prominent New Orleans citizens organized a Mexican Association for the purpose of collecting useful data on Mexico in case of a war with Spain. Clark certainly knew of the aims of the Mexican Association, and he may have introduced its leaders to Aaron Burr.[32]

The scope of Aaron Burr's schemes in 1805 and 1806 is almost impossible to determine; the former vice-president revealed a different plan to every person he involved. Clark's self-serving defense of his actions during this period, written several years later, casts doubt on his actual participation in Burr's schemes. "Never," he claimed, would he have "been fool enough to expose a large fortune and a respectable standing to certain destruction on an impractible scheme." Instead, when Colonel Bellechasse, then commandant of the territorial militia, told Clark that he, "several members of the territorial legislature, the clerk of the legislative council, and the captain of the port [Samuel B. Davis]" had been asked to join "an association to undertake some enterprise against Mexico," Clark dissuaded his friends from participating in the venture. In a statement that sounds as if Clark was preparing a defense of his own actions, he told Colonel Bellechasse that he "feared [his friends'] mutual antipathy toward Governor Claiborne would incline them to such action," but that he had "entreated them to forget their prejudices and sacrifice their personal feelings towards the governor, and to render the government every support in their power for its defense."[33]

31. Daniel Clark to James Wilkinson, Sept. 7, 1805, in Wilkinson, *Memoirs,* 2: appendix no. 14; Clark to Wilkinson, Apr. 14, 1806, ibid., 2: 83–4.

32. Wilkinson, *Memoirs,* 2: 17; *Orleans Gazette,* Nov. 1, 1805, p. 2; Hatcher, *Edward Livingston,* 123–4; Jacobs, *Tarnished Warrior,* 221; Kendall, *History of New Orleans,* 1: 79.

33. Daniel Clark, *Proofs,* 92–3, 97–8; *Louisiana Gazette,* Apr. 8, 1808, p. 2.

Clark did make a report about Spanish defenses in Vera Cruz to the secretary of war, but business problems had provided the primary reason for his trips to Mexico. The commercial contracts he concluded in this "land of promise" proved quite profitable for the firm of Coxe & Clark. Trading Louisiana sugar for a cargo of cochineal (a dye) that was reexported to England added almost $160,000 to the accounts of the partnership. The infusion of money was desperately needed. The resumption of European hostilities had endangered American trade with foreign ports. Failure of Barclay's, one of Coxe & Clark's corresponding brokers in London, put an additional financial strain on the firm. Clark's letters to his Philadelphia partner after his return to New Orleans in April 1806 constantly referred to their precarious financial situation.[34]

Ignoring Clark's pleas of business necessity, Governor Claiborne seized on the reports of Clark's involvement with Burr to discredit the merchant with President Jefferson. "If there be any serious disaffection to the American Government in this Territory," Claiborne promised the president, "it may . . . be attributed to the Intrigues of a few designing, discontented, restless men," of whom Daniel Clark was a "conspicuous and zealous member." The governor apparently feared that Clark would be more successful in damaging Claiborne's reputation in Washington than in scheming to dismember the United States. Clark's selection (over another candidate favored by Claiborne) in the spring of 1806 as the first territorial representative from Louisiana to Congress caused the governor to worry that as a delegate Clark would "most unquestionably say much and do much" to injure the career Claiborne had carefully built. The governor claimed that this "unprincipled, ambitious, avaricious, and artful . . . character," was "collecting materials for his attack," especially "all the Abu-

34. Deposition of John Graham, Esq., delivered to the Court of Inquiry in Washington, D.C., . . . 1808, quoted in Wilkinson, *Memoirs*, 2: 84–5; Daniel Clark, *Proofs*, 94–5; Daniel Clark to Daniel W. Coxe, Apr. 3, 1806, reprinted in *Transcript of Record, Gaines v. City of New Orleans*, 2: 1539; Clark to Coxe, May 15, 1806, ibid., 2: 1544; Clark to Coxe, June 11, 1806, ibid., 2: 1545. Approximately one-third of the profits of the voyage ($56,000) remained in Vera Cruz when Clark left. He intended to return for the balance the following year. Historians who claim that Clark was an emissary from Burr to the Spanish government of Mexico see this sum and Clark's visits as evidence of his involvement. Clark argued that he would never have left such a large amount of money in Mexico where it could be easily confiscated by the Spanish government, if he had been personally connected to any plan of Aaron Burr. Daniel Clark, *Proofs*, 92–3, 107; Matthew L. Davis, ed., *Memoirs of Aaron Burr* (New York: Harper, 1837), 1: 382.

sive pieces, which were published against [Claiborne] during [his] administration in the Mississippi Territory."[35]

Claiborne's apprehensions were unjustified. Although he sometimes chastised Claiborne, Jefferson trusted the Louisiana governor and generally followed his advice. The president naturally saw Louisiana through Claiborne's eyes, since most of his information about the territory came from the governor's official reports. And Clark actually had written General Wilkinson in June asking for damaging information about Claiborne. He told Wilkinson that his reason for accepting the nomination as territorial delegate was solely "to oppose Governor Claiborne's Creatures and schemes with success." But Clark's efforts to persuade Congress and the president of the loyalty of Louisianians and their readiness for statehood failed. The hints of his involvement with Burr, added to the past accusations of changes in his citizenship and his association with congressional opponents of the president (such as John Randolph of Virginia), ended any residual hopes Clark might have held about his political future under a Jefferson or Madison administration.[36]

Burr's plots continued to shadow Clark after the close of 1806. If James Wilkinson had ever entertained thoughts of linking his fortune to that of Aaron Burr, he had changed his mind by November. After warning President Jefferson of a conspiracy to seize Louisiana, the general rushed to New Orleans, where his prediction that Burr would attempt to take the city threw the residents "into the wildest state of excitement and perturbation." Wilkinson's decision to impose martial law on the city drew initial opposition from Claiborne, but the general's decisive measures soon gained the governor's approval. Claiborne, at least, believed that Burr intended to destroy the union of states: "[I]t ought to be a subject of great joy that this intrigue is defeated," he advised his superiors in Washington; "the objects were, the destruction of our Government and the dismember-

35. Malone, *Jefferson the President,* 4: 358; William Claiborne to Thomas Jefferson, June 21, 1806, *Official Letter Books of W. C. C. Claiborne,* 3: 339–40; Claiborne to Jefferson, July 9, 1806, *Territorial Papers of the United States,* 9: 67; Claiborne to Jefferson, July 15, 1806, ibid., 9: 673; Hatcher, *Edward Livingston,* 120–1.

36. Daniel Clark to James Wilkinson, June 16, 1806, *Territorial Papers of the United States,* 9: 660; Newton, *Americanization of French Louisiana,* 79, 146; Wohl, "Not Yet Saint nor Sinner," 199–200. In the *Louisiana Gazette* of Feb. 20, 1807, Clark reported to the territorial legislature on his efforts to gain repeal or redress of the decision to register land titles in Louisiana. Clark had little success; although he presented several petitions from landholders, the certification of land titles continued.

ment of the union—objects which perhaps were not communicated to all the partisans of Burr but which would certainly have been attempted (and with a considerable force, too) had not the agents of the Government acted with promptitude and Energy." If Wilkinson's "zeal" had "betrayed him into some errors," the governor assured President Jefferson, only the "purest motives of honest patriotism" motivated his actions.[37]

Wilkinson's denunciation ended Burr's hopes—of what, historians still disagree—and the former vice-president abandoned his "terrifying horde of three-score unstable amateurs in small boats" on the Mississippi River and fled. Lieutenant Edmund Pendleton Gaines intercepted Burr near the Tombigbee River; escorted to Richmond, Burr stood trial for treason, with Wilkinson as a principal witness against him.[38]

Although Clark was in Washington throughout the winter of 1806–1807, Governor Claiborne placed him securely at the center of the plot, and he seized on the accounts of Clark's connection with Burr to discredit the merchant with President Jefferson. When reports reached the governor of comments made by Clark critical of the United States, Claiborne passed them on to Washington. Leading citizens—Dr. John Watkins (mayor of New Orleans) and Mr. J. W. Gurley (attorney general of the territory)—had heard the merchant exclaim that, had he children, "the first words he would teach them to speak, would be to damn the government of the United States." These unpatriotic sentiments were enough for Claiborne to accuse Clark. When Dr. Watkins suggested that Clark's intemperate language was due "more to the impulse of some momentary passion rather than to deliberate reflection," Claiborne reluctantly reconsidered his earlier charge. He was, he declared, willing to "render justice to everyone— even my greatest enemy."[39]

The feud between Clark and Claiborne boiled over upon Clark's return to New Orleans in April 1807. A tumultuous welcome greeted the delegate. Incensed at the "splendid dinner" given Clark, the governor suggested that

37. William Claiborne to the secretary of war, Mar. 3, 1807, *Territorial Papers of the United States* 9: 712; Claiborne to President Jefferson, Mar. 3, 1807, ibid., 9: 730; Gayarré, *History of Louisiana,* 4: 162; *Orleans Gazette,* Dec. 18, 1806, p. 2.

38. Marshall Smelser, *The Democratic Republic, 1801–1815* (New York: Harper & Row, 1968), 117; James Wilkinson to Thomas Jefferson, Mar. 1, 1807, Wilkinson, *Memoirs,* 2: 102; Hatcher, *Edward Livingston,* 135.

39. William Claiborne to Secretary of State Madison, Dec. 5, 1806, *Official Letter Books of W. C. C. Claiborne, 1801–1816,* 4: 43; deposition of George Mather in Wilkinson, *Memoirs,* 2: 80; Gayarré, *History of Louisiana* 4: 161.

those who honored him desired a violent return of the "late proceedings here." Not content with their own entertainment, Claiborne fumed, "the Gentlemen propose that their *Wives* should do so likewise, and the Ladies, I understand, contemplate giving him a grand fête in a few Days." The extravagant reception of Clark, coupled with the urging of several of the governor's supporters, pushed Claiborne into challenging Clark to a duel.[40]

Although against the law in Spanish Louisiana, duels were common and rarely resulted in criminal penalties. When Louisiana became part of the United States the territorial legislature enacted more stringent antidueling laws. No one paid any attention. Until the Civil War almost every man active in public affairs had fought at least one duel; most had engaged in several. The more prominent his position, the more likely a man would have to fight at some time. A "gentleman" who refused to fight would be "posted" or publicly branded a coward. Daniel Clark had fought several duels and was considered a fine shot. Claiborne had publicly expressed opposition to the practice after his brother-in-law fell in a duel in 1804. But despite his dislike of settling disputes on "the field of honor," Claiborne issued a challenge to Clark.[41]

The governor took exception to remarks Clark had made before the U. S. House of Representatives the previous December denouncing Claiborne's neglect of the territorial militia. Territorial citizens had "offered their services to the United States, and had been disregarded by the man put over them, and a preference given to another corps." Clark claimed that "the militia were in an unorganized state—there were indeed, no militia in the Territory." Coming so soon after the Burr fiasco, with Wilkinson's imposition of martial law still very much on the minds of New Orleans residents, Clark's criticism stung. A report of the speech in the *Orleans Gazette* attributed even more inflammatory language to Clark. According to the paper, Clark claimed that the governor had given a "Standard" to a corps of free blacks while ignoring the offers of the Creole population to be of service to their new country.[42]

40. William Claiborne to Thomas Jefferson, June 1, 1807, *Territorial Papers of the United States*, 9: 742–3.

41. John Kendall, "The Humors of the Duello," *Louisiana Historical Quarterly* 23 (1940): 449; Asbury, *French Quarter*, 145.

42. William Claiborne to Daniel Clark, May 23, 1807, *Territorial Papers of the United States*, 9: 738; U.S. Congress, *Debates and Proceedings* (Washington, D.C.: U.S. Government Printing Office, 1834–1856), 9th Cong., 2nd sess. (Dec. 24, 1806), 215; *Orleans Gazette*, Feb. 2, 1807, p. 2; William Claiborne to Daniel Clark, May 23, 1807, *Territorial Papers of the United States*, 9: 738.

When Clark refused to retract or explain his statement, Claiborne demanded satisfaction. Clark was convinced that others around the governor had provoked the challenge—he named particularly "one Gurley [John W. Gurley] who has always hated me for my contemptuous treatment of him"—and that Claiborne agreed, "driven to despair by the flattering reception I met with on arrival." Following the prescribed practice of the code of honor, the two named their seconds: John Gurley for Claiborne and Richard R. Keene for Clark. The seconds exchanged letters, first attempting to settle the dispute peacefully, then arranging a time and place for the confrontation. Since the governor of the territory should be expected to uphold its laws, the men decided to fight outside the Orleans Territory. To keep the matter secret, Claiborne planned to leave New Orleans on June 3, Clark following three days later. Somehow, news of the projected duel leaked out (Clark blamed the governor's supporters), and Clark left New Orleans the day after Claiborne, pursued by the sheriff for ninety miles, all the way to the Iberville River, until the duelists had passed out of the territorial jurisdiction. On Monday, June 8, at one o'clock in the afternoon, they met. According to Clark, "we fired almost at the same instant, at 10 paces, and the Governor fell, shot thro' the thigh, and with a most severe contusion on the other." Clark received no injury. Claiborne privately assured General Wilkinson that both "before and after the shot (while on the ground) Mr. Clark and I were mutually polite to each other."[43]

An exultant Clark returned to New Orleans to receive what he termed "the congratulations . . . of the public on the occasion . . . mixed with . . . some bitter reproaches that I should have *dared* to risk [my] life, which, they think, ought to be reserved for them." Clark may have overstated the appreciation of the Creoles for his bravery; Claiborne was not as bereft of friends as Clark believed. Moreover, the fortitude with which the governor bore the pain of his wounds won the admiration of the citizens of the territory. He did not heal quickly. On June 17 he wrote President Jefferson that he continued to be "confined to my room, and experience considerable

43. J. W. Gurley to Richard Keene, May 31 and June 1, 1807, and Keene to Gurley, May 31 and June 1, 1807, Jefferson Papers, Library of Congress; Daniel Clark to Thomas Jefferson, May 24, 1807, Jefferson Papers, Library of Congress; Clark to Daniel W. Coxe, June 12, 1807, *Transcript of Record, Gaines v. Relf, Chew, and Others,* 756; William Claiborne to James Wilkinson, June 17, 1807, quoted in Henry C. Castellanos, "Duels and Dueling: The Claiborne-Clark Combat—A Chapter in Louisiana History," *New Orleans Times-Democrat,* Oct. 21, 1894, p. 18.

pain—but the wound now suppurates profusely and my Surgeon gives me reason to believe that in three weeks I shall be enabled to walk." His surgeon was too optimistic; not until September was Claiborne able to resume his duties as territorial governor.[44]

Although their feud continued, played out on the pages of New Orleans newspapers, the duel between Clark and Claiborne marked a turning point in the political futures of both men. Claiborne's understanding of the Creole population improved, and his smiling acceptance of his defeat in the duel with Clark—he felt he had been "sufficiently punished for [his] imprudence"—proved that an American could be as gallant on the field of honor as any Creole. As Claiborne mended his connections with the Creole community, Clark's acceptance as their spokesman diminished. One year later, in the next election for territorial delegate to Congress, his handpicked successor, Dr. Watkins, failed to defeat the governor's candidate, Julien Poydras of Pointe Coupée (one of the wealthiest and most influential Creoles in New Orleans). After 1808, Daniel Clark held no more political office in Louisiana.[45]

In the years following Clark's duel with Claiborne a new feud with an old friend occupied much of his attention. General James Wilkinson and

44. Daniel Clark to Daniel W. Coxe, June 14, 1807, *Transcript of Record, Gaines v. Relf, Chew, and Others*, 758; Clark to Coxe, June 12, 1807, ibid., 756; William Claiborne to Thomas Jefferson, June 17, 1807, *Territorial Papers of the United States*, 9: 743.

45. William Claiborne to Thomas Jefferson, June 28, 1807, *Territorial Papers of the United States*, 9: 743; Newton, *Americanization of French Louisiana*, 79. The newspaper war between supporters of Clark and supporters of Claiborne involved bitter invective on both sides. The *Louisiana Courier*—generally pro-Claiborne (and Wilkinson)—claimed that "the intrigues of Clark are crossing and multiplying in every direction" as Clark "cajoles and splendidly entertains" the Creoles on his plantation *(Courier, Aug. 27, 1810, p. 2)*. The *Louisiana Gazette*—equally pro-Clark—sought the source of accusations against Clark, asking "how many doubloons, bright from the mint, have been fixed as the promised price of [the] ridiculous tergiversation and impotent scurility?" Editorial, *Louisiana Gazette*, no date, quoted by Michael Wohl, "Not Yet Saint nor Sinner," 202–3. See also Newton, *Americanization of French Louisiana*, Chapter 3. George Dargo suggests an additional reason for Clark's loss of support among New Orleans citizens. The municipal government of the city wished to connect the streets between the Old City and the new Faubourg St. Mary, but a "ropewalk" owned by Clark and Samuel B. Davis ran the entire length of Canal Street and blocked the crossing. Clark refused a request by the city council to dismantle the ropewalk, and when it burned to the ground in 1806, he insisted on rebuilding it. His intransigence cost him considerable support among the city leaders and may have contributed to the "coolness" that developed between Clark and Davis after Myra's birth. Dargo, *Jefferson's Louisiana*, 64, 205 (note 78).

Clark engaged in a very public squabble over their individual involvement in Burr's conspiracy, each blaming the other for participation in a plan to dismember the Union. Clark's intimacy with Wilkinson had begun with Wilkinson's arrival in New Orleans in 1787. The information Clark relayed to his uncle and Wilkinson from the Spanish governor's offices proved essential to their success in forcing open New Orleans trade for western American farmers. The friendship continued for thirty years; Clark and Wilkinson corresponded regularly and speculated in western land to their mutual benefit. Clark wrote to Wilkinson seeking damaging information that could be used against Governor Claiborne, and when accused of financing Burr's plots, Clark turned to Wilkinson for aid in refuting the charges.

The alliance fell apart in the aftermath of Burr's arrest for treason in the spring of 1807. The general appeared as the chief witness against Burr, and Clark was summoned to Richmond as a witness for Burr, although he never actually testified. By fall each had accused the other of complicity in Burr's schemes, and the level of invective accelerated over the next few years. In 1809 Clark published his *Proofs of the Corruption of General James Wilkinson, and of his connexion with Aaron Burr*. He proclaimed Wilkinson a "fawning sycophant . . . [a] trembling coward . . . [and a] sanguinary traitor" whose "unexampled depravity [and] unheard of meanness" were examples of "wickedness unparalleled in the annals of treachery." In his *Memoirs* (published in 1816 after Clark's death), Wilkinson replied with equally intemperate language: Clark was an "ostentatious, vain, vindictive, and ambitious" man who had "squandered" vast sums by "hiring presses [and] procuring witnesses" to "persecute Wilkinson."[46]

Continuing his diatribe against Clark, General Wilkinson hinted that their mutual vendetta had begun not with a question of culpability in Burr's schemes, but with the hand of a lady. Sent to Washington as territorial delegate in 1806, Daniel Clark made time to enjoy eastern society. His unacknowledged connection to Zulime Carrière did not hinder further romantic adventures. Letters from friends mention the attraction the handsome and wealthy bachelor from New Orleans had for the women of several East Coast cities. Daniel Coxe's wife, Margaret, noted Clark's attention to a "Miss Lee" and hoped that she would at last see Clark a

46. Clark, *Proofs*, 42–3; Wilkinson, *Memoirs* 2: 78.

married man. From Baltimore came a letter of thanks for a small favor from Mrs. Richard Caton, closing with wishes for Clark's "health and happiness," wishes that her daughter Louisa also expressed. Samuel White, senator from Delaware, wrote from Washington that "the ladies" are "infinitely" at a loss for Clark's society, concluding that rumor linked his name with a "Miss L. of Georgetown" and a "Miss D. of Pa. Ave." If Clark had married Zulime in 1802, he did not act like a married man during his sojourn in Washington. His actions during the next year as he courted first one and then another society belle were important parts of the testimony against Myra's claims many years later. All of Clark's friends united in their belief that he was "too much the gentleman" to court one woman when he was already married to another.[47]

The woman with whom Clark's name was most often linked was Louisa Caton, daughter of Richard Caton and granddaughter of Charles Carroll, a signer of the Declaration of Independence and the first senator from Maryland. Clark's introduction to the Carroll and Caton families probably came through his New Orleans partner, Beverly Chew. Senator Carroll's wife was the daughter of Benjamin Chew, Beverly's grandfather. Or perhaps the introduction came from Clark's friend Robert Goodloe Harper, a leader of the Federalist Party before Jefferson's election in 1800. Harper married Catherine Carroll, a sister of Mrs. Caton (Polly Carroll) and actively promoted a match between Clark and his niece.[48]

The beautiful Caton sisters were "stars in the famous constellation of [Baltimore] beauties," and Daniel Clark's attraction to the youngest sister drew comments from his correspondents. By January of 1808 Daniel Coxe had heard rumors of an engagement between the two and chided Clark for omitting any "syllable of your engagement to Miss C." from his letters. Clark, with uncharacteristic modesty, replied that the "conjectures in my

47. Margaret Coxe to Daniel Clark, Feb. 14, 1807, *Transcript of Record, Gaines v. City of New Orleans,* 2: 1931; Mrs. Caton to Clark, Apr. 16, 1807, ibid., 2: 1931; Samuel White to Clark, Dec. 2, 1807, ibid., 2: 1930; deposition of W. W. Montgomery, June 18, 1849, ibid., 2: 1489.

48. George C. Keidel, "Catonsville Biographies," *Maryland Historical Magazine* 17 (1922): 75–6; Anne Hollingsworth Wharton, *Social Life in the Early Republic* (Philadelphia: J. B. Lippincott, 1902), 145; Mary Caroline Crawford, *Romantic Days in the Early Republic* (Boston: Little, Brown, 1912), 253; Elizabeth Ellet, *The Court Circles of the Republic; or, The Beauties and Celebrities of the Nation* (1869; reprint, New York: Arno Press, 1975), 25.

favor are so [far] devoid of foundation." He did have hopes of gaining the lady's affections, he wrote, but could not enter into any engagement until his business affairs could be settled.[49]

Although he did not yet know it, revelations made by General Wilkinson had doomed any hopes Clark might have had of marrying a daughter of the illustrious Caton family. In the fall of 1807 the general had visited at a Maryland plantation; among the guests were several men well acquainted "with Clark's real character and circumstances." A "gentleman from Baltimore" overheard conversation reflecting on Clark's financial standing, conversation "not designed to injure Clark, but which would not recommend him." After the Baltimore gentleman insisted on an explanation, Wilkinson disclosed that Clark, a "merchant of great enterprise," had inherited a plantation from his uncle that "would produce twelve thousand dollars a year, under good management." But, in New Orleans the previous March, the general had been offered a note of Clark's "due in nine months, at a discount of one-third." The deep discount indicated a lack of confidence in the merchant's ability to meet his obligations and was "a bad sign . . . a very bad sign," according to the gentleman from Baltimore. Although General Wilkinson asserted that he "was surprised to learn that Clark was courting this man's daughter," the general blamed the subsequent rupture between himself and Clark on Clark's belief that the disclosure was intentional.[50]

Apparently Clark did intend to propose to Louisa Caton. On February 9, 1808, Clark left for her home in Annapolis, hoping to find her "as favorably inclined toward [him]" as Daniel Coxe had hinted. He would "endeavor so to secure her affections as to permit me to offer myself to her at my return [to the East Coast] in the course of the ensuing winter." First, he planned to return to New Orleans and settle his business affairs with

49. Daniel Coxe to Daniel Clark, Jan. 6, 1808, *Transcript of Record, Gaines v. Relf, Chew, and Others,* 568; Clark to Coxe, Jan. 4, 1808, *Transcript of Record, Gaines v. City of New Orleans,* 2: 1566.

50. James Wilkinson, *Aaron Burr's Conspiracy Exposed and General Wilkinson Vindicated* (Washington, D.C.: printed for the author, 1811). Wilkinson may have been responsible for the failure of Clark's courtship, but his attribution of their mutual hatred to this tale must be incorrect. Clark made his public denunciation of Wilkinson, including his accusation that Wilkinson had served as a Spanish spy in the 1790s, in Congress on Dec. 31, 1807, two months before Clark proposed and was rejected by Miss Caton. Gales and Seaton, *Annals of the Congress of the United States* (Washington, D.C., 10th Cong., 1st sess.), Dec. 31, 1807.

Relf and Chew. Unfortunately for the anxious suitor, Richard Caton heeded General Wilkinson's warning and demanded a substantial prenuptial settlement on his daughter before giving consent to her marriage. Clark considered Caton's demand excessive, and "his affair . . . forever ended." By February 14, Clark was back in Washington and requested that Coxe never again mention Miss Caton's refusal.[51]

Clark intended to settle his affairs with Zulime Carrière, too, before proposing to Louisa Caton. With her marriage to DesGrange ended by the New Orleans court in November 1806, Zulime had followed Clark east. According to Daniel Coxe, "Madame Carrière" arrived in Philadelphia in January 1807, "under a fallacious hope which can not be realized." Did Zulime expect that Clark would now acknowledge her as his wife, as Myra Gaines's lawsuit claimed she was? Or did Zulime only hope that Clark would redeem a promise to marry her, as Daniel Coxe testified? Her presence in Philadelphia was "really an unfortunate thing," Coxe wrote his partner; better that she should return to New Orleans than "remain in a land of strangers, a tax on yourself, and a burden to herself and me."[52]

Clark's continued refusal to "promulgate his marriage" with Zulime may have been prompted by his preoccupation with the Burr treason trial, but his failure "very much fretted and irritated her feelings." Zulime did return to New Orleans in late winter, Clark following at the end of April 1807. In June, knowing that he was to fight a duel with Governor Claiborne, Clark dispatched Zulime and her sister back to Philadelphia, placing them again under the care of Daniel Coxe. A letter from Coxe to Clark recounts the arrival of the sisters in early July 1807; they took "a snug little house . . . which suits them perfectly" and waited for Clark to follow

51. Daniel Clark to Daniel Coxe, Feb. 9, 1808, *Transcript of Record, Gaines v. City of New Orleans,* 2: 1790; Clark to Coxe, Feb. 14, 1808, ibid., 1791. Although Louisa was not allowed to marry Daniel Clark, her marital history was distinguished. After a tour of Europe, she married first Colonel Sir Felton Hervey; widowed, she wed the marquess of Caermarthen, afterwards duke of Leeds. A "famous beauty," the duchess died at Hampton Court in 1853. Her sister, Mary Ann, married Robert Patterson (brother of Elizabeth Patterson Bonaparte); after his death she married the marquess of Wellesley. The beautiful Caton sisters formed the vanguard of a "transatlantic invasion" of American women who found husbands among the British nobility in the nineteenth century. Keidel, "Catonsville Biographies," 86–9; A. M. W. Stirling, "A Transatlantic Invasion of 1816," *Nineteenth Century and After,* 39 (1909): 1058.

52. Daniel Coxe to Daniel Clark, Jan. 5, 1807, *Transcript of Record, Gaines v. Relf, Chew, and Others,* 567.

in September. During the fall of 1807, as Clark courted Louisa Caton in Washington and Annapolis, Zulime and Sophia lived on Swanson Street in Philadelphia in the house provided by Coxe, and Clark continued to provide for their "welfare and comfort."[53]

Testimony in the Gaines case provides contradictory interpretations of Zulime's reaction when she learned of Clark's attentions to Louisa Caton. According to Sophia, gossip linking Clark's name to the Baltimore belle came to Zulime's ears, distressing her since "she knew herself to be his wife" and causing a quarrel in which each accused the other of infidelity. Pierre Baron Boisfontaine supported this account of a rift and claimed that "interested persons had produced a false state of things between them." Sophia testified that Zulime heard the rumors of Clark's attachment to Miss Caton while still in New Orleans, and her decision to search for legal proof of her marriage to Clark prompted the second trip to Philadelphia. Coxe's 1807 letter makes Sophia's memory suspect; if hints of an engagement to another did upset Zulime, they must have come after her arrival in Philadelphia that summer, because the letter to Clark indicates that the sisters eagerly anticipated Clark's arrival in Philadelphia that fall.[54]

If Zulime hoped to find documents that would sustain her claim to Clark's name, her search failed. Sophia testified to the despair her sister felt upon learning that the priest who had performed the ceremony had returned to Ireland and that no record of the marriage had been filed with the church in Philadelphia. When Zulime sent for Daniel Coxe, he informed her that she would never be able to "establish her marriage with Mr. Clark if he were disposed to contest it." Sophia declared that Coxe then offered to send "legal counsel" to advise the women. A "Mr. Smith" arrived and, after telling Zulime that she could never prove her marriage to Clark, "pretended to read to her a letter in English (a language then unknown to [Zulime]) from Mr. Clark to Mr. Coxe stating that he was about to marry Miss Caton."[55]

Disputing Sophia's version, Coxe claimed that the hints of Clark's interest in Louisa Caton angered Zulime and caused her to leave Clark's

---

53. Deposition of Sophia Despau, Mar. 19, 1849, *Transcript of Record, Gaines v. City of New Orleans,* 2: 1348; Coxe to Clark, July 16, 1807, *Transcript of Record, Gaines v. Relf, Chew, and Others,* 569.

54. Deposition of Sophia Despau, Mar. 19, 1849; Coxe to Clark, July 16, 1807.

55. Deposition of Sophia Despau, Mar. 19, 1849. Sophia's reference to the letter from Clark dates this interview after Feb. 9, 1803, since that is the date of Clark's letter to Coxe mentioning his intentions toward Miss Caton.

protection and the house he had provided. She and her sister moved to lodgings in Walnut Street provided for "Miss Carrière" by Dr. James Gardette. During an interview held at her new quarters, Coxe asserted that Zulime told him only that Clark's courtship was a violation of his promise to marry her, adding that "she now considered herself at liberty to connect herself with another person." And, according to Coxe, that other person was waiting in the next room. As Zulime announced her belief that she was no longer bound to Clark, Dr. Gardette entered and disclosed his intention to marry Zulime.[56]

Dr. James Gardette was a well-known and well-to-do Philadelphia surgeon-dentist, much sought after for his innovations. His discoveries included a "lever instrument for the easy and expeditious extraction of teeth," which received an "award of merit," and a new method of securing artificial teeth to the gums. He first met Zulime in 1802 when she and Sophia visited Philadelphia seeking proof of DesGrange's prior marriage. Gardette was the witness they sought, and the sisters claimed that Gardette's assurance that he had been present at DesGrange's marriage had prompted Clark to urge matrimony on Zulime.[57]

On August 2, 1808, Zulime married Dr. Gardette in a ceremony conducted before the Catholic bishop of the diocese of Philadelphia, the Right Reverend Michael Egan, in St. Joseph's Church. Zulime's marriage to Gardette considerably complicated her daughter's later claim that a valid marriage had existed between her and Clark. Zulime apparently believed that a marriage that had not been recorded and that one party denied was invalid and no barrier to another union. She signed the marriage certificate as "Marie Zulime Carrière." Zulime was twenty-seven when she became the third wife of the fifty-two-year-old Gardette. He had a daughter and two sons by his first wife, three daughters and two sons by his second, and he and Zulime had two sons of their own. For the next twenty-one years the couple lived in Philadelphia. Their marriage appeared happy; many of their Philadelphia acquaintances testified to Zulime's exemplary character and position as the wife of the prominent dentist. Seemingly, none of their friends knew of Zulime's connection with Clark. As far as Philadelphia

56. Deposition of Daniel Coxe, Aug. 25, 1849, *Transcript of Record, Gaines v. City of New Orleans*, 2: 1502.

57. Émile Gardette, *Biographical Notice of (the Late) James Gardette, Surgeon Dentist of Philadelphia* (Philadelphia, 1850) in the Henry D. Gilpin Papers, Historical Society of Pennsylvania, Philadelphia.

society knew, she had been "Miss Carrière of New Orleans" before her marriage to Gardette. In 1829 the couple moved to France, where Dr. Gardette died in 1831. In 1835 Zulime returned to New Orleans, where she continued to live with her son by Dr. Gardette (also a Dr. James Gardette) until her death in 1853. Although both Caroline and Myra lived in Philadelphia during the years of Zulime's marriage to Dr. Gardette, she had no contact with either daughter. Nor did she ever appear as a witness in any Gaines lawsuit. One possible explanation for her failure to testify is a reluctance to allow questions of legitimacy to affect the children of her marriage to Gardette.[58]

Daniel Clark returned to New Orleans in the summer of 1808, having lost both Louisa Caton and Zulime. A changed political climate in the booming city forced him to acknowledge also the loss of his domination in that area. More and more Americans reached New Orleans, eagerly seeking to build fortunes and political influence. The newcomers gravitated to Governor Claiborne's councils and shunned Clark, too tainted with Burr's plots for their taste. The court of inquiry summoned to investigate the charges Clark had brought against General Wilkinson cleared the general with scant ceremony. President Jefferson and the ranking officers of the army were anxious to vindicate the top army officer of the slur cast on his loyalty by the territorial delegate from New Orleans. And Clark would be territorial delegate no longer. When he realized the powerful opposition organized against him by Governor Claiborne, Clark withdrew from the contest and cast his support for Dr. Watkins, the former mayor of New Orleans. In spite of Clark's support and that of most of the Creole community, Watkins lost.[59]

Renewed interest in his daughter Myra, his business speculations, and his quarrel with Wilkinson occupied Daniel Clark's last years. Myra was four years old when Clark returned to New Orleans from Washington in

58. Deposition of Émileus Braiser, July 6, 1849, *Transcript of Record, Gaines v. Relf, Chew, and Others*, 546.

59. Daniel Clark, *Proofs*, 6–7; Martin, *History of Louisiana from the Earliest Period*, 344, 354–5. Jefferson had no difficulty deciding which man to believe. Wilkinson had delivered Burr, and Jefferson refused to listen to those who criticized the general. "Your enemies have filled the public ear with slanders, and your mind with trouble," the president wrote to General Wilkinson. "The establishment of their guilt will let the world see what they ought to think of their clamours. . . . No one is more sensible than myself of the injustice which has been aimed at you." Jefferson to Wilkinson, June 21, 1807, in Wilkinson, *Memoirs*, 2: 16.

1808. She lived with the Davis family in a rented house located "down the coast" about three miles from the city. A second house built on the same lot but separated by a fence was the home of the Reverend Philander Chase, rector of Christ Episcopal Church in New Orleans. Testifying forty years later, the now Bishop Chase recalled seeing the affection Clark demonstrated for his little daughter as he visited her at the Davis home. "Almost every day" a nurse brought Myra outside to greet her father. Bishop Chase had no doubt that Myra was Clark's daughter; he openly claimed his parentage, and Chase knew the little girl as Myra Clark. She was always "spoken of as his heiress," Chase remembered.[60]

Others also remembered the kindness Clark showed to his little daughter. Colonel Bellechasse recalled that Clark mentioned many times that Myra would be heiress to all his fortune and that he laid great emphasis on her legitimacy. Pierre Baron Boisfontaine swore that Clark had expressed great sadness that a breach had occurred between Zulime and himself. He had been deluded by enemies who had succeeded in separating them. Clark did not blame Mme. Gardette, of whom he spoke "with great regret," and he assured Boisfontaine that he would "never give Myra a stepmother."[61]

Other testimony in the Gaines cases provided a slightly different picture. Rather than pining for Zulime, several witnesses reported that Clark was on the verge of marriage when he died suddenly in 1813. Delphine Trépagnier positively declared that Clark was engaged to her elder sister Héloise at the time of his death. The engagement began in 1812, and Mme. Trépagnier could give no reason why the marriage did not immediately take place. Another witness, Mrs. Julia Wood, was just as certain that Clark was on the verge of matrimony with her aunt, "Miss Chew," a sister of Beverly Chew. The two women did agree that "all New Orleans" believed Clark a bachelor at the end of his life.[62]

Daniel Clark died on August 16, 1813, at his home on the Bayou Road in New Orleans. An inventory of the contents of the house indicates the

60. Deposition of the Right Reverend Philander Chase, Presiding Bishop of the Protestant Episcopal Church of the United States of America, May 3, 1849, reprinted in *Transcript of Record, Gaines v. Relf, Chew, and Others*, 473.

61. Deposition of Josef Bellechasse, Aug. 24, 1834, *Transcript of Record, Gaines v. City of New Orleans*, 2: 1832; deposition of Pierre Baron Boisfontaine, May 29, 1835, ibid., 2: 1847.

62. Deposition of Delphine Trépagnier, May 28, 1849, ibid., 2: 1459; deposition of Mrs. Julia Wood, Sept. 7, 1849, ibid., 2: 1616.

luxury of his surroundings. The two-story brick house, situated on a lot seventy feet deep by fifty feet wide contained a large room (the *grande salle*) and three smaller chambers with two fireplaces among them. The second floor repeated the arrangement of rooms, and a large gallery ran across the entire length of the front of the house. The large upper chamber, Clark's bedroom, held his high-post cherry bedstead with three mattresses of Spanish moss and ticking, a small walnut bureau-bookcase, two small cherry tables, and a wardrobe of "yellow wood." A pair of horse pistols, a silver mounted dagger, and a brass saber mounted on the wall completed the furnishings. The most prominent feature of the lower room was Clark's library, which testified to his erudite and eclectic tastes in literature. The 703 volumes included books of English history; the works of Milton, Swift, and Shakespeare; the *Odyssey* and Sophocles' *Tragedies* in Greek; Plutarch's *Lives* in Latin; *Don Quixote* in Spanish; English, Spanish, and Italian dictionaries; miscellaneous volumes in French; and a fifty-four-volume English encyclopedia.

Clark's funeral demonstrated that the New Orleans community remembered and respected his contributions to the city. Even Governor Claiborne put aside his animosity and walked in the cortege beside Colonel Bellechasse. The funeral procession ended at the St. Louis Cemetery where the body was interred in a large stone vault. A Latin epitaph placed on the tomb by Richard Relf recorded Clark's achievements:

> Here Lies
> Daniel Clark
> A Native of Sligo in Ireland,
> And an Inhabitant from Boyhood
> Of Louisiana and of this City.
> While it was under the Spanish Government
> He was Consul of the United States,
> Appointed on account of his Illustrious Virtues.
> Afterward by the Unanimous Vote
> Of the People of the Territory of Orleans,
> He sat as the First Delegate
> In the Congress of the American People.
> His great Wealth,
> Accumulated without Fraud,
> He used in Relieving
> The Necessities of the Poor;
> Nevertheless Becoming Richer,

By His Liberality.
He died, wept of all Good men,
August 16, 1813,
In the Forty-seventh year of his Age.
A Friend to a Friend
Has Erected This Monument.[63]

63. Clark epitaph in Latin, *Transcript of Record, Gaines v. Relf, Chew, and Others,* 1149, trans. in Harmon, *Famous Case of Myra Clark Gaines,* 153. Clark's tomb, in St. Louis Cemetery No. 1, can still be seen by visitors to New Orleans.

VI

A Romance in Real Life

In the years after Daniel Clark's death in 1813, as his friends and acquaintances reflected on the convergence of his public and private lives, they drew opposing pictures of this complex man. The ambiguity of his character required the judges, lawyers, participants, and spectators in the Gaines case to weigh the contradictory stories that emerged from the testimony of those who knew Daniel Clark and Zulime Carrière. Thus the case—like all litigation—became a competition between conflicting but allegedly truthful narratives of past events. With little documentary evidence to give a clear path to a definitive answer, both Gaines and her opponents could construct narratives that reflected their particular versions of fact, with each narrative providing a credible explanation for the relationship that bound Clark and Zulime. And the judges in the courts of law and the observers in the courts of public opinion could accept or reject each narrative based on their own attitudes toward the various institutions of marriage, motherhood, and family.[1]

1. Friedman, "Law, Lawyers, and Popular Culture," 1595; Laura Hanf Korobkin, "The Maintenance of Mutual Confidence: Sentimental Strategies at the Adultery Trial of Henry Ward Beecher," *Yale Journal of Law and the Humanities* 7 (1995): 18. Consideration of litigation as the construction, presentation, and interpretation of competing narratives is the subject of considerable analysis. See W. Lance Bennett and Martha Feldman, *Reconstructing Reality in the Courtroom: Justice and Judgment in American Culture* (New Brunswick, N.J.: Rutgers University Press, 1981); Robert Hariman, ed. *Popular Trials: Rhetoric, Mass Media, and the Law* (Birmingham: University of Alabama Press, 1990); Janice Schuetz and Kathryn Holmes Snedaker, *Communication and Litigation:*

* * *

Myra and William Whitney began to construct their narrative by challenging the probate of the will of 1811. Depositions from friends and associates placed the story of Clark's last will before the probate court. Harriet Harper Smythe, who had nursed Myra as a baby, testified to the contents of the lost will of 1813, completed only a month before Clark's death. Colonel Bellechasse bolstered her testimony as he recalled reading the will and remembered that Clark had declared Myra his legitimate daughter and heir. According to Bellechasse, Judge Pitot of the probate court and the chevalier Delacroix were also privy to its contents and were named with him as executors.[2]

Pierre Baron Boisfontaine, Clark's plantation manager and Colonel Davis's brother-in-law, gave essential information about Clark's last hours. The deathbed scene he described astounded the New Orleans community by suggesting that Richard Relf had destroyed the second will. Boisfontaine testified that on the day before he died, Clark spoke of Myra and of his relief that his new will had "insured his estate to her." Knowing that he was dying, Clark instructed Lubin, his "confidential servant," to carry the "little black case" containing his will and the schedule of his assets and liabilities that he had prepared that summer to Delacroix after his death. But a short time before Clark died, Boisfontaine saw Relf take a "bundle of keys from Mr. Clark's armoire," one of which he believed opened the little black case. Relf left the room with these keys, followed by Lubin. The slave saw Relf enter the office below and lock the door behind him.[3]

After Clark's death Richard Relf summoned Gallien Preval, a justice of the peace for the city of New Orleans, to gather all of the papers in the office and seal the room, a procedure known as a "*procès-verbal.*" Preval arrived quickly and completed his inventory by sundown. A moment be-

Case Studies of Famous Trials (Carbondale: Southern Illinois University Press, 1988); Bernard Jackson, *Law, Fact, and Narrative Coherence* (London: D. Charles Publications, 1988); and Bernard Jackson, "Narrative Theories and Legal Discourse" in *Narrative in Culture: The Uses of Storytelling in the Sciences, Philosophy, and Literature,* ed. Christopher Nash (New York: Routledge, 1990).

2. Deposition of Harriet Harper Smythe, Jan. 10, 1835, reprinted in *Transcript of Record, Gaines v. City of New Orleans,* 2: 1818; deposition of Josef Deville Degoutin Bellechasse, Aug. 24, 1834, ibid., 2: 1832.

3. Deposition of Pierre Baron Boisfontaine, May 29, 1835, ibid., 1847. Under Louisiana law, the slave Lubin could not testify against the executors.

fore Preval fixed the seals to the office door Richard Relf presented the official with the "olographic will of the deceased," which he had found "in a trunk." Preval took this will to deliver it to the court of probates. In 1834, during a hearing on creditor Shaumburg's petition to remove Relf and Chew as executors of the Clark estate, Preval testified that he vaguely recalled that Relf took the will from a trunk in the room, although it was not customary for anyone other than the justice of the peace "to examine the contents of trunks of deceased persons."[4]

The will produced by Richard Relf was the one made in 1811 naming Mary Clark as her son's heir. Bellechasse declared that he, Pitot, and Delacroix were astonished at the disappearance of the later will appointing them as executors (instead of Relf and Chew). As judge of the probate court, Pitot could not himself contest the will, but Delacroix could and did. Two days after the death of his friend, he requested Judge Pitot to order all the notaries in New Orleans to search their files for a "testament, or codicil, or any sealed packet" placed in their keeping by Daniel Clark. Delacroix swore that he had "strong reason to believe" that "the late Daniel Clark has made a testament or codicil posterior to that which had been opened before your honorable court." The notaries searched, but no sealed packet or second will appeared. Several days later, after appointing Louis Moreau-Lislet as attorney for Mary Clark of Philadelphia, Judge Pitot granted probate to the 1811 will and accepted Richard Relf and Beverly Chew as executors of the estate. Chew was in Virginia visiting his family at the time of Clark's death; for the next six months, Richard Relf acted alone.[5]

In the months after the death of Daniel Clark, Relf began to exercise his powers as executor and to dispose of the estate property. As he did so, he neutralized further opposition from anyone concerned about the disappearance of Clark's second will. On October 16, 1813, Delacroix bought twenty-three slaves from the estate for a total of $8,800. Delacroix made this purchase directly from the executor rather than at a public auc-

4. Procès-verbal, Succession of Daniel Clark, Aug. 16, 1813, Second District Court of New Orleans, reprinted in *Transcript of Record, Gaines v. Hennen,* 454; deposition of Gallien Preval, 1834, in *Shaumburg v. Relf and Chew,* Court of Probates of New Orleans, reprinted in *Transcript of Record, Gaines v. Relf, Chew, and Others,* 889.

5. Deposition of Josef Bellechasse, Aug. 24, 1834; Probate Proceedings, Succession of Daniel Clark, Aug. 17, 18, and 19, 1813, Second District Court of New Orleans, reprinted in *Transcript of Record, Gaines v. Hennen,* 454.

tion as required by the probate court. Matching the names of the slaves recorded in the deed of sale to Delacroix with their names and estimated worth listed on the inventory of the estate prepared by Gallien Preval indicates that the chevalier bought his slaves at a discount of about one-third. A few months later he bought another thirty-four slaves, again at a substantial discount. Judge Pitot, another executor of the lost 1813 will—but who, as probate judge, accepted the earlier will—was a creditor of the Clark estate in the amount of $45,500. Pursuing the question of the missing will would delay repayment of the money the estate owed him. He, too, accepted Relf's assurances that Clark must have destroyed the later will. Lubin, who should have received his freedom under the 1813 will, was sold along with the Cannes Brulées plantation on November 8, 1813. Colonel Bellechasse, who seemed more concerned for Myra than did either Judge Pitot or the chevalier, left New Orleans in 1814, pursued by rumors of disloyalty to his adopted country. Bellechasse always blamed Relf for his exile. With the witnesses who might object to their actions neutralized, Richard Relf and his coexecutor, Beverly Chew, gradually liquidated the Clark estate over the next twenty years. No accounting of their transactions was ever filed with the probate court, nor did Clark's mother benefit from her position as his heir. Claiming that the drop in land values caused by the War of 1812 had bankrupted the estate, the executors disbursed less than $20,000 to Mary Clark and nothing at all to her own heirs after her death in 1823.[6]

With the consistent testimony of Harriet Harper Smythe, Colonel Bellechasse, and M. Boisfontaine, Myra and William Whitney hoped to persuade the New Orleans court to void the probate granted to the will of

6. Sale of Slaves to F. D. Delacroix by Richard Relf as Executor of the Estate of Daniel Clark, Oct. 16, 1813, reprinted in *Transcript of Record, Gaines v. City of New Orleans,* 2: 2165; Inventory of the Estate of Daniel Clark, prepared by Gallien Preval, Justice of the Peace, Aug. 18, 1813, ibid., 2: 2171; Schedule of Debts and Credits of the Estate of Daniel Clark, Mar. 3, 1814, prepared by the Executors, ibid., 2: 1716; Sale of Plantation and Slaves to Michael Fortier and Omer Fortier, Nov. 8, 1813, ibid., 2: 2001; deposition of Josef Bellechasse, Aug. 24, 1834. Nolan Harmon, author of a 1946 history of the Gaines case, mistakenly placed the value of Delacroix's slave purchases at $50,000. According to the inventory of the estate compiled after Clark's death, their value equaled approximately one-half that amount, and Delacroix paid a total of $18,128.00. Harmon also states that Pitot owed the Clark estate for "a very valuable tract of land" purchased shortly before Clark's death. This is also a mistaken reading of the inventory. Clark bought New Orleans property *from* Pitot and, at his death, still owed the judge about one-third of the purchase price. *Famous Case of Myra Clark Gaines,* 148–52.

1811 and to accept their testimony as proof of the validity of the second will of 1813. The Whitneys were quickly disappointed. Judge Bermudez of the probate court was not at all disposed to help Myra. Many prominent citizens, including two justices of the Louisiana Supreme Court, had purchased land in the previous twenty years either directly or indirectly from the Clark estate. If a later will superseded the one under which Richard Relf and Beverly Chew had acted as executors, then all land sales from the estate had clouded titles.

William Whitney began by asking the court to compel Richard Relf to produce all of the remaining papers and letters of Daniel Clark for the Whitneys to examine. The inventory prepared by Gallien Preval listed a large number of letters, mortgages, deeds, and other miscellaneous legal papers found in two small trunks, all of which Preval had turned over to the executors. Whitney wanted to see those papers and to search in the bundles of documents for the missing will. Through their attorney, the executors replied that many of the requested documents were no longer in their possession, "some having been furnished to different tribunals . . . others have been furnished to the heirs," and some were lost or "destroyed by moisture."[7]

After several delays, Judge Bermudez ruled on the request for documents on June 8, 1836. The judge refused the Whitneys' petition, declining "to compel the production of what is lost or destroyed by moisture." Bermudez announced that he did not want "the character and reputation of one of our respectable citizens [Relf]" questioned further, and the judge ordered an immediate trial on the challenge to the probate of the 1811 will. Since Relf and Chew (and their attorneys) were ready for trial and the Whitneys (because they had been denied access to Clark's papers) were not, Judge Bermudez dismissed the complaint, commenting that the probate court could not probate a will unless that will was produced "in open court."[8]

In the course of two years, Myra and William had fought two suits in Louisiana courts. Both Judge Watts of the Louisiana District Court and Judge Bermudez of the state probate court had proved hostile to Myra's

7. Request for Documents, May 24, 1836, *W. W. Whitney and Wife v. O'Bearn, et al.*, case no. 843, Second District Court of New Orleans, reprinted in *Transcript of Record, Gaines v. City of New Orleans*, 2: 1867; Ruling on the Request for Documents, June 8, 1836, ibid., 2: 1870.
8. Ibid.

claims. Since the Whitneys were citizens of another state (New York), they had access to the federal court system, although their experience in the United States District Court for Louisiana (during William's trial for libel) did not offer much more hope for a favorable verdict. Nevertheless, three weeks after their loss in the probate court, Myra and William Whitney opened the Gaines case in federal court.

Up to this point the prime mover in the lawsuit had been William Whitney. Motivated at first by a spirit of adventure, his desire for justice for his wife kept the young lawyer undaunted by threats of disgrace or further imprisonment. But in 1837 the scourge of the summer months in New Orleans attacked. Before the federal court could rule, William Whitney fell victim to an epidemic of yellow fever.

Yellow fever epidemics ravaged New Orleans at regular intervals, beginning in late spring or early summer and ending with the first frost, usually in November. The first recognized cases of yellow fever in New Orleans occurred in 1796. Spanish intendant Morales described the epidemic that "terrified and [kept] in a state of consternation the whole population" of the city. Fifteen to twenty persons died each day, despite heroic efforts at treatment that often proved more deadly than curative. Between 1822 and 1861 yellow fever was an annual and dreaded visitor to the city. More than two thousand deaths each year gave New Orleans a deserved international reputation as a "plague-spot."[9]

Lack of understanding of disease causation prevented effective treatment. Doctors identified sufferers of yellow fever by their symptoms: "black vomit" caused by regurgitation of partially digested blood, and the jaundiced or yellow hue of the skin and eyes. Medical literature abounded with articles and monographs advocating or condemning various therapeutic methods. Some doctors advocated a cold-water treatment that placed semidelirious patients into a bathtub while doctors and nurses poured buckets of cold water over them. Other physicians, adopting the maxim, "desperate diseases require desperate remedies," turned to mercury compounds or bloodletting to the point of unconsciousness. The use of mercury as a treatment for yellow fever was controversial; supposedly

9. Duffy, "Pestilence," 100; Gayarré, *History of Louisiana,* 3: 375; Kendall, *History of New Orleans,* 1: 174. See also, generally, Jo Ann Carrigan, *The Saffron Scourge: A History of Yellow Fever in Louisiana, 1796–1905* (Lafayette: Center for Louisiana Studies, University of Southwestern Louisiana, 1994).

the excessive salivation produced by the mercury cured the patient. A doctor in 1838 commented that many victims might have actually died of mercury overdoses, since "a sore mouth did not always save them." Bloodletting was equally deadly. The Reverend Theodore Clapp commented that in the epidemic of 1837 he saw a physician bleed a sick man until he fainted, cupping more than fifty ounces at one time. The doctor then ordered the patient, who had been ill only four hours, to swallow three hundred grains of "calomel and gambage." That patient died. During the epidemic of 1837 the most widely used treatment involved the alkaloid quinine, derived from cinchona bark. But even when administered in high doses to patients in the early stages of the disease, it proved no more effective than any other treatment.[10]

During the 1837 epidemic, Reverend Clapp estimated that ten thousand cases of yellow fever resulted in five thousand deaths. Cannon were shot and barrels of tar burned in the streets to "clarify the atmosphere and disintegrate the miasmas." To prevent further spread, residents burned the bedding and clothing of patients and fumigated their homes with sulfuric acid. Despite these efforts, burial details could not keep up with the number of bodies and were forced to dump many corpses into the river. In an earlier epidemic of 1822, the tolling of church bells for the dead rang with such "maddening and monotonous frequency" that the city council passed an ordinance prohibiting the ringing of funeral bells between July and December. The chanting of priests at funerals was likewise forbidden for fear that such "doleful sounds" would terrorize the populace. By 1837 bodies of the dead were hauled away silently to the graveyards.[11]

After an illness of only three days, William Whitney died on September 13, 1837, his fifth wedding anniversary. He was not quite twenty-seven years old. His death left his widow and three children (William Jr., Rhoda, and a recently born daughter named Julia after William's mother) in difficult financial straits. Much of Whitney's own fortune had been expended on the legal costs of Myra's case; now she lacked even the funds to ship his body home to Binghamton.[12]

10. Duffy, "Pestilence," 98–104; Fossier, *New Orleans,* 397–8; Theodore Clapp, *Autobiographical Sketches and Recollections during a Thirty-Five Years' Residence in New Orleans* (Boston: Phillips, Sampson, 1857), 206–7.

11. Clapp, *Autobiographical Sketches,* 203; Fossier, *New Orleans,* 398; J. Clark, *New Orleans,* 278.

12. Pierce, *Whitney Genealogy,* 568–9; Myra Clark Whitney to General Joshua Whitney, Apr. 21, 1838, Joshua Whitney Papers, Broome County Historical Society, Binghamton, New York.

William's early death marked a turning point in Myra's legal odyssey. It is difficult to determine the extent of her personal involvement in the litigation filed in her name up to 1837. The early cases in the United States courts were filed as William W. Whitney and Wife, since married women had no legal standing except as adjuncts to their husbands. The Jacksonian era expected—even demanded—wifely submission. New husbands, such as William Whitney, often submerged themselves in politics or business and ignored their wives. Describing the attributes of the "true woman," historian Barbara Welter comments that "men were the movers, the doers, the actors. Women were passive, submissive responders," expected to submerge their own talents in whatever activity consumed their husbands. It is impossible to visualize Myra Whitney as such a wife; her later determination to fight for her "rights" led her to break down barrier after barrier erected to keep "ladies" in their proper place: at home. Like most nineteenth-century women, she was helpless to control many aspects of her life—her fertility, the mortality of her children (little Julia, born just before her husband's death, died in childhood), or her widowhood—but she did not passively allow tragedy to end her quest. The understanding that Myra demonstrated of the intricacies of her legal situation after the death of her husband indicates that she must have been an active participant in planning the litigation long before 1837.[13]

After her husband's death, Myra continued the lawsuits in her own name. Letters to William's family in Binghamton indicate the extent of her active participation and her understanding of the legal technicalities involved. As she explained to Virgil Whitney, her husband's brother, her financial difficulties began when a creditor of the Clark estate seized the property deeded to her by Colonel Bellechasse as repayment for his debt.

13. Welter, "Cult of True Womanhood," 159; Pease, *Ladies, Women, and Wenches*, 21, 37–8. Operating under the state civil code, Louisiana courts offered women more access to legal proceedings. The Spanish legal heritage granted single and married women more control over their own property than was available to women in other parts of the United States where the courts followed the tradition of English common law. Records of Louisiana courts provide many examples of women who sued or answered in their own right. But since most of the Gaines cases originated in the federal courts in Louisiana, the common law tradition held sway, and the early Gaines cases were filed under William Whitney's name. After her widowhood, Myra Gaines continued her suits under her own name. By 1848, several common-law states began to pass Married Women's Property Acts, giving married women more control over their own property. I am indebted to Louisiana attorney and legal historian Richard Kilbourne for pointing out to me the extent of women's participation in the Louisiana court system.

Myra directed her lawyer to "lay an injunction" to keep the property from being sold, but this action meant that she would have to bring a separate lawsuit to recover the property. Myra never doubted that the harassment and the financial problems would eventually end and she would be victorious. Continuing the case, however, meant more and more legal expenses. During her widowhood she began to mortgage any future funds she might gain from her father's estate to pay legal bills. Almost all of the lawyers who worked on the Gaines case took their payment as contingency fees based on a future settlement.[14]

Paying her lawyers was only one problem confronting Myra Whitney; actually bringing the case to trial proved equally difficult. The Whitneys had failed to convince the Louisiana probate court to recognize Clark's second will and revoke the probate granted to the will of 1811. Now, the petition they entered in the United States court before William's death asked the federal court to accept Myra as the "true heir" of Daniel Clark and to order the return of the property sold by the executors. When William and Myra Whitney had first challenged the probate of the 1811 will, they had restricted the defendants to the executors and the heirs of Mary Clark. Their new petition added twenty-five other purchasers of property from the estate, widening the impact of the litigation.

The delaying tactics adopted by her opponents frustrated Myra's hopes of success. The other defendants followed the lead of Richard Relf and Beverly Chew, and the executors had no intention of allowing the suit to come to trial. Rather than building their own narrative of events or attacking Myra's version, the defendants chose to use various legal technicalities to wear down their opposition. Such procrastination was especially effective because Myra Whitney lacked the financial backing necessary to wait for the legal process to slowly dispense with the impediments created by her antagonists.

The continued use of the French language by much of the populace of New Orleans complicated courtroom procedures. One observer explained the intricate maneuvers necessary to accommodate jurors who did not understand both French and English. An interpreter who spoke Spanish, French, and English translated, when necessary, the evidence and the charge of the court to the jury. He did not, however, translate the attorneys' arguments. If, for example, arguments opened in English, those in

14. Myra Whitney to Virgil Whitney, June 2, 1838, Joshua Whitney Papers, Broome County Historical Society, Binghamton, New York.

the jury who did not know the language withdrew from the jury box to the gallery; when these jurors returned to listen to the French counsel, the English-speaking jurors withdrew. Customarily, when a case involved both English- and French-speaking litigants, a jury evenly divided between these ethnic groups heard the case. Both groups went together into the jury room, "each contending the argument he had listened to was conclusive, and they finally agreed on a verdict in the best manner they could."[15]

Building on the confusion created by the multiple languages, the defendants in the federal court suit asked that a copy of all "Plans, Acts of Sale, Certificates of Survey, and Documents purporting to be Inventories, Schedules, Wills, and Probate of Wills" be translated into French and a copy provided to each of the eleven defendants who claimed that French was "the mother tongue of each of them." This request was a shrewd move designed to delay the case indefinitely, if not block it entirely. Compliance meant that each document would need to be translated and laboriously copied by hand eleven times. The expense would be considerable. Despite objections by Myra's counsel, Judge Samuel Harper ordered the translations prepared before the case could come to trial.[16]

The Louisiana judges (whether in state or federal court) who heard the early arguments in the Gaines case were anything but impartial. The defendants named in the petition numbered among them members of the "first society" of New Orleans, including the two members of the Louisiana state supreme court who had bought land from the estate. The executors, Richard Relf and Beverly Chew, were leaders in the New Orleans business community. Although the Whitneys had hoped that the transfer to federal court would blunt the hostility they had found in the state courts, they were disappointed. In 1834 Judge Harper of the United States District Court had ruled against Myra and William when they tried to recover the $2,500 Colonel Davis repaid to the executors. In 1837, the same judge had presided over William's conviction for libel and also ruled against the Whitneys on the necessity of the transcripts. But Judge Harper died before he could strike again, and he was replaced on the newly created United States circuit court bench by a Judge Lawrence. From Myra's viewpoint, the replacement was no improvement; when the case finally

15. Alcée Fortier, *A History of Louisiana* (New York: Goupil, 1904), 2: 58–9.
16. Petition by Respondents (n.d.), *William W. Whitney and Wife v. Richard Relf, et al.,* Circuit Court of the United States, Eastern District of Louisiana, General Case Files no. 3823, Record Group 21, National Archives, Southwest Region, Fort Worth, Tex.

came up in May 1837, Judge Lawrence refused to hear the case at all. He refused not only to recognize a protest made by her attorneys but also to have the motion and his refusal recorded in the minutes of the court proceedings. When the clerk of the court sought to make the proper entries, the judge denied permission.[17]

Such arbitrary behavior by Louisiana judges was not uncommon. The complicated combination of legal heritages embodied in the new civil code of 1825 and the Code of Civil Practice meant that the legal profession in Louisiana was a lucrative one. American merchants and landowners needed the guidance of Louisiana lawyers to interpret the complexities of the codes. Lawyers from all over the country headed for New Orleans to open their practices; since court procedures were conducted in French and English, each side usually employed both a French and an American attorney. New Orleans newspapers frequently attacked the conduct of the courts, questioned the ability of lawyers, and attributed the lack of judicial responsibility to "the low grade of lawyers who became judges because poor pay prevented the better ones from seeking the position." The *New Orleans Bee* editorialized in 1835 that "there is no state in which there is less efficiency and more diversity in the administration of the laws. . . . The judges are badly paid and are perfectly irresponsible. . . . Judges hold sessions of their courts as they please [and] connive at the failures of the attorneys [who] must in turn shelter the judges." The editor ended his diatribe by calling for a "reform of the judiciary . . . and that reform should be radical."[18]

Judge Lawrence demonstrated his lack of impartiality by announcing a change in the "rules of practice" for his court. Myra and William had filed their petition "at equity" and not "at law," a common practice in other parts of the United States in cases alleging acts of fraud. Even though the circuit court was a United States court, the judge declared that the "mode of proceeding in all civil cases" should conform to the code of practice in Louisiana. The purpose of the ruling was to deny "equity jurisdiction" in the United States courts in Louisiana.[19]

The question of equity versus civil practice, which eventually sent the Gaines case to the U.S. Supreme Court, may appear to be no more than

17. *Ex parte Whitney*, 13 Peters 404 (1839), at 406.
18. Fossier, *New Orleans*, 143; Fortier, *History of Louisiana*, 2: 147–8; *New Orleans Bee*, July 31, 1835, p. 2, Aug. 3, 1835, p. 2, and Aug. 5, 1835, p. 2.
19. *Ex Parte Whitney*, 406.

a legal technicality, but it was essential to the Gaines litigation. The legal system transmitted from England to the colonies drew primarily on English common law, the principles of which had evolved to meet the needs of a feudal society in which legal status was an expression of property relationships between political superiors and inferiors in the feudal hierarchy. Judges decided cases based on precedents and applied the principles of a law "common" to all. "Equity" emerged as a response to the perceived inflexibility of the common law. It was not so much a system of law as a way of applying law, an attempt to make law "supple enough to do substantial justice throughout the broad range of human experience accessible to the power of the state."[20]

As English society grew increasingly complex, the system of law grounded in feudalism proved inadequate. The equity courts, or courts of chancery, gradually emerged as an independent judicial institution in the fourteenth and fifteenth centuries, deriving their power from the traditional role of the king as the font of justice. But because the chancery courts became associated with the royal will of the monarch (the "royal prerogative"), they became targets of opposition in the seventeenth century. "Equity is a roguish thing," commented one legal critic; "for law we have a measure . . . [but] equity is according to the conscience of him that is Chancellor, and as that is larger or narrower, so is equity. 'Tis all one as if they should make the standard for measure a Chancellor's foot."[21]

Puritan opponents of the Stuart kings objected to the discretion equity allowed in its application to specific cases; a magistrate might "judge by a personal standard instead of by 'standing' laws." For this reason, legal scholar Roscoe Pound asserts, equity was never popular in America. The objection, however, was more to the separate chancery courts than to the principles of equity law. Gradually, American courts began to act both "at law" and "at equity." In the first half of the nineteenth century, United States courts could try cases at law, and their judges could also act as "chancellors" of equity courts.[22]

20. Rabkin, *Fathers to Daughters*, 21; Michael Katz, "The Politics of Law in Colonial America: Controversies over Chancery Courts and Equity Law in the Eighteenth Century," *American Historical Review* 97 (1992): 258–9.

21. Katz, "Politics of Law in Colonial America," 261, quoting John Selden, *Table Talk* (London, 1821).

22. Roscoe Pound, *The Formative Era of American Law* (1938; reprint, Boston: P. Smith, 1960), 155; Katz, "Politics of Law in Colonial America," 265.

Such was not the case in Louisiana. Because of its French and Spanish heritage, the legal system and court procedures in Louisiana differed from those in other parts of the United States. The Franco-Spanish population of Louisiana drew its legal traditions from European civil law. The French had governed by the "Custom of Paris," made applicable to the province in 1717. When France transferred Louisiana to Spain in 1763, Spanish governor Don Alejandro O'Reilly abolished French law and substituted, in 1769, the Spanish colonial law (the "Law of the Indies") operating in other parts of the empire.[23]

When Americans tried to introduce English common law into Louisiana after the cession in 1803, they met with opposition from the Creole population. Innovations in the criminal code—trial by jury, habeas corpus, and prevention of cruel and unusual punishments—were readily accepted; but civil practice resisted change. The congressional statutes accepting the Louisiana Territory as part of the United States provided that the civil law should "continue in force until altered, modified, or repealed by the governor and judges." In 1805 the territorial legislature of Orleans appointed Louis Moreau-Lislet and James Brown to codify the civil law and rectify its contradictions into a single, practical system. The territorial legislature adopted the *Digest of Civil Laws now in force in the Territory of Orleans, with Alterations and Amendments Adapted to its Present System of Government* on March 21, 1808. When Louisiana became a state, its constitution provided that "all laws now in force in this territory, not inconsistent with this constitution, shall continue and remain in full effect until repealed by the legislature." In 1817 the Supreme Court of Louisiana interpreted the Code of 1808 to mean that the Spanish laws were still operating in Louisiana.[24]

The opinion of the Louisiana court that Spanish laws remained in force meant that Louisianians were "obliged in many cases to seek our Laws in an undigested mass of ancient edicts and Statutes . . . the whole rendered more obscure by the heavy attempts of commentators to explain them." On March 14, 1822, the Louisiana legislature selected Edward Livingston,

23. Ferdinand Stone, "The Law with a Difference and How It Came About," in *Past As Prelude*, ed. Carter, 43; Hatcher, *Edward Livingston*, 245–6. On Louisiana law in general, see Edward Haas, ed., *Louisiana's Legal Heritage* (New Orleans: Published for the Louisiana State Museum by Perdido Bay Press, 1983).

24. Hatcher, *Edward Livingston*, 246–7; Louisiana Constitution of 1812, Art. IV, Sect. 11, in *Constitutions of the State of Louisiana and Selected Federal Laws*, ed. Benjamin W. Dart (Indianapolis: Bobbs-Merrill, 1932); *Cottin v. Cottin*, 5 Martin 93 (1817).

Louis Moreau-Lislet, and Pierre Derbigny to revise the *Civil Digest,* draw up a commercial code, and "formulate a treatise on the rules of civil actions and a system of practice to be observed before the courts." The committee announced that they would base their revision on the Spanish *Partidas,* the *Digest of 1808,* the English common law, the *Code Napoléon,* and the commentaries of French jurists on Roman law. As expressed by the finished civil code, adopted by the legislature in 1825, Louisiana law resembled that of other states in areas such as administrative and constitutional law, negotiable instruments, and incorporation. But important differences existed in the areas of property and family law—the two matters of most concern to the Gaines case. The Code of Civil Practice adopted at the same time did not provide for separate equity jurisdiction in Louisiana state courts, because the civil code itself was supposed to be "equitable," flexible enough to cope with specific problems that, in common-law states were generally handled by equity courts.[25]

Although the federal judges who heard the Gaines case based their decisions on the family-law provisions of the civil code, the practice of Louisiana federal courts normally followed that of United States courts in other states, allowing both "at law" and equity practice. Judge Lawrence's ruling to deny equity practice in the Louisiana federal court was a blow to the Whitneys' case. Equity remedied "defects" in the common law and could administer relief according to the true intentions of the parties involved in a dispute. It was especially applicable to cases concerning fraud, accident, mistake, or forgery. Myra and William Whitney asked the federal circuit court judge to exercise his "equity jurisdiction" because courts of equity allowed procedures not always available "at law": unique powers of examining witnesses (through writs of subpoena, the interrogatory

25. Edward Livingston, Louis Moreau-Lislet, and Pierre Derbigny (compilers), "To the Honorable the Senate and the House of Representatives of the State of Louisiana, in General Assembly Convened. The Subscribers, Jurists, appointed for the Revision of the Civil Code, Respectfully Report" (New Orleans, 1823), in Hatcher, *Edward Livingston,* 247; ibid., 248, 251–2; Stone, "Law with a Difference," 68–9; Dargo, *Jefferson's Louisiana,* 13–4; William Wirt Howe, "Memoir on François-Xavier Martin," Preface to Martin, *History of Louisiana from the Earliest Period,* xxii. See also William K. Dart, "The Louisiana Judicial System," *Louisiana Digest Annotated* 1 (Indianapolis, 1917): 21; Henry P. Dart, "The Sources of the Civil Code of Louisiana," in *Report of the Louisiana Bar Association* 13 (1911); Charles E. Fenner, *The Genesis and Descent of the System of Civil Law Prevailing in Louisiana* (New Orleans: L. Graham, 1887); and Henry P. Dart, "The Influence of the Ancient Laws of Spain on the Jurisprudence of Louisiana," *American Bar Association Journal* 18 (1932): 125–9.

process, and discovery of evidence); judgment without jury trial; injunction; imprisonment for contempt; and administration of estates.[26]

Probating a will that no longer existed with accusations of fraud against the previous executors called for the kind of "supple justice" available in equity but not necessarily in common law. Most of the testimony obtained in the Gaines cases came from witnesses who never actually appeared in the trial court. The usual method sent a "commission" to a local civil authority (a mayor, a sheriff, or, in the case of Colonel Bellechasse in Cuba or the chevalier Delacroix in Paris, the local United States consul) requesting that he ask and record the answers to a series of questions (the "interrogatories" and "cross-interrogatories"). These depositions became part of the trial record, and over one hundred were filed in the Gaines case. Equity also allowed the Whitneys to ask the chancery judge to force Myra's opponents to answer her petition (through a writ of subpoena), and thus allow the case to come to trial.

When Judge Lawrence refused to order Relf, Chew, and the other defendants to answer the petition, he blocked Myra's access to a legal remedy. When he announced that equity (or chancery) jurisdiction would no longer be followed in his court, the only avenue remaining was a "suit at law," and under the common law there was no basis for overturning a will already granted probate. Myra Whitney's appeal of Judge Lawrence's ruling, *Ex parte Whitney,* brought her case to the attention of the United States Supreme Court for the first time.

Prior to 1860 the Supreme Court met in a small room directly below the old Senate chamber in the capitol building. British traveler Harriet Martineau described in her travel diary the "badly lighted and ventilated" courtroom, "less fitted for its purposes than any other in the building." The nine justices sat before a bank of windows, making their "countenances . . . indistinctly seen." Visitors sat behind the attorneys and opposite the justices. Martineau disdainfully noted that American judges did not wear wigs, although other observers considered that the "nine judges in their robes of office presented a very imposing appearance."[27]

The sight of the "most exalted legal tribunal in the land" impressed

26. Katz, "Politics of Law in Colonial America," 259–60.

27. Harriet Martineau, "Life in Washington, D.C. in 1835," in *American Social History As Recorded by British Travellers,* ed. Allan Nevins (New York: H. Holt, 1923), 155; Ellet, *Court Circles of the Republic,* 329.

contemporary commentators. In 1837 Chief Justice Roger Taney, a "tall, spare man, with a striking intellectual countenance," led the court. His colleagues considered him a jurist of "large experience . . . great independence of character, and . . . unquestioned integrity." Justice Joseph Story sat on Taney's right. The "great Federalist" was the court's authority on equity. Next to Story was Justice John McLean of Ohio, a former postmaster general. A "stately and finelooking man," he had a "clear head and strong mind." Beside Justice McLean sat the "handsomest man on the bench," James M. Wayne of Savannah, Georgia. Justice McKinley of Alabama, "a plain, unpretending, quiet gentleman, whose thoughts were sound and sensible," filled the last place on the chief justice's right side. To Taney's left normally sat Justice Smith Thompson of New York, "thin and spare, almost to the point of emaciation, . . . strictly legal in all his tastes and pursuits, skillful in weighing the arguments of counsel." Thompson, absent due to family illness, did not hear Myra's appeal. Next to Thompson's empty chair sat Justice Henry Baldwin of Pennsylvania. A former member of Congress, Baldwin drew praise for his "logical mind." Farthest along the row of high-backed chairs to the left of the chief justice was John Catron of Tennessee. Like Justice Wayne, Catron was a Jackson appointee and relatively new to the court.[28]

Ex parte Whitney was Myra's first chance to place her narrative of events before the Supreme Court. Her appeal asked the court to order Judge Lawrence in Louisiana to proceed with her case according to the rules of equity (or chancery) practice. A technical question of legal procedure may have brought the Gaines case before the high court, but the justices demonstrated their fascination with its intricacies by continuing to review it as it appeared before them again and again over the next half century.

Myra's attorney for this first presentation to the Supreme Court was General Walter Jones of Virginia, a well-known Washington figure who had appeared before the high court on many occasions. A very small man whose "brilliant and expressive brown eyes" enlivened his "irregular features," Jones had a "silvery voice . . . easily heard in the largest assembly room." His clear tones outlined the story of Daniel Clark and Zulime, calling it a "true romance of litigation" which the little lawyer hoped would intrigue the court. Jones concluded by reminding the justices that in 1822 their body had announced that chancery practice should operate

28. Ellet, *Court Circles of the Republic,* 329–30.

in all United States courts. "This case is kept from the final decision of this court by the entire disregard of his duties by the judge of the Circuit Court," General Jones declared. The Supreme Court should issue a "writ of mandamus" to Judge Lawrence compelling him to proceed with the case.[29]

Justice Story delivered the court's opinion, and it did not please Myra and General Jones. Story appeared unmoved by the dramatic recitation of the "injured orphan's" history; his opinion addressed only the question of equity jurisdiction in Louisiana and the proper role for the Supreme Court. Story concluded that Judge Lawrence should allow the case to be tried in equity, but that the high court could not interfere directly in his conduct of his court. However irregular that conduct, the judge was "proceeding in the cause." Once Lawrence entered a decision in the case, then Myra could appeal to the Supreme Court for redress. Until then, even if Judge Lawrence's actions seemed "harsh" or "oppressive," she must seek some other remedy.[30]

Temporarily blocked, Myra recognized that winning would be easier if she could marshal public support for her claims. Northern newspaper editors and their readers had already expressed their fascination with the "romantic" aspects of the case. The favorable publicity convinced Myra Whitney to court public opinion by adopting a strategy that emphasized the congruency between her story and those of popular "sentimental" novels.[31]

The dry legal language of the bill of complaint filed on July 28, 1836,

29. Joseph Packard, "General Walter Jones," *Virginia Law Register* 8 (1901): 233–4; *Ex parte Whitney,* 407.

30. *Ex parte Whitney,* 408. The interest of the judges in the facts of the Gaines case kept it before the Supreme Court for many years. In recent years, the high court has generally restricted its docket to cases that raise important constitutional questions. The Constitution, however, gives the court appellate jurisdiction, "both as to Law and Fact," over cases arising out of disputes between citizens of two different states. United States Constitution, Art. 3, Sect. 2. The Supreme Court claimed that it exercised its discretion to hear the Gaines case because it "consider[ed] that justice will best be obtained by that course." Opinion of Justice James Wayne, *Patterson v. Gaines,* 6 Howard 550, at 584.

31. Lawrence Friedman defines popular culture as "the norms and values held by ordinary people (non-intellectuals) as opposed to high culture, or the culture of intellectuals." It includes books, songs, movies, plays, television—works of imagination whose intended audience is the public as a whole. The numbers of the mass reading public, who constituted Myra's intended audience, greatly expanded during the nineteenth century. Friedman, "Law, Lawyers, and Popular Culture," 1579.

in the United States circuit court in New Orleans could not disguise the dramatic accusations the petition made against Relf and Chew. Courtroom narratives can be analyzed in terms of plot, characters, and rhetoric. Myra and her attorneys knew that to win this case they had to transform the complex and ambiguous testimony of the witnesses into a persuasive narrative that was coherent, consistent, and believable. If the narrative also appealed to easily recognized stereotypes and commonly held moral values, she could draw support from the public, who enthusiastically followed reports of the litigation in the penny press. By suggesting that the facts of her case constituted a familiar plot to readers of popular fiction, she could create a clear moral framework to guide judges and spectators alike in evaluating the evidence and the credibility of witnesses.[32]

Nineteenth-century sentimental fiction divided the world into the morally unambiguous categories of victim and perpetrator. Cast as the "injured orphan," Myra denounced the executors who had "falsely and fraudulently" kept her in ignorance of "her real name, parentage, and true history." The Whitneys' first bill of complaint recapitulated the story of Zulime Carrière and Daniel Clark, describing their marriage, Myra's birth, and their subsequent parting. The dramatic disappearance of Clark's second will naming Myra as his true heir followed in the best melodramatic tradition of contemporary novels, and her theatrical discovery of her true parentage conformed to the well-known conventions of formula fiction.[33]

The genre of the seduction novel provided the necessary story form familiar to those who avidly followed the case in their newspapers. Most popular in America before 1820, by midcentury its stock characters had become conventional stereotypes. The standard seduction novel told the story of a virtuous young woman who fell prey to an unscrupulous rake and was abandoned when she became pregnant. Plots of the two best-known American examples of this genre, *Charlotte Temple: A Tale of Truth* by Susannah Haswell Rowson (1791) and *The Coquette* by Mrs. Hannah Foster (1797), illustrate the precarious plight of women in a male-dominated society. At fifteen, Charlotte Temple is seduced by Montraville, a young officer who promises her marriage. Having met a richer and thus

32. Korobkin, "Maintenance of Mutual Confidence," 13–4.
33. Bill of Complaint, *W. W. Whitney and Wife v. Relf, Chew, et al.*, case no. 122, Circuit Court of the United States, Eastern District of Louisiana, reprinted in *Transcript of Record, Gaines v. City of New Orleans*, 2: 1105.

more suitable woman, Montraville readily accepts reports of Charlotte's infidelity from a jealous rival and deserts her. Charlotte, who had followed Montraville to America, bears her child in a hovel and expires, lingering only long enough to reconcile with her father. *The Coquette* describes another rebellious, pleasure-loving young girl seduced and abandoned by a glamorous military officer; in the best sentimental tradition, she also dies destitute and alone after bearing her lover's child.[34]

After 1820 the gothic or melodramatic novel replaced the seduction novel as the most widely read romantic genre. Characters in gothic novels faced a variety of exciting adventures: duels, suicides, murders, and kidnappings abounded; separated relatives were reunited; wills were lost, stolen, or forged. Author Susannah Rowson satirized the fashionable novels by providing the following recipe for literary success: "Be sure you contrive a duel; and, if convenient, a suicide might not be amiss—lead your heroine through wonderful trials. . . . Manage your plot in such manner as to have some surprising discovery made—wind up with two or three marriages, and the superlative felicity of all the *dramatis personae*." In an early example of the genre, Sally Barrell Wood's villain Dorval commits bigamy, fraud, theft, kidnapping, and multiple murders but is ultimately foiled by the plucky heroine, Aurelia. The happy ending was the most important difference between the earlier seduction novels and the melodra-

---

34. Lucy M. Freibert and Barbara A. White, eds. *Hidden Hands: An Anthology of American Women Writers, 1790–1870* (New Brunswick, N.J.: Rutgers University Press, 1985), 2, 13–6; Helen Waite Papashvily, *All the Happy Endings: A Study of the Domestic Novel in America, the Women Who Wrote It, the Women Who Read It, in the Nineteenth Century* (New York: Harper & Brothers, 1956), 26–31; Earnest, *American Eve*, 30; Mrs. Rowson (Susannah Haswell Rowson), *Charlotte Temple: A Tale of Truth* (Windsor, Vt.: Preston Merrifield, T. M. Pomroy, 1815); Hannah Webster Foster, *The Coquette; or, The History of Eliza Wharton: A Novel Founded on Fact* (Boston: W. P. Fetridge, 1855). Both male and female authors wrote seduction novels—Samuel Richardson's *Pamela* (1741; reprint, New York: New American Library, 1980) is the earliest English example. Male writers emphasized the seducer; women writers built their entire novels around the act of seduction, an experience that, by itself, destroyed the heroine's life. The authors justified the indelicate content of their works by characterizing them as warnings that would save young readers from immorality (Freibert, *Hidden Hands*, 2). Rowson and Foster based their novels on contemporary scandals. *Charlotte Temple* was Charlotte Stanley, seduced from her home in England by Colonel John Montresor (Rowson's cousin) and abandoned by him in New York. The seduction and suicide of Elizabeth Whitman, a young woman of Hartford, Connecticut, suggested the plot of *The Coquette* to Hannah Foster. Rumor identified Elizabeth's seducer as either Aaron Burr or Pierpont Edwards, son of Jonathan Edwards (Earnest, *American Eve*, 30).

mas that followed. Death seemed the only solution to the heroines of the seduction stories; having broken the rules of established society, neither "ignorance, gullibility, stupidity, silliness, [nor] rebellion" could excuse their moral lapses. Women novelists in the gothic tradition broke away from the victimization pattern of the seduction novel. Aurelia and her sisters not only escaped countless dangers but triumphed over violent males, often reforming them in the process.[35]

This new kind of heroine was no passive sufferer, but a "radiant, vigorous, active" young woman who flouted conventional ideas of "pious, pure, domestic, and submissive" womanhood. The most famous nineteenth-century gothic novel, Mrs. E. D. E. N. Southworth's *The Hidden Hand* (1859), contains one murder; two duels; two prison breakouts; three miraculous escapes from certain death; a carriage accident; a shipwreck; and two deathbed confessions. Her heroine, Capitola, is witty, independent, and unwilling to submit to male authority. After saving a more passive young woman from a villain, foiling the kidnappers, and capturing the robbers, Capitola even fights a duel, "the most astounding thing that ever a woman of the nineteenth century or any former century attempted," according to the author.[36]

The trial narrative devised by Myra and her lawyers drew from both seduction and gothic fiction. With its plot that included a story of betrayed love, a lost will, a missing heir, and fraud by a young woman's "natural protectors," the Gaines case could take its title from one of Mrs. Southworth's tales: *The Discarded Daughter, The Lost Heiress,* or *The Deserted Wife.* In 1860 Beadle's Dime Novel Press published *Myra: The Child of Adoption, A Romance in Real Life,* loosely based on the story of Clark and Zulime. Author Ann Sophia Stephens placed the familiar characters (slightly disguised) of the Gaines case into their proper roles of victim and villain. "Ross," a fiend of "slow and calculating passions," deceives "Zulima," who, in "the first bud and bloom of her womanly beauty," has married Clark, a man of "stern and lofty pride," and drives the lovers apart by "foul slanders." Only after she has married another do Clark and Zulima learn of Ross's treachery. Near death, Clark desperately tries to pro-

35. Sally Sayward Barrell Keating Wood, *Dorval; or, The Speculator: A Novel Founded on Recent Facts* (1801; reprint, Portsmouth, N.H.: Nutting & Whitlock, 1970); Freibert, *Hidden Hands,* 3, 51; Papashvily, *All the Happy Endings,* 31–2.

36. Mrs. Emma Dorothy Eliza Nevitte Southworth, *The Hidden Hand: A Novel* (1859; reprint, New York: A. L. Burt, 1920); Papashvily, *All the Happy Endings,* 128–9.

tect the child of his unacknowledged marriage. But Ross destroys the new will that, by proclaiming the legitimacy of Clark and Zulima's child, Myra, threatens to destroy the work of his years of deceit. The Clark fortune falls into his hands. Years later a new threat to the villainous executor surfaces—Myra, grown into a "fair young beauty" and married to "Whitney," an "estimable young man, full of talent and generous feeling," whose manly attractions include a "figure, tall . . . athletic, and yet full of subtle grace." After surmounting the schemes of Myra's adoptive father, "Mr. D.," who wished to marry Myra to a man of his own choosing, the couple learn of Myra's true heritage. Told of the "frauds practiced on the infant heiress," Myra and Whitney determine to erase the doubt that "had been craftily thrown on her own legitimacy and thus on the fair name of her mother." This "high-spirited and proud young woman" sought only to retrieve "the wrongs heaped on her mother, and to wrest the honorable name of a father, whom she worshipped even in his memory, from the odium that had been fastened upon his actions."[37]

Stereotyped heroines were familiar to the scores of women who made the "domestic" novels early best sellers. Despite Nathaniel Hawthorne's caustic comment to his publisher about that "damned mob of scribbling women," novels of sensibility but little sense were enormously popular in the first half of the nineteenth century. By modern standards their plots, ranging from trite and predictable to wildly improbable, contain many flaws. But the pleasure of popular reading lay not so much in its instructional value or in its depiction of real life, as in its ability to provide sensations of excitement and escape for its audience.[38]

The correspondence between popular fiction and Myra's version of

37. Mrs. Emma Dorothy Eliza Nevitte Southworth, *The Discarded Daughter* (Philadelphia: T. B. Peterson, 1855), *The Lost Heiress* (Chicago: M. A. Donohue, 1912), *The Deserted Wife* (Philadelphia: T. B. Peterson, 1875); Ann Sophia Winterbotham Stephens, *Myra: The Child of Adoption, A Romance of Real Life* (N.Y.: Beadle Press, 1860), 6, 8, 12, 111–2; Frances B. Cogan, "Weak Fathers and Other Beasts: An Examination of the American Male in Domestic Novels, 1850–1870," *American Studies* 25 (1984): 11; Papashvily, *All the Happy Endings,* 113.

38. Nathaniel Hawthorne to William D. Tichnor, Jan. 19, 1855, *Letters of Hawthorne to William D. Tichnor, 1851–1864* (Newark, N.J.: Carteret Book Club, 1910), 1: 73–5, quoted in John T. Frederick, "Hawthorne's 'Scribbling Women,'" *New England Quarterly* 48 (1975): 231; Freibert, *Hidden Hands,* xii; Tony Davies, "Transports of Pleasure: Fiction and Its Audiences in the Later Nineteenth Century," in *Formations of Pleasure* (London: Routledge and Keagan Paul, 1983), 57; Papashvily, *All the Happy Endings,* 35.

"what really happened" explains the enduring appeal of the Gaines case. Set in a location deemed exotic by most Americans—New Orleans—and following the lurid outlines of the seduction plot, the tale of faithless romance told by Myra's narrative caught and held public attention. For fifty years the Gaines case made headlines in newspapers from New Orleans to New York. Magazines such as *Harper's Weekly* and *Putnam's* featured reports of the case, and they uniformly followed the lead of Myra's interpretation. Zulime, seduced by Daniel Clark and married to him but then betrayed and abandoned, was a modern Charlotte Temple. And Myra appeared in the press accounts as the new kind of heroine, "gay, daring, and confident," a devoted daughter kept in ignorance of her true heritage and now seeking to foil the evil executors, repair her mother's soiled reputation, and claim her rightful legacy.[39]

Myra Whitney gained additional leverage with editors and readers through her remarriage in 1839 to General Edmund Pendleton Gaines, the "Hero of Fort Erie" and one of the top-ranking officers in the United States Army. As a young subaltern in 1806 Gaines had captured Aaron Burr and escorted him to trial in Richmond. At some point the young officer met Daniel Clark, perhaps in Richmond at Burr's trial, or possibly on an earlier occasion while he was stationed in Natchez, where Clark owned a plantation. In 1839 Gaines commanded the Department of the West, headquartered in New Orleans. Calling on Mrs. Whitney, the general attributed his concern for her welfare to his friendship with her father.[40]

Myra Clark Whitney was almost thirty years younger than her distinguished second husband. The general was familiar with Myra's legal troubles—he never doubted that she was truly the legitimate daughter of his old friend—but the extent of their acquaintance before they married is unknown. After their marriage both Myra and the general remained on excellent terms with William Whitney's family in Binghamton. The tone

39. Papashvily, *All the Happy Endings,* 128-9.
40. James W. Silver, *Edmund Pendleton Gaines: Frontier General* (Baton Rouge: Louisiana State University Press, 1949) is the standard biography of General Gaines. See also "Edmund Pendleton Gaines" in *Dictionary of American Biography,* ed. Allen Johnson and Dumas Malone (New York: Charles Scribner's Sons, 1960), 4: 92-3. Myra Whitney was the third wife of General Gaines. He married first Frances Toulmin, daughter of Judge Harry Toulmin, and second Barbara Blount, daughter of Senator William and Mary (Granger) Blount of Tennessee, who died in Mobile on Nov. 29, 1836. *Dictionary of American Biography,* 93; Silver, *Edmund Pendleton Gaines,* 156-7.

of the letters exchanged between General Gaines and the family of Myra's first husband provides some evidence that Gaines knew Myra and William before the latter's death.[41]

Although older than his bride, General Gaines still stood erect, "straight as the arrow of an Indian warrior," wrote one observer, with thick, "snow-white" hair and a "sparkling" eye. The gallant general was widely admired for the polish of his manners, likened to those "of many old Frenchmen of high rank." His attention to proper decorum was such that one officer who visited the ailing general found him lying in bed "with his military collar on, and his sword by his side." He was a great favorite with the ladies, who particularly appreciated his ability on the floor of a ballroom. A "mirror of courtesy to the fair sex," an English visitor to Washington, D.C., reminisced; "no gentleman handl[ed] a lady's fan with greater dexterity. . . . Either sitting or standing he never forgot to relieve her of the task of fanning herself." The general's foppish behavior drew smiles from some of his contemporaries, but no one doubted his bravery.[42]

Born in 1777 in Culpeper County, Virginia, Gaines was the son of James Gaines, a lawyer who also served as presiding judge of Virginia's state court of appeals. As a member of the Virginia legislature, James Gaines voted to ratify the United States Constitution. In 1790 the Gaines family moved to East Tennessee, and at age eighteen Edmund Gaines began his military career with an election to a lieutenancy in a Tennessee rifle company. In January 1799, Gaines received an appointment as an ensign in the United States Army on the recommendation of a fellow Tennessean, William C. C. Claiborne, then a member of the Tennessee congressional delegation. In 1801 Gaines's superiors assigned him to survey the topography from Nashville to Natchez prior to the building of a military road along the old Natchez Trace. Three years later he was ordered to Mobile to maintain a United States presence in the West Florida

41. See letters from Myra Clark Gaines and General Edmund Pendleton Gaines to General Joshua Whitney, 1840–1847, Joshua Whitney Papers, Broome County Historical Society, Binghamton, New York.

42. Erasmus Darwin Keyes, *Fifty Years Observation of Men and Events* (New York: Charles Scribner's Sons, 1884), 172–3; John S. Jenkins, *Daring Deeds of American Heroes: A Record of the Lives of American Patriots and Heroes Including Full and Accurate Biographies of the Most Celebrated American Generals* (New York: D. W. Evans, 1860), 86–7; Ellet, *Court Circles of the Republic*, 399, quoting "Mrs. Maury," an English visitor to Washington in 1846. E. D. Keyes was a young West Point graduate who served on Gaines's staff during the War of 1812.

territory, then in dispute with Spain. From his post at Fort Stoddard, thirty-six miles north of Mobile, Lieutenant Gaines arrested Aaron Burr and escorted him to trial in Richmond. Once there, Gaines was appointed temporary marshal for the court, charged with summoning witnesses to Burr's trial.[43]

The War of 1812 provided Gaines with a national reputation. A commendation for bravery in the St. Lawrence campaign of 1813 earned him a promotion to brigadier general. On August 5, 1814, he took command of the army troops at Fort Erie, New York. British officers expected that a victory over the poorly constructed and exposed fort would force the withdrawal of all United States troops from Canadian territory. On August 7, a British cannonade began the bombardment of Fort Erie, "the earth shaking for miles around." Gaines's force (about 2,500 men) was outnumbered two to one. When Gaines allowed a night attack by British troops to approach the fort, American artillery and muskets opened fire, repulsing the enemy. Reports of the battle praised the general who led his men with "dauntless courage." A young staff officer later described the general, "in the pride of manhood, when he stood unmoved, gazing with an unblenched eye on the carnage around him, and issuing orders with an unfaltering lip, amid the whirling balls and blazing shells, on the ramparts of Fort Erie." British losses amounted to 157 killed, 308 wounded, and 186 prisoners—the largest number of British troops lost in any engagement of the war except the Battle of New Orleans. Gaines's troops suffered only 17 killed, 56 wounded, and 11 missing in action. Among the most severely wounded was the general himself.[44]

General Gaines's gallant defense of Fort Erie earned him the rank of major general, and "the Press . . . hailed Gaines's victory at Fort Erie as the only gleam of sunshine in our War for a long time." Congress presented him with a gold medal for bravery, and the states of Tennessee, Virginia, and New York awarded him gold-hilted swords valued at between $1,000 and $2,000 each in honor of his victory.[45]

After the war Gaines served under Andrew Jackson in the Creek War, and his reputation for bravery and aggressive leadership grew. He refused

43. Jenkins, *Daring Deeds of American Heroes,* 61–6; Silver, *Edmund Pendleton Gaines,* chapters 1 and 2.

44. Jenkins, *Daring Deeds of American Heroes,* 73–8; Keyes, *Fifty Years Observation,* 174; Silver, *Edmund Pendleton Gaines,* chapter 3.

45. John B. Brownlow to John Wesley Gaines, Apr. 15, 1919, Edmund Pendleton Gaines Papers, Tennessee Historical Association, Nashville.

to leave the battlefield even when a spent bullet knocked out two teeth; "it is only a little rough dentistry," he assured his aide and continued to lead his column. In 1821 President Monroe appointed Gaines commander of the western military division, and by 1828 he was a candidate (along with Winfield Scott) for the position of general-in-chief of the army. The two generals argued over their respective priority of rank, and each wrote a "very exceptional and violent" letter to President John Quincy Adams claiming the office. Deciding to favor neither, Adams ultimately appointed General Alexander Macomb to the coveted post. The quarrel between Gaines and Scott led to "an unfortunate estrangement" between them that lasted until Gaines's death.[46]

The general's courtship of Myra Whitney and their subsequent marriage became national news. He was "the best representative living of the old army of the revolution," and she was the heroine of a "true-life romance." Responding to a query from the *New York Gazette,* the editor of the *Nashville Republican Banner* replied that "the general has won a field lately that has covered him all over with wealth and laurels—a field hardly fought and hotly won in the teeth of a hundred young, handsome, and spirited gallants. It's a fact, Mr. *Gazette,* General Gaines is in New Orleans—a conqueror of a fair widow's heart."[47]

Remarriage solved many problems for the new Mrs. Gaines. Her financial position had grown increasingly precarious and her legal situation ever more complicated. The lawsuits had consumed most of William Whitney's money; his family continued to be supportive, but no funds had been obtained from the Clark estate. Myra's only asset, the lots in the Faubourg St. John transferred to her by Colonel Bellechasse in 1833, were now also the subject of litigation. Her half-sister Caroline, Caroline's hus-

46. Brownlow to John Wesley Gaines, Apr. 15, 1919; Allan Nevins, ed., *Polk: The Diary of a President, 1845–1849: Covering the Mexican War, the Acquisition of Oregon, and the Conquest of California and the Southwest* (London: Longmans, Green, 1929), 187 (Jan. 19, 1847). At a Washington, D.C., party, a matron posed this riddle to her friends: "The one dislikes what most men pursue, ——; the other, though a descendent of a Caldonian [*sic*], hates the ——." She gave no solution to the riddle, but it apparently refers to the feud between Gaines and Scott—"gains" being "what most men pursue" and "the Scot" being what the Caledonian incongruously hates—and indicates that their rivalry was the subject of considerable gossip. Ellet, *Court Circles of the Republic,* 236–7.

47. Fayette Robinson, *An Account of the Organization of the Army of the United States with Biographies of Distinguished Officers . . .* (Philadelphia, E. H. Butler, 1848), 1: 285; *Nashville (Tenn.) Republican Banner,* May 10, 1839, p. 3.

band John Barnes, and the other heirs of Mary Clark under the will of 1811 had sued in the Louisiana courts to reclaim the property in the faubourg. When the sheriff, Frederick Buisson, took possession of the square in question, Myra sued him. But with few friends and little money, her ability to continue the pursuit of what she deemed her rights dimmed.[48]

Myra gratefully accepted General Gaines's offer of his heart and hand. No letters exchanged between the two have survived; like so many aspects of the Gaines case, assumptions about their relationship are only conjecture. Possibly Myra married the general because his private fortune was large enough to finance her continuing legal battle. The prospect of improving her social position may also have weighed heavily in the general's favor. Nineteenth-century women took their social status from their husband's position or family. In New York, the Whitney family occupied a prestigious place in society, but the Louisiana social world had shunned Myra and William Whitney, in part because their lawsuits threatened the property of the New Orleans elite, but also because of their "foreign" background. As the wife of the general who commanded every army post on the Mississippi River, Myra Gaines could no longer be ignored. Moreover, the general's connections in Washington might be helpful when—as seemed certain—the Supreme Court decided her case.[49]

Equally likely, however, is that Myra appreciated the general's reputation for honesty and stubborn persistence. His disdain for higher authority was well known. Upon receiving an order from the secretary of war to find a place on his staff for a young officer, the general replied, "I will not do it, Sir, and I am astonished that the Sec. of War should have issued such an order. You go back to the Sec. of War and tell him that the position of a staff officer is a confidential one and I would as soon permit the Sec. of War to select a wife for me as a staff officer." Such a husband would be unlikely to be cowed by the well-connected and powerful enemies arraigned against his wife.[50]

On April 19, 1839, Myra married General Gaines at the home (described by one guest as a "bizarre mansion") of Don Louis Bringier on Esplanade Avenue in New Orleans. Their marriage, which lasted ten

48. Myra Whitney to Virgil Whitney, June 2, 1838; *Barnes v. Gaines,* Louisiana Annual Reports, 5 Robinson (1843), 314.

49. Pease, *Ladies, Women, and Wenches,* 1.

50. John Brownlow to James W. Gaines, Apr. 4, 1911, Edmund Pendleton Gaines Papers, Tennessee Historical Association, Nashville.

years, appeared very happy. Mrs. Clement Clay, wife of the senator from Alabama, recalled meeting the couple in 1848 in New Orleans. The general, although "well-advanced in age," had a "dignified and military air." Mrs. Clay was struck by the marked disparity between this tall, commanding soldier and the very small young woman who hung upon his arm "like a reticule or a knitting pocket." "Never did woman exhibit more wifely solicitude," Virginia Clay remembered. "From the beginning of that dinner Mrs. Gaines became the General's guardian. She arranged his napkin, tucking it carefully in the 'V' of his waistcoat, read the menu and selected his food, waiting upon him as each course arrived, and herself preparing the dressing for his salad. All was done in so matter of fact, and quiet a manner that the flow of General Gaines's discourse was not once interrupted."[51]

"Wifely solicitude" aside, the Gaines's marriage was a true partnership from the beginning, with two overriding goals—the advancement of his military career and victory for Myra in the courts. Three days before their wedding the prospective bride and groom signed a prenuptial contract. General Gaines listed property in land and slaves worth a total of $107,000. Styling herself Myra Clark, daughter of Daniel Clark and widow of the late William Wallace Whitney, Myra claimed ownership of land in the Faubourg St. John worth $100,000 and "her rights and claims as sole heir to the estate . . . of her deceased father Daniel Clark, the amount whereof cannot be ascertained, it being now in litigation." She did not, however, intend to relinquish control of her property; the agreement stipulated that she retained the right to "alienate or encumber . . . all property belonging to her." Since both Myra and the general expected that he would "have considerable trouble and expense in attending to her lawsuits," Myra gave the general a future claim for $100,000 on any money obtained from the Clark estate. General Gaines never collected on this debt, and he spent most of his own fortune defending his wife's lawsuits.[52]

After their marriage the couple took up residence at the St. Charles Hotel. "Situated on an angular piece of ground, hemmed in by lofty stores and narrow streets, and shadowed by neighboring balconies," the hotel

51. Virginia Clay-Clopton, *A Belle of the Fifties: Memoirs of Mrs. Clay of Alabama Covering Social and Political Life in Washington and the South, 1853—* (New York, De Capo, 1969), 82–3.

52. Prenuptial Contract between Edmund Pendleton Gaines and Myra Clark, Apr. 16, 1839, reprinted in *Transcript of Record, Gaines v. City of New Orleans*, 2: 1665.

was the gathering place for visitors and the local American elite. It was also located on land Myra claimed as part of her father's estate. One resident of the St. Charles noted that his rooms "were fitted up in the French style, with muslin curtains and scarlet draperies." The public "drawing room" was furnished "à la Louis Quatorze" and opened onto "a large dining room with sliding doors." The English earl of Carlisle, concluding his American tour in New Orleans, proclaimed the St. Charles to be "the only good thing" in the city.[53]

Having studied law in Tennessee, General Gaines considered himself "something of a lawyer as well as a military man" and planned to take an active part in the case, throwing his prestige and fortune with a vengeance into the quest. Six weeks after their wedding, the Gaineses petitioned the circuit court to continue the lawsuit that would now bear the general's name. From 1839 on, the newspapers, which had eagerly reported on the litigation, now expanded their coverage of the Great Gaines Case. Myra's marriage endowed her with a social prominence that gave an added fillip to the true-life romance that continued to enthrall a nation.[54]

53. Nevins, *American Social History*, 235–6; Hall, *Manhattaner in New Orleans,* 8–9, 13; Hill, "French Traveler's View," 338; G. W. F. Howard, earl of Carlisle, *Travels in America* (New York: G. P. Putnam, 1851), 61–2.

54. Silver, *Edmund Pendleton Gaines*, 157–8; progress of case no. 122, Circuit Court of the United States, Eastern District of Louisiana, reprinted in *Transcript of Record, Gaines v. City of New Orleans*, 2: 2042–45.

VII

A Most Unusual Woman

In the early 1840s Washington was a struggling small town, "unlike any other that was ever seen." One English visitor compared the United States capital to a Potemkin village—a "card-board city" that when Congress recessed was "taken down and packed up again til wanted." The large number of temporary structures built to house transients created the impression that everyone was a bird of passage in Washington. Congress and the diplomatic corps rarely stayed after the legislative sessions ended, and even the clerks and other government officials were "mere lodgers." The climate appalled visitors; "nine days out of ten" it was "simply detestable." Rain turned the unpaved streets into "sloughs of liquid mud"; during the dry season, clouds of dust enveloped the same thoroughfares. Pennsylvania Avenue was the closest approximation to a real street. Lined with rows of houses, the avenue led from the Capitol to the White House. These two buildings were, in the opinion of one German visitor, the "only two specimens of architecture in the whole town, the rest being merely hovels."[1]

The capital's two newest transients were General Edmund Pendleton Gaines and his bride, already notable as the "heroine of a prolonged and interesting lawsuit." The earliest physical descriptions of the new Mrs. Gaines come from the Washington dowagers, who generally approved of

1. Ellet, *Court Circles of the Republic*, 581–3; Francis J. Grund, *Aristocracy in America: From the Sketchbook of a German Nobleman* (1839; reprint, New York: Harper & Row, 1959), 229.

her. She "is of medium height," declared one, "slender but well-rounded in form. Her brown hair is thick and clustered with curls. Her eyes are dark and brilliant, her complexion fair and clear. Her features are regular and she is beautiful beyond criticism. Full of life and animation, fresh in feeling and impulse, with a store of information and a mind well-cultivated, possessing rich humor and spirit with manners cordial, piquant, and winning, she is a universal favorite in society, and has a court of gentlemen about her wherever she moves." Another matron reported her meeting with General Gaines and his "tiny, frisky wife." The "pompously stately" general always appeared in public in full uniform, "epaulettes, sword, and what not"; his wife, "all smiles and ringlets and flounces," hung upon his arm "like a pink silk reticule."[2]

If Myra Gaines pleased Washington society, Washington society in turn pleased Myra. She wrote General Whitney that she had "received much kindness from strangers as well as public officers and other acquaintances." Public opinion, she believed, was decidedly "in our favor." Congressmen from both parties "took a quiet interest in the matter [her lawsuits] . . . and cordially wish for our success." Myra met president-elect William Henry Harrison at a ball given before his inauguration. She could not help boasting in the hearing of "a number of ladies and gentlemen," that General Harrison regretted that he did not dance, "else he would select me for his partner in preference to all others." But such flattery meant little, and Myra revealed what was truly important to her in her response. She would have "appreciated the compliment much more highly if he had desired me to name a friend for one of the appointments to be made by him and promised to support whoever I might recommend." Perhaps she had in mind a future vacancy on the Supreme Court.[3]

Myra had quickly discovered that Washington society gossip centered around patronage. General Gaines's refusal to identify with any political party limited the extent of his influence in the power struggles of Washington politics. The general was, in his wife's words, not a "Party man," and his recommendations met with less attention than those of men subject to party discipline. Myra had hoped to aid the Whitney family by obtaining

2. Wharton, *Social Life in the Early Republic*, 287; Ellet, *Court Circles of the Republic*, 563; Eliza Moore Chinn McHatton Ripley, *Social Life in Old New Orleans: Being Recollections of My Girlhood* (1912; reprint, New York: Arno Press, 1975), 170.

3. Myra Clark Gaines to General Joshua Whitney, Feb. 18, 1841, and Dec. 31, 1841; Myra Clark Gaines to Virgil Whitney, Feb. 6, 1841, all in Joshua Whitney Papers, Broome County Historical Society, Binghamton, New York.

an appointment to West Point for one of Virgil Whitney's sons (her nephew by her first marriage). Since "there [was] not the slightest disposition in the high public functionaries of the Government here to favor any application made by General Gaines," Myra had to tell her brother-in-law that she could not help his son.[4]

The old soldier's indifference to higher authority was well known, and he had made a considerable number of enemies over the course of many years' service. In 1839, the year of his marriage to Myra, General Gaines presented to the War Department a new plan for the defense of port cities against fleets of "steam-powered warships." His proposal recommended the use of "floating batteries" for harbor defense, rather than ships of the line; carrying heavier guns, drawing less water, and costing much less, the batteries could link land and naval forces using railroads for transport. The War Department was unimpressed and informed Gaines that no funds for the construction of floating batteries would be released. Nor would the general be reimbursed for the expenses he incurred collecting information about construction of his batteries. Opposition had the same effect on General Gaines as on his wife; refusing to accept defeat, he sent a memorial to Congress on December 31, 1839, proposing that the government fund his harbor defenses. Congress referred his memorial to Secretary of the Navy James K. Spaulding, who passed his recommendation to a navy board of commissioners. The board rejected the floating batteries as too expensive to construct and maintain. Gaines, they concluded, was an "interloper" who meddled in areas not any of his concern.[5]

Repulsed by the War Department, Congress, and the navy, the general took his cause to the country with a vengeance. In lecture halls all over the eastern half of the country, he spoke of his plan for improved defenses. Dressed in the full uniform of a major general, he used his drawn sword to point at a diagram of the watershed of the Mississippi River hung on the wall behind him. Following the general's address at every stop came the real attraction that drew capacity audiences everywhere. "Amid immense cheering," Myra Clark Gaines rose from the audience, stepped onto the platform, and addressed the crowds on "The Horrors of War."[6]

4. Myra Clark Gaines to Virgil Whitney, Dec. 31, 1841.

5. Edmund P. Gaines to Samuel J. Peters, Jan. 22, 1839, Edmund P. Gaines Papers, Tennessee State Library and Archives, Nashville; Charles Morris to Secretary of the Navy James K. Spaulding, Apr. 25, 1840, quoted in Silver, *Edmund Pendleton Gaines,* 229.

6. Silver, *Edmund Pendleton Gaines,* 230; Ellet, *Court Circles of the Republic,* 279–80.

* * *

Myra Gaines's public appearances represented a departure from conventional expectations for women. Speaking from a public platform contravened accepted behavior for middle- and upper-class females. In the mid-nineteenth century, social mores denied women the opportunity to express themselves on major issues before audiences composed of members of both sexes. Speaking before such "promiscuous" audiences invited accusations of impropriety, even immorality—formidable barriers for women who sought a public platform.[7]

Rarely had women lectured to mixed audiences before Gaines did so. They had ventured into the realm of public speaking as early as 1787. A "Miss Mason," the salutatorian of the Philadelphia Female Academy (the first secondary school for girls in the United States), welcomed parents and guests to the academy's graduation ceremonies "with a speech defending a woman's right to use her talents and to contribute to the public dialogue." A few others followed. In 1802 Deborah Sampson Gannett lectured in Massachusetts on her Revolutionary War military record, offering to explain her "unwomanly behavior." In 1828 Frances Wright lectured throughout the United States on the basic principles of democracy. Ten years before Myra Gaines spoke, Maria W. Miller urged her fellow Boston African Americans to oppose the colonization movement and demand their citizenship rights.[8]

Despite these precedents, few women dared face the censure that public speaking aroused. Public speech placed a woman "outside a mystical geometric entity called 'woman's sphere.'" In 1837 the General Association of the Massachusetts Congregational Church distributed a pastoral letter

7. Lillian O'Connor, *Pioneer Women Orators: Rhetoric in the Ante-Bellum Reform Movement* (1954; reprint, New York: Columbia University Press, 1979), vii; Susan Zaeske, "The 'Promiscuous Audience' Controversy and the Emergence of the Early Woman's Rights Movement," *Quarterly Journal of Speech* 81 (1995): 191. Glenna Matthews notes that the term "promiscuous" was repeatedly used to characterize audiences composed of both men and women. *The Rise of Public Women: Woman's Power and Woman's Place in the United States, 1630–1970* (New York: Oxford University Press, 1992), 100, note 18. Kenneth Cmiel argues that the term "promiscuous audience" is used only when women spoke to both men and women; when men spoke to the same assemblage, the term was not used. *Democratic Eloquence: The Fight over Popular Speech in Nineteenth-Century America* (New York: William Morrow, 1970), 70.

8. Karlyn Kohrs Campbell, Introduction to *Women Public Speakers in the United States, 1800–1925: A Bio-Critical Sourcebook* (Westport, Conn.: Greenwood Press, 1993), xiv.

denouncing women who spoke from a public platform. Such women lost their "indirect, delicate, charming female influence," a woman's "genuine power." Horace Mann's "Hints to a Young Woman" warned that "when a young woman . . . appears on the forum and makes speeches she unsexes herself." Francis Hosford, historian of Oberlin College, found that reproofs for public speech came from all sides: "the religious called it unscriptural, . . . the cultured thought it unseemly, the cynical found in it material for their bitterest sneers, the evil-minded felt free to make a woman orator the target of vulgarity."[9]

Even women whose chief goal was the education of their own sex believed that their pupils should be "frail, lovely, yielding," and shrink "from publicity and observation." No one expected female students to face a public assembly or address a "promiscuous multitude." Although elocution was a required course at the Troy Female Seminary, led by Emma Willard, the young ladies never read their own essays—this would place "too great a strain on [their] modesty." Should a young lady student read another's essay, she "never raised her eyes from the paper, her voice usually being so low as to be inaudible to all except the very closest, and she was supported throughout her ordeal of reading aloud by another girl upon whom she leaned heavily."[10]

The admonitions against addressing promiscuous audiences threatened the social identity of women speakers. A "lady" was "pious, pure, domestic, and submissive"; speaking in public meant loss of virtue and position in the social stratum. Deeply rooted myths of the enticing powers of the female sex reinforced this prohibition. Women were irrational and could persuade only through seduction. Thomas Jefferson echoed this common perception in an 1816 letter. Even in a "pure democracy," he wrote, women should be excluded from participation, because "[w]omen, to prevent depravation of morals and ambiguity of issue, could not mix promiscuously in the public meetings of men." By casting a woman who spoke

9. Zaeske, "Promiscuous Audience," 195; Horace Mann quoted in O'Connor, *Pioneer Women Orators*, 31; Mae Elizabeth Harveson, *Catherine Ester Beecher, Pioneer Educator* (1932; reprint, New York: Arno Press, 1969), 199; Frances J. Hosford, *Father Shipherd's Magna Charta: A Century of Co-education in Oberlin College, 1837–1937* (Boston: Marshall Jones, 1937), 81.

10. Welter, "Cult of True Womanhood," 152; Alma Lutz, *Emma Willard: Daughter of Democracy* (Boston: Houghton Mifflin, 1929), 101, 184–5.

in public as immoral, men defended their monopoly of public platforms and of political power.[11]

This outcry effectively kept most women off public platforms. Women speaking to women was acceptable; the proper role for women speakers confined them to prayer groups and sewing circles. If it should be necessary to step outside their female groups—as did early women educators seeking funds for their schools—propriety dictated that the woman recruit a man to deliver her speech. Catherine Beecher secured the services of her younger brother Thomas to deliver her appeals for school funding while she sat silently by his side. The public scorn that showered on "strong-minded females" who dared address a mixed audience also deterred Emma Willard, whose address at a citizens' meeting on behalf of public schools was delivered by Mr. Elihu Burritt. In Mrs. Willard's opinion, "for a woman to read her own address before such an assembly" would place "too great a strain on the proprieties." Nor did Dorothea Dix, whose life's work lay in rousing public interest in the conditions of asylums, prisons, and hospitals, ever speak to "mixed" audiences, despite the widely held belief that she made public speeches to spread her message. Her procedure for addressing her memorials to state legislatures or congressional committees imitated that of Catherine Beecher or Emma Willard; she requested a male supporter to deliver her speech. She "laid great stress on preserving her womanly dignity" and did not want to "vulgarize a cause and its representative by a pushing and teasing demeanor."[12]

Myra Gaines did not shun the public spotlight; she knew well the value of the publicity she and the general garnered from their lecture tour. Hav-

11. Zaeske, "Promiscuous Audience," 197–8; Karlyn Kohrs Campbell, *Man Cannot Speak for Her: A Critical Study of Early Feminist Rhetoric* (New York: Praeger, 1989), 1: 9–10; Thomas Jefferson to Samuel Kercheval, 1816, quoted in Zaeske, "Promiscuous Audience," 193. Jefferson, like many husbands and fathers, classed women with infants and slaves—the part of the population that had no will of its own and was incapable of forming opinions and being represented in public assemblies.

12. O'Connor, *Pioneer Women Orators*, 24, 27–8; Alice Stone Blackwell, *Lucy Stone: Pioneer of Women's Rights* (Boston: Little, Brown, 1930), 114; Willystine Goodsell, *Pioneers of Women's Education in the United States* (1939; reprint, New York: McGraw-Hill, 1970), 131–2; Lutz, *Emma Willard*, 211. In 1854 Catherine Beecher's older brother, Henry Ward Beecher, commented that he would "rather have seen his mother or sister in their graves" than making a speech on a public platform. Henry Ward Beecher to Gerrit Smith, in the *Liberator*, Nov. 24, 1854, quoted in O'Connor, *Pioneer Women Orators*, 26.

ing sought to link her story with that of popular fictional heroines, she could ensure her hold on public sympathy by her national appearances, but not if critical attacks charged her with immorality or unfeminine behavior. The technique she used to defuse censure allowed her to occupy a prominent public position yet remain a properly "pious, pure, domestic, and submissive" wife. While listening to her husband, who spoke first, Myra sat in the audience. Upon the conclusion of the general's remarks, she was escorted to the platform. Dressed in "a black velvet pelisse, made to fit tight," wearing "earrings and diamonds in her hair," with a "rich silk hat ornamented with a waving plume of bird of paradise feathers," she presented a picture of femininity. While she read her lecture, General Gaines, in full regimentals, stood behind her. His willingness to share the floor with his wife indicated his support for her actions outside of the usual "cloistered seclusion" of the women's sphere.[13]

Mrs. Gaines began her remarks by acknowledging the "novel and uncommon scene" of a "lady addressing a large audience." Well aware that many might consider it "wrong for a lady to speak in a public assembly," since by doing so she "trangress[ed] the boundaries of strict female reservedness," Myra claimed the right to speak "in the presence of [her] liege lord" and on a subject dear to his heart. "[W]hat wife," she asked, "can be blamed in taking a deep interest in the affairs of her husband?" Having undermined any opposition by her demeanor and by acknowledging the unconventional nature of the activity, Myra delivered her speech. By depicting "how deeply the female sex with their little children have reason to apprehend and deplore the 'Horrors of War,'" Myra supported her husband's theme: in peace, prepare for war. Her peroration ended with a ringing call for a patriotic defense of an "America . . . now placed on the pinnacle of glory . . . the summit of happiness," and prayed that "scenes of blood" might never "pollute our happy country."[14]

As several reviewers mentioned, Myra Gaines had no firsthand experience of the "horrors of war." Nevertheless, her appearances before "promiscuous audiences" drew little criticism and excited no cries of immorality. By casting her actions in terms acceptable to the dominant conception of a woman's role, Myra disarmed her critics. Philadelphia pa-

13. *New Orleans Daily Picayune*, Jan. 29, 1841, p. 2.

14. Myra Clark Gaines, "The Horrors of War," in *The New-Orleans Book, Extracts . . . from the Journals, the Pulpits, the Bench, and the Bar of New-Orleans,* ed. Robert Gibes Barnwell (New Orleans, 1851), 37–9.

pers praised the lectures delivered in that city by General Gaines and "his accomplished lady." Describing the audience assembled to hear the pair, the *Daily Standard* proclaimed that "all the beauty and fashion of this peerless city are to be present, to learn military tactics. The General is popular—Madame is immensely popular." Their lectures filled the largest hall in town to capacity, and many who hoped to hear the Gaineses were turned away at the door. The *Daily Standard* wasted no time repeating the content of either speech; its readers were much more interested in "domesticalities." The general's daily early-morning walk of five or six miles earned him the title of "greatest pedestrian in town." Reporting Myra's age as thirty-two (she was at least thirty-five), the *Daily Standard* assured its readers that she "look[ed] much younger." The general's "lady . . . is very beautiful," the paper advised; "her eye resembles that of the *ci devant* Fanny Kemble, but is brighter—lit up no doubt with military ardor."[15]

The *Daily Standard's* reference to the actress Fanny Kemble demonstrated that Myra Gaines had attained the celebrity status she sought— status that allowed her to overstep traditional limits on female behavior, an action that would draw criticism if performed by a woman of less renown. Her lectures kept her and her case in the public eye. It was not necessary, and would even be counterproductive, to speak on her legal situation; Myra's audiences were familiar with her romantic history and were eager to see the heroine of a true-life romance.

Not every spectator was equally effusive with praise. Although the *New York Sun* declared Myra "decidedly the better speaker of the two," the *Signal* (also a New York paper) suggested that she gave a "poor performance" and demonstrated "no adequate grasp of the subject." Even the *Signal* agreed, however, that Myra delivered her address in a "clear, sweet voice" that proved she possessed "all the accomplishments requisite to constitute the ornament and charm of woman's appropriate sphere." Diarist Philip Hone provided a more acerbic commentary on the lecture tour: "General Gaines and his wife have been making fools of themselves. . . . He has given a lecture . . . upon 'National Defense,' and she follows him with most marvelous incongruity upon the 'Horrors of War.' . . . They began this ridiculous career of vanity and silliness at the South and taking the applause which was given for the novelty of the exhibition as a crite-

15. *New Orleans Daily Picayune*, Jan. 14, 1841, p. 2, quoting the *Philadelphia Daily Standard*, Dec. 31, 1840.

rion of the public opinion of its merits, they came here an itinerant Punch and Judy show, and drew a great crowd to the Tabernacle."[16]

The public who flocked to hear the general and his lady did not share Philip Hone's sardonic impression of their performance. The widespread support evident for Myra Gaines demonstrated that her entry into a traditionally masculine preserve had not detracted from her public persona as a persecuted heroine. Her relentless adherence to the accepted standards of outward feminine appearance diminished criticism of her actions.

Myra Gaines knew that appearances counted with her public. On one memorable occasion twenty years later she made clear her strategy for straddling the gendered spaces of nineteenth-century culture. Coming out of the United States Patent Office in the late 1860s, she met Dr. Mary Walker, an advocate of "rational dress" for women. Dr. Walker, a graduate of Syracuse Medical College in 1853, adopted the "infamous loose trousers" popularized by Amelia Jenks Bloomer in the mid-1850s. Walker served as a Civil War surgeon under George H. Thomas, despite strong protests from the medical director of the Army of the Cumberland and the men of the 52nd Ohio Regiment to which she was assigned, and wore the same uniform as that of her fellow officers. When she encountered Myra Gaines, Dr. Walker was experiencing a brief moment as a war celebrity, and bystanders eagerly watched the meeting between the two outspoken women. A description of their conversation appears in a gossipy memoir of Washington society at midcentury, Elizabeth Ellet's *Court Circles of the Republic*. When Mrs. Gaines approached Dr. Walker, she stopped, requested the name of the woman in the "peculiar dress," and asked permission to "give her a little advice." Dr. Walker's pantaloons "shock[ed] the moral sentiment" of the community, Myra Gaines announced; her dress placed "her sex in a false position, in a light to be ridiculed and treated with contempt by the other sex." Such evasion of community standards could only be counterproductive; Gaines assured her acquaintance that "[h]ad I assumed your garb, I should have failed to obtain the sympathy of the virtuous and good throughout the country, in this great struggle for my rights."[17]

16. *New Orleans Daily Picayune*, Feb. 2, 1841, p. 2, quoting the *New York Sun* (n.d.) and *New York Signal* (n.d.); Philip Hone, *The Diary of Philip Hone, 1828–1851*, ed. Allan Nevins (New York: Dodd, Mead, 1927), 2: 247.

17. Louis Filler, "Mary Edwards Walker," in *Notable American Women, 1607–1950: A Biographical Dictionary*, ed. Edward T. James, Janet W. James, and Paul S. Boyer (Cambridge, Mass.: Belknap Press of Harvard University, 1971), 3: 532–3; Ellet, *Court Circles of the Republic*, 574–7.

Gaines was not the only unconventional woman to acquiesce in certain social customs while resisting others. Elizabeth Cady Stanton, also attracted to the Bloomer costume, wore her trousers only a few times before realizing that the public ridicule they provoked interfered with her message about votes for women. Cultural historian Karen Halttunen depicts nineteenth-century America as a culture grasping uncertainly for new standards of behavior in an increasingly fluid social world. Dress became a reliable sign of character, and many middle-class Americans turned to fashion as a key indicator of personal worth. Gaines and Stanton's assessment of their reception had they adopted unconventional garb indicated that each woman understood the symbolic nature of her attire.[18]

General and Mrs. Gaines appeared on platforms throughout the United States (St. Louis, Cincinnati, and Philadelphia between November and December 1840 and New York City, Baltimore, and again Philadelphia in January 1841), always playing to packed houses. As they toured, the Gaines case continued to meander slowly through the Louisiana federal court. Myra Gaines's marriage improved her social position and gave her access to a wider audience than she had had as a widow, but it did little to settle the vexing problem presented by Judge Lawrence's repeated refusals to hear her case as a suit in equity. What the general called "these long-contested quibbles" over "chancery jurisdiction [and] copies in the French language" came before the United States Supreme Court twice more, in 1841 and 1844. After the court held in 1841 that the Louisiana court must "conform to the [chancery practice] adopted and established in the other States," an elated Myra wrote General Whitney of her "triumph over my miserable enemies, Relf and Chew."[19]

When even that decision proved an inadequate goad for the Louisiana court, Myra tried a little discreet lobbying of the United States Supreme

18. Fishburn, *Women in Popular Culture,* 18; Karen Halttunen, *Confidence Men and Painted Women: A Study of Middle-Class Culture in America, 1830–1870* (New Haven, Conn.: Yale University Press, 1982), passim; Daniel Cohen, "The Murder of Maria Bickford: Fashion, Passion, and the Birth of a Consumer Culture," *American Studies* 31 (1990): 9.

19. Edmund P. Gaines to Virgil Whitney, Feb. 2, 1841; Myra Clark Gaines to General Joshua Whitney, Feb. 18, 1841; Joshua Whitney Papers, Broome County Historical Society, Binghamton, New York. The second and third appearances of the Gaines case before the Supreme Court are *E. P. Gaines and Wife v. Relf, Chew, et al.,* 15 Peters 9 (1841) and *E. P. Gaines et ux. v. Chew, Relf, et al.,* 2 Howard 619 (1844).

Court. The Gaineses had begun to spend their winters in Washington, as the court heard appeals in the capital during December and January. In the midst of the January term of 1843, several of the justices called on General Gaines and his lady. Myra "playfully observed" that she hoped "the Decision upon the merits of my cause would be given this Term" as the court "had so promised last winter." "Did we indeed?" replied her visitors. "Well, well, we shall certainly do something about it." Myra, however, had to wait another year for the court to finally dispense with the technical questions of jurisdiction and rule that the Gaineses were entitled to "full and explicit answers from the defendants."[20]

While they waited for the U. S. Supreme Court to rule, Myra's other opponents pressed their case in the Louisiana courts. Caroline Barnes and her husband, Dr. John Barnes, joined by the other heirs of Mary Clark, sued Myra for possession of the Faubourg St. John land formerly held in trust for her by Colonel Bellechasse. Since the Barneses chose to bring their suit "at law" in a Louisiana district court, a jury would hear the arguments.

Mrs. Barnes's role in the Gaines case is puzzling. Myra and her Carrière aunts always claimed that Caroline was Myra's half-sister, the daughter of Zulime and Jerome DesGrange. Recognizing that Caroline was the daughter of Clark might mean that the estate would be split between the two daughters. Myra, however, was equally concerned with the reputation of her mother. Admitting that Caroline was illegitimate would seriously injure the "betrayed woman" image that Myra sought to create for Zulime.

The executors Relf and Chew, Clark's business partner Daniel Coxe, and Caroline herself believed she had been born in Philadelphia in 1802, the illegitimate daughter of Zulime and Daniel Clark. Clark's family in Philadelphia recognized Caroline as the "natural daughter" of their son, and old Mrs. Clark provided an allowance for the young girl. After Mary Clark's death in 1823, her will divided her estate (which consisted mainly of her expected inheritance from son Daniel) in equal shares among her daughters, Eleanor O'Bearn and Jane Green, and her granddaughters, Sarah Campbell and Caroline Clark. Mary Clark's will also recognized "Mira Clark, commonly called Mira Davis" as another "natural daughter" of Daniel Clark, but Myra received only two hundred dollars, "to purchase a jewel as a remembrance of me." Mary Clark was not aware of Myra's existence until William Hulings and Daniel Coxe informed her in 1817, and she intended the small bequest to serve as "recognition of Mira's parentage." Daniel's mother would have left this third granddaughter an equal share of her estate had not Dr. Hulings assured her that Myra's future "had already been provided for." In a deposition, Hulings admitted that Mrs. Clark's statement referred to the lots held by Colonel Bellechasse for Myra.[21]

Barnes v. Gaines provided Myra with an opportunity to demonstrate her grasp of the complexities of her claims by arguing the case personally. In the middle of the nineteenth century it was almost unprecedented for a woman to act as an attorney in any court, state or federal. Rarely did women even appear as witnesses. Historians Richard Wightman-Fox and Michael Grossberg have noted that nineteenth-century judges usually refused to accept female testimony. A woman was less able than a man to speak reasonably or truthfully; her words were not "rooted in the sort of controlled discourse that made possible the rational operation" of the courtroom. Women were above such mundane matters and were "too spiritual" to render competent judgments about the affairs of the (men's) world. In two other well-known nineteenth-century trials, neither of the female principals ever spoke for herself in court. In the Beecher-Tilton adultery trial, her lawyers refused to allow Elizabeth Tilton to speak because, as a woman, she was "irrational and unreliable." Nor was Ellen Sears d'Hauteville allowed to speak in the courts deciding her divorce and child-custody dispute in the early 1840s. In these cases, however, the women probably had no desire to speak for themselves. Even in the Gaines case, lawyers customarily presented petitions and arguments while Myra Gaines watched from the audience. Her presence was unusual, but by this time Myra was a familiar figure to habitués of Louisiana courtrooms. When presented with an opportunity to speak for herself, Myra let no complaint of female delicacy stand in her way.[22]

The tale of Myra's presentation to the Louisiana jury became part of

21. Will of Mary Clark and Probate Record (1825), reprinted in *Transcript of Record, Gaines v. City of New Orleans*, 2: 1629; Daniel Coxe, deposition of May 5, 1835, ibid., 2: 1878; Dr. William Hulings, deposition of June 11, 1835, ibid., 2: 1881.

22. Fox, "Intimacy on Trial," 128–9, 131; Grossberg, *Judgment for Solomon*, passim.

the legend of the Gaines case and appears in several contemporary accounts. During the trial, her counsel John R. Grymes "fell into a wrangle with the judge and withdrew from the courtroom." General Gaines rose, dressed as usual in his uniform with his sword at his side. As the husband of the defendant and a "member of the bar of the United States," he claimed the right to represent his wife's interests. Unfortunately, having studied law "under a very different system of jurisprudence," he "felt out at sea in the courts of a civil law state." Therefore, he requested that his wife, the "lady defendant," who was "better acquainted with the remarkable facts of her history than anyone else," should be allowed to present her case to the jury. When Judge Buchanan agreed that "the lady had a right to argue her own case," the general, "with that grand dignity for which he was so distinguished," led his wife forward.[23]

How Myra felt at finally having an opportunity to express her own arguments can only be imagined; no surviving Gaines letters mention this incident. Once begun, however, she apparently was reluctant to stop. Having "addressed the jury at length," Myra continued reading document after document in the face of Judge Buchanan's efforts to end her presentation. A "disagreeable contest" ensued. Myra charged the judge "with having an interest against her," and he retorted "with temper." When Myra persevered in her address, Judge Buchanan informed General Gaines that "he was expected to control his wife in court." The stately old soldier rose to his "full height of six feet three, and assuming the position of a commander of grenadiers, and gracefully touching the belt of his sword," answered the judge. "May it please your honor," he thundered, "for everything that lady shall say or do, I hold myself personally responsible in every manner and form known to the laws of my country or the laws of honor." Gaines's threatening gesture toward his sword and his intemperate tone further incited the temper of the judge. "This court," shouted Buchanan, "will not be overawed by military authorities." No less incensed, the general replied, "Rest assured, your honor, that when an attempt of that sort is made, the sword which I wear . . . will be quickly unsheathed to defend the rights and dignity of your honor and all the civil tribunals of my country."[24]

With that declaration, peace was restored to the courtroom. Myra sat

23. Several nineteenth-century sources on the Gaines case recount this story. The fullest description is found in Elizabeth Ellet's *Court Circles of the Republic,* 572–4.
24. Ibid.

quietly while her husband and the judge wrangled. Her point had been made; for the first time in any Gaines case, a Louisiana jury returned a verdict in Myra's favor. Judge Buchanan refused the Barneses' motion for a new trial, saying that such an "extraordinary effort" had been made to influence public opinion through the newspapers that finding an unbiased jury would be impossible. He might not have ordered a new trial, but Judge Buchanan publicly announced that he thought the verdict "contrary to both law and evidence."[25]

The Gaineses' victory in Louisiana added to their recent triumph before the United States Supreme Court. Their third appearance before the high court had led to the justices' declaration that Myra's opponents should "answer" her petition—that is, admit that a cause for action existed. With a victory in the Supreme Court and another in a Louisiana court, a final vindication of Myra's claims seemed imminent. But finding anyone who had bought land from the Clark estate willing to contest her claims in court proved difficult. On April 14, 1840, the Gaineses offered to reduce the amount they might ultimately claim (should a trial be decided in Myra's favor), if a defendant would "meet us in a fair trial in Chancery." Only one purchaser came forward to accept the offer. Charles Patterson quickly consented to a speedy trial on the merits of Myra's claims. Patterson had purchased his family home and several adjacent lots through Relf and Chew. His answer asserted that the land, the property of Daniel Clark during his lifetime, was left to Clark's mother and sole heir, Mary Clark, and had been legally sold by the executors of the Clark estate in 1820.[26]

The Patterson case came quickly to trial, since the trial judge admitted the record of the probate court proceedings as evidence and no additional depositions were taken. Myra Gaines claimed Patterson's property as Daniel Clark's only legitimate child, not only through the lost will of 1813 (as his "universal heir") but also under the will of 1811. The civil code of 1808 prohibited a father from disinheriting his legitimate child—no more than one-fifth of an estate could be willed away from his children. Since the Supreme Court had indicated that the 1813 will had to be probated before Myra could claim Clark's estate under it, she and General Gaines

---

25. *Barnes v. Gaines,* Louisiana District Court, General Case Files no. 3663, Record Group 21, National Archives, Southwest Region, Fort Worth, Tex. The Barneses' appeal to the Louisiana Supreme Court also failed to secure a new trial, despite Judge Buchanan's move from the trial court to the appellate bench.

26. Notice to Purchasers and Present Claimants of the Estate of Daniel Clark, Apr. 14, 1840, reprinted in *Transcript of Record, Gaines v. Relf, Chew, and Others,* 832.

decided to base their arguments on Myra's status as Clark's legitimate daughter and his "forced heir" under the 1811 will. If successful, she could obtain four-fifths of her father's estate, and the remaining one-fifth would be divided among the heirs of Mary Clark.[27]

Before the Supreme Court could hear Patterson's appeal, the Mexican War interrupted the Gaineses' concentration on Myra's litigation. General Gaines commanded the Department of the West, but because of his age he was not sent to Mexico. Reacting with "a high flush of enthusiasm" to the news of Zachary Taylor's confrontation with Mexican troops near Brownsville, Texas, Gaines decided to call on the governors of states in the Mississippi River valley to raise volunteers to aid Taylor before a declaration of war passed the Congress. Thousands responded eagerly to the call to relieve the "embattled Americans on the Rio Grande." Companies formed throughout the South and West; volunteers bought brightly colored uniforms and boarded steamboats for New Orleans or marched overland to fight the Mexicans. General Gaines, however, had no authority from the War Department to call out volunteers. Most of the enlistments ran for three or six months, and few would volunteer for a longer term. When the soldiers reached the Rio Grande, Taylor had no supplies to support the unexpected troops, so the men camped on the hot, sandy beach of the Texas coast and grumbled. The War Department ordered "Gaines's Army" home before serious fighting began, and "its name became in the familiar speech of the Mississippi Valley for a generation, an accepted symbol of futility."[28]

Secretary of War William H. Maxey relieved Gaines of his command and ordered him to report before a court of inquiry at Fortress Monroe. Maxey and Gaines had clashed before because of Gaines's dislike of War Department bureaucracy. In one official report, the general had replied to Maxey's orders, "I carelessly submit to them as they seem to be a source of pleasure to the War Department and certainly inflict no injury on me." This time, however, the department's order threatened to end the general's military career. As the Gaineses made preparations to leave New Orleans, they met the officers of the "Louisville Legion," about to embark for the Brazos. In his usual grandiloquent fashion, General Gaines told them,

27. Louisiana Civil Code of 1808, Chapter 3, Section 1, Article 19; *Patterson v. Gaines,* 6 Howard 550 (1848), at 551.
28. Robert Selph Henry, *The Story of the Mexican War* (1950; reprint, New York: Da Capo Press, 1989), 74; Jenkins, *Daring Deeds of American Heroes,* 85.

"Gentlemen, we are in diametrically opposite positions, glorious to you but painful in the extreme to me. You go to meet the foe. I for the first time in my life am compelled under the hard obligations of duty and under superior orders to turn my back on him."[29]

Relieved of his command but unsubdued, General Gaines continued to sign up officers to fight in the Mexican War. This only increased the exasperation of President Polk and his cabinet. General Winfield Scott openly said that he thought Gaines was "crazy." At Fortress Monroe, Gaines defended his actions, insisting that since the War Department allowed General Taylor to raise volunteer forces, he, who as a major general outranked Taylor, ought also to have that right. By this time, General Gaines was one of the oldest serving officers in the country; his quarrels with his superior officers had "enlivened army circles for a generation." The younger officers on the board of inquiry recognized that the general's "pure and praiseworthy" motives mitigated his action, and recommended no further sanctions. President Polk reluctantly agreed. He confided in his diary on August 15, 1846, that "the court recommended in consideration of his long service and the supposed patriotism and purity of his motives, that no further proceedings be had. . . . It is evident from the finding of the court that they have labored to give a construction to General Gaines's conduct most favorable to him. . . . General Gaines is now a very old man . . . [and] I determine in lenity . . . to yield to the recommendation of the court of inquiry. . . . His late conduct at New Orleans greatly embarrassed the government."[30]

In recognition of Gaines's long years of service, the War Department reassigned him to command the Department of the East, far away from the theater of war. Forced to sit idle while his rival General Scott and his friend and cousin General Taylor earned fame in Mexico, Gaines continued to annoy his superiors in Washington. In late January 1847 Zachary Taylor wrote a letter to Gaines highly critical of the Polk administration, and Gaines gave permission to the *New York Express* to publish the letter with its recipient's name deleted. The letter received wide publicity from

29. John B. Brownlow to John Wesley Gaines, Apr. 15, 1919, Edmund Pendleton Gaines Papers, Tennessee State Library and Archives, Nashville; *New Orleans Daily Picayune,* Jan. 10, 1885, p. 1.

30. Nevins, ed., *Polk,* 139 (Aug. 15, 1846); Robinson, *Account of the Organization of the Army,* 1: 330; Henry, *Mexican War,* 66–7.

those who felt that General Taylor's accomplishments had been over-
looked. President Polk angrily wrote in his diary that the letter uttered
"unfounded complaints" and gave "publicity to the world of plans of campaign contemplated by the government, which it had . . . desired to keep
concealed from the enemy." The president considered the letter "highly
unmilitary," and he had no doubt who was responsible for its publication.
General Gaines wrote the president admitting that the letter had been addressed to him and that he given permission for its publication. The next
day the cabinet unanimously condemned Taylor "for writing such a letter"
and Gaines for publishing it, "as being not only unmilitary and a violation
of their duty as officers, but calculated seriously to embarrass and injure
the pending military operations in Mexico."[31]

The military fortunes of her husband suffered from his quarrel with the
War Department and the president, but Myra's legal contest benefitted
from their move to the East Coast. With the Patterson suit pending before
the Supreme Court, Myra reestablished her contacts with Washington society. One observer of the Washington social scene commented that "the
small, slight figure and keen dark eyes of Myra Gaines were familiar to
Washingtonians," and society met the general and his wife everywhere. At
a congressional dinner party, "Mrs. Linn of Missouri and Mrs. Gaines,
the distinguished wife of the General, presided as matrons at the ceremo-
nial," an occasion at which "almost the entire *beau monde* was present."
Myra used every opportunity to "advocate her case in and out of court,
to the judges, in public and in private, in every place and under all circumstances." Washington society seems to have accepted Myra Gaines on her
own terms. Almost every contemporary commentary expressed admiration for "her confidence, her equanimity, her earnest zeal and unflagging
energies." She displayed to the world "the most remarkable example of
courageous devotion and resolute persistency which can be found in the
history of the severest of all trials of human patience and endurance."[32]

31. Nevins, ed., *Polk*, 191–2 (Jan. 25, 1847); Henry, *Mexican War*, 166.
32. Wharton, *Social Life in the Early Republic*, 287; Ellet, *Court Circles of the Republic*, 332–3, 574.

VIII

A "Prolonged and Interesting Lawsuit"

The appeal of the Patterson case came before the Supreme Court in its January term, 1848. Since Myra Gaines, in conjunction with her husband, had decided to claim Daniel Clark's estate as his "forced heir" under the accepted will of 1811, the issue of Gaines's birth status became the center of controversy. Determination of legitimacy was a serious problem for post-Revolutionary American courts, both in common-law states and under the Louisiana civil code. English common law used matrimony to separate legitimate from spurious issue—the latter was *filius nullius,* the child and heir of no one. The bastard, a child born outside of marriage or the offspring of an adulterous union, had no recognized legal relationship to his or her parents—neither for maintenance, custody, nor inheritance. The only heirs of bastards were those "of their own body." Common law set up barriers to full family membership to protect family lineage and property and to promote matrimony by punishing misbegotten offspring.[1]

After 1776, republican views of children raised concerns over the treatment of bastards, and a strong reluctance to stigmatize children helped foster changes in bastardy law. A Virginia statute of 1785 was the first to grant an illegitimate child inheritance rights to the mother's estate. By the 1830s, thirteen states, including Louisiana, had joined Virginia in modifying their inheritance laws. American courts also modified the English prac-

1. Michael Grossberg, *Governing the Hearth,* 196; Carole Shammas, Marylynn Salmon, and Michel Dahlin, *Inheritance in America, from Colonial Times to the Present* (New Brunswick, N.J.: Rutgers University Press, 1987), 71.

tice regarding legitimization of children after the marriage of their parents. English common law provided that a child could be legitimized only by an act of Parliament—a lengthy, difficult, and expensive undertaking. Civil law, such as operated in Louisiana before 1803, accepted that the subsequent marriage of the parents legitimated the child. After the Revolution, American lawmakers began to follow the civil-law tradition. The 1785 Virginia statute was the first to reverse the common-law practice, and Louisiana continued its continental tradition through its civil codes of 1808 and 1825.[2]

Lack of reliable records, informal registration of births, and conflicting laws and customs encouraged nineteenth-century judges to adopt liberal standards of evidence when answering questions of legitimacy. In 1834 a Pennsylvania court declared that the court should "make every intendment in favor of the plaintiff's legitimacy, which was not necessarily excluded by proof." Judges also placed great faith in parental actions toward their children, especially parental statements acknowledging legitimacy. Several states changed their inheritance laws to accept the legitimization of children born outside of wedlock but made exceptions for the offspring of incestuous, bigamous, or adulterous unions. In Louisiana the civil law allowed a father to legitimize his bastard child by a formal statement before a notary, but not in the case of an "adulterous bastard." The Louisiana Code of 1808 defined adulterous bastards as those children "born from an unlawful connection between two persons who at the time the child was conceived were either of them, or both, connected by marriage with some other person." Such children could not be legitimated by the subsequent marriage of their parents. Nor could the natural father or mother bequeath property to their adulterous or incestuous children, even if acknowledged, beyond what was necessary for the maintenance of the child, "or to procure them an occupation or profession by which to support themselves." Should a parent attempt to make a bequest to his adulterous bastard beyond that allowed by the code, that "disposition . . . shall be null."[3]

Louisiana's adherence to the practices of its civil code complicated the

2. Grossberg, *Governing the Hearth,* 196–7, 201, 204, 211–2; Shammas, *Inheritance in America,* 71–2.

3. *Senser v. Bower,* 1 Pa. 450 (1834), quoted in Grossberg, *Governing the Hearth,* 201; ibid., 368, note 11; Louisiana Code of 1808, Art. 5, p. 44; Art. 46, p. 156; Art. 15, p. 212; and Art. 17, p. 212.

determination of Gaines's status. If Clark and Zulime Carrière had wed—both of them free from other contracts—and Myra was their child—born after their union—then her legitimacy was established, and by Louisiana law she would inherit, at a minimum, four-fifths of the Clark estate. It was not necessary for the 1811 will to mention Myra, since a Louisiana father could not disinherit his legitimate child. Conversely, if Clark and Zulime married, but their union was bigamous because Zulime's prior marriage to DesGrange was still valid, then Myra was an adulterous bastard and could never inherit from her father, even at his specific bequest. If, however, Zulime's marriage to DesGrange was invalid because he had been married (and not divorced) previously, a child of Daniel and Zulime might still inherit (even if no proof of the marriage existed) if the father had made a declaration of her legitimacy. And several witnesses swore that Clark had made such a declaration before he died.

Caroline's position increased the confusion. Although born before any marriage between Clark and Zulime, if she was their daughter (as she, Dr. Hulings, and Daniel Coxe claimed), then she could also be legitimate and entitled to share the estate with Myra. This assumes that Clark and Zulime married subsequent to her birth, both of them free to contract a legal marriage. In part, this explains why Gaines always claimed that Caroline was the daughter of DesGrange.

As the arguments presented in *Patterson v. Gaines* scrutinized Gaines's pretensions of legitimacy, they led to the concurrent question of the existence of a valid marriage between Zulime and Daniel Clark. English common law required a five-step process before a marriage could be considered valid: espousal (by formal contract); published banns; execution of the espousal contract in church; celebration; and sexual consummation. Yet eloping couples, dissenters, and impoverished suitors often ignored these provisions. Judges cited the failure to follow the prescribed format for legal marriages as the cause of property disputes, bigamy, and disruption of family continuity. In 1753 Lord Hardwick's Marriage Act made religious ceremonies compulsory in England and fixed formal requirements for parental consent, registration, and publication of banns for all legal unions. As a result marriage became an institution subject to strict statutory controls. Hardwick's act did not apply to Scotland, where Gretna Green, the first town over the border along the Great North Road, became the destination of eloping couples. English law recognized a Gretna Green marriage—no more than a simple statement before a witness (often the local blacksmith) of the intention to become man and wife—as valid, thus allowing couples wishing to be married but unwilling or unable to comply with the provisions of the Marriage Act an alternative.[4]

The Council of Trent had established similar restrictions on informal unions for civil-law countries. Eighteen years after it convened in 1545, the council issued the *Decretum de Reformatio,* declaring that marriages must be performed after the publishing of banns, before (but not necessarily by) a priest, and in the presence of two to three witnesses. Zulime's marriage in 1794 to Jerome DesGrange conformed to these requirements. Having brought witnesses to support his statements that he was a bachelor, a Roman Catholic, and a resident of the parish, DesGrange received a civil license to marry; after publication of banns (only two and not three, as was customary), the church authorities granted permission for the ceremony.[5]

As in colonial Louisiana, early English colonies tried to regulate marriages by requiring compliance with certain legal formalities, usually publication of banns and a requirement that a minister or justice of the peace perform the ceremony. An engaged couple posted their banns in a conspicuous place for a specified number of days before the actual wedding. Family-law historian Michael Grossberg terms banns a "community warning system" that allowed parents, guardians, or neighbors to prevent undesirable marriages. Yet banns appeared as an invasion of privacy to many post-Revolutionary couples, who preferred to use licenses as a means of registering (but not restricting) their unions. As a replacement for banns, licenses could still serve to announce both community and parental sanction of the union.[6]

As the mobility of individuals meshed with the growth of urban areas across the country, banns and licenses became less useful as a method of social regulation. Couples routinely flouted the community controls and married informally. Dissenters might question traditional religious practices; frontier couples might have no access to proper religious and/or lay

4. Stuart J. Stein, "Common-Law Marriage: Its History and Certain Contemporary Problems," *Journal of Family Law* 9 (1969): 274–6; Grossberg, *Governing the Hearth,* 65; *Marriage Act* (1753), 26 Geo. II, c. 33.

5. Stein, "Common-Law Marriage," 273; Marriage Record of Geronimo DesGrange and Zulime Carrière, reprinted in *Transcript of Record, Gaines v. City of New Orleans,* 2: 2141.

6. Grossberg, *Governing the Hearth,* 67, 77–8.

officials; and some couples might not be able to afford the marriage fee or simply dislike bureaucratic interference. The post-Revolutionary solution to these "irregular marriages" eased the rules governing proof of valid unions. As interpreted by American jurists, the common law emphasized the private nature of contracts, including marriage, and relied on self-regulation. Grossberg concludes that official recognition of irregular marriages "acted as a further step from the patriarchal families of the eighteenth century and a step toward the republican concept of the household as a voluntary collection of separate individuals."[7]

Demonstrating this altered standard, in 1816 William Tilghman, chief justice of the Pennsylvania State Supreme Court, reversed a lower-court ruling that denied a dower to a "common-law" widow. "We have no established church," he declared. "A certificate of the bishop, therefore, is out of the question. We have no law compelling the keeping of a register by all persons who perform the marriage ceremony. Our marriages are celebrated sometimes by clergymen, sometimes by justices of the peace, and sometimes before witnesses, without the intervention of clergymen or justices. . . . To hold a woman, therefore, to proof of her actual marriage might be productive of great inconvenience, without any advantage." Since the purported marriage of Clark and Zulime took place in Philadelphia, Justice Tilghman's decision meant that if Clark and Zulime exchanged vows before witnesses, they were legally married, with or without any record of the marriage being kept (assuming Zulime was free to marry).[8]

The federal structure of the United States government, which allowed each state to set its own marriage laws, spawned a variety of judicial interpretations of the validity of common-law marriages. Most state courts chose to follow either New York chancellor James Kent's ruling in *Fenton v. Reed* or Massachusetts chief justice Theophilus Parson's decision in *Milford v. Worcester*. In *Fenton*, Elizabeth Reed sought a pension from the Provident Society on the Revolutionary War record of her second husband, William Reed. Her first husband, John Guest, had deserted her in 1785, and she had remarried in 1792 after hearing rumors of Guest's death. Soon after the second marriage, the first husband returned but did not try to reclaim his wife. Guest died in 1800, and Elizabeth and William Reed continued to live together as man and wife until his death. Chancel-

7. Ibid., 83.
8. *Chambers v. Dickson*, 2 S. & R. 475, at 477 (Penn. 1816), quoted ibid., 79–80.

lor Kent held that during John Guest's lifetime, Elizabeth's marriage to William Reed was void, but that a valid common-law marriage existed for the years after Guest's death. "A marriage," he announced, "may be proved, in other cases, from cohabitation, reputation, acknowledgment of the parties, reception in the families, and other circumstances from which a marriage might be inferred. No formal solemnization . . . was requisite." One authority cited by the chancellor for his decision, *Reed v. Passer,* found that a witness's testimony of the fact of a marriage was sufficient to "raise a valid assumption of such a marriage." Gaines based her claim of legitimacy on the testimony of her aunt Sophia Despau that a marriage had occurred between Clark and Zulime, causing Chancellor Kent's criteria for establishing a common-law marriage to become an issue in the Gaines case.[9]

One year later, Chief Justice Parsons of the Massachusetts high court came to an opposite conclusion. His decision in *Milford* resolved a dispute between two towns over the support of paupers Stephen and Rhoda Temple (residents, respectively, of Worcester and Milford) and their six children. If a marriage existed, Worcester would be responsible for the support of the whole family, since matrimony conferred Stephen's residence on his wife. The couple had filed their intent to marry, and then stumbled across a justice of the peace in a tavern. When he refused to perform a ceremony for them, they exchanged vows in his presence and then lived together as man and wife. Justice Parson's decision nullified the marriage. Marriage might be a civil contract, but its nature required public supervision and sanction. In a statement that seems directed specifically at Zulime Carrière, Justice Parsons warned, "Every young woman of honor ought to insist on a marriage solemnized by a legal officer and shun the man who prates about marriage, condemned by human laws, as good in the sight of heaven. This cant, she may be assured, is a pretext for seduction; and if not condemned, will lead to dishonor and misery."[10]

Justices Kent and Parsons were both staunch Federalists seeking to use the law to maintain social order. Both emphasized the role of matrimony in preserving the stability of society. But Kent argued in *Fenton* that sanctioning irregular marriages provided the surest method of binding couples

9. *Fenton v. Reed,* 4 Johns 52 (N.Y. 1809), quoted in Stein, "Common-Law Marriage," 277; *Reed v. Passer,* Peakes Cases *nisi prius* 23 (1793), quoted ibid., 279.

10. *Milford v. Worcester,* 7 Mass. 4 (1810), quoted in Stein, "Common-Law Marriage," 277.

together. Marriage was a private act, not a public event that had to be monitored by the state. Parsons, in *Milford*, saw matrimony as a public responsibility, and believed that state guidelines for matrimony were necessary for the protection of society. Prevention of immorality, fraud, and the protection of property rights provided sufficient reasons for the state to ban irregular marriages. As the Gaines case developed, these two decisions would be cited by justices holding opposite opinions on the validity of any marriage between Daniel and Zulime.[11]

A legal marriage, formal or informal, between Zulime Carrière and Daniel Clark presupposed the invalidation of her union with DesGrange. Followers of the Gaines case in the popular press recognized Myra Gaines's characterization of DesGrange as a "confidence man," a status-conscious social climber posing as something he was not: the bachelor son of a French noble family. Myra's trial narrative played on fears aroused by reports in the sensational press of male bigamists who preyed on unsuspecting young women. Bigamy was a plot staple of sentimental fiction, used as a "moral signpost warning readers of the sexual dangers and illicit deceptions of urban life." By linking her mother's fate to that of the bigamist's victims, Myra gained sympathy for her mother.[12]

Bigamy, marrying one spouse while another mate still lived, was a canonical offense made a crime by both Parliament and American colonial assemblies. Considered by the courts as an "outrage upon public decency," bigamy became a common ingredient in American criminal codes, with harsh penalties following its exposure. Pennsylvania in 1705 ordered that bigamists be whipped, have their second union nullified, and be imprisoned for life. Despite the threat of such retribution, bigamous unions occurred frequently in the mobile structure of nineteenth-century American society. Many couples treated bigamy as an informal means of common-law divorce. Judicial divorce was expensive and, since courts recognized few grounds, was rarely granted. Most bigamists were never discovered; only when one party tried to end the relationship or filed an estate claim was the bigamous marriage revealed.[13]

Bigamy was hard to prove. Most communities were lax in keeping par-

11. Grossberg, *Governing the Hearth*, 72–3.

12. Timothy J. Gilfoyle, "The Hearts of Nineteenth-Century Men: Bigamy and Working-Class Marriage in New York City, 1800–1890," in *Prospects: An Annual of American Cultural Studies*, ed. Jack Salzman (Cambridge: Cambridge University Press, 1995), 19: 135–6.

13. Grossberg, *Governing the Hearth*, 120–1.

ish records of marriages. Substitution of licenses for banns meant fewer in a community knew of a proposed marriage, and the transience of the population made monitoring of sexual history difficult. In the Gaines case, DesGrange's first marriage allegedly took place in New York City. If he and Barbara D'Orsi did exchange vows, they appear to have considered their separation a common-law divorce, since both subsequently married other partners.[14]

Common-law states considered bigamous marriages void and their issue illegitimate. Texas and Louisiana, however, adopted the civil-law doctrine of "putative marriage," which became an added complication for the Gaines case. A putative marriage allowed that if one party to a marriage had acted in "good faith," not knowing that the other had a prior marriage, then the innocent victim and any children of the putative marriage were "entitled to the full civil benefits of matrimony, along with the first family." If Clark and Zulime believed Zulime's first marriage void, then any children of the second union were legitimate. Claiming a "putative marriage," Myra needed only to prove that Clark and Zulime thought their ceremony was legal.[15]

As judges attempted to determine the legality of irregular marriages, community, class, and sexual standards affected their decisions. In 1799 a North Carolina judge affirmed a marriage in which "there was . . . no positive proof . . . [but] the witnesses say she was a woman of irreproachable character before [she co-habited with her common-law husband]. If so, a presumption arises that she would not have co-habited with the other defendant unless a marriage had previously been solemnized." Myra Gaines would use this argument to support the existence of a marriage between her parents, and her opponents would try to blacken the character of Zulime, claiming that Clark would never have married his mistress.[16]

The post-Revolutionary judiciary understood that marriage was an unequal institution and demonstrated "solicitude for wronged female virtue." In 1869 a Pennsylvania judge validated a secret marriage between a University of Pennsylvania professor from an upper-class family and an Irish servant. "Marriage, followed by the birth of issue," he held, "lies at the very base of the social fabric. . . . We feel unwilling to suffer an acknowledged marriage and parentage of children to be overthrown by

14. Gilfoyle, "Hearts of Nineteenth-Century Men," 138.

15. Grossberg, *Governing the Hearth*, 345, note 40.

16. *Fetts v. Foster*, 2 Hayward 102 (N.C. 1799).

weak and inconclusive reasons drawn from the position in life, and from conduct readily explained by the circumstances of the parties." Denying that the professor's decision to hide his marriage from his family invalidated it, the court declared, "Mystery may surround its origins, suspicion may linger in its circumstances, and slight doubt may disturb its clearness, but the policy of the state demands that this relation should not be lightly discredited and the issue bastardized." Mystery surrounded Clark's relationship with Zulime, and the narrative created by their daughter emphasized the importance to society of the protection of marriage and family.[17]

The willingness to protect women from "male perfidy" and to see them as "paragons of wronged virtue" animated several of the justices who heard the Gaines case before the United States Supreme Court, but not all. In the course of the nineteenth century a decided shift occurred in judicial attitudes toward women plaintiffs seeking redress in breach-of-promise suits. As the century progressed, women came under increasing suspicion of being fortune hunters and mercenaries who sought lifetime support through the courts. After the middle of the century it became harder for a woman to sustain a breach-of-promise action, as the court's willingness to accept statements from friends and relatives as supporting evidence waned. By 1872 an Illinois court refused to grant a pension to a woman whose only proof of the supposed marriage was her own statement to her sister. The Gaines case demonstrates the midpoint of these opposing judicial attitudes, as the justices on the Supreme Court grappled with changing standards.[18]

Charles Patterson's willingness to answer the Gaineses' claim to the property he occupied provided the high court with its first opportunity to rule on the merit of Myra Gaines's assumption of legitimacy. *Patterson v. Gaines* moved quickly through the New Orleans circuit court. Based on the testimony presented in the depositions recorded in the old probate court suit, the trial judge ruled in Gaines's favor and ordered Patterson to turn over the disputed property. This decision by a Louisiana court surprised no one, since Patterson had reserved his defense for an appeal to the Supreme Court, an action supported by Myra and Edmund Gaines. The Gaineses hoped that a favorable decision by the appellate court on the

17. *De Armaell's Estate*, 2 Brew 239, at 246 (Penn. 1869), quoted in Grossberg, *Governing the Hearth*, 80.

18. Ibid., 49–57. For breach-of-promise suits, see *McPherson v. Ryan*, 59 Mich. 33 (1886) and *Walmsey v. Robinson*, 63 Ill. 41 (1872).

merits of the case would allow them to return to New Orleans and settle
with the remaining defendants.[19]

Arguments presented in trials provide clues about what a society considers
important public values. As the lawyers for both sides constructed their
courtroom stories before the Supreme Court, they drew on the story forms
most familiar and powerful in the culture of their time. The determination
of Myra's legitimacy became the central issue in *Patterson v. Gaines,* and
the attorneys sought to shape their narratives of events to conform to popular stereotypes found in the familiar romances of sentimental fiction.[20]

The narrative structure adopted by Myra's opponents evoked a vivid
mental picture of the "dark and adulterous intrigue" between Clark and
Zulime. "How often is it that the innocent offspring are made to suffer
for the acts of the parent?" began Henry May, counsel for Charles Patterson. The attorney's presentation spared neither parent. Clark's actions
demonstrated that he knew that Myra was "the fruit of an adulterous intercourse." The secrecy with which he guarded her birth, the haste with
which he "tore the tender infant from her mother's breast," refusing to
allow the child to "dwell under his roof," all testified to the illegitimacy
of Myra's birth. Henry May admitted that as Clark's affection for "his
natural child" increased he attempted to provide for her by conveying
property to Bellechasse, Delacroix, and Davis "on blind trust." Why
should he hazard the property designated for his "helpless and lawful
child" when he could guard her interests much more certainly by a will?
Only Clark's knowledge that Myra was not his lawful child could explain
his conduct. He knew that Louisiana law prohibited a father from be-
queathing his estate to an illegitimate child; that restriction forced him to
rely on the honor and conscience of his friends for his daughter's protection. May argued that Clark's desire to "efface the stain which his own
wild passions had placed upon his child at her birth" led him to perpetrate
a "pious but posthumous fraud" on his own family and make a will naming Myra his legitimate heir. Admitting that "there is evidence to prove
that Clark made a will some weeks before his death," his guilt as he con-

19. Decision of the Circuit Court of the United States, Eastern District of Louisiana,
in *Gaines and Wife v. Patterson,* reprinted in *Transcript of Record, Gaines v. City of New
Orleans,* 2: 1755.

20. Friedman, "Law, Lawyers, and Popular Culture," 1595; Korobkin, "Maintenance of Mutual Confidence," 13.

templated his "fraud on society" convinced him to destroy the will "with his own hands." His deathbed statements about its disposition were merely ravings caused by the "delirium of fever."[21]

Henry May painted Zulime as an adventuress and an unnatural mother—"a mother who, for the world's false esteem, would discard from her maternal breast two helpless infants, and never look again upon her own offspring; a mother who . . . stands convicted of adultery before her pretended marriage with Clark, and with bigamy afterwards; such a mother is above the judgment of human tribunals." Gaines was the innocent victim of this "web of destiny," but the "dreadful past" could not be changed, and the actions of her parents proclaimed her illegitimacy.[22]

Myra Gaines's attorneys were equally eloquent. Reverdy Johnson of Baltimore joined Walter Jones in summarizing the history of the Gaines case. "The annals of jurisprudence will probably not present again a cause so momentous as this," the attorneys began. Jones told the court that he would attempt to unravel the "exciting, extraordinary, and mysterious" events that surrounded the love affair between Clark and Zulime. Clark, "a man of handsome fortune," possessed a "well-balanced mind" and an "energy and perseverance . . . only surpassed by his almost unbounded hospitality and munificence." At the beginning of the century he met Zulime, "a lady of many charms, personal and intellectual." This "transcendently beautiful Creole" married "a dashing fellow of many pretensions and fine address" who had "wickedly imposed himself upon her and her family as an unmarried man," an action that brought "inexpressible suffering upon an innocent and confiding woman."[23]

Johnson continued Jones's flamboyant narration by describing the "intimacy" that developed between Clark and Zulime during DesGrange's absence from New Orleans. When "rumor with its thousand tongues" accused DesGrange of bigamy, Clark's passion for Zulime led him to propose, but she would not accept until proof of the invalidity of her former marriage could be obtained. Zulime and her sister left for Philadelphia where they met Dr. James Gardette, "a gentleman of high respectability," who assured the sisters that rumor had not lied—DesGrange had married

21. *Patterson v. Gaines*, 6 Howard 550 (1848), at 576, 578, 581.

22. Ibid., 581.

23. The arguments of Gaines's attorneys are not reported in the record of *Patterson v. Gaines*, but their statements are repeated in Alexander Walker, *A Full Report of the Great Gaines Case in the suit of Myra Clark Gaines vs. Chew, Relf, & Others* . . . (New Orleans, 1850), 7–8.

another woman in New York and he, Gardette, had been a witness to the ceremony. Clark then exclaimed, "Now you have no longer any reason to refuse being married to me!" Their marriage took place immediately, according to the laws of Pennsylvania, but Clark insisted that their union "should be preserved as a profound secret" until Zulime obtained a judicial annulment of her former marriage. At this point the two separated: Clark left for Europe and Zulime returned to New Orleans.[24]

Johnson and Jones recognized that Clark's refusal to acknowledge his wife was inconsistent with the picture they drew of his character. It was, however, "by no means a solitary and isolated instance . . . of the most reprehensible weakness and littleness combined with the most exalted and admirable attributes." Reports that Clark had "addressed Miss Caton of Maryland," a lady of "renowned family and distinguished accomplishments," deeply distressed Zulime, and she and her sister quickly set out for Philadelphia to find "written evidence of her marriage." Unable to locate the priest who had performed the ceremony, Zulime "was advised by those in whom she had misplaced her confidence" that she could never prove her marriage if Clark "was disposed to contest it." She then married Dr. Gardette and lived with him until his death in 1831, always recognized and received in "society of the highest respectability." In later life, the attorneys suggested, Clark "dwelt with the emotions of keen regret upon the train of circumstances which prevented him from doing complete justice to his injured wife and child, the victims of his caprice, . . . his inordinate vanity and pride, and overleaping ambition." He had listened with "blind confidence to the wicked machinations of his professed friends," and his "beloved wife" had been "driven from his side by his own rash folly." Only by recognizing Myra, the "sole offspring" of their marriage, could Clark soothe the "anguish which tortur[ed] him continually."[25]

Johnson and Jones concluded by affirming the determination of Myra Clark Gaines to remove the stain of bastardy from her name. "Every petty circumstance that could possibly be used" to defeat the interests of their client had been tried; ridicule in "every shape and form that the ingenuity of the parties could invent" had been used; yet Gaines was undeterred in the pursuit of her rights. Her attorneys admitted that the "peculiarity of her position and the novelty of her case" had thrown Myra before the public in "an unusual attitude to be occupied by females." But, they urged,

24. Ibid., 9.
25. Ibid., 10.

her public notoriety should not be grounds to deny her legal rights, "from the possession of which she has so long been legally debarred."[26]

Not all members of the Supreme Court heard the arguments in *Patterson v. Gaines*. Chief Justice Taney excused himself because his brother-in-law, Francis Scott Key, had represented Mrs. Gaines in an earlier hearing before the Court. Mr. Justice Catron did not hear the case because of illness, but the record provides no reason for the absence of Mr. Justice McLean. Of the six justices who did hear the arguments, no dissent is recorded to the opinion written and delivered by Justice James Wayne. Justice Wayne became a great partisan of Myra Clark Gaines and his first opinion in a Gaines case demonstrated that his sympathies lay with the "lone woman fighting valiantly for her rights."[27]

James Wayne was born in Savannah, Georgia, in 1790, the twelfth child of a wealthy rice planter. After serving in the Georgia congressional delegation and on the Georgia supreme court, he was appointed by President Andrew Jackson to the United States Supreme Court in 1835. At forty-five, Wayne was the youngest justice and the first to be born after the adoption of the Constitution. His handsome appearance and elegant manners made him a desirable addition to the Washington elite, and he and his wife were prominent figures on the social circuit. A visitor to the high court in 1850 described Wayne as "an exceedingly handsome man—about five feet, ten inches high, of stout but graceful figure, ruddy complexion, fine teeth, and clustering wavy hair, now mingled with gray." The "model of an elegant, cultivated, and courtly gentleman," his "overflowing courtesy" made Wayne a favorite with the ladies but not with all court observers. His selection excited criticism from Whig newspapers in his home state. Characterizing Wayne as a "second-rate lawyer . . . [and] a third rate judge," the *Columbus (Georgia) Enquirer* blamed his appointment on the "wages of political sin and sycophancy." Other commentators reserved judgment. Boston's *Mercantile Journal* noted that "Judge Wayne has always been a distinguished politician and on that account, perhaps, the nomination is objectionable. . . . He has many excellent qualities, however."[28]

26. Ibid.
27. *Patterson v. Gaines*, 605.
28. Alexander A. Lawrence, *James Moore Wayne: Southern Unionist* (Chapel Hill: University of North Carolina Press, 1943), 7, 83, 128–30; ibid., quoting *Columbus (Ga.) Enquirer*, Jan. 23, 1835, 80; *Boston Mercantile Journal*, Jan. 12, 1835, 81; and *New York*

Wayne served on the Supreme Court for thirty-two years. During that time he authored 135 majority opinions (not a large number) and issued twenty-five dissents. Comments on his opinions varied. The *Washington (D.C.) Daily Morning Chronicle* considered him "extremely conscientious in his opinions" and praised the "great personal attention and study" he brought to his decisions. The *Southern Quarterly Review* disagreed: "the learned justice's style, bad as is that of some of his associates, is still worse. . . . It is overloaded with words; scarcely any of his sentences convey a distinct idea; and some of them are quite beyond the pale of criticism." A measured biography of Wayne concluded that he had not been "one of the great men on the Court," but had been no worse than most of the justices who served during his tenure. Alexander Lawrence wrote that Wayne's common sense made him "particularly effective"; he does seem to have possessed more ability than most credited.[29]

Wayne's judicial philosophy indicated the direction of his rulings in the Gaines case. A few years before he joined the high court, a colleague in Congress had accused Wayne of "entertaining advanced views" on the nature of government. The judge drew this criticism by declaring that the national government was "formed by the people in their aggregate character and without any reference to their political being as members of separate and independent communities." Wayne's opinions illustrate this commitment to judicial nationalism. In *Dodge v. Woolsey* Wayne explained that "[t]he foundation of the right of citizens of different states to sue each other in the courts of the United States is not an unworthy jealousy of the impartiality of the state tribunals. It has a higher aim and purpose. It is to make the people think and feel . . . that their relations to each other were protected by the strictest justice, administered in courts independent of all local control or connection with the subject matter of the controversy between the parties of a suit." Myra Gaines certainly agreed.[30]

Legal scholars call the prevailing focus of appellate opinions in the

---

Tribune, Feb. 4, 1850, and Mar. 17, 1857, 81. Wayne's biographer argues that his candidacy for the Supreme Court was aided by his kindness to Peggy Eaton, whose part he had taken in the Cabinet War and "whose vanity he sometimes flattered with complimentary speeches." Lawrence, *James Moore Wayne*, 79.

29. *Washington (D.C.) Daily Morning Chronicle*, July 6, 1867, quoted in Lawrence, *James Moore Wayne*, 114–5; *Southern Quarterly Review* 16 (1850): 501.

30. *Gales and Seaton's Debates*, 22nd Cong., 2nd sess., 1833, p. 1886, Feb. 28, 1833; *Dodge v. Woolsey*, 18 Howard 331 (1856).

nineteenth century an "instrumental" conception of law—that is, judges tried to use law as an "instrument" of change. An associate on the Supreme Court, Justice John Campbell (another supporter of Myra Clark Gaines) commented that Wayne "regarded the constitution and law of the country as an expanding and improving law and was willing to make a precedent to make possible the conditions of the development of the country, though the letter of the constitution had not provided for the precedent." As the appellate courts developed a new concept of domestic relations law, judges like Wayne used their opinions to create new forms of legal protection for women, families, and children. "No Judge on the bench," wrote Campbell, "so habitually acted on the principal of developing the law of the nation through the courts of judication" as did Wayne.[31]

Wayne's opinion in *Patterson v. Gaines* reflected the direction of the developing structure of domestic relations law that saw women as a dependent class with a special claim on judicial protection. As a contract between individuals, marriage presupposed equality between the contracting parties. Yet judges like Wayne recognized that "the delicacy of [the female] sex, which happily in this country gives man so much advantage . . . in the intercourse which leads to matrimonial engagements, requires for its protection and continuance the aid of the laws."[32]

This judicial philosophy guided Justice Wayne's declaration that the evidence of Madame Despau, who testified that she had witnessed the marriage between her sister and Clark, satisfactorily established proof of the marriage. The numerous statements by Clark's friends that they thought him a bachelor were insufficient to "impeach the testimony of one witness swearing positively to the fact of the marriage." Madame Despau's testimony added to the "declarations of the father, and his affectionate treatment of his child from her birth to his death," provided "conclusive proof" of Myra's legitimacy.[33]

Turning to the issue of Zulime's marriage to DesGrange, Wayne relied on the testimony of Madame Louise Benguerel. Madame Benguerel and her husband knew DesGrange well; her husband had been one of the wit-

31. Lawrence M. Friedman, *A History of American Law* (New York: Simon & Schuster, 1973), passim; Eulogy of James Moore Wayne by Justice John Campbell, *New Orleans Daily Picayune*, July 7, 1867, p. 2.

32. Michael Grossberg, "Crossing Boundaries: Nineteenth-Century Domestic Relations law and the Merger of Family and Legal History," *American Bar Foundation Research Journal* 4 (1985): 810.

33. *Patterson v. Gaines*, 589.

nesses who swore that DesGrange was unmarried before he received a license for his marriage to Zulime. In her testimony, Madame Benguerel remembered that the accusations of bigamy against DesGrange "were notoriously known in New Orleans." When the Benguerels reproached him "for his baseness in imposing on Zulime," DesGrange endeavored to excuse himself by saying that when he married Zulime he had "abandoned his lawful wife and never intended to see her again." This indirect confession of bigamy by DesGrange satisfied Wayne that Zulime's first marriage was invalid.[34]

Justice Wayne's opinion overflowed with sympathy for the beautiful Creole. The Pennsylvania marriage of Clark and Zulime needed no "sentence of dissolution" by a Louisiana court of Zulime's union with DesGrange to be a true marriage. Wayne recognized, however, that the lack of such a judicial determination of the nullity of the first marriage would be adequate reason for a man of Clark's "pride and temper" to refuse to acknowledge his wife until a "judicial sentence had restored [her] to the unequivocal condition enjoyed by her before the imposition of DesGrange." The justice recognized that "men of the world shun more than anything else the exposure of their follies." Noting that many men had died without disclosing an imprudent marriage, and "women have been found to bear it," Wayne concluded that concealment alone was not enough to "repeal any presumption" of legitimacy.[35]

Zulime's subsequent marriage to Dr. Gardette, although "inexcusable conduct," was also insufficient to discredit her marriage to Clark. The "irritation and impositions to which this female had been subjected from her girlhood, and her well founded fears of the fidelity of Mr. Clark," increased the justice's compassion for Zulime. She was, Wayne knew, "very deficient in her apprehension of the sacredness of marriage"; which did raise "a suspicion against the marriage," but that suspicion could not be allowed to "prevail over the legitimacy of her child." The justice concluded "this most curious and original chapter of domestic life," by declaring Myra Clark Gaines the legitimate daughter of Daniel Clark by a "lawful marriage contracted in Pennsylvania," and the "forced heir" of four-fifths of his estate.[36]

34. Deposition of Louise Benguerel, May 27, 1836, reprinted in *Transcript of Record, Gaines v. City of New Orleans,* 2: 1876; *Patterson v. Gaines,* 598.
35. *Patterson v. Gaines,* 592–3.
36. Ibid., 597, 602.

Justice Wayne delivered his opinion to a packed courtroom. The number of spectators fascinated news reporters present, who considered it "a thrilling scene . . . quite unusual in the presence of that solemn and dignified bench." Daniel Webster, Henry Clay, and many other prominent lawyers and congressional leaders filled the tiny chamber in the Capitol basement. The eminent jurists present approved of Wayne's opinion, terming it a decision that "illustrat[ed] the high character and value of the Supreme Judicial Bench and the efficiency of the laws in settling the rights of property." Gaines sat in the midst of a group of admiring ladies, accepting the congratulations of her supporters. Twelve years of litigation had earned her the title to four-fifths of two small lots in New Orleans. She hoped this decision would be the key that unlocked the legal barriers that had blocked her way for so long.[37]

37. *Virginia Historical Register* 1 (1848): 43; Lawrence, *James Moore Wayne*, 125; *New York Times*, Mar. 15, 1861, p. 1.

IX

The Supreme Court Changes Its Mind

In 1849 Myra and Edmund Gaines returned to New Orleans fresh from their victory in the Supreme Court. With Zachary Taylor in the White House, the general was once again back in favor, and his old friend reappointed him commander of the Department of the West. The Gaineses soon brought the *Patterson* decision to the new federal courthouse in New Orleans. The old, dingy, two-story building on Canal Street—the scene of the earlier litigation—had been demolished the year before. The new courthouse bustled with sheriffs, clerks, advocates, clients, witnesses, jurors, and assorted hangers-on. Once Myra Gaines reappeared, the courthouse became even busier.[1]

Justice Wayne's opinion in *Patterson* held that Relf and Chew had no authority under the 1811 will to sell any property from the estate; their role as executors had ended, and the deeds they had issued were void. Technically, *Patterson* applied only to the land occupied by Charles Patterson, but Myra intended to use that decision as a *res adjudicata* (a closed judgment, which allowed no appeal), against all the other defendants who still held property bought from the Clark estate. She and her attorneys expected that the New Orleans courts would, at last, follow the lead of the Supreme Court. They would be disappointed.

The Supreme Court's ruling in *Patterson* stunned the Crescent City community. New Orleans citizens were convinced that the "infamous"

---

1. Castellanos, *New Orleans As It Was*, 150; Hall, *Manhattaner in New Orleans*, 75.

ruling, the "disgraceful and outrageous fraud," must have been imposed on the court by an "unscrupulous, scheming, and unstinted perjury." Their suspicions appeared vindicated when Charles Patterson revealed the collusive character of his defense in the Supreme Court. Desperate to bring the case to trial, Myra and her husband had sought one of the many defendants who would agree to abandon the delaying tactics and answer their bill of complaint. When Louisiana state supreme court judge François-Xavier Martin angrily declined their offer, the Gaineses turned to Patterson. They promised that he would not lose his land if he agreed to provide an opportunity for the United States Supreme Court to rule on the merits of their case. If the court decided against Patterson, Myra and the general assured him that they would bear all costs, including lawyers' fees, and that his property would not be taken. Soon after *Patterson v. Gaines* concluded, the Gaineses expressed their appreciation for Patterson's willingness to "meet us upon the MERITS OF THE CASE." Gaines and her husband realized that Patterson had "incurred the displeasure of many of the lawless holders of the estate," and they assured him that his "long and strenuous opposition," though often "harassing," was "unavoidable, and perhaps essential" to the "full and perfect establishment of our rights . . . without some years more of acrimonious controversy."[2]

All New Orleans rose in indignation at the strategy Myra and General Gaines had adopted to bring their case to trial. In later testimony, Patterson swore that the Gaineses had urged him to "use my best exertions with the aid of the best counsel, to make every defense in my power to this suit." In his opinion, the couple had acted out of a desire to come to a speedy trial with one of the defendants. Patterson noted that when his attorneys wished to enter the record of the probate court as evidence, Myra and the general overruled the objections of their own attorneys and insisted that all possible evidence be introduced—that way, their victory would be more "glorious."[3]

The Gaineses may have intended for Patterson to mount an earnest defense, but, earnest or not, most New Orleanians considered the suit collusive, and their belief tainted the victory. Most residents thought the

2. Speech of Colonel Preston, reprinted in Walker, *Full Report of the Great Gaines Case*, 41; Edmund Pendleton Gaines and Myra Clark Gaines to Charles Patterson, May 11, 1848, reprinted in *Transcript of Record, Gaines v. Relf, Chew, and Others*, 1147.

3. Charles Patterson, deposition of June 19, 1849, reprinted in *Transcript of Record, Gaines v. Relf, Chew, and Others*, 678.

Gaineses and Patterson had conspired to obtain a verdict from the Supreme Court that would allow Myra Gaines to foreclose on property owned by many eminent citizens of New Orleans. Tempers flared, and threats were made against Myra's life. When she appeared in public, menacing crowds surrounded her carriage. On one occasion an angry mob blocked her progress down a New Orleans street. Curses filled the air, and scowling faces pressed against the carriage windows. Urged by Myra, the shaken coachman whipped his horses into motion and quickly bore her out of danger. As a souvenir of this and other such occurrences, Myra kept her small silk bonnet with a bullet hole shot cleanly through the brim.[4]

During 1849 Myra and Edmund Gaines continued to live at the St. Charles Hotel while they and their attorneys prepared new briefs summoning the occupants of houses and land once owned by Daniel Clark to New Orleans courtrooms. It was the slow season in New Orleans. Summer months could be dangerous, and in early June cholera struck General Gaines. Put to bed on June 5, the old soldier did not have long to live. New Orleans newspapers described the deathbed scene for their readers. The general assured his aide that he had "nothing on his conscience" and was not afraid to die. "I am an old man," he admitted calmly, "and have probably lived long enough." His last words were for Myra—"My dear wife, farewell. You cannot imagine how much I love you."[5]

"With infinite pain," the *Daily Picayune* recorded the death of Edmund Pendleton Gaines at 3:00 A.M. on June 6, 1849. For two days visitors thronged the Ladies' Parlor of the St. Charles where the general's body lay in state, "dressed in the full uniform of his rank with his battlesword buckled at his side." The *Picayune* suggested that stores and businesses close during the funeral ceremony as a mark of the city's respect. After a public funeral on June 8, a military procession escorted the body to the depot of the Pontchartrain railroad. Following a rail journey of one hour, the soldiers placed the general aboard the steamer *Oregon,* which carried him to Mobile for burial. Later in 1849, the War Department announced that a new post on the farthest reaches of the Mississippi River would be christened Fort Gaines.[6]

4. Harmon, *Famous Case of Myra Clark Gaines,* 318. Nolan Harmon attributes this story to his father who heard it from Myra Gaines.

5. "Death of Major-Gen. Gaines," *New Orleans Daily Picayune,* June 6, 1849, p. 1.

6. Ibid.; "Funeral Honors to the Late Gen. Gaines," *New Orleans Daily Picayune,* June 7, 1849, p. 2; "The Funeral of Gen. Gaines," *New Orleans Daily Picayune,* June 8, 1849, p. 2; Silver, *Edmund Pendleton Gaines,* 270–1.

No report of the general's death or funeral service in the New Orleans papers mentions Myra, nor did the Reverend Theodore Clapp make more than a slight reference to the grieving widow in his funeral oration. News stories reviewed the military service of Edmund Gaines, glossing over the Mexican War period to express the city's gratitude for "his devoted patriotism" during his long service in Louisiana. Reverend Clapp's only allusion to Myra came when he reminded his listeners that Gaines's character was "never tarnished by the slightest taint of dishonor." Such a character was "worth more than all the silver and gold in the universe. Contrasted with such a character . . . how insignificant are the boastful possessions of worldly ambition," he concluded.[7]

Myra Gaines had no time to grieve for her husband. Her opponents decided that, notwithstanding the adverse decision in *Patterson,* she was vulnerable. When called to surrender the property she claimed, her defiant antagonists, still led by Richard Relf and Beverly Chew, decided to fight. No more delays, postponements, or demurrers; now the case would come to trial on its merits, but this time with real opposition. Each side began a desperate search for new evidence to support its claims. Between May and August of 1849 more than one hundred depositions were taken. Myra's aged aunts again gave evidence. Sophia Despau, claiming her age as seventy-one (which would make her only seven at her wedding in 1785), repeated her story of Zulime's marriage; her sister Rose, age eighty-three, added her testimony. For the last time, Colonel Davis and Daniel Coxe, both now eighty-one, appeared in a Gaines lawsuit.

One witness never testified—neither side ever called Zulime Carrière. The little evidence available about Myra's mother provides an ambiguous picture of the woman the newspapers portrayed as a betrayed and abandoned wife. After Zulime married Dr. Gardette in 1808, the couple lived in Philadelphia until 1829. Numerous witnesses attested to their social prominence. One acquaintance described the Gardettes as "genteel and respectable people," and his wife added that Zulime was "a kind and affectionate stepmother" with no "slur on her character." Dr. Gardette's daughter (by an earlier marriage) disagreed. Adile Gardette Burnos was nine years old when her father married Zulime. She resented her stepmother, whom Adile blamed for destroying her own relationship with Dr.

---

7. "Remarks Made at the Funeral of General Gaines by Reverend Theodore Clapp," *New Orleans Daily Picayune,* June 10, 1849, p. 1.

Gardette. Zulime was "always very unkind . . . and unjust." Adile complained that she had "suffered greatly under her," and at the first opportunity, she "went away never to return." Although she and her father corresponded for two years after her departure in 1817, she heard nothing more from him from 1819 until his death in 1831.[8]

In 1829 the Gardettes left Philadelphia for Bordeaux, and Zulime remained there after her husband's death in August 1831. Friends in Philadelphia, New Orleans, and various French cities sent Zulime gossipy letters filled with family news and details of visits and social events. The only children mentioned in the surviving letters are those of Zulime and Dr. Gardette. In 1835 Zulime left France for New Orleans, where she joined her son, also Dr. James Gardette, who had established a successful dentistry practice in the Crescent City.[9]

Zulime's return to New Orleans came at an opportune time for her daughter. No indication appears in the trial records that Zulime and Myra communicated before the widow's arrival in the city, but they certainly made contact immediately afterwards. On May 7, 1836, "Madame Maria Julie Carrière, widow Gardette" transferred to her daughter "Myra Clark Whitney" all the "right, title, interest, [or] claim" that Zulime had, or might have in the future, to the "estate, property, or succession of Daniel Clark." This assignment did not indicate by what right Zulime might claim the estate of Clark; neither did she call herself the widow of Clark. The document was not registered with a notary in New Orleans for eight years. On June 10, 1844, Zulime signed another document prepared by Myra's attorneys, accepting a "community interest" in the estate of Daniel Clark as his widow. She signed the acceptance as "Marie Zulime Carrière,

8. Émileus Braiser, deposition of July 6, 1849, reprinted in *Transcript of Record, Gaines v. Relf, Chew, and Others,* 546; Elizabeth Braiser, deposition of Oct. 26, 1849, reprinted in *Transcript of Record, Gaines v. City of New Orleans,* 2: 1417; Émile B. Gardette, *Biographical Notice of (the Late) James Gardette, Surgeon Dentist of Philadelphia* (Philadelphia, 1850), 22–3, pamphlet belonging to the Henry Dilworth Gilpin Papers of the Historical Society of Pennsylvania, vol. 29, no. 4; deposition of Adile Tauzia [Gardette] Bournos, June 19, 1849, *Myra Clark Gaines v. F. D. Delacroix,* General Case Files no. 2619, National Archives, Southwest Region, Fort Worth, Tex.

9. L. née Bouligny to Zulime Gardette, Mar. 3, 1833, June 16, 1833, July 1, 1833, and Aug. 4, 1833, reprinted in *Transcript of Record, Gaines v. City of New Orleans,* 2: 2150–3; Fanny Duchaufour to Zulime Gardette, Oct. 22 [1833 or 1834], Nov. 28, 1833, ibid., 2: 2155–6; S. de Raffinac to Zulime Gardette, July 20 [1834 ?], Oct. 19, 1834, ibid., 2: 2150.

V've [widow of] Clark." Four days later notary William Christy also recorded the 1836 assignment.[10]

These legal devices, intended to eliminate any question of Zulime's claim on the Clark estate, demonstrate that Gaines and her mother were in cordial contact, although there is nothing more in the record of the Gaines case or in Myra or Zulime's letters to characterize their relationship. Anna Clyde Plunkett, granddaughter of one of Gaines's attorneys, claimed that Gaines had "little sympathy" for her mother and felt "only hot resentment of what her mother had brought on her." Plunkett's memoir of her grandfather, Franklin Perin, suggested that Zulime was "unpredictable, unstable, and easily confused." Family stories of her grandfather's role in the Great Gaines Case formed the basis of Plunkett's memoir. Written more than one hundred years after Zulime's death when Plunkett was in her seventies, its reliability is questionable. According to his granddaughter, Perin believed that Relf and Chew never called Zulime as a witness because they feared she would convincingly proclaim herself Clark's widow. Perin, however, never called Zulime because he feared the "charmingly stupid" Creole would become flustered and deny any marriage to Clark. Plunkett's memoir declared that Perin met Zulime just before her death and found her a "broken, bewildered woman, older than her years, possessing all the pathetic signs of an aging woman who had drunk too deeply of life, depending solely upon physical charms . . . with no backlog of intelligence, culture, or talent." Few traces remained of the "overwhelming beauty of face and body of the Lorelei whose siren had lured Daniel Clark to the rocks."[11]

In January 1850 Gaines's opponents attempted to take Zulime's testimony. They submitted questions to Gaines's attorneys for Zulime to answer under oath, but apparently the solicitors never gave the questions to her. She did make a statement—not under oath and not subject to cross-examination—that was published as part of a summary of the evidence in 1850. In this statement she corroborated the testimony of her sister (Mme. Despau) about her relationship to Daniel Clark. According to Zulime, both Caroline and Myra were her daughters; Caroline's father, however,

10. Donation by Madame Gardette of her Interest and Title in and to the Estate of Daniel Clark to Madame Myra Clark Whitney, May 7, 1836, recorded June 14, 1844, reprinted in *Transcript of Record, Gaines v. Hennen,* 881; Acceptance of Community by Marie Zulime Carrière, V've Clark, June 10, 1844, reprinted in *Transcript of Record, Gaines v. City of New Orleans,* 2: 1747.

11. Plunkett, *Corridors by Candlelight,* 63.

was not Clark but Jerome DesGrange. Zulime claimed to have met Clark in 1802 or 1803, after the publication of notices of DesGrange's bigamy. She said she had married Clark in 1802 in Philadelphia and returned to New Orleans to press bigamy charges against her former husband. Des-Grange's escape from prison foiled that attempt. Since Clark insisted that Zulime's marriage to DesGrange be declared void before their own union could be revealed, she brought suit against DesGrange in 1806 and received a judicial declaration of nullity.[12]

Zulime's statement also explained her actions after Myra's birth. Clark's continued refusal to announce their marriage "fretted and irritated" Zulime, and she became seriously alarmed when reports reached her that Clark was courting Miss Caton of Baltimore. Upon his return from Washington (in 1807, just before the duel with Governor Claiborne) Zulime reported their relationship altered. "Instead of meeting me with that feeling of affection he had ever evinced towards me, his manner was entirely changed," she insisted. Gossip had deceived Clark about Zulime's conduct during their separation, and, she declared, "[h]e reproached me . . . that my conduct in his absence had been of such a nature as would ever prevent his promulgating his marriage with me." Clark's "undeserved" slurs angered Zulime, who became "excessively indignant" and accused him of using gossip as an excuse to avoid acknowledging her as his wife so that he could marry another, more socially important woman. Dramatically, Zulime announced that "as much as I loved him . . . did I now hate him [and] we must part forever."[13]

Zulime believed that "those whom [she] had regarded as [her] friends" maliciously spread false tales of her misconduct, designed to "produce a breach" between her and Clark. Their "diabolical plan" succeeded. When Zulime and her sister sailed for Philadelphia they could find no proof of the marriage. Daniel Coxe confirmed the rumors of Clark's engagement to Louisa Caton and disclosed that, although Clark had told him of the private marriage, Zulime could never prove it, "if Mr. Clark was disposed to contest it."[14]

Zulime's statement asserted that Daniel Coxe brought Dr. Gardette to visit her and encouraged her to accept Gardette's proposal. "Such was my situation," she explained, "that I was induced to marry him." Two months

12. Walker, *Full Report of the Great Gaines Case*, 83.
13. Ibid., 83–4.
14. Ibid., 84.

later, Clark appeared in Philadelphia to ask "my forgiveness for having for a moment believed those calumnies that my enemies had circulated against me." Too late, Zulime replied, and "his grief can well be imagined when I told him . . . I had been married to Dr. Gardette two months." A distraught Clark assured Zulime that their daughter Myra would remain under his protection and that he would make a will declaring her his legitimate child and heiress of his "immense estate."[15]

Caroline, Zulime claimed, was DesGrange's child, but when Clark had married her he had promised "that he would act always the part of a father" to Caroline nonetheless. When Daniel Coxe took Caroline to old Mrs. Clark, proclaiming her as Clark's "natural child," the announcement "shocked" Zulime. Caroline's birth in Philadelphia was, Zulime explained, the result of her "delicate" health prior to the child's birth. Claiming that she had been "advised by our physician to travel"—which, despite her assertions to the contrary, seems a made-up excuse for getting out of town to bear an illegitimate child—Zulime and Sophia journeyed to Baltimore and Philadelphia, where Caroline was born two months prematurely. "Not having any milk to nourish my infant," Zulime left Caroline in Philadelphia in the charge of "an intimate friend," intending to "return for her the following year." Her statement does not reveal if she ever saw Caroline again.[16]

According to Zulime, she and Clark remained in contact after their separation. In 1812 she claimed that Clark wrote to tell her that the Davis family had returned to Philadelphia, taking Myra with them. Although Clark had not intended, he said, to allow Myra to leave New Orleans, the tears and pleadings of Mrs. Davis had convinced him to accept her departure. Zulime then frequently visited Myra in the Davis home and even hoped to take the child into her new household. Colonel Davis dissuaded her, insisting that Mrs. Davis was "devotedly attached" to the child, who believed the Davises to be her parents. "It would be cruel to undeceive her," the colonel protested. If Zulime would relinquish her child, and "never speak of Myra" as her daughter, Colonel Davis promised to "leave [Myra] all his fortune, which was estimated to be near $600,000." Otherwise, although Davis "knew Myra was a legitimate child," Myra would be considered illegitimate, since the marriage had never been acknowledged. Davis further informed Zulime that Clark "had died insolvent" without

15. Ibid.
16. Ibid.

enough funds to pay the debts of the estate. Pressed by Davis, Zulime consented. "I sacrificed my feelings for her future," she proclaimed.[17]

Zulime's statement is not supported by the letters exchanged between Clark and his various correspondents, nor do the trial records of the ecclesiastical court in 1802 or the civil courts in 1805 and 1806 corroborate her story. Depositions from Davis and Coxe also contradict it in important ways. Zulime's tale of the star-crossed lovers played no part in any judicial decision made in the Gaines case. Subjected to no cross-examination, it never appeared as evidence in any trial. The statement seems designed solely for publication, and may well have been written by Gaines to answer the defamation of her mother's character unveiled in the opposition arguments in *Patterson v. Gaines*. Newspapers adopted Zulime's version, and several years later it became the basis for the Beadle Dime Novel *Myra, Child of Adoption*.[18]

Zulime died in September 1853, and the obituary notices that appeared in newspapers from New Orleans to New York evince Gaines's successful portrayal of her mother as a "heroine of [a] romance in real life." The *New-York Daily Times* followed Zulime's statement precisely as it recounted the "intensely interesting" background of the Gaines case. Its obituary concluded by praising Myra Clark Gaines, who had "prosecuted her claim to the property of Daniel Clark, as his lawful heir, with a zeal, earnestness, and energy, which have rarely been equaled in the annals of litigation."[19]

Lacking testimony from the person most able to resolve the question of Myra's legitimacy, both sides in the lawsuit redoubled their efforts to locate new evidence and witnesses to bolster their interpretations of the chain of events. And when the trial of *Gaines v. Relf, Chew, and Others* opened in 1850, both sides had found surprising new information. Three sets of documents were introduced at this point. Usually called the "ecclesiastical record," the "mutilated record," and the "Latin certificate," the documents became the center of new controversy.

Myra and General Gaines had long sought the record of the 1802

17. Ibid., 84.
18. Motion by Defendants, Jan. 22, 1850, *Gaines v. Relf, Chew, and Others*, reprinted in *Transcript of Record, Gaines v. City of New Orleans*, 2: 2042.
19. *New Orleans Weekly Delta*, Sept. 25, 1853, p. 7; *New-York Daily Times*, Sept. 29, 1853, p. 6.

church trial of DesGrange. In 1840 the general employed C. W. Drechsler to make a "very extensive and most diligent search" for a copy of the prosecution of Jerome DesGrange for bigamy. Drechsler reported failure; all Spanish records of such proceedings had been removed by Spanish authorities to Spain or Cuba after the transfer of Louisiana in 1803. The few papers left in the city were lost or in "bad condition" from fire damage. Drechsler also searched the files of the *Moniteur de la Louisiane,* the only newspaper published in New Orleans up to 1804, and found that volume three, covering the suspected period, was missing.[20]

In 1849 the missing record reappeared, discovered in the archives of the St. Louis Cathedral "in one of the armoires" by Archbishop Antoine Blanc. Father Blanc admitted that he had "never found any other similar record among these archives," but he believed the document genuine. The record of the bigamy trial included the testimony of Barbara Jeanbelle D'Orsi and the seamstress Maria Yllar, both of whom denied marriage with DesGrange; the testimony of Marie Julie Carrière stating that she did not believe the reports of her husband's (DesGrange) bigamy; and a statement of innocence from Jerome DesGrange himself. Gaines's response to the ecclesiastical record called the document an obvious forgery, planted in the cathedral archives for Bishop Blanc to find. Both sides introduced notaries, engravers, and other handwriting experts who questioned or supported the record's veracity.[21]

Lawyers for Relf and Chew next introduced the mutilated record of the two suits by Zulime against DesGrange in 1805 and 1806. The first petition asked for "alimony" on grounds of desertion, and the default judgment granted Zulime $500 per year. The defendants stressed that this ruling meant that Zulime had admitted in 1805 that she still considered herself the wife of DesGrange. Gaines's answer countered that what Zulime really wanted from the court was a divorce, and DesGrange's failure to respond to her petition was the reason for the default judgment. In support, her attorneys offered the fragmented record from the court files of 1806. Unfortunately, the petition of Zulime in this case could not be found, but this time DesGrange's answer contended that no damages could be assessed until the court ruled on the existence of their marriage.

20. C. W. Drechsler, deposition of Apr. 24, 1840, reprinted in *Transcript of Record, Gaines v. City of New Orleans,* 2: 1341.
21. Reverend Antoine Blanc, deposition of July 6, 1849, ibid., 2: 1590.

Myra's lawyers claimed that the court had declared the marriage void and granted damages of $100 to Zulime for DesGrange's "imposition" of marriage on her while still the husband of another.[22]

Zulime's son, Dr. James Gardette, had discovered the third document while he and Zulime "looked over the papers" of his father. This was a certificate, in Latin, declaring that a marriage between "Jacobum Des-Grange and Barbara M. Orci," took place on July 6, 1790. Signed by William O'Brien, priest of the Church of St. Peter in New York City, on September 11, 1806, the Latin certificate described the ceremony the priest had performed sixteen years earlier. Depositions from Father O'Brien's niece and the pastor of St. Peter's Church in 1852 supported the accuracy of the signature and form of the certificate. But the defendants now cried forgery, and more testimony was introduced to prove or disprove the certificate's authenticity. No one ever explained how the certificate of Des-Grange's first marriage had appeared among the elder Dr. Gardette's papers.[23]

New witnesses also appeared whose testimony supported or repudiated Gaines's contentions. Attorneys for Relf and Chew attacked the testimony of Mme. Despau by assailing her morals. They produced an order for a judicial separation, obtained by Sophia Despau's husband in 1805, charging her with "leading a wandering and rambling life" and "living in open adultery." William Despau also disclosed that his wife had "several times deserted [his] bed and board." By branding Zulime's sister, the only witness to her marriage, an "adulteress," the lawyers hoped to convince the court that her testimony was not "worthy of belief." In response, many who knew Sophia swore to her irreproachable conduct. One added that "the husband of Madame Despau . . . was an unprincipled man."[24]

22. Argument of John A. Campbell, *Gaines v. Relf, Chew, and Others,* case no. 122, Circuit Court of the United States, Eastern District of Louisiana, reprinted in Walker, *Full Report of the Great Gaines Case,* 49–50.

23. Dr. James Gardette, deposition of May 7, 1849, reprinted in *Transcript of Record, Gaines v. Relf, Chew, and Others,* 347–8; Ellen Guinan, deposition of 1846, and John Power, deposition of 1846, reprinted in *Myra Clark Gaines v. Relf, Chew, and Others,* 12 Howard 472 (1852), at 475.

24. Petition for Separation, *Despau v. Despau,* June 10, 1805, reprinted in *Transcript of Record, Gaines v. City of New Orleans,* 2: 1652; argument of Colonel Preston, *Gaines v. Relf, Chew, and Others,* case no. 122, Circuit Court of the United States, Eastern District of Louisiana, reprinted in Walker, *Full Report of the Great Gaines Case,* 40; Maria Clara Lassabe Truffin, deposition of Aug. 15, 1849, reprinted in *Transcript of Record, Gaines v. City of New Orleans,* 2: 1423.

The parade of testimony continued as each side questioned the reputations of their opponents' witnesses. To challenge Myra's identity as the child of Daniel Clark, the defendants resurrected a rumor, begun by the *Louisiana Courier* during the newspaper war between Clark and Claiborne, accusing Clark of impotence. Testimony from several gentlemen repeated the rumor, supposedly spread by some *"femmes galantes."* Clark, they hinted, spent "so much time . . . in the company of ladies" to refute the allegations of impotence. Other witnesses noted that gossip credited Clark with numerous mistresses; still others exposed Zulime as the *"amanté"* of Clark, declaring that she was "very *coquette et légère,"* and lived with him in "an amorous and illicit connexion." Even more came forward to declare that Clark stood on the brink of matrimony with several women when he died in 1813. Caroline Stanard, sister of Beverly Chew, disclosed that Clark had given her "every proof of [his unmarried status] that a gentleman could give to a lady." But Delphine Trépagnier insisted that Clark was engaged to her sister, the widowed "Madame Lambert." Most of the character witnesses for both sides seem to have had little impact on the outcome of the Gaines case.[25]

Three witnesses, however, did influence the judicial determination of Gaines's legitimacy. Horatio Davis, son of Colonel Davis, swore that Myra was Daniel Clark's "natural daughter," and that he and his whole family knew it. Davis bolstered his testimony by introducing a petition filed by his father in 1817. The colonel had asked the executors of the Clark estate for "maintenance" for Myra as Clark's illegitimate child, all that Louisiana law allowed the estate of a natural father to provide for an adulterous

25. For charges of impotence, see P. J. Tricou, deposition of June 23, 1849, reprinted in *Transcript of Record, Gaines v. Relf, Chew, and Others,* 649; Jacob Hart, deposition of June 28, 1849, ibid., 658; Jean B. Dejan Sr., deposition of July 6, 1849, ibid., 687; and Hilary Julian Domingon, deposition of July 6, 1849, reprinted in *Transcript of Record, Gaines v. City of New Orleans,* 2: 1499. On Clark's many mistresses, see Louis Bouligny, deposition of July 3, 1849, reprinted in *Transcript of Record, Gaines v. Relf, Chew, and Others,* 685; Jean Canon, deposition of June 28, 1849, ibid., 660; and Hilary Julian Domingon, deposition of July 6, 1849. On Zulime's relationship with Clark, see Louis Bouligny, deposition of July 3, 1849; Joachim Courcelle, deposition of June 20, 1849, reprinted in *Transcript of Record, Gaines v. Relf, Chew, and Others,* 678; P. J. Tricou, deposition of June 23, 1849; Hillary Julian Domingon, deposition of July 6, 1849; Étienne Carraby, deposition of June 4, 1849, reprinted in *Transcript of Record, Gaines v. City of New Orleans,* 2: 1473. On Clark's prospective brides, see Mrs. Caroline Matilda Stanard, deposition of Sept. 11, 1849, reprinted in *Transcript of Record, Gaines v. City of New Orleans,* 2: 1618; Delphine Trépagnier, deposition of May 28, 1849, ibid., 2: 1459.

bastard. Colonel Davis's petition contradicted his earlier testimony that he had never asked for support for Myra from the estate, but his son indicated that the importance of its statement that Myra was "the natural daughter of Daniel Clark" overbore any reluctance he felt to gainsay his father's word. The petition added support to the statement of chevalier Delacroix, who testified that Clark had told him of Myra's illegitimate birth.[26]

The second new witness, Dr. John Barnes, husband of Caroline Clark (who had died in 1845), produced two letters exchanged between Clark and his sister in England, Jane Green, in 1805–1806. Mrs. Green had filled a request by her brother for an "elegant lady's toilette" and could not help teasing Clark about its intended recipient. Clark had replied that there was no person "likely to become Mrs. Clark . . . for some time to come." This declaration of his bachelor status in 1805 (after his purported marriage to Zulime) aided the defense's challenge to Mme. Despau's testimony.[27]

The third witness testified through a letter written in 1842 to Daniel Coxe. Étienne Mazureau, a noted New Orleans attorney, had represented Richard Relf in his 1834 libel suit against William Whitney, and "felt a very natural delicacy" about appearing as a witness in a case "that has since made so much noise." His letter reported a consultation among Clark, Edward Livingston, and himself "to ascertain whether [Clark] could make some provision by will for Myra, his supposed illegitimate daughter." According to Mazureau, Clark had prepared a will declaring Myra his "natural daughter" and made her his "universal heir," leaving his own mother an annual income of $3,000. When asked the identity of the mother of Myra, Clark replied, "You know the lady; it is Madame DesGrange. . . . [S]he was married, I know, and what matters it? . . . the ruffian (who kept a confectionery shop here) had deceived that pretty woman; he was married when he courted her and became her husband; and . . . he ran away afterwards for fear of being prosecuted. So, you see, this marriage was null." Mazureau disagreed. Until so declared by a competent tribunal, he told Clark, the marriage existed, and the child "is of such a class of bastards (an adulterine bastard) as not to be capable by our

26. Horatio J. Davis, deposition of June 25, 1849, reprinted in *Transcript of Record, Gaines v. Relf, Chew, and Others,* 651; Petition of Myra Clark for Support from the Estate of Daniel Clark, filed by her guardian, S. B. Davis, June 24, 1817, reprinted in *Transcript of Record, Gaines v. City of New Orleans,* 2: 1646.

27. Dr. John Barnes, deposition of July 20, 1849, reprinted in *Transcript of Record, Gaines v. City of New Orleans,* 2: 1621.

laws of receiving by will from her supposed father anything beyond what may be necessary for her sustenance and education." Mazureau then showed Clark the Louisiana Code of 1808 and the Spanish laws; although disappointed, Clark apparently understood that his proposed will would not be valid. The attorney also explained that "the girl could not be legitimated or even acknowledged as his child by subsequent marriage or otherwise." There was, however, an alternative. "Sir," Mazureau suggested, "if you have friends in whom you can place your confidence . . . convey them secretly some of your property, or give them money for the use of the child, to be given to her by them when she comes of age." Afterward, Mazureau heard from both Clark and from Colonel Bellechasse that "he had done what he told me he would do." Mazureau's letter, given by Daniel Coxe to the defendants, provided a persuasive explanation for Clark's provisions for Myra before his death and cast doubt on his declaration of her legitimacy in the alleged will of 1813.[28]

The latest installment of the Great Gaines Case, as the New Orleans papers began to call *Gaines v. Relf, Chew, and Others*, opened on Wednesday, January 20, 1850, before an overflow crowd in the United States circuit court. Justice John McKinley was the member of the United States Supreme Court assigned to the Eastern District of Louisiana, and he joined Judge McCaleb of New Orleans on the bench. It took four days to read all the depositions entered as evidence. Not until the following Monday did the attorneys begin their presentations. Although Gaines's counsel would normally begin the arguments, Colonel Issac Preston, representing the defendants, requested as a personal favor that he speak first so that he might return to his duties as a member of the Louisiana legislature in Baton Rouge. The colonel gained the immediate sympathy of the crowd as he depicted the feelings of the defendants "when suddenly a lady appears in this city, and startles the whole community by claiming all this property." Colonel Preston summarized the evidence against the "monstrous pretension" of Myra Clark Gaines to be the legitimate daughter of Daniel Clark: the ecclesiastical record; the 1817 suit by Colonel Davis for Myra's maintenance; the mutilated record of 1805 and 1806; the charges of immorality against Sophia Despau (an "adulteress"), which discredited her truthfulness; the letter from Jane Green to her brother; Delacroix's reports of Clark's declarations of Myra's bastardy and Horatio Davis's

28. Étienne Mazureau to Daniel Coxe, May 1, 1842, ibid., 1549.

knowledge of her birth; the testimony of many witnesses that Clark had been "too proud" to marry his mistress ("the cast-off wife of a poor, miserable French syrup maker"); the testimony of many others that he had contemplated matrimony with the daughter of a prominent family (Louisa Caton)—an unthinkable action had he actually married Zulime Carrière; the Mazureau letter and Clark's subsequent actions; and the testimony of Daniel Coxe about Zulime's relationship with Clark and her marriage to Dr. Gardette. Colonel Preston's often vituperative address concluded by asking the court to disregard the "infamous *Patterson* decision, a disgraceful and outrageous fraud" on the record of justice.[29]

In reply, Gaines's attorneys, P. C. Wright and John Grymes of New Orleans and John Campbell of Alabama, centered their arguments on the *Patterson* decision in favor of Myra's legitimacy. Campbell was a new addition to Gaines's legal team. The case had attracted considerable interest, and the forty-year-old Campbell sought to build his practice in New Orleans by impressing the crowds who came to hear the sessions. The New Orleans newspapers admired his "force of logic, clearness of style and vigor of thought that seemed to carry conviction with all the listeners and greatly to startle the defendants who have all along reposed very confidently on the strength of their case." Each day of the trial the *Daily Picayune* reprinted Campbell's speech and praised his argument for "its logical, clear, and forcible reasoning," concluding that "an abler effort has seldom been seen in our judicial halls."[30]

Campbell dismissed the allegations of Clark's impotence as the "idlest bar-room and brothel gossip"; Clark's treatment of Myra clearly marked her as his own child. His statements confirming her legitimacy to Harriet Harper Smythe and in his will of 1813 were sufficient proof of her status. Campbell noted that Clark and Zulime both erroneously believed that only a publicly recorded marriage was authentic; because they each thought their private union invalid, their subsequent conduct—Zulime's marriage to Dr. Gardette and Clark's courtship of Louisa Caton—was understandable. Madame Despau's testimony adequately established the fact

29. Argument of Colonel Isaac Preston, in Walker, *Full Report of the Great Gaines Case*, 39.

30. Robert Saunders Jr., *John Archibald Campbell, Southern Moderate, 1811–1889* (Tuscaloosa: University of Alabama Press, 1997), 108; Henry G. Connor, *John Archibald Campbell: Associate Justice of the United States Supreme Court, 1853–1861* (Boston: Houghton Mifflin, 1920), 11–2, quoting an unnamed New Orleans newspaper; *New Orleans Daily Picayune*, Feb. 1, 1850, p. 1.

of the marriage in Pennsylvania, and by Pennsylvania law such a private exchange of vows was perfectly legal.[31]

Other attorneys also had their opportunity to speak. John R. Grymes, at the end of a flamboyant career spanning five decades, held the floor for seventeen hours over three days as he outlined the Gaines case. Twice Grymes felt "too fatigued to proceed," and argument continued on the next day. Greer Duncan, for Relf and Chew, also spoke at length. Despite the protracted speeches, the crowds remained. The *Daily Picayune* reminded its readers to arrive early. The courtroom was "perfectly crammed," it warned; many who could not gain admission had left "much disappointed."[32]

Considerable speculation surrounded the decision. Most spectators hoped that a Louisiana judge would be willing to rule against the Supreme Court's *Patterson* decision, but since Justice McKinley sat on the court that had decided *Patterson*, he would surely hold that the decision bound the Louisiana court. When the judges announced their ruling, surprise rippled through the packed courtroom. After conferring, McKinley and McCaleb announced that they disagreed on the binding nature of *Patterson*. Since they both held firmly to their positions, Justice McKinley had decided to step aside and allow Judge McCaleb to decide the case. McKinley did so because he foresaw an appeal to the Supreme Court, and he would have to sit on the case when it came before that tribunal. He commented that he had never known a case in which the Supreme Court overruled its own decision, but he believed the case should come to the high court with an opinion written by a judge "familiar with the peculiar jurisprudence" of Louisiana.[33]

In his decision, McCaleb did rely on Louisiana's "peculiar jurisprudence." The judge included a long dissertation on the Spanish laws of marriage, which, he noted, still operated in the state by the 1808 code. A "clandestine marriage" kept secret for the entire lifetime of one of the couple "manifests the shame . . . [of] concubinage" rather than "the dignity of marriage." Children born of such a marriage could not inherit. McCaleb explained that in areas where the "law of community" prevailed (such as

31. Argument of John Campbell, in Walker, *Full Report of the Great Gaines Case,* 45.

32. *New Orleans Daily Picayune,* Feb. 8, 1850, Fri. morning edition, p. 4, Fri. evening edition, p. 1.

33. *New Orleans Daily Picayune,* Feb. 21, 1850, p. 1.

Louisiana) too much confusion would result "if parties are permitted to
contract a matrimonial alliance and never make it known to the world."
McCaleb indicated that Louisiana law did not attach so much importance
to the clandestine solemnization of the marriage "as to the keeping of that
marriage secret." For that reason, McCaleb judged that the argument that
Clark and Zulime's marriage had taken place in Pennsylvania and should
be governed by Pennsylvania law "applies no further than to the form or
ceremony of the contract. Its effects must be governed by the laws of Louisiana."[34]

McCaleb's declaration echoes the civil law's bias toward family solidar-
ity. The civil law, he instructed, "greatly concerns the interests of families,
that marriage contracts should be preserved inviolate." For that reason
Zulime's marriage to DesGrange—bigamous or not—could not be void
until a competent court had declared it so. And, he noted, that the Louisiana Supreme Court had consistently held that a child of a woman "deceived by a man, who represented himself as single," was entitled to all
the rights of a legitimate child.[35]

Considering the depositions of the witnesses, Judge McCaleb admitted
the difficulty of evaluating the testimony of persons never seen by the
court. Some of the witnesses had testified several times over a period of
twenty years; others could only testify posthumously through depositions
taken while they still lived. Under the necessity of determining fact (a job
McCaleb believed truly belonged only with a jury), the judge declined to
credit the testimony of Madame Despau, M. Boisfontaine, Mrs. Harriet
Harper Smythe, and Colonel Bellechasse. As he considered the new evidence, McCaleb announced that Gaines's attorneys had not succeeded in
creating a convincing explanation of Clark's actions. McCaleb declared
that "ambitious as he doubtless was," it was not conceivable that Clark
would consider marriage to Louisa Caton "if there were the slightest risk
of his being exposed to the world as a bigamist." The letter from Mazureau also demonstrated that Clark regarded Myra only as his illegitimate
child. Nor was Zulime's marriage to Dr. Gardette "reconcilable with common decency." Could it be reasonable, he asked, "to suppose that if this
female was at the time married to Daniel Clark, she would, with so little

34. Opinion of Judge McCaleb, *Gaines v. Relf, Chew, and Others,* Circuit Court of
the United States, Eastern District of Louisiana, reprinted in Walker, *Full Report of the
Great Gaines Case,* 79–81.
35. Ibid., 81–2.

ceremony or hesitation, have formed a matrimonial alliance with another man, and that, too, in violation of the laws of Pennsylvania, which punished with severity the crime of bigamy!" Such "facts and circumstances," Judge McCaleb concluded, "dispose of the case."[36]

Turning to the *Patterson* decision, the judge assured the courtroom that he respected the "high tribunal" that had handed down that ruling. But, he continued, "I feel most solemnly convinced that the merits of the present case, have not been fully and fairly settled by that decision." The testimony of Charles Patterson indicated that his agreement with Myra and her husband created a collusive case, and that no serious contest had come before the court. The "taint of collusion" rendered the judgment in *Patterson* "of no binding force as *res adjudicata*."[37]

The judge's decision devastated Gaines, but she made immediate plans to appeal to the United States Supreme Court. The court had changed little since the Patterson case; only one new justice, Benjamin R. Curtis, sat on the bench. So well received had been the arguments of John A. Campbell that Gaines chose to have him join Reverdy Johnson and reprise his presentation to the high court. Her opponents decided to take no chances; Greer Duncan and his brother Lucius would prepare the case as they had for the circuit court, but for the presentation to the Supreme Court, Relf and Chew retained Daniel Webster, the most renowned active lawyer in the country. *Gaines v. Relf, Chew, and Others* would be the last case argued by Webster before the Supreme Court.[38]

The arguments presented to the court differed little from those offered to the circuit court. As they endeavored to transform the perplexing and equivocal data into a persuasive narrative, counsel for plaintiff and defendants again debated the validity of the DesGrange marriage, the testimony of Madame Despau, and Clark's declaration of Myra's legitimacy in the will of 1813. As a narrative competition, the Gaines case demonstrates the difficulty of creating a "coherent, consistent, believable, and unambiguously moral" story that could convince its audience that the litigant deserved to win (or lose) the case.[39]

On March 1, 1852, defendants' attorney Greer Duncan sat in the Su-

36. Ibid., 76, 79.

37. Ibid., 73.

38. *The Papers of Daniel Webster: Legal Papers*: vol. 3, *The Federal Practice, Part II*, ed. Andrew King (Hanover, N. H.: Published for Dartmouth College by the University Press of New England, 1989), appendix 1, 1066.

39. Korobkin, "Maintenance of Mutual Confidence," 10.

preme Court chamber waiting for the decision to be announced. As he waited he wrote to a fellow attorney in New Orleans describing the tense atmosphere in the crowded courtroom. "The moment," he wrote, "is nigh at hand. It is to be the first and only opinion delivered today. I commence these lines to relieve the inescapable rush of feeling, which at this moment, is gushing through my mind and heart!" Noon arrived, and the justices entered the chamber. At eighteen minutes past, Justice Catron began reading the opinion of the court. Duncan's elation is evident in his letter. "The Opinion is a noble one—," he wrote hurriedly. "—it dodges nothing—rips the testimony of the Aunts of Mrs. Gaines all to tatters—calls things by their right names, denounces the whole as a gross fiction, supported by the basest perjury! Every point opined by me is fully and broadly sustained. The story of Madame Despau is denounced as disgraceful. The review of the testimony of Plaintiff's witnesses is a thousand times more indignant even than the language in Judge McCaleb's opinion." Greer Duncan's letter did not exaggerate; the Supreme Court had indeed changed its mind.[40]

The court's reversal of *Patterson* indicates that the justices had become suspicious of the motives of Gaines and her female supporters. Catron's decision suggests that judicial concern for womanly weakness had turned to misgivings about women who sought financial security through legal actions. Like Gaines's great champion on the bench, Justice Wayne of Georgia, Catron was a Jackson appointee to the court, a southern unionist, and a Democrat, but his opinion in the Gaines case demonstrated the collision of their differing positions on the necessity of legal protection for women.[41]

*   *   *

40. G. B. Duncan to James McConnell, Mar. 1, 1852, McConnell Family Papers, Box 11, Folder 1, Howard-Tilton Memorial Library, Tulane University, New Orleans. Daniel Webster had advance knowledge of the court's decision. A letter to Webster attributed to Justice John McLean, dated Feb. 26, 1852, informed the lawyer that the "decision in the Gaines Case will be made at Monday next at 12. Judge Catron delivers the opinion—Judge Wayne dissenting and delivers a long argumentative opinion adverse to the Majority . . . this information is strictly Confidential, being so given to me." The anxious letter from Greer Duncan to his friend in New Orleans makes clear that Webster did not share his early information about the decision with his fellow attorney. *Papers of Daniel Webster*, 1043.

41. Gilfoyle, "Hearts of Nineteenth-Century Men," 151; Grossberg, *Governing the Hearth*, 54.

Over six feet tall, with a large frame, John Catron presented a command-ing presence. He had "penetrating black eyes, ample dark hair, a large nose, and a square jaw." Born in Virginia in 1781, he moved with his family to Tennessee in 1804. He was largely self-educated, his legal educa-tion consisting of a few years of reading law in the office of Nashville at-torney George Gibbs. He was no orator, did not have a "pleasing voice," nor did he make "graceful gestures," but his common touch gave Old Hickory valuable support. With Felix Grundy, James K. Polk, and Cave Johnson, he became one of the "four pillars of Jacksonianism" in Ten-nessee.[42]

Catron's acquaintance with Andrew Jackson began during his service in the Creek War, in which he fought at Fort Strother and attained the rank of sergeant major. Incapacitated by the "hardships and privations" of the war, he returned to Tennessee and began his public career by winning election as attorney general for the Third Judicial Circuit in 1815. Ca-tron's biographer stresses the difficult life of a circuit court judge: traveling on horseback equipped with pistols ("chiefly but not entirely for show") and staying in taverns where he could meet fellow lawyers and judges. Catron returned to the practice of law during the Panic of 1819—a disas-trous time for businesses but a bonanza for lawyers. With a backlog of two thousand cases in the Nashville courts, Catron soon had a busy office. His practice before the Nashville bar specialized in conflicting titles to land, experience he would bring to his decision in the Gaines case.[43]

In 1824 Tennesseans elected Catron justice of their Court of Errors and Appeals. Since appellate judges in Tennessee also held the chancery courts, Justice Catron obtained considerable experience sitting as chancellor in the equity courts. Soon afterwards he rose to the Tennessee state supreme court, and from there, in 1837, Andrew Jackson appointed Catron to the Supreme Court of the United States, where he became the first Tennessean to serve on that court.[44]

During his service on the Tennessee supreme court, Catron participated in a decision (*Grisham v. State*) invalidating a common-law marriage. Un-

---

42. Walter Chandler, *The Centenary of Associate Justice John Catron of the United States Supreme Court. Address Given at the Fifty-Sixth Annual Session of the Bar Associ-ation of Tennessee at Memphis, Friday, June 11, 1937*, Printed in the Congressional Re-cord of June 17, 1937 (Washington, D.C.: United States Government Printing Office, 1937), 3.

43. Ibid., 4–5.

44. Ibid.

like Justice Wayne's home state of Georgia, which recognized irregular marriages, Catron's Tennessee did not. With the adoption of the new state constitution in 1831, the state became an early proponent of legislative creation of law by statute. Catron and his fellow Tennessee justices held that where a state law prescribed requirements for marriages, couples who failed to comply with the prerequisites of the statutes could not claim a legal marriage. This legal formalism, or reference to statutory law, contrasted with Wayne's instrumental approach, which encouraged judges to mold judicial precedents to fit the occasion. Catron's Tennessee background predisposed him to refute the profession of marriage between Clark and Zulime, just as Wayne's encouraged him to credit the existence of an irregular marriage between the two.[45]

Judge Catron's opinion for the majority in *Gaines v. Relf, Chew, and Others* reflected his Tennessee bias in favor of formally established marriage. "The great basis of human society throughout the civilized world," he wrote, "is founded on marriages and legitimate offspring." Zulime married Jerome DesGrange in 1794 in a cathedral ceremony, with a properly issued civil license, and lived with him as his wife "for seven or eight years." If Zulime remained the lawful wife of DesGrange at the point of her "alleged" marriage to Daniel Clark, "then the marriage with Clark is . . . void; and it is immaterial whether it did or did not take place." Catron placed the burden of proof on Gaines to establish that the DesGrange marriage had been bigamous.[46]

Catron dismissed the rumors of DesGrange's bigamy as the creations of Zulime and her sisters. Catron's sympathy with the Frenchman is palpable. DesGrange "was a man somewhat advanced in life; he kept a humble shop selling liquors and confectionery . . . his sole business." His twenty-two-year-old wife, Zulime, was "uncommonly handsome." DesGrange was a "lone man in New Orleans" with no friends or relations beyond his wife and her family. These relations concocted a "plausible tale of fiction" to conceal the adultery of the wife and her delivery of an illegitimate child. This action, Catron averred, demonstrated a "highly dangerous and criminal character." On their return from Philadelphia, Zulime "presented herself to society as an innocent and injured woman, and public indignation was turned on her husband for a supposed crime against her." Catron

45. *Grisham v. State*, 2 Yerg. 589 (Tenn. 1831).
46. *Myra Clark Gaines v. Relf, Chew, and Others*, 12 Howard 472, at 506, 534.

dismissed the "Latin certificate" of DesGrange's marriage to Barbara D'Orsi as "dangerous hearsay evidence." Issued sixteen years after the purported marriage, the certificate did not, in Catron's view, substitute for a properly recorded license or register of marriage. Allowing any clergyman or justice of the peace to hand out such certificates as evidence of marriage "would open a door to frauds that could not be guarded against." Calling the accusation of bigamy a "mystery," the justice asked, why "an humble shopkeeper should be of sufficient consequence to excite public indignation . . . [and] be the object of general and gross reproach?" Catron credited "the unintelligent condition of much of the population of New Orleans of that day" for this "absurd public opinion." His solution to the mysterious bigamy charges found "Madame DesGrange and her sisters and friends" determined to "drive DesGrange from the country, so that his wife might indulge herself in the society of Clark, unencumbered and unannoyed by the presence of an humble and deserted husband." When DesGrange returned to New Orleans in 1805, his wife "immediately sued him for alimony . . . and again drove him away." Catron concluded that "we cannot shut our eyes on the truth and accord belief to this fiction."[47]

Catron ended his opinion by considering the nature of the *Patterson* case. The justice described the litigation between the Gaineses and Charles Patterson as "amicable"; since Patterson stood to lose nothing he was "indifferent to what evidence might be introduced." General and Mrs. Gaines used his name to carry the appeal to the Supreme Court, where their object was "to obtain a favorable opinion and decree." As such, the case represented "no earnest litigation." The additional evidence entered by the defendants projected "an aspect altogether different" and was sufficient to allow the court "to produce a different decree from that given in Patterson's case."[48]

The judge finished with a word of sympathy for Myra Gaines. "The harshness of judicial duty," he acknowledged, "requires that we should deal with witnesses and evidence . . . as we find them, and we have done so here. But we sincerely regret that it could not be satisfactorily done without making exposures that would most willingly have been avoided." Catron's opinion stood for the majority of five: Catron, Baldwin, Grier,

47. Ibid., 527, 532–3, 535.
48. Ibid., 537–9.

Curtis, and—surprisingly—John McKinley, who had decided after all that he could change his mind.[49]

Two justices, Wayne and Daniel, entered dissents. Wayne, Gaines's champion from *Patterson,* did not allow the challenge to his earlier decision to go unanswered. He placed in the record one of the longest dissenting opinions ever delivered by a Supreme Court justice. Characterizing his fellow justices' ruling as a "capricious and unregulated judgment," he reviewed the reasons he had given in *Patterson* for maintaining that "Myra Clark Gaines is the only child of her father, Daniel Clark, by his marriage with her mother, Zulime Carrière." He reserved special ire for the attack on Madame Despau's credibility. Perhaps she did conceal the purpose of Zulime's first trip to Philadelphia. She did so "at most, only as the attendant of a frail sister to aid her in her travail, and to shelter her and her family from disgrace." Wayne's sympathy for Zulime and her sister places him firmly among the early-nineteenth-century judiciary who drew from the evolving common law a special judicial protection for women. "The testimony of women," he declared, "is weighed with caution and allowances for them [made] differently from that of men, but never with the slightest suspicion that they are not as truthful." No witness, he declared, could disprove the facts Madame Despau stated, and "her character for veracity rose above the attempt to assail her general reputation."[50]

Justice Wayne closed his dissent with a prophetic warning:

> Those of us who have borne our part in the case will pass away. The case will live. . . . The case itself presents thought for our philosophy, in its contemplation of all the business and domestic relations of life. It shows the hollowness of those friendships formed between persons in the greediness of gain, seeking gratification in a disregard of all those laws by which commerce can only be honestly and respectably pursued. It shows how carelessness in business and secret partnerships . . . to run the risk of unlawful adventures may give to the latter its spoils and impoverish those whose capital alone gave consequence to the concern. It shows how a mistaken confidence given to others by a man who dies rich, may be the cause of diverting his estate into an imputed insolvency, depriving every member of his family of any part of their inheritance.

49. Ibid., 539. Justice Roger Taney did not hear *Gaines v. Relf, Chew, and Others* for the same reason he did not sit in the Patterson case: his brother-in-law Francis Scott Key had once represented Myra Gaines.

50. Ibid., 540, 550–1.

We learn from it that long continued favors may not be followed by any sympathy from those who receive them for those who are dearest to our affections. It shows if the ruffian takes life for the purse which he robs, that a dying man's agonies soothed only by tears and prayers for the happiness of a child, may not arrest a fraudulent attempt to filch from her her name and fortune. We can learn from it, too, that there is a kindred between virtue and lasting respectability in life, and that transgressions of its proprieties or irregular yieldings to our passions in forming the most interesting relation between human creatures, are most likely to make them miserable and to bring ruin upon children. . . .

"I, the Lord God, am a jealous God, and visit the sins of the fathers upon the children unto the third and fourth generation of them that hate me, and show mercy unto thousands of those who love me and keep my commandments."[51]

51. Ibid., 597.

X

Victory at Last

At the midpoint of the nineteenth century New Orleans was a bustling, brawling, sprawling port city—the fourth largest in the United States. Boom time came to the Cotton South, and New Orleans boomed along with it. Steamboats plied the Mississippi River, and newspaper reports of the accidents and explosions that made river traffic dangerous did little to deter the mobility of the populace. The population of New Orleans had doubled since 1840, filling the new houses and stores that appeared everywhere almost overnight. "Carnival" embodied the robust spirit of the thriving city, and both Creole and American residents enthusiastically embraced the annual revelry. New Orleans kept its European atmosphere, but the old faubourgs coalesced into "the City," the antagonism between old and new districts gradually subsiding as all benefitted from the prosperous economy. After the Supreme Court's decision in *Gaines v. Relf, Chew, and Others,* owners of the old Clark estate property relaxed, believing their titles no longer shadowed by litigation. The property sold and sold again as the building craze continued and various owners enjoyed their new prosperity.[1]

As the Gaines case moved into its third decade, the numbers of those who could remember Daniel Clark and Zulime Carrière slowly dwindled. Boisfontaine and Bellechasse had died during the 1840s, but the chevalier Delacroix, although approaching ninety, remained. Harriet Harper Smythe and Myra Gaines's two aunts passed away early in the 1850s. Zul-

1. Kendall, *History of New Orleans,* 2: 202, 213–4.

ime died in 1853, and Colonel Davis in 1854. Of the two executors, only Richard Relf still lived.[2]

Defeat in the Supreme Court meant that the attorneys scattered. John R. Grymes died soon after the conclusion of the appeal of *Gaines v. Relf, Chew, and Others.* Walter Jones retired. Isaac Preston, whose speech in 1850 helped sway the Louisiana court, lost his life in a steamboat explosion on Lake Pontchartrain in 1851. Reverdy Johnson became a Maryland senator, then accepted an appointment as solicitor general from President Franklin Pierce. Daniel Webster died, but not before he charged the defendants in *Gaines v. Relf* a fee of fifty thousand dollars for his successful defense and brought suit in New Orleans to collect it. John Campbell moved onto the Supreme Court in 1853. His arguments in the Gaines case, though unsuccessful, had so impressed the justices that when a vacancy occurred on the court, they recommended to President Pierce that Campbell be named to fill it.[3]

Myra Gaines had spent the last twenty years of her life caught in the shadow of the law. Mathew Brady's photograph of her at forty-seven reveals a middle-aged woman with shadowed eyes and firmly set mouth. Her loss before the Supreme Court and Justice Catron's designation of her suit as a "colossal fraud," had had little effect on her legions of supporters. Particularly in the North, her friends continued to exhibit a degree of partisanship that amounted to wild enthusiasm for her cause. Daniel Webster ruefully noted that "she has a band of sympathizers throughout the land that is more powerful than an army arranged with banners." The *Southern Quarterly Review* declared that the Gaines case "attracted a larger share of public attention and has inspired a stronger feeling of interest, than any other in all the records of the American courts." *Putnam's Magazine* featured a summary of the litigation favorable to Gaines and concluded that "nobody could listen to her for fifteen minutes without sharing in her enthusiasm and perfect conviction of ultimate success."[4]

2. Harmon, *Famous Case of Myra Clark Gaines,* 368; John S. Kendall, "The Strange Case of Myra Clark Gaines," *Louisiana Historical Quarterly* 20 (1937): 36. Beverly Chew died Jan. 13, 1851.

3. Connor, *John Archibald Campbell,* 17; *Washington (D.C.) Evening Star,* Jan. 31, 1855, p. 3.

4. Daniel Webster, Opening Speech, *Gaines v. Relf, Chew, and Others,* quoted in *Argument of George M. Paschau before C. Delano, Secretary of the Interior . . . , Nov. 4, 1870* (Washington City, 1870), 11; S., "The Gaines Case," *Southern Quarterly Review* 9 (Apr. 1854): 274; "The Romance of the Great Gaines Case," 210.

Myra Clark Gaines continued to be a fixture on the Washington social circuit. Invited to the Pierce White House, she met Mrs. McNeill Potter, a niece of the president, and the women established a friendship that lasted for the rest of their lives. Gaines did not hesitate to use her intimacy with the president's family to urge the appointment of friends and family to government positions. In 1853 she wrote Pierce recommending the appointment of William H. Allman as a purser in the United States Navy. She also seconded the justices' suggestion of John Campbell for the Supreme Court vacancy—in this, at least, she and Justice Catron agreed.[5]

Money was a persistent problem. Loss in the Supreme Court meant that Gaines paid both her own and her opponents' costs. The fortune of her first husband, William Whitney, and the property held in trust for her by Colonel Bellechasse had long since been gobbled up by the expenses of litigation. By her prenuptial agreement with General Gaines, Myra received $100,000 from his estate, which was exhausted by expenses incurred in *Gaines v. Relf*. The Whitney family continued to provide support, and other friends also lent money. Gaines's situation grew so desperate that she applied to Congress for an increase from $25 to $50 per month in the pension she received as the widow of General Gaines. The two senators from Louisiana, John Slidell and Judah Benjamin, opposed the increase; one supporter of Gaines wrote that "their friends were personally interested in robbing the widow of her rights in New Orleans real estate." Slidell had represented Relf and Chew in one of the case's earlier incarnations, and a member of Benjamin's family was a defendant. When the senators spoke disparagingly of General Gaines's military record, Jefferson Davis rose to defend his former commander. Davis, now a Democratic leader in the Senate, had served on the general's staff as a young officer just out of West Point. He was seconded by William H. Seward, leader of the Republicans, who praised the "splendid service" of General Gaines. The speeches and support of Davis and Seward procured for

5. Surrogate's Court, Kings County [New York], *General Term. Second Judicial Department, In the Matter of the Probate of the Last Will and Testament of Myra Clark Gaines, Deceased. Julietta Perkins and Marie P. Evans, Appellants. Record of Appeal* (Washington, D.C., 1896), 1: 412; Myra Clark Gaines to President Franklin Pierce, Mar. 17, 1853, Ferdinand J. Dreer Autograph Collection, Misc. MSS no. 1, Historical Society of Pennsylvania, Philadelphia. The Kings County litigation, which will hereafter be cited as *Evans Will Record,* contains much of the surviving correspondence of Myra Clark Gaines, as well as testimony from those who knew her in the last twenty-five years of her life.

Gaines her additional pension. A friend suggested that this was the only time the two opposing party leaders ever agreed.[6]

Myra Gaines never lacked money for lawyers, even if other bills went unpaid. When necessary, she mortgaged her hoped-for inheritance to pay their fees. Soon after her return to New Orleans in 1852, she retained a new attorney. For the next eleven years, until his death in 1863, Franklin Perin devoted most of his time and all of his considerable intellect to the resurrection and ultimate triumph of the crusade for Myra Gaines's rights.[7]

Perin graduated from law school at the University of Cincinnati in the early 1840s. According to his granddaughter, Anna Clyde Plunkett, Perin left the Midwest for New Orleans because of his fascination with the legal drama of the "case that was rocking the nation." He entered into partnership with Judge James Malcolm Smiley, and the firm of Smiley & Perin established its legal practice at 44 Camp Street in New Orleans. In 1846, Governor Isaac Johnson appointed Perin district attorney of the Third Judicial District of Louisiana, but after 1852 the representation of Myra Clark Gaines consumed all his energy.[8]

A new attack orchestrated by Perin began on May 19, 1852, just two months after the adverse ruling from the Supreme Court in *Gaines v. Relf, Chew, and Others*. Gaines placed an advertisement in a New Orleans paper warning occupants of property once in the Clark estate that she would file suit in the probate court "to recover the estate of her father" under his will of 1813. The previous defendants can be pardoned if they seemed skeptical about Gaines's new tack. Claiming to be Clark's "universal heir," she and Perin planned to probate a will that existed only in the recorded testimony of former witnesses now deceased.[9]

Almost twenty years earlier Myra and William Whitney had asked the New Orleans probate court to revoke the probate granted to Clark's will of 1811 and accept the testimony of Harriet Harper Smythe, Boisfontaine, and Bellechasse as proof of a later will drawn a month before Clark's death. The court had refused. In 1844 the Supreme Court declared that

6. John B. Brownlow to John Wesley Gaines, Apr. 15, 1919, Edmund P. Gaines Papers, Tennessee State Library and Archives, Nashville.

7. Plunkett, *Corridors by Candlelight*, 51.

8. Ibid., 51–2.

9. *New York Daily Times*, June 16, 1852, p. 3, quoting an unnamed New Orleans paper.

Gaines could make no claim on the estate as heir under the 1813 will unless and until a "duly constituted" court in Louisiana accepted that device
as Daniel Clark's last testament. Having once failed in the probate court,
Myra and General Gaines decided to rely on the Louisiana Code of 1808,
which prevented a father from disinheriting his legitimate child, and to
claim the estate as "forced heir" under the 1811 will. That strategy had
brought success in the 1848 *Patterson* decision. When the court declared
four years later, however, that *Patterson* was collusive (and thus not binding) and that new evidence disputed Myra's legitimacy, Myra's expectations as forced heir ended.

But did the decision in *Gaines v. Relf* mean that Gaines could still use
Clark's alleged bequest to her in the later will—as his legitimate child—to
claim his estate? Myra and Perin thought she could, and they proceeded to
construct a hypothetical version of the missing will. Based on the detailed
remembrances in the depositions of Harriet Harper Smythe and the other
witnesses who claimed to have read the will, they framed an instrument
on which Myra Gaines placed all her hopes. On January 18, 1855, Smiley & Perin presented Gaines's petition to the Second District Court of
New Orleans (the designated probate court). They requested probate for
"the last will" of Daniel Clark, "which was in substance and to the effect
following":

New Orleans, July 13, 1813
In the name of God, amen. I, Daniel Clark, of New Orleans, do make this
my last will and testament.

Imprimus. I order that all my just debts be paid.

Second. I do hereby acknowledge that my beloved Myra, who is now
living in the family of Samuel B. Davis, is my legitimate and only daughter,
and that I leave and bequeath unto her, the said Myra, all the estate, whether
real or personal, of which I may die possessed, subject only to the payment
of certain legacies hereinafter named.

Third. It is my desire that my friend, Chevalier François Dusuau Delacroix, shall have the charge of my said daughter Myra, and I do appoint and
constitute him tutor to her.

Fourth. I give and bequeath unto my mother, Mary Clark, now or recently of Germantown, in the State of Pennsylvania, an annuity of two thousand dollars, which is to be paid out of my estate during her life. I further
give and bequeath an annuity of five hundred dollars to Caroline DesGrange
until she arrives at the age of majority, after which I give and bequeath her
a legacy of five thousand dollars.

Fifth. I hereby nominate and appoint my friends François Dusuau Delacroix, James Pitot, and Joseph D. D. Bellechasse, my executors, with full
power to execute this my last will, and to settle everything related to my
estate.

In addition to the formal wording, Gaines's petition declared that the
will also provided several other legacies: $5,000 to a son of James Pitot;
$5,000 to the son of "Mr. DeBuys"; and freedom and a sum of money for
his maintenance to Clark's slave Lubin. The original was an "olographic"
will—written, dated, and signed entirely in Clark's own handwriting. At
the time of Clark's death, Gaines claimed, it lay among Clark's papers at
his residence. Since then, the will had been "mislaid, lost, or destroyed,"
and its loss prevented the provision of greater accuracy in detailing the
contents.[10]

Circumstances had altered the district courts in Louisiana since Myra
Gaines's last appearance in a probate hearing. Judge J. N. Lea, who received the petition, opened the session "with an air of meticulous and impartial exactness" not often exhibited by a Louisiana judge in a Gaines
case. On January 27, 1855, Judge Lea ordered Clark's 1813 will "proved"
before him. Three "interested parties" asked permission to contest the
probate of the will. Richard Relf, as an executor of the previous will, filed;
so did the ninety-year-old chevalier Delacroix, whose statement indicated
that he had no desire to assume the executorship and that, moreover, he
had "no knowledge, information, or belief" of any Clark will made in
1813. The third opposition came from the City of New Orleans. For the
first time, the city entered the case as a municipal corporation. Twenty
years before, New Orleans had bought the "Blanc Tract" from the Clark
estate. The city still owned a considerable portion of the property and was
directly interested in the outcome of the probate action.[11]

Gaines and Perin pulled out all the old depositions again. James Gardette testified to the deaths of his aunts; Thomas Harper confirmed the
death of his mother and certified her signature on her depositions; and
Louis T. Beauregard testified to the exemplary character of his mother's
friend, Harriet Harper Smythe. The nearly blind chevalier tottered into

10. Will of Daniel Clark, July 13, 1813, reprinted in *Transcript of Record, Gaines v. City of New Orleans*, 2: 14.
11. Harmon, *Famous Case of Myra Clark Gaines*, 374; Petitions of Intervention of F. D. Delacroix, Richard Relf, and the City of New Orleans in the Question of Probate, Feb. 10, 1855, reprinted in *Transcript of Record, Gaines v. City of New Orleans*, 2: 7130.

court on the arm of his elderly son. Despite the petition entered in his name denying knowledge of a second will, the ancient Frenchman willingly recalled the long-ago day in 1813 when Clark had exhibited the sealed packet marked with the words *"pour être ouvert en cas de mort."* The *procès-verbal* signed by Gallien Preval recorded no such marking on the will presented by Richard Relf.[12]

Delacroix's "solemnity and earnestness" impressed the spectators, but not Judge Lea. His opinion was determinedly bipartisan. Myra Gaines had proved the existence of a will made by Clark in 1813, he held. The charge that Clark had destroyed or revoked his second will was "satisfactorily rebutted." But the Code of 1808 had demanded two creditable witnesses, who could swear that they recognized the testament as "entirely written, dated, and signed in the testator's handwriting, having often seen him write during his lifetime." The code also required that an olographic will be dated, and no witness had specified a date; the petition merely estimated the date of July 13. Lea denied probate.

The decision seemed to block Gaines's action. Her witnesses were dead. They could not be questioned about their knowledge of his handwriting. None claimed to have seen Clark sign the will in their presence and none had mentioned a specific date. One option remained—an appeal to the state supreme court. An appeal required an expensive bond, and the costs of the probate petition had depleted Gaines's funds. As had happened so often before, her family came to her aid. Her half-brother James Gardette furnished the necessary bond, and the case was set for a hearing.

Then came a stroke of good fortune for Gaines. An assault on Thomas Slidell, chief justice of the Louisiana supreme court and the brother of Senator John Slidell, injured the judge so severely that he resigned from the bench. A special election was announced to fill the state's highest judicial position at a time when the Gaines case appeal waited to be heard. Most of New Orleans thoroughly detested Myra Gaines for the disruption she had caused to property transactions in the city, but in the rest of Louisiana, as across the nation, she had supporters who admired her unfaltering courage and stubborn perseverance. So Myra went into politics.[13]

* * *

12. Dr. James Gardette, deposition of Oct. 29, 1857; Thomas Harper, deposition of July 14, 1849; and Louis T. Beauregard, deposition of Oct. 30, 1857, General Case Files no. 2619, Record Group 21, National Archives, Fort Worth, Tex.; *New Orleans Times-Democrat*, Jan. 10, 1885, p. 2.

13. Henry Plauché Dart, "The History of the Supreme Court of Louisiana," *Louisiana Historical Quarterly* 4 (1921): 14; Kendall, *History of New Orleans*, 1: 206.

Under John Slidell, the Democratic Party gave Louisiana "its first taste of machine politics," to the dismay of many. Slidell's candidate to replace his brother on the high court bench was J. K. Elzee. The opposition—mostly Whigs but with heavy support from the anti-Catholic Know-Nothings—nominated Edwin T. Merrick from East Feliciana Parish. Although Merrick had no stake in the property disputes of Orleans Parish, Myra Gaines may have known that he favored her position. His wife, Caroline, knew and admired Gaines. In any case, since almost anyone was preferable to a Slidell candidate, Myra campaigned vigorously for Merrick, even making speeches in his behalf. After a bitter campaign, with the *Louisiana Courier* screaming at the Know-Nothings in French on one page and in English on the other, Merrick won by a large margin.[14]

Joining the newly elected judge on the state bench was Judge Lea, who had issued the adverse ruling in the lower court; Judge A. M. Buchanan, who had tried to stop Myra's speech to the jury years before; and two judges, Voorhies and Spofford, who had no previous connection to the Gaines case. Before the hearing, Judge Buchanan declined to hear the case, citing his prior involvement, but Judge Lea decided to stay and uphold his previous judgment.[15]

In 1836, while rejecting Myra's demand for chancery jurisdiction in her suit, Judge Lawrence had indicated that the Louisiana Code was designed to be equitable, or fair and flexible, and thus Louisiana needed no separate equity courts. Now Judge Merrick proceeded to demonstrate that this code could be as supple as necessary. "The rules for the opening and proof of testaments," he declared, "nowhere say that other cases may not arise to which the strict letter of these rules may be inapplicable, and that the Judge may not receive in extraordinary cases other equally satisfactory proof that the requirements of law have been fulfilled." Citing the long period that had elapsed since the death of Daniel Clark as sufficient reason to accept secondary evidence as proof of the will, Judge Merrick announced that the "will of Daniel Clark, dated New Orleans, July 13, 1813 [would] be recognized as his last will and testament." Myra Gaines and Franklin Perin had successfully probated her father's will—one that many still believed never existed at all—forty-three years after his death.[16]

14. "Edwin Thomas Merrick," *Dictionary of American Biography*, 4: 555; Caroline Merrick, *Old Times in Dixie Land: A Southern Matron's Memories* (New York: Grafton Press, 1901), 13–4.

15. Succession of Daniel Clark, 11 Louisiana Reports 124 (1856).

16. Ibid., 138; *Louisiana Courier*, Dec. 19, 1855, p. 2.

The news rippled through New Orleans: the Gaines case was back. One month later Greer Duncan, who had written so triumphantly of the 1852 decision against Gaines, stood again before Judge McCaleb. "Five years ago," Duncan admitted, "I . . . ventured to address to your Honor a few words of congratulations that . . . the Supreme Court had . . . finally, entirely and without reservation put an end to the [Gaines] controversy. Well, sir, the case is *here.* The controversy is not ended. . . . And I think I may safely say that the controversy never will be ended if the complainant can help it." Greer was correct. Using the newly probated will, Gaines began to gather in the property owned by her father at his death so many years before. She sued the chevalier Delacroix for the seventy-five slaves he bought from the estate, and also claimed that "more than 300 slaves have been born from the female slaves . . . the slaves now living and their increase are worth $300,000; . . . the hire of said slaves . . . amounts to $300,000, and that the interest due . . . amounts to $500,000." Gaines made similar claims against all the purchasers of Clark property. She did not merely seek the reversion of title; she wanted the improvements made by the occupants, the full value of rents for the use of the property since its original sale from the estate, and interest on the total.[17]

Another suit followed against the City of New Orleans. Since that corporation admitted its interest in blocking the probate of Clark's will because of its ownership of the Blanc Tract, Gaines sued the city to recover the "rents, fruitage, and titles" of the land in question. A third suit claimed ownership of several lots between Poydras and Perdido Streets owned by Manuel Lizardi, John Slidell, Alfred Hennen, and fifteen others. Judge McCaleb presided over the trial of these next three incarnations of the Gaines case. Predictably, he held that Myra's claim under the 1813 will was no different from her earlier claim under the 1811 will; the Supreme Court decision in *Gaines v. Relf* covered both cases. Gaines quickly made plans for her appeal to Washington. *Gaines v. Hennen,* the only one of the three to actually reach the Supreme Court, represented the sixth appearance of the Gaines case before that tribunal.[18]

Before the Supreme Court could hear the *Hennen* appeal, Richard Relf died. For over a quarter century Relf had led the opposition to Gaines's claims. Neither he nor Beverly Chew ever testified in a Gaines case, nor were they ever charged with fraud for their actions as executors. Perhaps Gaines had learned from her first husband's long-ago libel trial that a

17. *Myra Clark Gaines v. New Orleans, Delacroix et al.* (Washington, D.C., 1858).
18. *Gaines v. Hennen,* 24 Howard 555 (1860).

criminal case would be tried before a New Orleans jury, who would surely exonerate Relf. The testimony presented in the civil trials of the Gaines case clearly indicates that Clark did make a second will, and that testimony also persuasively argues for the destruction of that second will by Richard Relf. In 1813 the firm of Chew & Relf experienced serious cash-flow problems due to the war with Great Britain. As partners of Clark, the firm's own funds were mingled with those of his estate. The Clark fortune provided the financial cushion that allowed Chew & Relf to meet their creditors' demands and continue to operate. If Relf believed (or knew) that Clark had willed his property to an illegitimate child (Myra), he could expect that the will would be challenged by Clark's mother and her own heirs (the beneficiaries of the earlier will). The estate would exist in legal limbo until the question of Myra's birth could be answered, and without access to the estate funds his own firm would fail. Possibly he rationalized the will's destruction as a simple answer to a potentially disastrous situation, especially if he believed that Clark had made other provisions for his daughter. Or perhaps Relf was the archvillain portrayed in Gaines's trial narratives, the scoundrel who stole an orphaned child's birthright. Whatever the explanation for his actions, Relf never ceased to regard the Gaines case as a diabolical plot to deprive him and his partner of their reputations and fortunes.[19]

Two years before Relf's death in 1859, the husband of Gaines's daughter Rhoda visited Relf and suggested that the two adversaries bury the hatchet. Robert Strother's overture was a surprise to both Relf and his mother-in-law. Relf replied by letter to Gaines that though he had "never entertained any other than the kindest feelings toward you personally" or had forgotten his "fondlings with you in your childhood," other considerations, "the obligations of a sacred trust committed to me by one whose memory you should revere, and justice to third parties," compelled him to refuse the olive branch. In answer, Gaines insisted that Strother tell Relf that the offer of compromise came from him alone. She did, however, "freely forgive [Relf] for all the wrongs and persecutions he had inflicted on her." The bitterness revealed by this exchange explains the resolve of both opponents to keep the Gaines case alive.[20]

19. On the intermingling of business between Daniel Clark and the firm of Chew & Relf, see *Partnership Agreement between Daniel Clark and Relf & Chew,* June 19, 1813 (filed Apr. 12, 1841), reprinted in *Transcript of Record, Gaines v. City of New Orleans,* 2: 1791.

20. Richard Relf to Mrs. Myra Clark Gaines, May 13, 1857, reprinted in *Transcript of Record, Gaines v. Hennen,* 199.

When Gaines returned to Washington to hear her attorneys argue the latest version of her case, she discovered that the Supreme Court had moved upstairs in the Capitol building; now it occupied the old Senate chamber, a room more in keeping with its increasing importance. George Townsend, in his memoirs of life in the capital city, called the new hearing room the "noblest apartment in proportion and architecture, considering its small size, in the United States." The room was semicircular; along the diameter, on a raised platform, stood the cushioned, high-backed chairs of the justices. Behind the row of chairs a screen of Ionic columns supported a gallery of windows curtained in red. Raised over all was a half dome, with the apex centered over the chief justice's chair. The furniture came from the old Senate chamber—desks, bookcases, tables, all made of rosewood or mahogany. Townsend tried one of the justice's chairs and found it "wonderfully introductory to sleep." One justice agreed, and told Townsend that "the greatest trial he had was to keep awake."[21]

Supreme Court justices stood at the top of capital society, even more sought after than cabinet members. Invited everywhere, they found a welcome at all the great weddings, dinners, receptions, and balls. Mrs. Clement Clay remembered that the justices and their wives formed a "charmed circle into which the merely light-minded would scarcely have ventured." Myra Gaines felt at home in that world where she met the "wittiest and weightiest minds of the capital . . . discussed philosophies, inventions, history, perhaps, and the arts; seldom the fashions, as seldom the *on dits*." Her persuasive voice could be heard explaining the details of her litigation to anyone who would listen. One who encountered Gaines reported that her favorite technique was to hold on to a gentleman's lapel so that he could not escape her arguments.[22]

When the *Hennen* case came before the Supreme Court in December 1860, Franklin Perin moved his whole family to Washington, where they lived at number six on 4 1/2 Street, commonly known as "Lawyers' Row." Myra Gaines lived with the Perins in Washington, and the family considered her a useful but tedious guest: useful in assisting with hostess duties (Perin's wife, Mary, was frequently ill) and tedious because she constantly talked of her case and its newspaper coverage. Perin's granddaughter con-

21. George A. Townsend, *Washington, Outside and Inside* (Chicago: James Betts, 1873), 300–5.

22. Lawrence, *James Moore Wayne*, 130; Clay-Clopton, *Belle of the Fifties*, 137; "The Romance of the Gaines Case," *Putnam's Magazine*, 210.

sidered Myra "publicity-mad," and recounts that she was "never seen or known to read anything but newspapers." She "reveled in the gaze of the crowd," according to Anna Clyde Plunkett.[23]

The reappearance of the Gaines case brought new attorneys to the Supreme Court. In addition to Franklin Perin, Gaines retained Caleb Cushing. A distinguished politician, scholar, linguist, and soldier, Cushing had a tremendous practice before the high court. Aware of Gaines's financial troubles, Cushing demanded his fee up front: $25,000 for arguing the appeal of *Gaines v. Hennen*. Somehow, Myra paid. Alfred Hennen chose to represent himself and the other defendants; joining him was New Orleans attorney Louis Janin. Janin had participated on the periphery of Gaines cases but had never before directly argued the case in court. Over the next thirty years, he became one of Myra's most implacable opponents.[24]

In their arguments, Hennen and Janin relied on the 1852 *Gaines v. Relf* decision, Cushing and Perin on the newly probated will. The debate was familiar to the audience; the highest point of drama came when Franklin Perin collapsed in the middle of his opening speech. His granddaughter blamed the grueling work he had done in preparation. After regaining consciousness, Perin continued, and the court permitted him to sit during his presentation, "an unprecedented courtesy" allowed by Justice Wayne.[25]

The personnel of the Supreme Court had undergone changes, but Justices Wayne and Catron remained. These two judges continued to use the Gaines case to express their ideas about the relationship of family, marriage, and children to the law. But in the end, Wayne and Catron also differed over the facts of the case: Wayne always believed that Myra Gaines was truly Daniel Clark's legitimate child and his rightful heir, while Catron believed her identity was a "pious fraud." This time, when the court handed down its sixth Gaines decision on March 15, 1861, Wayne's view prevailed by a slim one-vote majority. Wayne's biographer calls the justice "Mrs. Gaines's judicial knight errant . . . a crusader in ermine" for her cause. Rarely had any justice "so tenaciously espoused a litigant's cause" as had Mr. Justice Wayne in the case of Daniel Clark's daughter. His sympathy for the "lone woman, fighting gallantly for her rights" is evident in both the opinions he authored. Joining him in declaring for Gaines's legitimacy were Justices Nelson and Clifford (new on the court

23. Plunkett, *Corridors by Candlelight*, 88–90.
24. Kendall, "Strange Case of Myra Clark Gaines," 47.
25. Plunkett, *Corridors by Candlelight*, 91.

since 1852), and Justice McLean (who, because of illness, had missed the last appearance of the case). Justice Campbell, Myra's former attorney, did not participate. Catron and Grier remained in opposition, now joined by Chief Justice Taney.[26]

Addressing the concerns of his colleagues, Wayne took care to distinguish the *Hennen* case from its predecessors. In this sixth appearance, the Gaines case "presents the controversy differently from what it has been before." Now Gaines came to the court with support from a Louisiana bench directing that the 1813 will of Daniel Clark "be recognized and executed as such." Wayne reprised the whole case, attacking all the arguments raised in the earlier cases as well as in *Hennen*. Even the old concern for the collusive nature of the *Patterson* complaint came under review. Wayne decreed that even if a "discreet arrangement" had existed, "it [had not been] one of intentional deception in contemplation of any undue advantage." He concluded with a sweeping declaration of Myra's legitimacy: she had been born of "lawful wedlock" with Zulime Carrière. In his last will, Clark had named Myra his "universal legatee," and the Louisiana civil code as well as the state supreme court's decision entitled her to her father's estate, subject only to the payment of legacies mentioned in the will. "After a litigation of thirty years," Wayne hoped that the U.S. Supreme Court had seen the last of the Gaines case. "This court," he proclaimed, "has adjudicated the principles applicable to her rights. . . . They are now settled."[27]

But he did not have the last word. Justice Catron issued a dissent that repeated all the arguments he had made against Myra's claims eight years earlier, and then added one more. "Ruin" would be the consequence of overturning the 1852 decision. "In a growing city like New Orleans much of the property supposed to be protected by our former decree must have changed hands," he wrote. "Large improvements must have been made in the nine years since that suit was decided. If the twenty odd defendants to this bill can be recovered against, so can the others." Catron's fears mirrored the concerns of those watching in New Orleans.[28]

In *Gaines v. Hennen,* one other justice entered a dissent, one of the shortest on record. Justice Grier did not think it necessary to review the history of the "scandalous gossip . . . buried under the dust of half a cen-

26. *Gaines v. Hennen,* 24 Howard 553; Lawrence, *James Moore Wayne,* 127, 170.
27. *Gaines v. Hennen,* 615.
28. Ibid., 626.

tury, and which a proper feeling of delicacy should have suffered to remain so." He, too, hoped to see the end of the Gaines case. But he considered the final decision, which allowed a will to be "established by the dim recollections, imaginations, or inventions of anile gossips, after forty-five years," and to "disturb the titles and possessions of the bona fide purchasers," indefensible and incomprehensible.[29]

"The decision in favor of Mrs. Gaines creates profound sensation," proclaimed the *New York Herald*. "Those who know the lady and have watched the unparalleled perseverance and ability with which she has prosecuted her case against the most extraordinary combination of talent and money that has ever been contended against, are rejoiced." Congratulations poured in from across the United States. The *New York Times* reported the "unusual excitement" that awaited the decision, and the gratification of Gaines's friends afterward. The decision, the *Times* assured its readers, gave Myra Gaines title to "many millions of dollars," making her "the wealthiest woman in America." The *Herald* agreed: "Unless public information is very much at fault, Mrs. Gaines is undoubtably the richest woman on this side of the Atlantic, and if wealth could give it, ought to be the happiest."[30]

The editor of the *Times* sounded a more moralistic note; Mrs. Gaines not only obtained a "fortune of fabulous amount," but "establishe[d] forever the honor of her mother." The *Times* praised her for the "honorable affection" she demonstrated for her mother's memory. Against the "most fearful odds," she had battled for her mother's honor, "evinc[ing] the most commendable spirit." Her "legal struggles, the attempted social ostracism, the treacheries, the sorrows," were too many to enumerate. When she had exhausted her fortune, when her friends, "convinced of the uselessness of further trial" were gone, all she had left was her "own indomitable spirit."[31]

Women everywhere admired Myra Gaines. The *Times* reported that a stream of callers left cards at Gaines's residence. The *Herald* understood that the ladies of three cities—New York, Washington, and Memphis—planned fitting testimonials in recognition of the "indomitable faith and perseverance of Mrs. Gaines in this most remarkable and protracted case." The *Herald* encouraged these fitting tributes "to one of their own sex,

29. Ibid., 631.
30. *New York Herald*, Mar. 15, 1861, p. 1; *New York Times*, Mar. 15, 1861, p. 1.
31. Editorial, *New York Times*, Mar. 15, 1861, p. 4.

who, against difficulties, delays, combinations and reverses that very few men would have had the moral courage to face, has thus achieved one of the greatest legal triumphs of this century."[32]

Several newspapers sounded a cautionary note. Louisiana had seceded from the Union the previous January. What would be the response of the Confederate state to a decree from the United States Supreme Court? Gaines had not long to wait. Although a special clause in the Louisiana secession proclamation exempted pending cases before United States courts from its decree of nullity directed at United States laws, exceptions could be made. The Louisiana legislature declared Gaines an "alien resident" so that the decree of the Supreme Court could be avoided.[33]

On April 14, 1861, Pierre G. T. Beauregard, fresh from hearing his father's testimony on Myra's behalf, ordered the guns of the Charleston battery to fire the opening salvos of the Civil War at Fort Sumter. Secession and war meant decisions for those involved in the Gaines case. Justices Wayne and Catron, both southerners and Jackson men, held to the Union, but in their last years they saw the nation they served "distracted by rebellion and scourged by civil war." Justice Wayne's son resigned his commission in the United States Army and returned to Georgia. Wayne, however, refused to resign from the court. Georgia's secession came three months before the March 1861 decision in *Hennen*. To resign, "to break up the Court," he explained, "would be to the injury of many private rights, involving much money, before it." Unquestionably, he was referring to the Gaines case.[34]

Judge Catron also chose to stay on the Supreme Court at the cost of many friendships in his home state. Catron, a Democrat, strongly opposed secession; when it came his fellow Tennesseans banished him from the state. Catron spent the early years of the war in Washington, telling friends that "his life would not be safe in his home state" since he remained loyal to the Union. Once Tennessee returned to Union control, Catron did go back to reopen its federal courts in 1862. He died in Nashville on May 30, 1865, prior to the next appearance of the Gaines before the Supreme Court.[35]

32. Ibid.; *New York Herald*, Mar. 15, 1861, p. 1.

33. *New York Herald*, Mar. 15, 1861, p. 1.

34. Lawrence, *James Moore Wayne*, 169–70. Wayne's decision proved costly. A Confederate court branded him an enemy alien and confiscated all his Georgia property. Bernard Schwartz, *A History of the Supreme Court* (New York: Oxford University Press, 1993), 98.

35. Chandler, "Centenary of Associate Justice John Catron," 13.

Alone among the southern justices on the high court, John A. Campbell resigned. He, too, did not believe in secession, but when Alabama seceded, he returned to the South. He joined the Confederate government at Richmond, accepted the post of assistant secretary of war, and spent the war years handling requisition orders and attending to the operation of the southern draft.[36]

The Perin family left Washington for New Orleans soon after Fort Sumter, but Gaines remained. She moved into a boarding house near Lawyers' Row while she awaited word from Perin on the attitude of Louisiana to the *Hennen* decision. Money problems continued to plague her. Evicted from her lodgings for nonpayment of rent and her trunks confiscated by the hotel's owner, Gaines decided to leave Washington and seek aid from the Confederacy.[37]

Once in Richmond, Myra Gaines found herself a less-than-welcome visitor. Writing to Franklin Perin early in 1862, she lamented that she had "passed a very unhappy summer." Twice she had been "placed on the list to be arrested." Dismayed, Gaines told Perin that she "had hoped [that] a person holding a high position would have been excluded." Nor did Richmond society open its arms to her. The "first families of Virginia" had received her with "ambivalence," she reported to Perin.[38]

Politics proved even less welcoming than society. Myra met with "Mr. MacFarland," the "most distinguished lawyer in Richmond," to ask about the possibility of a bill before the Confederate congress granting recognition to the decrees of the United States Supreme Court for cases involving residents of the southern states. MacFarland advised her that a general bill might pass, might even gain the support of the Louisiana delegation, but that any suggestion of special treatment for the Gaines case would fail.[39]

The animosity felt by Gaines's opponents spilled over onto her family. Gaines's son, William Whitney, fought in a Louisiana regiment during the

36. Connor, *John Archibald Campbell,* 247.

37. Plunkett, *Corridors by Candlelight,* 105. Plunkett asserts that Myra got through the Confederate lines by "a display of hysteria," a charge that fails to mesh with other indications of her character.

38. Myra Clark Gaines to Franklin Perin, Feb. 10, 1862, Myra Clark Gaines Collection, Manuscript Room, Howard-Tilton Memorial Library, Tulane University, New Orleans.

39. Myra Clark Gaines to Franklin Perin, Mar. 23, 1862, ibid.

Civil War. He enlisted as a private when his mother's efforts to get a commission for him failed. Gaines had directed her request to her friend John Campbell in the War Department, but an old opponent blocked the appointment. Campbell's superior, the Confederate secretary of war, was Louisianian Judah P. Benjamin. Gaines angrily wrote Perin that she "should have had [a lieutenancy for Whitney] but for that *miserable scum* Benjamin—he ought to have been dismissed from the Cabinet according to the wishes of the people. Never has there been so *overrated a man*."[40]

For the next year Gaines moved between Richmond and Warrenton, North Carolina, the home of her daughter Rhoda, now married to James Y. Christmas. In New Orleans Franklin Perin continued his efforts on Gaines's behalf. The Confederate courts opened in New Orleans on May 8, 1861, and Perin placed the first case on the docket. When Louisiana seceded and its two federal judges resigned, President Jefferson Davis appointed Edwin Warren Moise, a former state attorney general and a lawyer who had once represented Myra Gaines, as Confederate district judge for the Eastern Division at New Orleans. With Moise on the bench, Perin believed Myra might have a chance to establish her claims in the Confederate courts. *Myra Clark Gaines v. John M. Brown* was case number one in the new Confederate District Court, and 246 more Gaines lawsuits quickly followed.[41]

The cases Perin filed all described Gaines as "an alien citizen of the District of Columbia, now temporarily residing in Virginia," and asked the Confederate court to recognize her claim to the property now in the possession of the defendants named in the suits. Since he could not rely on the United States Supreme Court's decree, Perin chose to claim the lots under the decision of the Louisiana supreme court admitting Daniel Clark's 1813 will to probate in 1858. Charles Janin, Louis Janin's brother, represented most of the defendants. The exception he filed for each case denied that Gaines had any right to use the Confederate courts. She was "an alien enemy" who should be "deprived by law of any right of action or standing" in the southern courts. He reminded the court that by deci-

40. Ibid.
41. Statement of J. W. Gurley relative to the records of the District Court of the Confederate States, Mar. 14, 1877, reprinted in *Transcript of Record, Gaines v. City of New Orleans*, 1: 129; Henry Putney Beers, *The Confederacy; A Guide to the Archives of the Government of the Confederate States of America* (Washington, D.C.: National Archives and Records Administration, 1986), 2–3.

sion of the legislature, "all her estate, either real or person, within the Confederate States have been sequestered by the Confederate States and [are]
... under their exclusive control." Franklin Perin never argued any of the
cases he filed before the Confederate courts; the courts closed on March
6, 1862, as the forces of Admiral Farragut approached New Orleans. But
Perin remained active to the end. The 247th Gaines case was the last case
placed on the Confederate court docket.[42]

When the federal troops closed in on New Orleans, Perin's family left
for Ocean Springs, Alabama, to take advantage of the therapeutic waters
and allow Perin to restore his shattered nerves. After they left the city,
General Butler commandeered the Perin home and turned it into a hospital. The Civil War had divided Perin's family; an adopted southerner, his
own family members fought for the North against his wife's four brothers.
The strain of war, added to his devotion to Gaines's cause, ruined Perin's
health, and he died in Alabama on August 9, 1863. Although Anna Clyde
Plunkett later blamed the "driving, whiplashing domination of Myra
Gaines" for having shortened her grandfather's life, Gaines's gratitude for
Perin's ability kept her in close touch with his family. She always described
Perin as "the best friend she ever had—the lawyer who stood by her to the
very end of his life and achieved, ultimately, more success for her than any
other of the thirty big legal lights of the nation." Myra Gaines had agreed
to pay Perin $100,000 for his legal services, contingent on her victory.
Although she satisfied a portion of this sum by transferring ownership of
several pieces of New Orleans property, worth $35,000 in 1880, most of
Perin's fee was never paid.[43]

Once the federal courts reopened in New Orleans after the city's capture by Union troops, Gaines's residency in the Confederacy was a liabil-
ity. Her journey back through the Confederate lines ("in spite of Mr.
Stanton," was the acid comment of Louis Janin) was not without danger.
A Confederate patrol captured her near the tiny hamlet of Darkesville,
now in West Virginia. She always declared that she would have lost her life

42. Record of *Myra Clark Gaines v. Fuentes,* case no. 55, District Court of the Con-
federate States of America, District of Louisiana, reprinted in *Transcript of Record,
Gaines v. City of New Orleans,* 1: 125; Beers, 2–3; Gurley Statement, Mar. 14, 1877.
Gaines v. Fuentes is cited here as an example of the 247 suits filed for Myra Gaines in the
Confederate courts. The pleadings in all suits differ only in the names of the defendants
and the property descriptions. Confederate court records for Louisiana are located in
Record Group 21, National Archives, Southwest Region, Fort Worth, Tex.
43. Plunkett, *Corridors by Candlelight,* 97–8.

there if not for the gallantry of a southern colonel from Marietta, Georgia, named George W. Benson. The colonel secured her release and saw that she was safely conveyed through southern and northern lines. This episode seems too much like the romantic exaggerations that Myra Gaines often added to her personal history, but in her will, she made a bequest of ten thousand dollars to Colonel Benson "for saving her life."[44]

After spending the rest of the war years with family in Brooklyn, New York, Gaines returned to New Orleans. She was not unmoved by the trauma of "this wicked war," but her general attitude viewed the contest between North and South as merely a roadblock to her eventual success. In June 1865 she wrote to Mary Perin (Franklin's widow) that she had "to see that all my suits are transferred from the Confederacy to the District Court of the New Orleans Circuit—and all the other litigation of the last two years. What a siege of it have I not had!"[45]

In 1861, the *New York Times* had commented that Myra's victory ought to make her the happiest of women. That triumph, however, had produced not a single dollar or piece of land. During the war years she had made promises, given mortgages on land she did not yet control, and borrowed from anyone who would lend her money, but "vexatious delays"—as a friend euphemistically called them—continued to block her progress. Now she had to start back at the beginning. After the Louisiana Supreme Court granted probate to the 1813 will, Gaines had begun three suits to recover property from her father's estate. One, against Hennen, had been decided by the U.S. Supreme Court in her favor. The other two were still active. The old chevalier was dead, but his son continued his case, and the City of New Orleans was a very active participant. In 1865, the circuit court ruled against Myra in *Gaines v. The City of New Orleans* and *Gaines v. Delacroix,* demonstrating again that a Louisiana court did not consider itself bound by the actions of the United States Supreme Court. Two years later, *Gaines v. The City of New Orleans* itself reached the high court. The Gaines case was back again.

44. Testimony of Colonel George Benson, *Evans Will Record,* 3: 2; Harmon, *Famous Case of Myra Clark Gaines,* 397.
45. Myra Clark Gaines to Mrs. Franklin Perin, June 6, 1865, Myra Clark Gaines Collection, Manuscript Room, Howard-Tilton Memorial Library, Tulane University, New Orleans.

Conclusion

"The Most Remarkable Case"

When the Supreme Court convened for the 1867 winter term, two figures familiar to Myra Gaines were absent. Justice Catron had died in Nashville two years before, and Justice Wayne, Gaines's great advocate, had died of typhoid fever in the heat of the previous summer, on July 5, 1867. Justices Taney and McLean were also gone. Their replacements, Noah H. Swayne of Ohio, David Davis of Illinois, Cyrus Field's brother Stephen J. Field, and the new chief justice, Salmon P. Chase, had no prior acquaintance (in a formal, legal sense) with the Gaines case. Justices Nelson, Clifford, and Grier were still on the bench. No doubt, Grier was less than pleased to see the case he had dismissed—he hoped "for the last time"—before him again.

Gaines v. The City of New Orleans saw Louis Janin again representing the city and Caleb Cushing acting for Myra Gaines. The opinion of the court, written by Justice Davis, provides a summary that, for the modern reader, is the clearest explanation in any of the Supreme Court opinions of the evidence supporting Gaines's legitimacy. Davis began, as had many of his brother justices before him, by expressing his hopes that "the history of this litigation . . . will be closed by this decision." It was enough, he thought, that Myra Gaines had pursued her case through a third of a century, "with a vigor and energy hardly ever surpassed, in defiance of obstacles which would have deterred persons of ordinary mind and character."[1]

The key to resolving the controversy was the legitimacy of Myra

1. *Gaines v. City of New Orleans,* 6 Wallace 642 (1868), at 643.

Gaines. With the probate of the 1813 will, no court could deprive her of her father's estate if she was his legitimate daughter. Davis placed great stress on Clark's declaration of her legitimacy in his last will. He excused Clark's conduct in the last years of his life as the attempt to "repair the consequences of his folly." Clark had "contracted an unfortunate . . . and in many respects disreputable marriage, having married a person with whom he had previously lived improperly, who, without a divorce, had married again." The justice thought it natural that Clark, "possessed of commanding influence, and high position, and mingling in social intercourse with the best society of the country," should want to conceal his marriage to Zulime. But at the end of his life, it was also natural that he should wish to make amends to the child born of that marriage by a "deliberate acknowledgment" of her legitimacy.[2]

Davis pictured the "struggle in Clark's mind" after Zulime married Dr. Gardette. He could not, the justice considered, acknowledge their marriage without harming a woman "whom he had once loved and still professed to respect." Yet not to announce their marriage would "bastardize a child for whom he had great affection, and to see a large part of his estate go to others, who had no claims on his bounty." Before Clark's death, Justice Davis believed, "the better nature of this man of lofty pride and sensitive honor . . . gained the ascendency." By public acknowledgment in his will and by statements to Harriet Harper Smythe, Boisfontaine, and Bellechasse, Clark had "atoned in some measure for the errors of his past life."[3]

Davis's opinion illustrated that Myra Gaines succeeded in developing a trial narrative that convincingly appealed to the prevailing sense of public morality. As in every trial, the Gaines case represented a conflict between two supposedly truthful narratives. The argument that succeeded with its audience—whether judge, jury, or public—corroborated the audience's experiences and validated their prejudices. The Gaines case demonstrated the anxieties and concerns that confronted its century. Myra Gaines and her attorneys used the rhetorical strategy of sentimentality to "solve" the case's central credibility problem, and their success was evident in Davis's opinion.

"Courts . . . have rarely had to deal with a case of greater hardship, or more interesting character and history," than the Gaines case, Justice

2. Ibid., 698.
3. Ibid., 701–2.

Davis concluded. The Louisiana supreme court had established the validity of the will in Myra Gaines's favor executed by her father forty-three years before. The questions of law and fact at issue in the Gaines case had been determined seven years earlier in *Gaines v. Hennen.* "After argument by able counsel, and on mature consideration, we have reaffirmed that decision. Can we not indulge the hope," Davis pleaded, "that the rights of Myra Clark Gaines in the estate of her father, Daniel Clark, will *now* be recognized?"[4]

Public opinion, except in New Orleans, did recognize Myra Gaines as her father's heir. The remainder of the 1860s was the zenith of Gaines's popularity. Her legal victory "commanded the admiration and sympathy of the whole country." She was the focus of every gathering she attended; one gentleman remarked that she was the "most interesting conversationalist" he had ever known. Society columns never failed to mention her presence and describe her dress. At the Grant inaugural ball, amid the "struggling and suffering mass," she "commanded as usual, a very large share of attention." Her "black and gold lamé with gold fringe and embroidery," accessorized with a "blue bonnet and diamonds," excited admiring comments. Everywhere well wishers surrounded her and stopped her progress, so "delighted were her friends to recognize her."[5]

For much of her life Myra Gaines had remained apart from the various reform movements that attracted other women active in public life. Her participation in the preparation and presentation of the legal arguments in her extensive litigation left little time for other interests. Too, her awareness of the need to maintain the role of persecuted heroine precluded membership in activities that failed to secure wide support. But as she grew older, she used her celebrity status to draw attention to the post–Civil War campaign for women's suffrage. During the 1850s Gaines supported Edwin Merrick's election to the Louisiana state supreme court. Her inability to vote for Merrick herself, or to draw other women to the polls, lessened her impact on that election. In 1879 the "celebrated litigant" occupied a prominent position among the "notables" in a group of women petitioning the Louisiana state constitutional convention to grant women the franchise. Three years later in Washington, D.C., she joined the Woman's National Labor League and pledged to continue its work for women's

4. Ibid., 718.

5. Harmon, *Famous Case of Myra Clark Gaines,* 417; Ellet, *Court Circles of the Republic,* 571–2.

suffrage. Her belated conversion to women's rights, however, never became more than an adjunct to her continued concentration on collecting the fruits of her legal victory.[6]

As the Gilded Age opened, the public's fascination with the inherited wealth of Myra Gaines kept her case on the front pages of the newspapers. A popular magazine in 1868 commented to its readers that "Nothing marks the high civilization of the day more surely than an intense desire to be millionaires." Estimates of the worth of the property she now owned (but still did not control) in New Orleans topped $35 million. In comparison, the tax rolls of New York City listed the total taxable property (assessed at approximately one-third its actual value) of William B. Astor as $16,114,000. The next wealthiest New Yorker, William C. Rhinelander, had $7,745,000 worth of taxable property. Thus, the *New York Times* announcement that Myra Gaines was the wealthiest woman in the country does not seem unreasonable.[7]

The Supreme Court may have confirmed Myra Gaines's title to millions of dollars worth of New Orleans real estate, but delays and "vexatious" suits continued to keep her from actually taking possession of the property. She did not feel wealthy. Sale of the Hennen property brought only $2,600; Gaines owed hundreds of thousands of dollars. To finance the appeal of *Gaines v. The City of New Orleans* alone, she sold New Yorker James Emott a mortgage on property she hoped to obtain for $120,000. For twenty-five years she had paid her bills and borrowed from her friends on the expectations of her inheritance. Now, as funds slowly dribbled in, demands for repayment began.[8]

Family difficulties compounded Gaines's monetary woes. With the confirmation of her inheritance Davis's opinion provided, Myra's extended family expected to benefit from her new wealth. The two daughters of her old Aunt Despau, Caroline McMahon and Zulime Villerette, believed that their mother's testimony had secured Gaines's estate; they felt Myra owed

6. Merrick, *Old Times in Dixie Land*, 127; "A Recruit for the Labor League," *New York Times*, Sept. 29, 1882, p. 1.

7. T. W., "Our Millionaires," *Galaxy: An Illustrated Magazine of Entertaining Reading* 5 (1868): 529; *New York Times*, Mar. 15, 1861, p. 1.

8. Record of mortgages given by Myra Clark Gaines, in *Transcript of Record, Gaines v. City of New Orleans*, 1: 728; Myra Clark Gaines to Mrs. Franklin Perin, June 13, 1865, Myra Clark Gaines Collection, Manuscript Room, Howard-Tilton Memorial Library, Tulane University, New Orleans.

Sophia Despau's daughters a share of her "millions." Letter after letter came from Caroline, Zulime, or their husbands, pleading financial difficulties. Gaines replied to each letter assuring her cousins of her concern for their plight but explaining her lack of funds. "How hard a lot is mine," she wrote to Colonel McMahon, "with such an immense Estate and after fighting for it for so many long wearing years to be so situated that it is not in my power to return to those who I feel have legitimate claims?" In another letter, written in 1872, she explained her frustrating attempts to collect on her suits. "Although I have a judgment in my favor against the City of New Orleans for $120,000," she complained, "yet to this hour I have been unabled [sic] to obtain one dollar of it . . . in consequence of the various creditors insisting on their pro rata share."[9]

Gaines's decision not to evict the occupants of her property is one reason she found herself in financial difficulties. To turn out of their homes a number of widows, orphans, and elderly would destroy the carefully erected edifice of celebrity that Gaines enjoyed. But her letters also indicate a sincere concern for the innocent victims of the executors' fraud. A letter from Gaines's daughter Rhoda to Zulime Villerette explaining her mother's poverty admits that "Mother is one of the wealthiest persons in the United States, but we must have a little patience to realize the benefits accruing from the decision of the Court. . . . [H]er kind heart not to turn these people off her property is the reason of her not being better off. She says she could never be happy again were she to do it and she can better afford to wait than to turn them out of doors homeless." Gaines's generosity to her former opponents is amazing in light of her continued financial difficulties.[10]

Prompted by both her concern for the current residents and her money troubles, Gaines decided to offer "quit-claim" deeds to the individual occupants and pursue her claim against the city of New Orleans. Most of the city property involved in the dispute lay within the boundaries of the old Blanc Tract purchased by the city in 1834. Some of this land remained in the possession of the city; other portions had been sold with the city warranting the titles. On the basis of the *Hennen* decision, Gaines sought to recover not only the current value of the land, but rents computed year by year since the first occupation under the disputed title. One attorney

9. Myra Clark Gaines to Colonel McMahon, Sept. 6, 1866, and to Zulime Villerette, Aug. 28, 1872, Myra Clark Gaines Papers, Library of Congress.

10. Rhoda Christmas to Zulime Villerette, July 14, 1877, ibid.

for the city noted that "for a little piece of waste land sold in 1821 for $4,760 [by Relf and Chew to Évariste Blanc] to pay Clark's debts, and subsequently in the process of time, bought by the city, laid out in streets and squares and sold to hundreds of persons in such lots, [Myra Gaines] expects to obtain a decree from this tribunal making this little parcel of waste land realize for her the sum of two millions!"[11]

The city's financial position made settlement difficult. Reconstruction left the municipal government with an enormous civic debt. The task of repaying that debt was made more difficult by the Gaines litigation. The decisions rendered against the city compelled Mayor Wiltz to borrow $148,000 in 1874—an immense sum in those days. Nine years later the continuing legal actions forced the city to raise its tax rate to 3.17 percent just to pay off a judgment in favor of Myra Gaines. By 1883, the financial situation of the city was so desperate that the gas company threatened to cut off the lights and "plunge the city into darkness."[12]

The uncertainty surrounding land affected by the Gaines case slowed development in New Orleans at a time when the city sorely needed the increased tax revenue improved property would bring in. Louis Janin recounted one story in a court presentation. He told of a man who wished to buy a lot in the city, but before he accepted the deed the gentleman insisted that the sellers guarantee that Myra Clark Gaines would never claim it. In vain did the owners of the property assure him that the parcel was not part of the Clark land and had never been the subject of a Gaines suit. The man refused to listen. No one knew, he said, what Mrs. Gaines might claim![13]

In the years following Justice Davis's decision in *Gaines v. The City of New Orleans*, the two parties fought almost constantly in the courts. Justice Davis's plea that the Supreme Court had seen the last of the Gaines case went unheeded. Five more times the case returned. In 1880, a consultant retained by the city recommended terminating the "vexatious litigations already carried on for more than a third of a century at heavy expenses to and greatly to the detriment of the city, whose growth is seri-

11. Brief for Appellees, *Gaines v. City of New Orleans*, reprinted in *Transcript of Record, Gaines v. City of New Orleans*, 1: 536.

12. Joy J. Jackson, *New Orleans in the Gilded Age: Politics and Urban Progress, 1880–1896* (Baton Rouge: Published by the Louisiana State University Press for the Louisiana Historical Association, 1969), 3–4; Kendall, *History of New Orleans*, 1: 352, 443.

13. Harmon, *Famous Case of Myra Clark Gaines*, 434.

ously retarded by the cloud which hangs over so many of the titles to its real estate." Further resistance, the consultant suggested, was "an idle waste of time."[14]

But the city refused to back down. The final years of Myra Gaines's life were spent no differently from the rest of her adulthood, caught in the shadow of the law, suing and being sued by the city, her lawyers, and her creditors. Her celebrity status faded, and on her visits to the capital, fewer people stopped to speak. One who did left a memorable description of Myra Gaines three years before her death. She was "under five feet tall, thin [and] wiry, with small, bright restless black eyes, very red hair streaked with white, worn in bunches of little curls on either side of the forehead. She was always dressed in black with black mitts upon her hands, carrying with her a large black bag in which were papers connected with her many suits." Known as the "New Orleans Claimant," her increasingly eccentric figure became a fixture on the streets of the city. She kept her own office at number thirteen Exchange Place, in a building now demolished. From there she could reach her attorneys, keeping them "keyed up to the proper pitch by her presence, her enthusiasm, and her confidence, which never wavered."[15]

Family troubles continued to shadow her last years. Her daughter, Rhoda Christmas, died in 1879, and Gaines took over the care of her three grandchildren. She wrote a close friend that she feared she could "never recover my spirits from the death of my beloved daughter, the greatest affliction of my life." But greater trials were to come. Two years later, on June 25, 1881, her son-in-law, James Christmas, shot and killed Gaines's only son, William Whitney Jr. Whitney and his family had moved in with his mother the previous year and added three more children to the household that already contained Christmas and his children. During this time Gaines lived in Washington, D.C., in the Cataczy House at 1336 I Street. Originally built for Justice Campbell, the "large and commodious" house became the property of the Russian minister after the Civil War. After the Cataczys left Washington, the house became a respectable boarding house run by the Misses Harrover.[16]

14. E. Woolridge to the New Orleans Municipal Council, Sept. 1880, reprinted in *Transcript of Record, Gaines v. City of New Orleans,* 1: 563–4.

15. J. Carroll Payne, *A Celebrated Case: The Myra Clark Gaines Litigation: A Paper Read before the Fourteenth Annual Session of the Georgia Bar Association* (Atlanta, Ga.: Franklin Printing and Publishing, n.d.), 12–3; Kendall, *History of New Orleans,* 2: 23.

16. Myra Clark Gaines to Mrs. Perkins, May 18, 1880, *Evans Will Record,* 3: 146.

The headlines in the *Washington Evening Star* screamed "Fratricidal Affair" and recounted all the scandals of the Gaines case again. According to the testimony of Selina Wheat, another resident of Cataczy House, Christmas shot Whitney as he was coming down the stairs and Whitney was running up. Wheat did not see the actual shot, but reached Whitney immediately afterward and found him dead. Her husband, Reverend John Thomas Wheat, saw Whitney strike Christmas on the back of the neck with his fist. Then, Wheat testified, he saw Whitney "fumbling at his hip pocket as if to draw a pistol." Reverend Wheat did not see the shooting, either. Christmas admitted killing Whitney, saying he "was compelled to do it in self-defense." The two men, who were in business together, had quarreled over the money they expected to inherit from Gaines, and Whitney accused Christmas of trying to supplant him in his mother's affections. A Washington jury acquitted Christmas of murder. Six months after Whitney's death, Myra Gaines wrote a friend that "I have not seen him [Christmas] nor held any communication with him since that unfortunate tragedy." Eventually, she reconciled with her son-in-law, helped by a remembrance of her son's threats and a desire to remain close to her grandchildren.[17]

Gaines did not live to see the end of the lawsuit that consumed her life. As she grew increasingly frail, her family urged her to make her own will so that the property still under litigation might be distributed according to her wishes. For one who had spent her whole life fighting over a disputed will, she showed remarkable reluctance to make her own. In January 1885, Dr. William Holcomb, a well-known physician in New Orleans, where Gaines had returned to live, treated her for a serious cold and bronchitis. Her attorney, William H. Wilder, and her son-in-law James Christmas (again part of her household) asked Dr. Holcomb to encourage Gaines to make her testament, and the doctor complied, with little success. "I am not going to die, sir," he reported as her reply.[18]

As her condition worsened and her breathing grew more labored, Myra Gaines finally relented and consented to make a final disposition of the

17. Rhoda's first husband, Robert Strother, had died during the Civil War, and she married James Y. Christmas, by whom she had three children. Mrs. Selina Wheat and Reverend John Thomas Wheat, depositions of Feb. 28, 1882, *United States v. Christmas,* District of Columbia Criminal Court, General Case Files no. 3955, National Archives, Eastern Region, Maryland; Myra Clark Gaines to "My Dear Sir," Jan. 2, 1882, *Evans Will Record,* 3: 292.

18. Harmon, *Famous Case of Myra Clark Gaines,* 449.

estate she had claimed as her own inheritance. When Wilder arrived with a notary, Gaines refused to allow both men in her bedroom. Wilder interviewed the bedridden woman and called out her wishes to the notary sitting outside in the hall who wrote them down. After several special bequests, including the one to Colonel Benson, who had saved her life during the Civil War, she left the remainder of her estate to her grandchildren in equal shares. Having learned the value of a statement of legitimacy, she insisted that her will declare each child legitimate. A Dr. Harrison served as one of the witnesses. He later testified that Myra seemed "very reluctant to do that thing [sign the will]. . . . She couldn't believe she was going to die, and they were forcing something on her which she didn't like and like an old petulant woman she was angry at it."[19]

Myra Clark Gaines died four days later, on January 9, 1885. At her funeral many members of the New Orleans bar and judiciary joined family and friends to pay tribute to a remarkable woman. The funeral oration, delivered by Presbyterian minister B. M. Palmer, praised the "persistency of will and constancy of endeavor" that earned Gaines the admiration of the millions across the United States who had followed the progress of the Great Gaines Case for over half a century. Gaines had wished to be buried in the tomb of her father in the old St. Louis Cemetery No. 1. The newspapers reported that when gravediggers opened her father's tomb they found nothing: no bones, wood fragments, bits of cloth—nothing.[20]

The death of Myra Gaines shocked New Orleans. It seemed impossible that the indomitable old woman had not lived to see the end of her case. Even while newspapers assured their readers that the extent of her claims was exaggerated and predicted eventual victory for the city, they applauded her "splendid example of incessant and unremitting devotion" to her cause "against obstacles of so formidable a character and so many disastrous defeats." Even her enemies admitted that the Gaines case represented "the most interesting and romantic chapter in judicial history."[21]

Not even Gaines's death could end the Gaines case. The city of New Orleans continued to contest the decrees of both the United States and Louisi-

19. William H. Holcomb, Testimony, *Evans Will Record*, 1: 67.

20. *Washington (D.C.) Evening Star*, Jan. 12, 1885, p. 1.

21. *New Orleans Daily Picayune*, Jan. 11, 1885, p. 10; *Argument of George W. Pascall before C. Delano, Secretary of the Interior and W. T. Otto, Assistant Secretary, Delivered on the 26th Day of November, 1870, in Behalf of Myra Clark Gaines upon Her Claim for a Patent for Land in New Orleans* (1870), 8.

ana Supreme Courts awarding ownership of the disputed New Orleans property to Myra Gaines. Three more times the Gaines case reached the Supreme Court, carried there by her heirs in hopes of gaining something from the long litigation. Finally, in 1891, Justice Bradley wrote a decision that approved some of the more technical claims of the city of New Orleans but still compelled the city to pay the Gaines heirs $576,707.92 plus interest of 5 percent since 1881. The total amount of the award equaled $923,788. Immediately, creditors filed with the administrators of her estate for satisfaction of the loans made to Gaines over the years of her litigation, and lawyers who had never received their fees filed liens on the estate for payment. Totaling more than $860,000, the claims left little for her heirs to divide.[22]

Even that amount became the object of legal action. The will dictated to attorney Wilder became the subject of litigation when another will surfaced two days after Gaines's death. An olographic will, dated January 8, 1885, purporting to have been "written, dated, and signed" by Myra Clark Gaines was presented to the New Orleans probate court. On the same day, the will drawn by attorney Wilder and witnessed by Dr. Harrison was entered for probate in the same court. A "Mrs. Evans" told the court that the day before Gaines died she went to call on Myra but was not allowed to see her. Mrs. Evans returned three times to the house on Thalia Street, and on her final visit, a heavily veiled, shabbily dressed woman, standing on the lowest of the front steps, handed her an envelope wrapped in a handkerchief and said it came from Gaines. Mrs. Evans returned home, opened the envelope and found a will leaving some real estate to Julietta Perkins (Mrs. Evans's mother) and one-third of her estate to Mrs. Evans. The remainder went to the Gaines grandchildren.[23]

The probate court considered the two wills, and so did the surrogate's court in Brooklyn, New York, Myra Gaines's legal residence at the time of her death. The New Orleans court declared the Evans will a forgery, and denied probate to the other will because it was not executed and witnessed in the proper manner for nonresidents. The Brooklyn court also declared the Evans will a forgery but admitted the other will to probate. Naturally each decision was appealed to a higher court. The Louisiana Supreme Court heard the Evans will case six times; the Appellate Division of the New York Supreme Court heard it once; and the New York Court

22. *New York Times,* July 27, 1892, p. 1.
23. *New Orleans Times-Picayune,* Jan. 12, 1885, p. 1.

of Appeals heard it for the last time in 1897. The final decisions left standing the will dictated by Myra Gaines to her attorney four days before her death. The courts agreed that a woman so ill that she could only make a mark for her signature on January 5 could not write out an entire will only two days later. Gaines's grandchildren divided approximately sixty thousand dollars, a tiny remnant of the vast fortune their grandmother had sought. Sixty-three years after Myra and William Whitney filed the first suit against Relf and Chew, the Gaines case was finally over.[24]

Once settled, the Gaines case disappeared from the newspapers as public attention moved on to new scandals and a new century. Few lawyers remembered the case once termed the "most interesting . . . in the history of jurisprudence." Today, only attorneys researching land titles in New Orleans have any reason to consult the records of a lawsuit whose testimony filled eighty thousand pages and took three large trunks to hold.[25]

Yet the Great Gaines Case was more than merely a prolonged legal struggle. It occupied a point of transition in the nineteenth century where judicial concerns for women's welfare intersected with the emergence of one woman from her sheltered sphere. No other nineteenth-century female was as actively involved in the traditionally gendered arena of the courtroom as Myra Clark Gaines. By bringing her case to the courts and keeping it there, Myra Gaines supplied the issues that allowed the nineteenth-century judiciary to construct a new type of family law, which provided special protection for women, children, and marriages. By weaving together the strands of this emerging domestic-relations law and the plot twists of popular sentimental fiction, the Great Gaines Case created a true-life romance that remained on the front pages of newspapers for over fifty years. Justice James Wayne's designation of the Gaines case as "the most remarkable in the history of the [Supreme] Court" celebrates the courageous struggle of a very unusual woman.

24. Walter S. Holden, "Three Generations of Romance and Litigation: The Celebrated Gaines Will Cases," *Illinois Law Review* (1917): 488; *Julietta Perkins and Marie P. Evans v. Gaines Administrators*, New York Supreme Court Reports, 74 Hun 95; 83 Hun 225; and 84 Hun 520.

25. *Argument of George W. Pascall*, 11; *New York Times*, Oct. 20, 1883, p. 4.

Bibliography

CASE LIST: GAINES CASES

UNITED STATES SUPREME COURT CASES (IN CHRONOLOGICAL ORDER)

Ex Parte Myra Clark Whitney, 13 Peters 404 (1837)

Edmund P. Gaines and Wife v. Richard Relf, Beverly Chew, et al., 15 Peters 9 (1841)

Edmund P. Gaines et ux. v. Beverly Chew, Richard Relf, et al., 2 Howard 619 (1844)

Charles Patterson v. Edmund P. Gaines, et ux., 6 Howard 550 (1848)

Myra Clark Gaines v. Richard Relf and Beverly Chew, Executors, et al., 12 Howard 472 (1852)

Myra Clark Gaines v. Duncan N. Hennen, 24 Howard 553 (1861)

Myra Clark Gaines v. The City of New Orleans et al., 6 Wallace 642 (1868)

Myra Clark Gaines v. F. De La Croix, et al., 6 Wallace 719 (1868)

Myra Clark Gaines v. Manuel J Lizardi, et al., 6 Wallace 723 (1868)

City of New Orleans v. Myra Clark Gaines, 82 U.S. 624 (1873)

Myra Clark Gaines v. Joseph Fuentes, et al., 92 U.S. 10 (1876)

Samuel Smith, James E. Zunts, et al., v. Myra Clark Gaines, 93 U.S. 341 (1876)

Eliza Davis v. Myra Clark Gaines, 104 U.S. 386 (1881)

City of New Orleans v. James Y. Christmas, et al., 131 U.S. 191 (1889)

City of New Orleans v. James Y. Christmas and Hattie L. Whitney, Administrators of the Succession of Myra Clark Gaines, 131 U.S. 220 (1889)

City of New Orleans v. William Wallace Whitney, Administrator of the Succession of Myra Clark Gaines, and William Wallace Whitney, Administrator of the Succession of Myra Clark Gaines, v. The City of New Orleans, 138 U.S. 595 (1891)

Louisiana Supreme Court Cases (in chronological order)

Barnes v. Gaines, 5 Robinson 314 (1843)
Succession of Clark, 11 Louisiana Annual 124 (1856)
Heirs of Mary Clark v. Gaines, 13 Louisiana Annual 138 (1858)
De la Croix v. Gaines, 13 Louisiana Annual 177 (1858)
Van Wych v. Gaines, 13 Louisiana Annual 235 (1858)
White v. Gaines, 29 Louisiana Annual 69 (1871)
Fuentes, et al., v. Gaines, 25 Louisiana Annual 85 (1873)
Foulhouze v. Gaines, 26 Louisiana Annual 84 (1874)

United States District and Circuit Court Cases

National Archives, Southwest Region, Fort Worth, Texas
   Eighty-eight cases in the records of the Second District Court of Louisiana (Probate), the District Court of the United States for the Eastern District of Louisiana, and the latter's successor, the United States Circuit Court for the Fifth Judicial District and Circuit of Louisiana, involve Myra Clark Gaines, William Whitney, or Richard Relf. The original pleadings, summonses, depositions, exhibits, and letters entered in these cases are located in the General Case Files, Record Group 21, National Archives, Southwest Region, Fort Worth, Texas. An index to the case files is available.
   Portions of these records were compiled and published as:

Transcript of Record, Gaines v. Relf, Chew, and Others, case no. 122 in the Circuit Court of the United States, Eastern District of Louisiana, prepared for appeal to the Supreme Court of the United States. New Orleans: Clerk's Office, United States Circuit Court, 1858.

Transcript of Record, Gaines v. Hennen, comprising cases nos. 2619, 2695, 2715, and 2734 in the Circuit Court of the United States, Eastern District of Louisiana, entered in the appeal of *Gaines v. P. H. Monseaux,* case no. 3663 in the United States Circuit Court for the Fifth Judicial Circuit and District of Louisiana, to the Supreme Court of the United States. New Orleans: Clerk's Office, United States Circuit Court, Nov. 28, 1877.

Transcript of Record, Gaines v. The City of New Orleans, case no. 8825 in the United States Circuit Court for the Fifth Judicial Circuit and District of Louisiana, on appeal to the Supreme Court of the United States, 8 vols. New Orleans: Clerk's Office, United States Circuit Court, Oct. 1883.

   A copy of the *Transcript of Record, Gaines v. Relf, Chew, and Others* is located in case no. 2695, and a copy of the *Transcript of Record, Gaines v. Hennen* in case no. 2715 of the General Case Files, Record Group 21, National Archives, Southwest Region, Fort Worth, Texas.

A copy of the *Transcript of Record, Gaines v. The City of New Orleans* is available in the Howard-Tilton Memorial Library, Tulane University, New Orleans, Louisiana.

National Archives, Eastern Region, College Park, Maryland
Barret v. Gaines, no. 4711 at Law (1861)
William D. Colt v. Myra Clark Gaines (1867)
Dodderidge v. Gaines, no. 5691 at Law (1868)
Gaines v. Tenney, no. 5706 at Law (1869)
United States v. James Y. Christmas, no. 13955 in the Criminal District Court (1881)

NEW YORK PROBATE AND SUPREME COURT

Julietta Perkins and Marie P. Evans v. Gaines Administrators, New York Supreme Court Reports, 74 Hun 95, 83 Hun 225, 84 Hun 520

The record of appeal of the Evanses' litigation over the will of Myra Clark Gaines was published as:

Supreme Court (Surrogate's Court), Kings County.—General Term. Second Judicial Department. In the matter of the Probate of the last Will and Testament of Myra Clark Gaines, Deceased. Julietta Perkins and Marie P. Evans, appellants. Record of Appeal. 4 vols. Washington, D.C., 1896. A copy of the Evans Will Record is located in the Nolan Harmon Papers, Emory University, Atlanta, Ga.

CASE LIST: OTHER CASES

Reed v. Passer, Peakes Cases *nisi prius* 23 (1793)
Fetts v. Foster, 2 Hayward 102 (N.C. 1799)
Fenton v. Reed, 4 Johns 52 (N.Y. 1809)
Milford v. Worcester, 7 Mass. 4 (1810)
Chambers v. Dickson, 2 S. & R. 475 (Pa. 1816)
Cottin v. Cottin, 5 Martin 93 (La. 1817)
Grisham v. State, 2 Yerg. 589 (Tenn. 1831)
Senser v. Bower, 1 Pa. 450 (1834)
Dodge v. Woolsey, 18 Howard 331 (1856)
De Armaell's Estate, 2 Brew 239 (Pa. 1869)
Walmsey v. Robinson, 63 Ill. 41 (1872)
McPherson v. Ryan, 59 Mich. 33 (1886)

MANUSCRIPT SOURCES

ARCHIVES OF THE CITY OF NEW ORLEANS

City Council of the City of New Orleans. Minutes of the Regular Meetings, City Hall.

UNITED STATES OFFICIAL PAPERS, NATIONAL ARCHIVES

Adjutant-General of the United States Army to the Honorable John W. Gaines, April 26, 1909, explaining the Court of Inquiry of 1846 in the Case of General Edmund P. Gaines.

Department of State, Foreign Relations (Record Group 59), Consular Despatches.

Department of War, Office of the Judge Advocate General, Record Group 153

Proceeding of the Court of Inquiry in the Case of General James Wilkinson, July 4, 1808.

Record of the Court of Inquiry in the Case of Major General Edmund Pendleton Gaines, Fortress Monroe, 1846.

PRIVATE PAPERS

Broome County Historical Society, Binghamton, New York
Whitney, Joshua. Papers.

Pitts Theology Library, Emory University, Atlanta
Harmon, Bishop Nolan. Papers.

Historical Society of Pennsylvania, Philadelphia
Clark, Daniel. Papers.
Coxe, Daniel. Papers.
Gilpin Family Papers.
Pile Family Papers.
Reed and Forde Letter Books.

Howard-Tilton Memorial Library, Tulane University, New Orleans
Gaines, Myra Clark. Papers.
McConnell Family Papers.

Library of Congress
Gaines, Myra Clark. Papers.
Jefferson, Thomas. Papers.

Tennessee State Library and Archives, Nashville
Gaines, Edmund Pendleton. Papers.

University of Texas at Arlington
Gaines, Edmund Pendleton. Papers.

Theses and Dissertations

Arena, Carmelo Richard. "Philadelphia–Spanish New Orleans Trade: 1789–1805." Ph.D. diss., University of Pennsylvania, 1959.

Dennis, David C. "The Image of Louisiana in America, 1800–1890." Master's thesis, University of Southwestern Louisiana, 1995.

Dugdale, Mattie Wood. "Travelers' Views of Louisiana before 1860." Master's thesis, University of Texas, 1938.

Echezabal, Elvina M. "The Public Career of W. C. C. Claiborne from 1795–1804." Master's thesis, Tulane University, 1935.

Grossberg, Michael. "Law and Family in Nineteenth-Century America." Ph.D. diss., Brandeis University, 1979.

Hatfield, Joseph T. "The Public Career of William C. C. Claiborne." Ph.D. diss., Emory University, 1962.

Jenkins, Wiley Woodrow. "William C. C. Claiborne, Governor of the Creoles." Ph.D. diss., University of Texas, 1951.

Klein, Selma Louise. "Social Interaction of the Creoles and Anglo-Americans in New Orleans, 1803–1860." Master's thesis, Tulane University, 1940.

Le Blanc, Howard. "Claiborne's Administration of Louisiana." Master's thesis, St. Mary's University, 1941.

Olsen, Susan Annette. "The Antebellum New Orleans Merchant Aristocracy, 1841–1850." Master's thesis, Texas A & I University, 1991.

Porter, Ausie Laurence. "W. C. C. Claiborne's Administration in Louisiana, Provincial, Territorial, and State." Master's thesis, Tulane University, 1932.

Reinders, Robert C. "A Social History of New Orleans, 1850–1860." Ph.D. diss., University of Texas, Austin, 1957.

Ryan, Frank W. "The Southern Review, 1842–1857: A Study in Thought and Opinion in the Old South." Ph.D. diss., University of North Carolina, 1956.

Scarboro, Louise. "George W. Cable's New Orleans with Special Reference to 'Old Creole Days' and 'The Grandissimes.'" Master's thesis, Duke University, 1944.

Toups, Gerard J. "William Charles Cole Claiborne and the Louisiana Interests, 1803–1806." Master's thesis, University of Southwestern Louisiana, 1969.

Vest, George Southall. "William Claiborne." Master's thesis, University of Virginia, 1947.

Vostorff, Vivian Virginia. "William Charles Cole Claiborne: A Study in Frontier Administration." Ph.D. diss., Northwestern University, 1932.

Wohl, Michael. "A Man in the Shadow: The Life of Daniel Clark." Ph.D. diss., Tulane University, 1984.

Yoakum, Doris L. "An Historical Study of the Public Speaking Activity of Women in America from 1828–1860." Ph.D. diss., University of Southern California, 1935.

PUBLISHED SOURCES: PRIMARY

Official Papers

American State Papers, Foreign Relations. 32 vols. Washington, D.C.: Gales and Seaton, 1832.

Bayou St. John Cemetery Records, 1835–1844. Online access, Sept. 29, 1997: http://home.gnofn.org/~nopl/inv/neh/nehff.htm#ff1.

Beers, Henry Putney. *The Confederacy: A Guide to the Archives of the Government of the Confederate States of America.* Washington, D.C.: National Archives and Records Administration, 1986.

Carter, Clarence Edwin, ed. *The Territorial Papers of the United States.* Vol. 9: *The Territory of Orleans, 1803–1812.* Washington, D.C.: United States Government Printing Office, 1940.

Dart, Benjamin, ed. *Constitutions of the State of Louisiana and Selected Federal Laws.* Indianapolis: Bobbs-Merrill, 1932.

Despatches from United States Consuls in New Orleans, 1798–1807. Washington, D.C.: National Archives and Records Service, 1958.

"Documents: Despatches from the United States Consul in New Orleans, 1801–1803: Part I," *American Historical Review* 32 (1927): 801–24.

"Documents: Despatches from the United States Consul in New Orleans, 1801–1803: Part II," *American Historical Review* 33 (1928): 331–59.

Dunbar, Rowland, ed. *Official Letter Books of W. C. C. Claiborne, 1801–1816.* 6 vols. Jackson, Miss.: State Department of Archives and History, 1983 [1917].

Fitzpatrick, John C., ed. *The Writings of George Washington from the Original Manuscript Sources, 1745–1799.* 39 vols. Washington, D.C.: United States Government Printing Office, 1931–44.

Ford, Paul Leicester, ed. *The Writings of Thomas Jefferson.* 12 vols. New York: George Putnam & Sons, 1892–99.

Forsyth, Alice, ed., *Louisiana Marriages: II, A Collection of Marriage Records from the St. Louis Cathedral in New Orleans during the Spanish Regime and the Early American Period, 1784–1806.* New Orleans: Polyanthos, 1977.

Gales and Seaton. *Annals of the Congress of the United States.* Washington, D.C.: 10th Cong., 1st sess.

King, Andrew, ed. *The Papers of Daniel Webster, Legal Papers.* Vol. 3, *The Federal Practice, Part II.* Hanover, N.H.: Published for Dartmouth College by the University Press of New England, 1989.

McDonald, William. *Select Charters and Other Documents Illustrative of American History, 1660–1775.* Ann Arbor, Mich.: University Microfilms, 1964.

Moser, Harold, David R. Hoth, and George H. Hoemann, eds. *The Papers of Andrew Jackson.* Vol. 4, *1821–24.* Knoxville: University of Tennessee Press, 1996.

United States Circuit Court (Fifth Circuit). *Opinion of Judge Theodore McCaleb, Presiding Judge of the District Court: Myra C. Gaines, complainant vs. F. Dusuau De La Croix, defendant delivered on the 17th day of April, 1858.* New Orleans, 1858.

United States Congress. House Committee on Private Land Claims. *In the Matter of the Claim of Mrs. Myra Clark Gaines for the Confirmation of Certain Land Claims Described in Executive Document no. 60.* 43rd Cong., 1st sess., 1874.

United States Congress. House Committee on Private Land Claims. *In the Matter of the Claim of Mrs. Myra Clark Gaines for the Confirmation of Certain Land Claims.* 45th Cong., 3rd sess., 1879.

United States Congress. Senate. *Debates and Proceedings,* Dec. 24, 1806. 9th Cong., 2nd sess.

United States Congress. Senate. *Proceedings of Military Courts of Inquiry in the Case of Major General Scott and Major General Gaines.* Washington, D.C.: W. Duane, 1837.

United States Congress. Senate. *Mississippi Question: Report of a Debate in the Senate of the United States on the 23rd, 24th, and 25th February, 1803,* 7th Cong., 2nd sess., 1802–1803.

United States Supreme Court. *In the Supreme Court of the United States, No. 188: Myra Clark Gaines, Appellant, vs. Richard Relf, Beverly Chew, et al.* Washington, D.C.: George S. Gideon, Printer, 1850.

United States Surveyor General for Louisiana. *Map of New Orleans and Jefferson Cities Showing the Claims of Mrs. Myra Clark Gaines.* 1870.

Washington, H. A., ed. *The Writings of Thomas Jefferson.* 9 vols. Washington, D.C.: Taylor and Maury, 1854.

Whitaker, A. P., ed. *Documents Relating to the Commercial Policy of Spain in the Floridas (with Incidental Reference to Louisiana).* Deland: Florida State Historical Society, 1931.

ARGUMENTS, PLEADINGS, AND BRIEFS ENTERED IN THE GAINES CASE

Billings, Edward C. *Myra Clark Gaines vs. The City of New Orleans: Opinion of Judge Edward C. Billings, pronounced May 3, 1883.* New Orleans: Circuit Court of the United States, Eastern District of Louisiana, 1883.

Bradford, Robert H. *Exposition of the Nullity of Myra Clark Gaines's Pretentions to the City of New Orleans: with copies and translations of the testimony abstracted from the government records, and suppressed by her or her confederates.* New Orleans: Steel, 1870.

Campbell, John A., Thomas J. Semmes, and Alfred Goldthwaite. *A Statement of Matters of Fact and Law in Behalf of the Appellees in this Suit. The City of New Orleans, Appellant, v. The Heirs of Myra Clark Gaines, Appellees.* Washington, D.C.: Press of Thomas McGill, Law Printers, n.d.

Chinn, R. H. *Suggestions on Behalf of Complainants. Edmund Pendleton Gaines and Myra Clark Gaines, complainants, vs. Richard Relf and B. Chew, executors of Daniel Clark, dec'd and Others, def'ts.* In Chancery. New Orleans, 1839.

Christy, William. *Brief submitted by Appellee in Patterson vs. Gaines,* on appeal to the Supreme Court of the United States, from the Ninth Circuit Court. New Orleans: Snethen and Brother, 1841.

City of New Orleans. *Brief submitted on Appeal from the Circuit Court of the United States, Eastern District of Louisiana. City of New Orleans, Appellant v. The Succession of Myra Clark Gaines, Appellee.* New Orleans, 1887.

Collens, T. Wharton. *Opinion of Judge T. Wharton Collens and the Decree of the Court, revoking and recalling as absolutely null and of no effect, the Decree of Probate of the alleged lost will of 1813, set up by Defendant as the Basis of her Title in suits in the United States Circuit Court and Declaring the said alleged will Invalid and Revoked. Jos. Fuentes, et al., vs. Myra Clark Gaines,* Second District (probate) Court, Parish of New Orleans. New Orleans: Hinck and Co., Stationers and Printers, 1872.

Coxe, Daniel. *Refutation, Sustained by Documentary Proofs, of the Pretended Claims of Mira Clark, Alias Mira Davis, Alias Mrs. Whitney, and Now Mrs. Gaines upon the Estate of the Late Daniel Clark.* New Orleans: published by the author, May 24, 1839.

Delacroix, François Dusuau. *Answer of the Defendant Dusuau de la Croix to the Bill of Complaint of Myra C. Gaines.* New Orleans: Printed at the Office of the *Picayune,* 1856.

Duncan, G. B. *Supplemental Brief.* Submitted by Counsel for Defendants, *Myra Gaines vs. Chew, Relf, and Others.* In the Circuit Court of the United States, Eastern District of Louisiana. New Orleans, 1850.

Duncan, Greer B. *Argument of G. Duncan, Esq. Myra Clark Gaines vs. City of New Orleans, de la Croix, et al.* In the United States Circuit Court. New Orleans: Printed at the *True Delta* Office, 1858.

Duncan, Greer B. *The Case of General Gaines and Wife versus Richard Relf and Beverly Chew, in the Circuit Court of the United States for the State of Louisiana. Answer, etc., of the Defendants, Relf, Chew, Ferrier, and Barnes and Wife.* New Orleans: J. Cohn, 1845.

Fellows, J. Q. A. *Writ of Error to the Supreme Court of Louisiana. Brief on Behalf of Plaintiff in Error. Myra Clark Gaines, Plaintiff in Error, vs. Joseph Fuentes, et al., Defendants in Error.* No. 104. In the United States Supreme Court, Oct. Term, 1875. Washington, D.C., 1875.

Fellows, J. Q. A., Mills, Race, Foster, and E. T. Merrick. *Brief for Appellant and Assignment of Errors. Joseph Fuentes, et al., Appellees, versus Myra Clark Gaines, Appellant. No. 3700.* In the Supreme Court, State of Louisiana. New Orleans: n.p., n.d.

Gaines, Myra Clark. *Appeal from the Circuit Court of the United States for the Eastern District of Louisiana to the Supreme Court of the United States.* No. 344, *Myra Clark Gaines, Appellant vs. F. D. De la Croix, et al., Appellees.* New Orleans, 1859.

Gaines, Myra Clark. *Record. Myra Clark Gaines versus Richard Relf, Beverly Chew, and Others.* New Orleans: Hinton, 1849.

Gaines, Myra Clark. *Synopsis of New Testimony, Speeches of Counsel, etc. Myra Clark Gaines vs. François Dusuau Delacroix and City of New Orleans.* Washington, D.C.: George S. Gideon, 1858.

Janin, Louis. *Explanation of the Fraudulent Character of the Claims of Mrs. Myra Clark Gaines, to the City of New Orleans with copies to be had at the office of Colonel J. B. Walton, Auctioneer, 162 Common St.* Washington, D.C., 1874.

McConnell, J. M., and Miles Taylor. *Brief for the Defendants and Appellees. Myra Clark Gaines, Appellant, vs. F. de la Croix, Appellee* (no. 81); *Myra Clark Gaines, Appellant, vs. The City of New Orleans, et al., Appellees* (no. 82); *Myra Clark Gaines, Appellant, vs. M. J. Lizardi, et al., Appellees* (no. 83). In the Supreme Court of the United States. Appeals from the Circuit Court, District of Louisiana. Washington, D.C., 1860.

McConnell, Jas. *The Gaines Case: A Letter from Jas. McConnell, Esq. To the Mayor and Board of Administrators of the City of New Orleans.* New Orleans: Democrat Print, 1881.

Paschal, George W. *Argument before C. Delano, Secretary of the Interior and W. T. Otto, Assistant Secretary, delivered on the 26th Day of November, 1870, in behalf of Myra Clark Gaines, upon her Claim to a Patent for Land in New Orleans.* Washington City: M'Gill & Witherow, 1870.

Paschal, George W. *Petition and Statement Submitted by Myra Clark Gaines to the City Council of New Orleans Embracing Decisions of the United States Supreme Court and Circuit Courts, A Tableau of Property in Dispute, Petitions of Occupants, etc.* New Orleans: Printed at the Office of the *Republican*, 1870.

Perin, Franklin. *The Present Position of Mrs. Gaines's Claim to the Estate of Her Father, Daniel Clark.* N.p., 1853.

Relf, Chew, and Others Ats. Gaines. In Chancery, Circuit Court of the United States in and for the Fifth Circuit and Eastern District of Louisiana. New Orleans: Joseph Cohn, 1850.

Report of the Finance Committee on the Petition of Mrs. Myra Clark Gaines, with accompanying Documents. To the Common Council of the City of New Orleans. New Orleans: Printed at the Crescent Steam Book and Job Office, 1868.

Sabourin, Ernest. *Report of the Master in Chancery in the Matter of Fruits, Revenues, and Value for Use and Improvements. Myra Clark Gaines vs. P. H. Monsseaux et al.* New Orleans, 1878.

Semmes, Thos. J. *Brief for Appellees. Succession of Myra Clark Gaines.* In the Supreme Court of Louisiana. No. 11,193. New Orleans: n.p., n.d.

Statement of the Gaines Case Now Pending before the Supreme Court of the United States. New Orleans: L. Graham & Son, n.d.

Walker, Alexander. *A Full report of the Great Gaines Case, in the Suit of Myra Clark Gaines vs. Chew, Relf, and Others. For the Recovery of the Property of the Late Daniel Clark, Involving Several Millions, in which the Legitimacy of the Plaintiff is Investigated, and Her Romantic and Interesting History Developed.* New Orleans: printed at the office of the *Daily Delta.* 1850.

White and Saunders, E. H. McCaleb (Attorneys for W. W. Christmas). *Succession of Myra Clark Gaines: Answer to Brief for W. W. Whitney.* Supreme Court of Louisiana. No. 10,508. New Orleans: T. H. Thomason, n.d.

Wright, P. C. *Brief for Complainant.* In Chancery: United States Circuit Court, Eastern District of Louisiana. *Myra Clark Gaines vs. Relf, Chew and Others.* No. 122. New Orleans: Printed at the *Crescent* Office, 1850.

MEMOIRS, PAMPHLETS, PRIVATE CORRESPONDENCE, ETC.

Burr, Aaron. *The Trial of Col. Aaron Burr on an indictment for treason. Before the Circuit Court of the United States, held in Richmond, Virginia, May term, 1807. Including the arguments and decisions on all the motions made during the examination and trial, and on the motion for an attachment against General Wilkinson.* Washington City: Westcott, 1807.

Castellanos, Henry C. *New Orleans As It Was: Episodes of Louisiana Life.* 1895; reprint, George F. Reinecke, ed., Baton Rouge: Published for the Louisiana American Revolutionary Bicentennial Commission by the Louisiana State University Press, 1978.

Clark, Daniel. *Deposition of Daniel Clark . . . in relation to the conduct of Gen. James Wilkinson.* City of Washington: A. & G. Way, 1808.

———. *Proofs of the Corruption of Gen. James Wilkinson, and of his connexion with Aaron Burr, with a full refutation of his slanderous allegations in relation to the character of the principal witness against him.* Freeport, N.Y.: Books for Libraries, 1970 [1809].

Clay-Clopton, Virginia. *A Belle of the Fifties: Memoirs of Mrs. Clay of Alabama Covering Social and Political Life in Washington and the South, 1853—.* New York: Da Capo Press, 1969.

Davis, Matthew L., ed. *Memoirs of Aaron Burr.* 2 vols. New York: Harper & Brothers, 1836–37.

Ellet, Elizabeth Fries Lummis. *The Court Circles of the Republic; or, The Beauties and Celebrities of the Nation.* New York: Arno Press, 1979 [1869].

———. *The Queens of American Society.* New York: Charles Scribner, 1867.

Everett, William. "Critical Notices: Beadle's Dime Books." *North American Review* 99 (1864): 303–9.

Gaines, Edmund P. *Memorial of Edmund Pendleton Gaines to the Senate and House of Representatives Assembled Relating to a System of National Defense.* Memphis, Tenn.: *Enquirer* Office, 1840.

Gaines, Myra Clark. "The Horrors of War." In *The New-Orleans Book, Extracts . . . from the Journals, the Pulpits, the Bench, and the Bar of New-Orleans,* ed. Robert Gibes Barnwell. New Orleans, 1851.

Gardette, Émile B. *Biographical Notice of (the late) James Gardette, Surgeon Dentist, of Philadelphia.* 1850. Henry D. Gilpin Papers, Historical Society of Pennsylvania, Philadelphia, Pa.

Graves, Mrs. A. J. *Woman in America: Being an Examination into the Moral and Intellectual Condition of American Female Society.* New York: Harper & Brothers, 1843.

Graves, H. A., ed. *The Family Circle: Its Affections and Pleasures.* Boston: Gould, Kendall & Lincoln, 1844.

History of the Yellow Fever in New Orleans, during the summer of 1853. Philadelphia: Kenworthy, 1854.

Holloway, Laura C. *Famous American Fortunes and the Men Who Have Made Them: A Series of Sketches of Many of the Notable Merchants, Manufacturers, Capitalists, Railroad Presidents, Bonanza and Cattle Kings of the Country.* New York: J. A. Hill, 1889.

Hone, Philip. *The Diary of Philip Hone, 1828–1851,* ed. Allan Nevins. 2 vols. New York: Dodd, Mead, 1927.

Jenkins, John S. *Daring Deeds of American Heroes: A Record of the Lives of American Patriots and Heroes Including Full and Accurate Biographies of the Most Celebrated American Generals.* New York: D. W. Evans, 1860.

Jewell, Edwin L. *Jewell's Crescent City Illustrated, the commercial, social, political and general history of New Orleans: including biographical sketches of its distinguished citizens, together with a Map and General Stranger's Guide.* New Orleans: E. L. Jewell, 1873.

Keyes, Erasmus Darwin. *Fifty Years' Observation of Men and Events.* New York: Charles Scribner and Sons, 1884.

Laussat, Pierre Clément de. *Memoirs of My Life to My Son during the Years 1803 and After, Which I Spent in Public Service in Louisiana as Commissioner of the French Government for the Retrocession to France of that Colony and for Its Transfer to the United States,* ed. Robert D. Bush. Translated by Sister Agnes-Josephine Pastwa, Order of St. Francis. Baton Rouge: Published for the Historic New Orleans Collection by the Louisiana State University Press, 1978.

March, Charles W. *Daniel Webster and His Contemporaries*. New York: Charles Scribner, 1852.

Merrick, Caroline. *Old Times in Dixie Land: A Southern Matron's Memories*. New York: Grafton, 1901.

Morrison, Andrew. *New Orleans and the New South*. N.p.: Metropolitan, Printed by L. Graham and Son, 1888.

New Orleans Directory for 1842, Comprising the Names, Residences, and Occupations of the Merchants, Businessmen, Professional Gentlemen and Citizens of New Orleans, Lafayette, Algiers, and Gretna. New Orleans: Pitts & Clarke, 1842.

New Orleans in 1805: A Directory and a Census. New Orleans: Pelican Gallery, 1960.

Nichols, Thomas Low. *Forty Years of American Life*. London: Longmans & Green, 1874.

Nugent, Henry P. *A Letter to His Excellency William C. C. Claiborne, Governor of the Territory of New Orleans. A Letter to James Brown, esq., Counsellor at Law. A Defense of the Honorable John Rowan and Daniel Clark, members of Congress, against the slanders of the tergirversant [sic] redacteur of the Courier*. New Orleans: printed for the author, 1808.

Parton, James. *General Butler in New Orleans: History of the Administration of the Department of the Gulf in the Year 1862*. New York: Mason Brothers, 1864.

Pierce, Frederick Clifton. *Whitney Genealogy*. Chicago: Conkey, 1895.

Polk, James K. *Polk: The Diary of a President, 1845–1849: Covering the Mexican War, the Acquisition of Oregon, and the Conquest of California and the Southwest*. ed. Allan Nevins. London: Longmans, Green, 1929.

Poore, Benjamin Perley. *Perley's Reminiscences of Sixty Years in the National Metropolis*. 2 vols. Philadelphia: Hubbard Brothers, 1886.

Ripley, Eliza Moore Chinn McHatton. *Social Life in Old New Orleans: Being Recollections of My Girlhood*. New York, 1912; , New York: Arno, 1975.

Robinson, Fayette. *An Account of the Organization of the Army of the United States with Biographies of Distinguished Officers . . .* 2 vols. Philadelphia: E. H. Butler, 1848.

Scott, Winfield. *Letter to the Secretary of War; or, Review of the Controversy on a Question of Rank between Generals Scott and Gaines*. New York, 1827.

Simon, Benedict, and William H. Wilder. *Map of New Orleans and Jefferson Cities, showing the claims of Mrs. Myra Clark Gaines*. 1870. Historic New Orleans Collection.

Smith, Jeremiah. *Cases on Selected Topics in the Law of Persons*. Cambridge, Mass.: Harvard Law Review Publishing Association, 1899.

Smith, William Stephens. *Remarks on the Late Infraction of Treaty at New Orleans*. New York: Vermilye and Crooker, 1803.

Some Celebrities of New Orleans. Louisiana Scrapbook, no. 2. Howard-Tilton Memorial Library, Tulane University, New Orleans.

Thornwell, Emily. *A Lady's Guide to Perfect Gentility in Manners, Dress, and Conversation.* . . . New York: Derby and Jackson, 1856.

Townsend, George A. *Washington, Outside and Inside.* Chicago: James Betts, 1873.

Wharton, Anne Hollingsworth. *Social Life in the Early Republic, with numerous reproductions of portraits, miniatures, and residences.* Philadelphia: J. B. Lippincott, 1902.

Wilkinson, James. *A Brief Examination of Testimony to Vindicate the Character of General James Wilkinson Against the Imputation of a Sinister Connexion with the Spanish Government, for Purposes Hostile to His Own Country.* Washington City: W. Cooper, 1811.

————. *Aaron Burr's Conspiracy Exposed and General Wilkinson Vindicated Against the Slanders of His Enemies on that Important Occasion.* Washington, D.C.: printed for the author, 1811.

————. *Memoirs of My Own Time.* 3 vols. Philadelphia: Abraham Small, 1816.

Willard, Frances E., and Mary A. Livermore, eds. *American Women: A Comprehensive Encyclopedia of the Lives and Achievements of American Women during the Nineteenth Century.* Rev. ed. New York: Mast, Crowell, and Kirkpatrick, 1897 [1893].

TRAVEL ACCOUNTS

Alexander, Captain Sir James E. *Transatlantic Sketches, Comprising Visits to the Most Interesting Scenes in North and South America.* 2 vols. London, 1833; reprint, Philadelphia: Key and Biddle, 1983.

Bernhard, Karl, His Highness, Duke of Saxe-Weimar-Eisenach. *Travels through North America during the Years 1825 and 1826.* 2 vols. Philadelphia: Carey, Lea, and Carey, 1828.

Buckingham, James Silk *America: Historical, Statistical, Descriptive.* London: Fisher, 1841.

————. "Life in Old New Orleans, 1846." In *American Social History As Recorded by British Travellers,* ed. Allan Nevins. New York: H. Holt, 1923.

————. *Travels through the Slave States of America.* 2 vols. London: Fisher, 1842.

Chevalier, Michel. *Society, Manners and Politics in the United States.* Boston: Weeks, Jordan, 1983 [1839].

Clapp, Theodore. *Autobiographical Sketches and Recollections during a Thirty-Five Years' Residence in New Orleans.* Boston: Phillips, Sampson, 1857.

Cobb, Joseph B. *Mississippi Scenes; or, Sketches of Southern and Western Life and Adventure.* Philadelphia: A. Hart, 1851.

Cuming, Fortescue. *Sketches of a Tour to the Western Country.* In *Early Western*

Travels, 1748–1846, ed. Reuben Goldthwaite. Cleveland: Arthur H. Clark, 1904.

de Tocqueville, Alexis. *Democracy in America: The Henry Reeve Text As Revised by Francis Bowen, now further corrected and edited, with introduction, editorial notes, and bibliographies, by Phillips Bradley.* 2 vols. New York: Knopf, 1948 [1835, 1840].

Dickens, Charles. *American Notes.* London: Chapman and Hall, 1842.

Didimus, Henry. *New Orleans As I Found It.* New York: Harper & Brothers, 1845.

Felton, Rebecca Latimer. *Country Life in Georgia in the Days of My Youth, also Addresses before Georgia Legislature, Woman's Clubs, Women's Organizations and other Noted Occasions.* Atlanta, Ga.: Index Printing, 1919.

Flint, Timothy. *History and Geography of the Mississippi Valley.* 2 vols. Cincinnati: E. H. Flint & L. R. Lincoln, 1833.

———. *Recollections of the Last Ten Years.* New York: Knopf, 1826.

Flugel, Felix. "Pages from a Journal of a Voyage Down the Mississippi to New Orleans in 1817." *Louisiana Historical Quarterly* 7 (1924): 27–38.

Gould, Emerson W. *Fifty Years on the Mississippi.* St. Louis, Mo.: Nixon-Jones Printing, 1889.

Grund, Francis J. *Aristocracy in America: From the Sketchbook of a German Nobleman.* New York: Harper & Row, 1959 [1839].

Hall, A. Oakley. *The Manhattaner in New Orleans; or, Phases of "Crescent City" Life.* New York: J. S. Redfield, 1851.

Hall, James. *Sketches of History, Life, and Manners in the West.* 2 vols. Philadelphia: Harrison Hall, 1835.

Hamilton, Thomas. *Men and Manners in America.* 2 vols. Philadelphia: Carey, Lea, & Blanchard, 1833.

Hill, Henry Bertram, and Larry Gara, "A French Traveler's View of Ante-Bellum New Orleans." Translation and revised edition of Henri Herz, *Mes Voyages en Amérique.* Paris, 1866. *Louisiana History* 1 (1960): 335–41.

Historical Sketchbook and Guide to New Orleans and Environs. New York: William H. Coleman, 1885.

Howard, G. W. F., Earl of Carlisle. *Travels in America.* New York: G. P. Putnam, 1851.

Ingraham, Joseph Holt. *The Southwest, By a Yankee.* 2 vols. New York: Harper, 1835.

Knight, Henry C. *Letters from the South and West.* Boston: Richardson and Lord, 1824.

Latrobe, Benjamin Henry. *Impressions Respecting New Orleans: Diary and Sketches, 1818–1820.* New York: Columbia University Press, 1973 [1951].

———. *The Journals of Benjamin Henry Latrobe, 1799–1820: from Philadelphia to New Orleans,* ed. Edward C. Carter II, John C. Van Horne, and Lee W.

Formwalt. 3 vols. New Haven, Conn.: Published for the Maryland Historical Society by Yale University Press, 1980.

Lee, William. *A Yankee Jeffersonian: Selections from the Diary and Letters of William Lee of Massachusetts, written from 1796 to 1840.* Cambridge, Mass.: Belknap Press of Harvard University, 1958.

Lyell, Charles. *A Second Visit to the United States of North America* [1849]. Vol. 2, Chapters 26, 27, and 28 reprinted in *America through British Eyes,* ed. Allan Nevins. Gloucester, Mass.: Peter Smith, 1968.

Marryat, Captain Frederick. *A Diary in America.* 2 vols. Philadelphia: Carey & Hart, 1839.

Martineau, Harriet. "Life in Washington, D.C. in 1835." In *American Social History As Recorded by British Travelers,* ed. Allan Nevins. New York: H. Holt, 1923.

———. *A Retrospect of Western Travel.* New York: Harper & Brothers, 1838.

———. *Society in America* [1839], Part 2, Chapter 5; reprinted in *America through British Eyes,* ed. Allan Nevins. Gloucester, Mass.: Peter Smith, 1968.

Montgomery, Elizabeth. *Reminiscences of Wilmington, in Familiar Village Tales, Ancient and New.* Philadelphia: T. K. Collins, Jr., 1851.

Nichols, Thomas Low. *Forty Years of American Life.* London: Longmans and Green, 1874.

Olmsted, Frederick Law. *A Journey through the Seaboard Slave States.* New York: Mason Brothers, 1858.

Pedrick, W. *New Orleans As It Is, with a Correct Guide to All Places of Interest.* Cleveland, Ohio: W. W. Williams, 1885.

Pickett, Albert James. *Eight Days in New Orleans in February, 1847.* Montgomery, Ala.: printed for the author, 1847.

Pope, John. *A Tour through the Southern and Western Territories of the United States of North America; the Spanish Dominions on the River Mississippi and the Floridas; the Countries of the Creek Nations and Many Uninhabited Parts.* New York: C. L. Woodward, 1888 [1792].

Power, Tyrone. *Impressions of America during the Years 1833, 1834, 1835.* 2 vols. London: R. Bentley, 1936.

Resident. *New Orleans As It Is: Its Manners and Customs. . . .* New Orleans, 1850.

Richards, T. Addison, ed. *Appleton's Illustrated Handbook of Travel, etc.* New York: D. Appleton, 1860.

Russell, William Howard. *My Diary, North and South, during the Civil War in America.* 2 vols. London: Bradbury & Evans, 1863.

Schultz, Christian. *Travels on an Inland Voyage . . . Performed in the Years 1807 and 1808.* 2 vols. New York: Isaac Riley, 1810.

Sibley, John. "The Journal of Dr. Sibley." *Louisiana Historical Quarterly* 10 (1927): 478–86.

Southwood, Marion. *"Beauty and Booty": The Watchword of New Orleans.* New York: M. Doolady, 1867.

Spear, Thomas. *Ancient and Modern New Orleans: A Description of the City and Its Environs, from their foundation to the present time.* New Orleans: Rea's, 1870.

Sterling, James. *Letters from the Slave States.* London: John W. Parker and Son, 1857.

Stoddard, Major Amos. *Sketches Historical and Descriptive of Louisiana.* Philadelphia: Matthew Carey, 1812.

Stuart, James. *Three Years in North America.* 2 vols. New York: J. & J. Harper, 1833.

Trollope, Frances. *Domestic Manners of the Americans.* London: Whittaker, Treacher, 1832.

Tudor, Henry. *Narrative of a Tour in North America, . . . with an Excursion to the Island of Cuba.* 2 vols. London: J. Duncan, 1834.

Two Months in the Confederate States, including a Visit to New Orleans under the Domination of General Butler. London: R. Bentley, 1863.

Walden-Pell, Orleana Ellery. *Recollections of a Long Life.* London: W. P. Griffith, 1896.

Wharton, George M. *The New Orleans Sketchbook.* Philadelphia: T. P. Peterson, 1899 [1800].

Whitaker, J. S. *Sketches of Life and Character in Louisiana, the Portraits Selected Principally from the Bench and Bar.* New Orleans: Ferguson and Crosby, 1847.

SENTIMENTAL FICTION

Foster, Hannah Webster. *The Coquette; or, The History of Eliza Wharton. A Novel Founded on Fact.* New ed., with an historical preface, and a memoir of the author. Boston: W. P. Fetridge, 1855.

Holmes, Mary Jane. *'Lena Rivers.* Halifax, England: Milner and Sowerby, 1857.

Richardson, Samuel. *Pamela; or, Virtue Triumphant.* New York: New American Library, 1980 [1741].

Rowson, Susannah Haswell. *Charlotte Temple: A Tale of Truth.* Windsor, Vt.: Preston Merrifield, T. M. Pomroy, 1815.

Southworth, Mrs. Emma Dorothy Eliza Nevitte. *The Deserted Wife.* Philadelphia: T. B. Peterson, 1875.

———. *The Discarded Daughter.* Philadelphia: T. B. Peterson, 1855.

———. *The Hidden Hand: A Novel.* New York: A. L. Burt, 1920 [1859].

———. *The Lost Heiress.* Chicago: M. A. Donohue, 1912.

Stephens, Ann Sophia Winterbotham. *Myra, The Child of Adoption, A Romance of Real Life.* Beadle's Dime Novels, #3. New York: Beadle Press, 1860.

Wood, Sally Sayward Barrell Keating. *Dorval; or, The Speculator: A Novel Founded on Recent Facts.* Portsmouth, N.H.: Nutting & Whitlock, 1970 [1801].

DAILY AND WEEKLY NEWSPAPERS

Baltimore Sun (1915)
Courrier de la Louisiane/Louisiana Courier (1810–55)
Louisiana Gazette (1804–26)
Moniteur de la Louisiane (1802)
Nashville Republican Banner (1839–42)
National Intelligencer and Washington Advertiser (1803)
New Orleans L'Abeille/Bee (1827–1900)
New Orleans Crescent (1848–49)
New Orleans Daily Democrat (1877)
New Orleans Daily Picayune (1839–1901)
New Orleans Times-Democrat (1883–1914)
New Orleans True Delta (1849–66)
New Orleans Union (1804)
New Orleans Weekly Delta [later *Daily Delta*] (1845–63)
New-York Daily Times (1852–54)
New York Evening Star/Sunday Star (1835)
New York Herald (1844–61)
New York Times (1861–1900)
Niles' Weekly Register (Baltimore) (1835)
Orleans Gazette (1807)
Philadelphia Gazette and Daily Advertiser (1832)
Washington (D.C.) Evening Star (1855, 1882–85)
Wilmington (Del.) Delaware Gazette (1854)
Wilmington (Del.) Delmarva Star (1921)
Wilmington (Del.) Every Evening (1914)

PUBLISHED SOURCES: SECONDARY

BOOKS

Abernathy, Thomas. *The Burr Conspiracy*. Oxford: Oxford University Press, 1954.
Abraham, Henry J. *Justices and Presidents: A Political History of Appointments to the Supreme Court*. 3rd ed. New York: Oxford University Press, 1991.
Adams, Henry. *History of the United States of America during the Second Administration of Thomas Jefferson*. New York: Scribner, 1931 [1893].
Adams, William H. *The Whig Party of Louisiana*. Lafayette: University of Southwestern Louisiana, 1973.
Altick, Richard D. *The English Common Reader: A Social History of the Mass Reading Public, 1800–1900*. Chicago: University of Chicago Press, 1957.

Armstrong, Nancy. *Desire and Domestic Fiction*. Minneapolis: University of Minnesota Press, 1987.

Asbury, Herbert. *The French Quarter: An Informal History of the New Orleans Underworld*. New York: Knopf, 1936.

Badinter, Elisabeth. *Mother Love, Myth, and Reality: Motherhood in Modern History*. New York: Macmillan, 1981.

Banner, Lois W. *American Beauty*. New York: Knopf, 1983.

Barbé-Marbois, François, Marquis de. *The History of Louisiana: particularly of the cession of that colony to the United States of America*. Philadelphia: Carey and Lea, 1830.

Bardes, Barbara, and Suzanne Gossett. *Declarations of Independence: Women and Political Power in Nineteenth-Century Fiction*. New Brunswick, N.J.: Rutgers University Press, 1990.

Basch, Norma. *In the Eyes of the Law: Women, Marriage, and Property in Nineteenth-Century New York*. Ithaca, N.Y.: Cornell University Press, 1982.

Baym, Nina. *Novels, Readers, and Reviewers: Responses to Fiction in Antebellum America*. Ithaca, N.Y.: Cornell University Press, 1984.

————. *Woman's Fiction: A Guide to Novels by and about Women in America, 1820–1870*. 2nd ed. Urbana: University of Illinois Press, 1993.

Bemis, Samuel Flagg. *Pinckney's Treaty: America's Advantage from Europe's Distress, 1783–1800*. Rev. ed. New Haven, Conn.: Yale University Press, 1960.

Bennett, W. Lance and Martha S. Feldman. *Reconstructing Reality in the Courtroom: Justice and Judgment in American Culture*. New Brunswick, N.J.: Rutgers University Press, 1981.

Berenson, Edward. *The Trial of Madame Caillaux*. Berkeley: University of California Press, 1992.

Berg, Barbara J. *The Remembered Gate: Origins of American Feminism: The Woman and the City, 1800–1860*. New York: Oxford University Press, 1978.

Berger, Max. *The British Traveler in America, 1836–1860*. New York: Columbia University Press, 1943.

Billings, Warren M., and Edward Haas. *In Search of Fundamental Law: Louisiana's Constitutions, 1812–1974*. Lafayette: Center for Louisiana Studies, University of Southwestern Louisiana, 1993.

Blackwell, Alice Stone. *Lucy Stone: Pioneer of Women's Rights*. Boston: Little, Brown, 1930.

Bloomfield, Maxwell H. *American Lawyers in a Changing Society, 1776–1876*. Cambridge, Mass.: Harvard University Press, 1976.

Bode, Carl. *The Anatomy of American Popular Culture, 1840–1861*. Berkeley: University of California Press, 1959.

Bowers, Claude G. *The Tragic Era: The Revolution after Lincoln*. New York: Halcyon, 1929.

Bragin, Charles. *Dime Novels, Bibliography*. Brooklyn, N.Y.: C. Bragin, 1938.

Branch, Edward Douglas. *The Sentimental Years, 1836–1860*. New York: D. Appleton-Century, 1934.

Brant, Irving. *James Madison*. 6 vols. Indianapolis: Bobbs-Merrill, 1953.

Brown, George R. *Washington, A Not Too Serious History*. Baltimore, Md.: Norman, 1930.

Brown, Glenn. *History of the United States Capitol, 1792–1900*. 2 vols. Washington, D.C.: United States Government Printing Office, 1900–03.

Bruce, William Cabell. *John Randolph of Roanoke*. New York: Octagon Books, 1970 [1922].

Bruchey, Stuart Weems. *The Roots of American Economic Growth, 1607–1861: An Essay in Social Causation*. New York: Harper & Row, 1965.

Buel, James W. *Metropolitan Life Unveiled; or, The Mysteries and Miseries of America's Great Cities: Embracing New York, Washington City, San Francisco, Salt Lake City, and New Orleans*. St. Louis, Mo.: Anchor, 1882.

Burson, Caroline M. *The Stewardship of Don Esteban Miró, 1782–1792: A Study of Louisiana Based Largely on the Documents in New Orleans*. New Orleans: American, 1940.

Cable, George W. *Creoles and Cajuns: Stories of Old Louisiana*. Ed. Arlin Turner. Garden City, N.Y.: Doubleday, 1959.

———. *The Creoles of Louisiana*. New York: Charles Scribner's Sons, 1884.

———. *Old Creole Days: A Story of Creole Life*. New York: Charles Scribner's Sons, 1921.

———. *Strange True Stories of Louisiana*. New York: Charles Scribner's Sons, 1907 [1889].

Campbell, Karlyn Kohrs. *Man Cannot Speak for Her: A Critical Study of Early Feminist Rhetoric*. New York: Praeger, 1989.

———, ed. *Women Public Speakers in the United States, 1800–1925: A Bio-Critical Sourcebook*. Westport, Conn.: Greenwood, 1993.

Capers, Gerald Mortimer. *Occupied City: New Orleans under the Federals, 1862–1865*. Lexington: University of Kentucky Press, 1965.

Carnes, Mark, and Clyde Griffin, eds. *Meanings for Manhood: Constructions of Masculinity in Victorian America*. Chicago: University of Chicago Press, 1990.

Carrigan, Jo Ann. *The Saffron Scourge: A History of Yellow Fever in Louisiana, 1796–1905*. Lafayette: Center for Louisiana Studies, University of Southwestern Louisiana, 1994.

Carson, Hampton Lawrence. *The History of the Supreme Court of the United States; with biographies of all the chief and associate justices . . . with portraits of the 58 judges*. 2 vols. New York: B. Franklin, 1971 [1902].

Cawelti, John G. *Adventure, Mystery, and Romance: Formula Stories As Art and Popular Culture*. Chicago: University of Chicago Press, 1976.

Chambers, Henry Edward. *A History of Louisiana*. 3 vols. Chicago: American Historical Society, 1925.

Chandler, Walter. *The Centenary of Associate Justice John Catron of the United States Supreme Court. Address Given at the Fifty-Sixth Annual Session of the Bar Association of Tennessee at Memphis, Friday, June 11, 1937.* Printed in the Congressional Record, June 17, 1937. Washington, D.C.: Government Printing Office, 1937.

Channing, Edward. *History of the United States.* 6 vols. New York: Macmillan, 1905–25.

Chroust, Anton-Hermann. *The Rise of the Legal Profession in America.* Norman: University of Oklahoma Press, 1965.

Chused, Richard H. *Private Acts in Public Places: A Social History of Divorce in the Formative Era of American Family Law.* Philadelphia: University of Pennsylvania Press, 1994.

Claiborne, J. F. H. *Mississippi As a Province, Territory, and State.* Jackson, Miss.: Power and Barksdale, 1880.

Clark, John Garretson. *New Orleans, 1718–1812: An Economic History.* Baton Rouge: Louisiana State University Press, 1970.

Clinton, Catherine. *The Other Civil War: American Women in the Nineteenth Century.* New York: Hill and Wang, 1984.

Cmiel, Kenneth. *Democratic Eloquence: The Fight over Popular Speech in Nineteenth-Century America.* New York: William Morrow, 1970.

Cogan, Frances. *All-American Girl: The Ideal of Real Womanhood in Mid-Nineteenth-Century America.* Athens: University of Georgia Press, 1989.

Cohen, Daniel A. *Pillars of Salt, Monuments of Grace: New England Crime Literature and the Origins of American Popular Culture, 1674–1860.* New York: Oxford University Press, 1993.

Colman, Edna Mary. *Seventy-Five Years of White House Gossip: From Washington to Lincoln.* New York: Doubleday, Page, 1925.

Connor, Henry G. *John Archibald Campbell, Associate Justice of the Supreme Court, 1853–1861.* Boston: Houghton Mifflin, 1920.

Conrad, Susan Phinney. *Perish the Thought: Intellectual Women in Romantic America, 1830–1860.* New York: Oxford University Press, 1976.

Cowie, Alexander. *The Rise of the American Novel.* New York: American Book, 1948.

Cox, Issac J. *The West Florida Controversy.* Baltimore: Johns Hopkins Press, 1918.

Crawford, Mary Caroline. *Romantic Days in the Early Republic.* Boston: Little, Brown, 1912.

Crété, Lilliane. *Daily Life in Louisiana, 1815–1830.* Trans. Patrick Gregory. Baton Rouge: Louisiana State University Press, 1981.

Cummins, Light Townsend. *Spanish Observers and the American Revolution, 1775–1783.* Baton Rouge: Louisiana State University Press, 1991.

Curtis, Nathaniel Cortlandt. *New Orleans: Its Old Houses, Shops, and Public Buildings.* Philadelphia: J. B. Lippincott, 1938.

Dally, Anne. *Inventing Motherhood: The Consequences of an Ideal.* New York: Burnett, 1982.

Dalziel, Margaret. *Popular Fiction 100 Years Ago.* London: Cohen and West, 1957.

Dargo, George. *Jefferson's Louisiana: Politics and the Clash of Legal Traditions.* Cambridge, Mass.: Harvard University Press, 1975.

Davis, Natalie Zemon. *The Return of Martin Guerre.* Cambridge, Mass.: Harvard University Press, 1983.

DeConde, Alexander. *This Affair of Louisiana.* Baton Rouge: Louisiana State University Press, 1976.

Degler, Carl. *At Odds: Women and the Family in America from the Revolution to the Present.* New York: Oxford University Press, 1980.

Delafield, Mrs. E. M. *Ladies and Gentlemen in Victorian Fiction.* New York: Harper & Brothers, 1937.

De Lamont, Sara, and Lorna Duffin, eds. *The Nineteenth-Century Woman: Her Cultural and Physical World.* London: Croom-Helm, 1978.

De Leon, T. C. *Belles, Beaux and Brains of the '60s.* New York: G. W. Dillingham, 1909.

A Dictionary of Louisiana Biography. Ed. Glenn R. Conrad. 2 vols. Lafayette: University of Southwestern Louisiana, 1989.

Douglas, Ann. *The Feminization of American Culture.* New York: Knopf, 1977.

Duff, Charles. *Ireland and the Irish.* New York: G. P. Putnam's Sons, 1954.

Duffy, John, ed. *The Rudolph Matas History of Medicine in Louisiana.* 2 vols. Baton Rouge: Louisiana State University Press, 1958, 1962.

Durham, Philip, ed. *Dime Novels.* New York: Odyssey Press, 1966.

Earnest, Ernest. *The American Eve in Fact and Fiction, 1775–1914.* Chicago: University of Chicago Press, 1974.

Epstein, Barbara Leslie. *The Politics of Domesticity.* Middletown, Conn.: Wesleyan University Press, 1981.

Faye, Stanley. *The Schism of 1805 in New Orleans.* New Orleans: T. J. Moran's Sons, 1939.

Fenner, Charles E. *The Genesis and Descent of the System of Civil Law Prevailing in Louisiana.* New Orleans: L. Graham, 1887.

Ferguson, Robert A. *Law and Letters in American Culture.* Cambridge, Mass.: Harvard University Press, 1984.

Fiedler, Leslie A. *What Was Literature? Class Culture and Mass Society.* New York: Simon & Schuster, 1982.

Fishburn, Katherine. *Women in Popular Culture: A Reference Guide.* Westport, Conn.: Greenwood, 1981.

Fortier, Alcée. *A History of Louisiana.* 3 vols. New York: Goupil, 1904.

Fossier, Albert. *New Orleans: The Glamour Period, 1800–1840.* New Orleans: Pelican , 1957.

Freiberg, Edna. *Bayou St. John in Colonial Louisiana, 1699–1803.* New Orleans: Harvey, 1980.

Freibert, Lucy M., and Barbara A. White, eds. *Hidden Hands: An Anthology of American Women Writers, 1790–1870.* New Brunswick, N.J.: Rutgers University Press, 1985.

Friedman, Lawrence M. *A History of American Law.* New York: Simon & Schuster, 1973.

Friedman, Leon, and Fred Israel, eds. *The Justices of the United States Supreme Court, 1789–1969: Their Lives and Major Opinions.* 4 vols. New York: Chelsea House, 1969.

Fuess, Claude M. *Daniel Webster.* 2 vols. Boston: Little, Brown, 1930.

———. *The Life of Caleb Cushing.* New York: Harcourt, Brace, 1923.

Garvey, Joan B. *Beautiful Crescent: A History of New Orleans,* 7th ed. New Orleans: Garner, 1994.

Gayarré, Charles. *The Creoles of History and the Creoles of Romance: A Lecture Delivered in the Hall of Tulane University, New Orleans.* New Orleans: Crescent Steam Print, 1885.

———. *History of Louisiana.* 4 vols. New York: William J. Widdleton, 1866.

Gehman, Mary. *Women and New Orleans: A History.* 3rd ed. New Orleans: Margaret Media, 1994.

Gilmore, Grant. *The Ages of American Law.* New Haven, Conn.: Yale University Press, 1977.

Goodsell, Willystine. *Pioneers of Women's Education in the United States.* New York: McGraw-Hill, 1970.

Green, Harvey. *The Light of the Home: An Intimate View of the Lives of Women in Victorian America.* New York: Pantheon Books, 1983.

Green, Thomas Marshall. *The Spanish Conspiracy: A Review of Early Spanish Movements in the Southwest, Containing Proofs of the Intrigues of James Wilkinson.* Gloucester, Mass.: Peter Smith, 1967 [1891].

Grossberg, Michael. *Governing the Hearth: Law and the Family in Nineteenth-Century America.* Chapel Hill: University of North Carolina Press, 1985.

———. *A Judgment for Solomon: The D'Hauteville Case and Legal Experience in Antebellum America.* New York: Cambridge University Press, 1996.

Haas, Edward. *In Search of Fundamental Law: Louisiana's Constitutions, 1812–1974.* Lafayette: Center for Louisiana Studies, University of Southwestern Louisiana, 1993.

Haas, Edward, ed. *Louisiana's Legal Heritage.* New Orleans: Published for the Louisiana State Museum by Perdido Bay Press, 1983.

Habermas, Jürgen. *The Structural Transformation of the Public Sphere: An Inquiry into a Category of Bourgeois Society.* Trans. Thomas Burger with Frederic Lawrence. Cambridge: Polity, 1989.

Hall, Kermit. *The Magic Mirror: Law in American History.* New York: Oxford University Press, 1989.

Hall, Mr. and Mrs S. C. *Ireland, Its Scenery, Character, and History.* Boston: Francis A. Niccolls, 1911.

Halttunen, Karen. *Confidence Men and Painted Women: A Study of Middle-Class Culture in America, 1830–1870.* New Haven, Conn.: Yale University Press, 1982.

Hamilton, Holman. *Zachary Taylor: Sword of the Republic.* Indianapolis: Bobbs-Merrill, 1941.

Hariman, Robert. *Popular Trials, Rhetoric, Mass Media, and the Law.* Birmingham: University of Alabama Press, 1990.

Harmon, Nolan B. *The Famous Case of Myra Clark Gaines.* Baton Rouge: Louisiana State University Press, 1946.

Harris, Barbara J. *Beyond Her Sphere: Women and the Professions in American History.* Contributions in Women's Studies, #4. Westport, Conn.: Greenwood, 1978.

Hart, James D. *The Popular Book: A History of America's Literary Taste.* Oxford: Oxford University Press, 1950.

Harveson, Mae Elizabeth. *Catherine Ester Beecher: Pioneer Educator.* New York: Arno, 1969 [1932].

Hatcher, William B. *Edward Livingston, Jeffersonian Republican and Jacksonian Democrat.* Baton Rouge: Louisiana State University Press, 1940.

Hay, Thomas Robson and M. R. Werner. *The Admirable Trumpeter: A Biography of General James Wilkinson.* New York: Doubleday, Doran, 1941.

Heitman, Francis B. *Historical Register and Dictionary of the United States Army.* 2 vols. Washington, D.C.: United States Government Printing Office, 1903.

Helsinger, Elizabeth K. *The Woman Question: Society and Literature in Britain and America, 1837–1883.* New York: Garland, 1983.

Henry, Robert Selph. *The Story of the Mexican War.* New York: Da Capo, 1989 [1950].

Hoff, Joan. *Law, Gender, and Injustice: A Legal History of United States Women.* New York: New York University Press, 1993.

Holmes, Jack D. L. *Gayoso: The Life of a Spanish Governor in the Mississippi Valley, 1789–1799.* Baton Rouge: Louisiana State University Press for the Louisiana Historical Association, 1965.

Horsman, Reginald. *The Causes of the War of 1812.* Philadelphia: University of Pennsylvania Press, 1962.

Horwitz, Morton J. *The Transformation of American Law, 1870–1960: The Crisis of Legal Orthodoxy.* New York: Oxford University Press, 1992.

Hosford, Frances J. *Father Shipherd's Magna Charta: A Century of Co-education in Oberlin College, 1837–1937.* Boston: Marshall Jones, 1937.

Hosmer, James Kendall. *The History of the Louisiana Purchase.* New York: D. Appleton, 1915.

Howe, Daniel Walker. *Victorian America.* Philadelphia: University of Pennsylvania Press, 1976.

Howe, William. *Municipal History of New Orleans.* Baltimore: N. Murray for Johns Hopkins University Press, 1889.

Hudson, Frederic. *Journalism in the United States from 1690 to 1872.* New York: Harper & Brothers, 1873.

Hurst, James Willard. *The Growth of American Law: The Lawmakers.* Boston: Little, Brown, 1950.

———. *Law and the Conditions of Freedom in the Nineteenth-Century United States.* Madison: University of Wisconsin Press, 1956.

———. *Law and Social Order in the United States.* Ithaca, N.Y.: Cornell University Press, 1977.

Hutcheson, Harold. *Tench Coxe: A Study in American Economic Development.* New York: Da Capo Press, 1969 [1938].

Jackson, Bernard. *Law, Fact, and Narrative Coherence.* London: D. Charles, 1988.

Jackson, Joy J. *New Orleans in the Gilded Age: Politics and Urban Progress, 1880–1896.* Baton Rouge: Louisiana State University Press for the Louisiana Historical Association, 1969.

Jacob, Kathryn Allamong. *Capital Elites: High Society in Washington, D.C., after the Civil War.* Washington, D.C.: Smithsonian Institution Press, 1995.

Jacobs, James Ripley. *Tarnished Warrior: Major-General James Wilkinson.* New York: Macmillan, 1938.

Johannsen, Albert. *The House of Beadle and Adams and Its Dime and Nickel Novels.* Norman: University of Oklahoma Press, vols. 1 and 2, 1950; vol. 3, 1962.

Kane, Harnett T. *New Orleans Woman: A Biographical Novel of Myra Clark Gaines.* Garden City, N.Y.: Sun Dial, 1948.

———. *Queen New Orleans: City by the River.* New York: W. Morrow, 1949.

Kasson, John F. *Rudeness and Civility: Manners in Nineteenth-Century America.* New York: Hill and Wang, 1990.

Kelley, Mary. *Private Woman, Public Stage: Literary Domesticity in Nineteenth-Century America.* Oxford: Oxford University Press, 1984.

———, ed. *Woman's Being, Woman's Place: Female Identity and Vocation in American History.* Boston: G. K. Hall, 1979.

Kempin, Frederick G. *Legal History: Law and Social Change.* Englewood Cliffs, N.J.: Prentice-Hall, 1963.

Kendall, John S. *History of New Orleans.* 2 vols. Chicago: Lewis, 1922.

Kerber, Linda. *Women of the Republic: Intellect and Ideology in Revolutionary America.* Chapel Hill: University of North Carolina Press, 1980.

King, Grace. *Balcony Stories.* Ridgewood, N.J.: Gregg, 1968 [1893].

———. *Creole Families of New Orleans.* New York: Macmillan, 1921.

———. *New Orleans: The Place and the People.* New York: Macmillan, 1895.

———. *Stories from Louisiana History.* New Orleans: L. Graham, 1905.

———. *Tales of a Time and Place.* New York: Garrett, 1969 [1892].

Knight, Alfred. *The Life of the Law: The People and Cases That Have Shaped Our Society, from King Alfred to Rodney King*. New York: Crown, 1996.

Koegel, Otto E. *Common Law Marriage and Its Development in the United States*. Washington, D.C.: J. Byrne, 1975 [1922].

Lawrence, Alexander A. *James Moore Wayne: Southern Unionist*. Chapel Hill: University of North Carolina Press, 1943.

Lerner, Gerda. *The Female Experience: An American Documentary*. Indianapolis: Bobbs-Merrill, 1977.

——. *The Majority Finds Its Past: Placing Women in History*. Oxford: Oxford University Press, 1979.

Lewis, William Draper, ed. *Great American Lawyers: The Lives and Influence of Judges and Lawyers Who Have Acquired Permanent National Reputation and Have Developed the Jurisprudence of the United States: A History of the Legal Profession in America*. 8 vols. Philadelphia: J. C. Winston, 1907–09.

Lutz, Alma. *Emma Willard: Daughter of Democracy*. Boston: Houghton Mifflin, 1929.

Lyon, Elijah Wilson. *Louisiana in French Diplomacy, 1759–1804*. Norman: University of Oklahoma Press, 1934.

——. *The Man Who Sold Louisiana: The Career of François Barbé-Marbois*. Norman: University of Oklahoma Press, 1942.

Lystra, Karen. *Searching the Heart: Women, Men, and Romantic Love in Nineteenth-Century America*. New York: Oxford University Press, 1989.

McCaleb, Walter F. *The Aaron Burr Conspiracy*. New York: Dodd, Mead, 1903.

McGrane, Reginald C. *The Panic of 1837: Some Financial Problems of the Jacksonian Era*. New York: Russell and Russell, 1965 [1924].

McLeister, Kathleen. *Nineteenth-Century Creole Society of New Orleans: A Cultural Inventory of Aspects of That Society, Final Report*. Prepared for the Jean Lafitte National Historical Park, New Orleans. Wayne, Pa.: K. McLeister, 1987.

McNall, Sally Allen. *Who Is in the House: A Psychological Study of Two Centuries of Women's Fiction in America, 1795 to the Present*. New York: Elsevier North-Holland, 1981.

Malone, Dumas. *Jefferson the President, First Term: 1801–1805*. Boston: Little, Brown, 1970.

Martin, François-Xavier. *The History of Louisiana from the Earliest Period*. New Orleans: J. A. Gresham, 1882.

Martinez, Raymond J. *Pierre George Rousseau, Commanding General of the Galleys of the Mississippi, with Sketches of the Spanish Governors of Louisiana (1777–1803) and Glimpses of Social Life in New Orleans*. New Orleans: Hope, 1965.

Matthews, Glenna. *The Rise of Public Women: Woman's Power and Woman's Place in the United States, 1630–1970*. New York: Oxford University Press, 1992.

Mintz, Steven, and Susan Kellogg. *Domestic Revolutions: A Social History of American Family Life*. New York: Free Press; London: Collier-Macmillan, 1988.

Mitchell, Sally. *The Fallen Angel: Chastity, Class, and Women's Reading, 1835–1880*. Bowling Green, Ohio.: Bowling Green University Popular Press, 1981.

Moore, Sally Falk. *Law As Process: An Anthropological Approach*. London: Routledge and Keagan Paul, 1978.

Mott, Frank Luther. *Golden Multitudes: The Story of Best Sellers in the United States*. New York: Macmillan, 1947.

Nelson, William Edward. *The Literature of American Legal History*. New York: Oceana, 1985.

Nevins, Allan, ed. *American Social History As Recorded by British Travellers*. New York: H. Holt, 1923.

Newmyer, R. Kent. *The Supreme Court under Marshall and Taney*. New York: Crowell, 1968.

Newton, Lewis William. *The Americanization of French Louisiana: A Study of the Process of Adjustment between the French and the Anglo-American Populations of Louisiana, 1803–1860*. New York: Arno, 1980.

Norton, Mary Beth. *Liberty's Daughters: The Revolutionary Experience of American Women, 1750–1800*. Boston: Little, Brown, 1980.

———, and Carol Berkin, eds. *Women of America*. Boston: Houghton Mifflin, 1976.

Nye, Russell B. *Society and Culture in America, 1830–1860*. New York: Harper & Row, 1974.

———. *The Unembarrassed Muse: The Popular Arts in America*. New York: Dial, 1970.

O'Connor, Lillian. *Pioneer Woman Orators: Rhetoric in the Ante-Bellum Reform Movement*. New York: Columbia University Press, 1979 [1954].

Oudard, George. *Four Cents an Acre*. Translated by Margery Bianco. New York: Brewer and Warren, 1931.

Papashvily, Helen Waite. *All the Happy Endings: A Study of the Domestic Novel in America, the Women Who Wrote It, the Women Who Read It, in the Nineteenth Century*. New York: Harper & Brothers, 1956.

Papke, David Ray, ed. *Narrative and the Legal Discourse: A Reader in Storytelling and the Law*. Liverpool: Deborah Charles, 1991.

Parmet, Herbert S., and Marie B. Hecht. *Aaron Burr*. New York: Macmillan, 1967.

Payne, J. Carroll. *A Celebrated Case: The Myra Clark Gaines Litigation*. Atlanta, Ga.: Franklin, n.d.

Pearson, Edmond. *Dime Novels; or, Following an Old Trail in Popular Literature*. Boston: Little, Brown, 1929.

Pease, Jane H., and William H. Pease. *Ladies, Women, and Wenches: Choice and*

Constraint in Antebellum Charleston and Boston. Chapel Hill: University of North Carolina Press, 1990.

Pessen, Edward. *Jacksonian America: Society, Personality, and Politics.* New York: Dorsey Press, 1969.

———. *Riches, Class, and Power before the Civil War.* New York: Heath, 1973.

Peterson, Merrill. *Thomas Jefferson and the New Nation.* New York: Oxford University Press, 1970.

Plunkett, Anna Clyde. *Corridors by Candlelight: A Family Album with Words.* San Antonio, Tex.: Naylor, 1949.

Pound, Roscoe. *The Formative Era of American Law.* Gloucester, Mass.: Peter Smith, 1960 [1930].

———. *Interpretations of Legal History.* New York: Macmillan, 1923.

Pritchard, Walter. *A Bibliography of Louisiana History.* Baton Rouge: Louisiana State University Press, 1936.

Proffatt, John. *Woman before the Law.* New York: G. Putnam's Sons, 1874.

Rabkin, Peggy A. *Fathers to Daughters: The Legal Foundations of Female Emancipation.* Contributions in Legal Studies, #11. Westport, Conn.: Greenwood, 1980.

Radway, Janice A. *Reading the Romance: Women, Patriarchy, and Popular Literature.* Chapel Hill: University of North Carolina Press, 1984.

Reep, Diana. *The Rescue and Romance: Popular Novels before World War I.* Bowling Green, Ky.: Bowling Green State University Popular Press, 1982.

Reinders, Robert C. *End of an Era: New Orleans, 1850–1860.* Gretna, La.: Pelican, 1989.

Robertson, James Alexander. *Louisiana under the Rule of Spain, France, and the United States, 1785–1807: Social, Economic, and Political Conditions of the Territory.* 2 vols. Cleveland, Ohio: Arthur H. Clark, 1911.

Rogers, Katherine, ed. *The Meridian Anthology of American Women Writers: From Anne Bradstreet to Louisa May Alcott, 1650–1865.* New York: Penguin, 1991.

Roman, Alfred. *Military Operations of General Beauregard.* 2 vols. New York: Harper & Brothers, 1884.

Rothman, Ellen K. *Hands and Hearts: A History of Courtship in America.* New York: Basic Books, 1984.

Rugoff, Milton. *America's Gilded Age: Intimate Portraits from an Era of Extravagance and Change, 1850–1890.* New York: Henry Holt, 1989.

Ryan, Mary P. *Cradle of the Middle Class.* Cambridge: Cambridge University Press, 1981.

———. *Womanhood in America: From Colonial Times to the Present.* 2nd rev. ed. New York: New Viewpoints, 1979.

———. *Women in Public: Between Banners and Ballots, 1825–1880.* Baltimore: Johns Hopkins University Press, 1990.

Saum, Lewis O. *The Popular Mood of Pre-Civil War America*. Westport, Conn.: Greenwood, 1980.

Saunders, Robert, Jr. *John Archibald Campbell, Southern Moderate, 1811–1889*. Tuscaloosa: University of Alabama Press, 1997.

Saxon, Lyle. *Fabulous New Orleans*. New York: Century, 1990 [1930].

Schudson, Michael. *Discovering the News: A Social History of American Newspapers*. New York: Basic Books, 1978.

Schuetz, Janice, and Kathryn Holmes Snedaker. *Communication and Litigation: Case Studies of Famous Trials*. Carbondale: Southern Illinois University Press, 1988.

Schwartz, Bernard. *A History of the Supreme Court*. New York: Oxford University Press, 1993.

Scott, Anne Firor. *The Southern Lady: From Pedestal to Politics, 1830–1930*. Chicago: University of Chicago Press, 1970.

Semmes, John E. *John H. B. Latrobe and His Times*. Baltimore: Norman, Remington, 1917.

Semmes, Thomas J. *The Civil Code As Transplanted in Louisiana*. New Orleans: Stansbury and Denis, 1882.

———. *History of the Laws of Louisiana and of the Civil Law*. New Orleans: M. M. Cohen and J. A. Quintero, 1873.

Seward, William Foote, ed. *Binghamton and Broome County, New York: A History*. 2 vols. New York: Lewis Historical Publishing, 1924.

Sexton, Richard. *New Orleans: Elegance and Decadence*. San Francisco: Chronicle Books, 1993.

Shammas, Carole, Marylynn Salmon, and Michel Dahlin. *Inheritance in America: From Colonial Times to the Present*. New Brunswick, N.J.: Rutgers University Press, 1987.

Shreve, Royal Ornan. *The Finished Scoundrel: General James Wilkinson, Sometime Commander-in-Chief of the Army of the United States, Who Made Intrigue a Trade and Terror a Profession*. Indianapolis: Bobbs-Merrill, 1933.

Siegel, Martin. *New Orleans: A Chronological and Documentary History, 1539–1970*. Dobbs Ferry, N.Y.: Oceana, 1975.

Silver, James W. *Edmund Pendleton Gaines, Frontier General*. Baton Rouge: Louisiana State University Press, 1949.

Sinclair, Harold. *The Port of New Orleans*. New York: Doubleday, Doran, 1942.

Sklar, Kathryn Kish. *Catherine Beecher: A Study in American Domesticity*. New Haven, Conn.: Yale University Press, 1973.

Smelser, Marshall. *The Democratic Republic, 1801–1815*. New York: Harper & Row, 1968.

Smith, Charles William. *Roger B. Taney: Jacksonian Jurist*. Chapel Hill: University of North Carolina Press, 1936.

Smith, Justin H. *The War with Mexico.* 2 vols. New York: Macmillan, 1919.

Smith, Merril D. *Breaking the Bonds: Marital Discord in Pennsylvania, 1730–1830.* New York: New York University Press, 1991.

Smith, Virginia Rogers. *Local History Collections for Louisiana Libraries.* Baton Rouge: State Library of Louisiana, 1995.

Smith-Rosenberg, Carroll. *Disorderly Conduct: Visions of Gender in Victorian America.* New York: Oxford University Press, 1985.

Soltow, Lee. *Men and Wealth in the United States, 1850–1870.* New Haven, Conn.: Yale University Press, 1975.

Sterne, Madeline B., ed. *Publishers for Mass Entertainment in Nineteenth-Century America.* Boston: G. K. Hall, 1980.

Stiner, B. C. *Life of Reverdy Johnson.* Baltimore: Norman, Remington, 1914.

Tallant, Robert. *The Romantic New Orleanians.* New York: E. P. Dutton, 1950.

Taylor, Joe Gray. *Louisiana: A Bicentennial History.* New York: Published for the American Association for State and Local History, Nashville, Tenn., by W. W. Norton, 1976.

Taylor, William R. *Cavalier and Yankee: The Old South and American National Character.* New York: Braziller, 1961.

Thernstrom, Stephen, and Richard Sennett, eds. *Nineteenth-Century Cities: Essays in the New Urban History.* New Haven, Conn.: Yale University Press, 1969.

Toledano, Roulhac, and Mary Louise Christovich. *New Orleans Architecture.* Vol. 6, *Faubourg Tremé and the Bayou Road.* Gretna, La.: Pelican, 1980.

Tompkins, Jane P. *Sensational Designs: The Cultural Work of American Fiction, 1790–1860.* New York: Oxford University Press, 1985.

Tooker, Elva. *Nathan Trotter, Philadelphia Merchant, 1787–1853.* Cambridge, Mass.: Harvard University Press, 1955.

Tregle, Joseph G. *Louisiana in the Age of Jackson: A Clash of Cultures and Personalities.* Baton Rouge: *Louisiana State University Press,* 1999.

Wade, Richard C. *The Urban Frontier: The Rise of Western Cities, 1790–1830.* Cambridge, Mass: Harvard University Press, 1959.

Walton, C. S. *The Civil Law in Spain and Spanish America.* Washington, D.C.: Lowdermilk, 1900.

Warbasse, Elizabeth B. *The Changing Legal Rights of Married Women, 1800–1861.* New York: Garland, 1987.

Warner, Sam Bass. *The Private City: Philadelphia in Three Periods of Its Growth.* Philadelphia: University of Pennsylvania Press, 1968.

Warren, Charles. *A History of the American Bar.* New York: H. Fertig, 1966.

———. *The Supreme Court in United States History.* 3 vols. Boston: Little, Brown, 1926.

Weems, John Edward. *Men without Countries: Three Adventurers of the Early Southwest.* New York: Houghton Mifflin, 1969.

Weibel, Kathryn. *Mirror, Mirror: Images of Women Reflected in Popular Literature.* Garden City, N.Y.: Anchor Books, 1977.

Welter, Barbara. *Dimity Convictions: The American Woman in the Nineteenth-Century.* Athens: Ohio University Press, 1976.

Whitaker, Arthur Preston. *The Mississippi Question, 1795–1803: A Study in Trade, Politics, and Diplomacy.* Gloucester, Mass.: Peter Smith, 1962 [1932].

———. *The Spanish Frontier, 1783–1795.* Gloucester, Mass.: Peter Smith, 1962.

Williamson, Jefferson. *The American Hotel: An Anecdotal History.* New York: Knopf, 1930.

Willson, Beckles. *America's Ambassadors to France (1777–1927): A Narrative of Anglo-American Diplomatic Relations.* London: J. Murray, 1928.

Wooster, Ralph A. *The People in Power: Courthouse and Statehouse in the Lower South, 1850–1860.* Knoxville: University of Tennessee Press, 1969.

Wright, Frank. *Two Lands on One Soil: Ulster Politics before Home Rule.* New York: St. Martin's, 1996.

ARTICLES

Abrams, Kathryn. "Hearing the Call of Stories." *California Law Review* 79 (1991): 971–90.

Allen, James Smith. "History and the Novel: *Mentalité* in Modern Popular Fiction." *History and Theory* 22 (1983): 233–52.

Andreano, Ralph. "American Economic Growth before 1840: An Explanatory Essay." In *New Views on American Economic Development,* ed. Ralph Andreano. New York: Schenkman, 1965.

"Ann Sophia Winterbotham Stephens." In *American Women Writers,* vol. 4., ed. Lina Mainiero. New York: Frederick Ungar, 1982.

Arena, Carmelo Richard. "Philadelphia–Spanish New Orleans Trade in the 1790s." *Louisiana History* 2 (1961): 429–45.

Basch, Norma. "Equity vs. Equality: Emerging Concepts of Women's Political Status in the Age of Jackson." *Journal of the Early Republic* 3 (1983): 306–8.

———. "Invisible Women: The Legal Fiction of Marital Unity in Nineteenth-Century America." *Feminist Studies* 5 (1979): 346–66.

Baughman, James P. "Gateway to the Americas." In *The Past As Prelude: New Orleans, 1718–1968,* ed. Hodding Carter. New Orleans: Tulane University, 1968.

Baym, Nina. "Portrayal of Women in American Literature, 1790–1870." In *What Manner of Woman? Essays on English and American Life and Literature,* ed. Marlene Springer. New York: New York University Press, 1977.

"The Beadle Dime Novel." *Publishers' Weekly* 57 (June 16, 1900): 1187–88.

Bispham, Clarence W. "Fray Antonio de Sedella." *Louisiana Historical Quarterly* 2 (1919): 24–37.

———. "New Orleans, a Treasure House for Historians." *Louisiana Historical Quarterly* 2 (1919): 237–47.

Blumin, Stuart M. "The Hypothesis of Middle-Class Formation in Nineteenth-Century America: A Critique and Some Proposals." *American Historical Review* 90 (1985): 299–338.

Bode, Carl. "The Scribbling Women: The Domestic Novel Rules the 'Fifties." In *The Anatomy of American Popular Culture, 1840–1861*, ed. Carl Bode. Berkeley: University of California Press, 1959.

Boyer, Paul S. "Myra Clark Gaines." In *Notable American Women, 1607–1950: A Biographical Dictionary*, ed. Edward T. James, Janet W. James, and Paul S. Boyer. Vol. 2. Cambridge, Mass.: Belknap Press of Harvard University, 1971.

Brown, Herbert Ross. "Home Sweet Home." In *The Sentimental Novel in America, 1789–1860*, ed. Herbert Ross Brown. Durham, N.C.: Duke University Press, 1940.

———. "Sex and Sensibility." In *The Sentimental Novel in America, 1789–1860*, ed. Herbert Ross Brown. Durham, N.C.: Duke University Press, 1940.

Bullard, Henry A. "A Discourse on the Life, Character, and Writings of the Honorable François-Xavier Martin, LL.D." *Louisiana Historical Quarterly* 14 (1936): 45–69.

Burke, Peter. "History of Events and the Revival of Narrative." In *New Perspectives on Historical Writing*, ed. Peter Burke. University Park: Pennsylvania State University Press, 1991.

Canning, Kathleen. "Feminist History after the Linguistic Turn: Historicizing Discourse and Experience." *Signs* 19 (1994): 369–404.

"Cap Français Account of the Fire of 1788, Extracts from the Minutes of November 18, 1896." *Louisiana Historical Quarterly* 1 (1896): 3–6.

Castellanos, Henry C. "Duels and Dueling: The Claiborne-Clark Combat, A Chapter in Louisiana History." *New Orleans Times-Democrat*, Oct. 21, 1894, p. 18.

———. "The Great Gaines Case: As Expounded by the United States Supreme Court: A Thrilling and Surprising Narrative." *New Orleans Times-Democrat*, May 26, 1895, pp. 18–9.

———. "Olden Times: Historical Recollections of Daniel Clark and Alexander Milne." *New Orleans Times-Democrat*, Jan. 13, 1895, pp. 17–8.

Chused, Richard. "Married Women's Property Law: 1800–1850." *Georgetown Law Journal* 71 (1983): 1359–1425.

"Clark, Daniel." *Dictionary of American Biography*, ed. Allen Johnson and Dumas Malone. Vol. 2. New York: Charles Scribner's Sons, 1960.

Cogan, Frances B. "Weak Fathers and Other Beasts: An Examination of the American Male in Domestic Novels, 1850–1870." *American Studies* 25 (1984): 5–20.

Cohen, Daniel. "The Murder of Maria Bickford: Fashion, Passion, and the Birth of a Consumer Culture." *American Studies* 31 (1990): 5–30.

Comaroff, John L. "Foreword." In *Contested States: Law, Hegemony, and Resistance*, ed. Mindie Lazarus-Black and Susan Hirsch. New York: Routledge, 1994.

"Commercial Cities and Towns of the United States: New Orleans and Its Trade and Commerce." *Merchants' Magazine and Commercial Review* (1844): 500–9.

Conway, Jill K. "Utopian Dreams or Dystopian Nightmare? Nineteenth-Century Feminist Ideas about Equality." *Proceedings of the American Antiquarian Society* 96 (1987): 285–94.

Cook, Frank G. "The Marriage Celebration in the United States." *Atlantic Monthly* 61 (1888): 521–9.

Cott, Nancy. "Divorce and the Changing Status of Women in Eighteenth-Century Massachusetts." *William and Mary Quarterly* 33 (1976): 598–610.

Cowie, Alexander. "The Domestic Sentimentalists and Other Popular Writers (1850–1870)." In *The Rise of the American Novel*, ed. Alexander Cowie. New York: American Book, 1948.

———. "The Vogue of the Domestic Novel, 1850–1870." *South Atlantic Quarterly* 41 (1942): 416–24.

Cox, I. J. "General Wilkinson and His Later Intrigues with the Spaniards." *American Historical Review* 19 (1913–14): 794–812.

———. "Hispanic American Phases of the Burr Conspiracy." *Hispanic-American Historical Review* 12 (1932): 146–75.

———. "Jefferson and Wilkinson." *Mississippi Valley Historical Review* 1 (1914): 212–39.

Curry, Leonard P. "Urbanization and Urbanism in the Old South: A Comparative View." *Journal of Southern History* 40 (1974): 43–60.

Curti, Merle. "Dime Novels and the American Tradition." *Yale Review* 26 (1937): 761–78.

Dart, Henry P. "The History of the Supreme Court of Louisiana." *Louisiana Historical Quarterly* 4 (1921): 14–71.

———. "Influence of the Ancient Laws of Spain on the Jurisprudence of Louisiana." *American Bar Association Journal* 18 (1932): 125–9.

———. "The Place of the Civil Law in Louisiana." *Tulane Law Review* 4 (1930): 163–77.

———. "The Sources of the Civil Code of Louisiana." *Report of the Louisiana Bar Association* 13 (1911).

Dart, William K. "The Justices of the Supreme Court." *Louisiana Historical Quarterly* 4 (1921): 113–24.

———. "The Louisiana Judicial System." *Louisiana Digest Annotated* 1 (Indianapolis, 1917): 21–43.

Davidson, Cathy N. "Mothers and Daughters in the Fiction of the New Republic." In *The Lost Tradition: Mothers and Daughters in Literature*, ed. Cathy N. Davidson and E. M. Broner. New York: Frederick Ungar, 1980.

Davies, Tony. "Transports of Pleasure: Fiction and Its Audiences in the Later Nineteenth Century." In *Formations of Pleasure*. London: Routledge and Keagan Paul, 1983.

"Davis, Samuel B." *Historical and Biographical Encyclopedia of Delaware.* Wilmington, 1882: 321.

De Rojas, Lauro A. "The Great Fire of 1788 in New Orleans." *Louisiana Historical Quarterly* 20 (1937): 578–81.

Duffy, John. "Pestilence in New Orleans." In *The Past As Prelude: New Orleans, 1718–1968,* ed. Hodding Carter. New Orleans: Tulane University, 1968.

Eley, Geoff. "Nations, Publics, and Political Cultures: Placing Habermas in the Nineteenth Century." In *Culture/Power/History: A Reader in Contemporary Social Theory,* ed. Nicolas B. Dirks, et al., Chapter 10. Princeton, N.J.: Princeton University Press, 1994.

"A Faithful Picture of the Political Situation of New Orleans, at the Close of the Last and Beginning of the Present Year, 1807," ed. James Wilson. *Louisiana Historical Quarterly* 11 (1928): 359–433.

Faye, Stanley. "Privateers of Guadeloupe and their Establishment in Barataria." *Louisiana Historical Quarterly* 23 (1940): 428–44.

Filler, Louis. "Mary Edwards Walker." *Notable American Women, 1607–1950: A Biographical Dictionary,* ed. Edward T. James, Janet W. James, and Paul S. Boyer. Vol. 3. Cambridge, Mass.: Belknap Press of Harvard University, 1971.

Fischer, David Hackett. "The Braided Narrative: Substance and Form in Social History." In *The Literature of Fact: Selected Papers from the English Institute,* ed. Angus Fletcher. New York: Columbia University Press, 1976.

Fitch, James M. "Creole Architecture, 1718–1860: The Rise and Fall of a Great Tradition." In *The Past As Prelude: New Orleans, 1718–1968,* ed. Hodding Carter. New Orleans: Tulane University, 1968.

"Forum. Beyond Roles, Beyond Spheres: Thinking about Gender in the Early Republic." *William and Mary Quarterly* 46 (1989): 565–85.

Fox, Richard Wightman. "Intimacy on Trial: Cultural Meanings of the Beecher-Tilton Affair." In *The Power of Culture: Critical Essays in American History,* ed. Richard Wightman Fox and T. J. Jackson Lears. Chicago: University of Chicago Press, 1993.

Frederick, John T. "Hawthorne's 'Scribbling Women.'" *New England Quarterly* 48 (1975): 231–40.

Friedman, Lawrence M. "Law, Lawyers, and Popular Culture." *Yale Law Journal* 98 (1989): 1579–1606.

"The Gaines Case." *Virginia Historical Register* 1 (1848): 43.

"Gaines, Edmund Pendleton." *Dictionary of American Biography,* ed. Allen Johnson and Dumas Malone. Vol. 4. New York: Charles Scribner's Sons, 1960.

Galpin, William Freeman. "The Grain Trade of New Orleans, 1804–1814." *Mississippi Valley Historical Review* 14 (1928): 496–507.

Gayarré, Charles. "The New Orleans Bench and Bar in 1823." *Harper's Monthly Magazine* 78 (1888): 889–900.

Geary, Susan. "The Domestic Novel As a Commercial Commodity: Making a Best

Seller in the 1850s." *Papers of the Bibliographical Society of America* 70 (1976): 365–95.

Gilfoyle, Timothy J. "The Hearts of Nineteenth-Century Men: Bigamy and Working-Class Marriage in New York City, 1800–1890." In *Prospects: An Annual of American Cultural Studies*, ed. Jack Salzman, vol. 19. Cambridge: Cambridge University Press, 1995.

Ginzburg, Carlo. "The Judge and the Historian." *Critical Inquiry* 18 (1991): 79–92.

Griswold, Robert L. "Law, Sex, Cruelty, and Divorce in Victorian America, 1840–1900." *American Quarterly* 38 (1986): 721–45.

Grossberg, Michael. "Battling over Motherhood in Philadelphia: A Study of Antebellum American Trial Courts As Arenas of Conflict." In *Contested States: Law, Hegemony, and Resistance*, ed. Mindie Lazarus-Black and Susan F. Hirsch. New York: Routledge, 1994.

———. "Crossing Boundaries: Nineteenth-Century Domestic Relations Law and the Merger of Family and Legal History." *American Bar Foundation Research Journal* 4 (1985): 819–32.

———. "Guarding the Altar: Physiological Restrictions and the Rise of State Intervention in Matrimony." *American Journal of Legal History* 26 (1982): 197–226.

———. "Who Gets the Child? Custody, Guardianship, and the Rise of a Judicial Patriarchy in Nineteenth-Century America." *Feminist Studies* 9 (1983): 235–60.

Gunderson, Joan R. "Independence, Citizenship, and the American Revolution." *Signs* 13 (1987): 59–77.

Hall, Stuart. "Notes on Deconstructing 'the popular.'" In *People's History and Socialist Theory*, ed. Raphael Samuel. London: Routledge and Keagan Paul, 1981.

Harris, Launcelot Minor. "The Creoles of New Orleans." *Southern Collegians*. Washington and Lee University, Jan. 1898: 1–12.

Hart, James D. "Home Influence." In *The Popular Book: A History of America's Literary Taste*, ed. James D. Hart. New York: Oxford University Press, 1950.

Hartog, Hendrik. "Mrs. Packard on Dependency." *Yale Journal of Law and the Humanities* 1 (1988): 79–103.

Harvey, Charles M. "The Dime Novel in American Life." *Atlantic Monthly* 100 (July 1907): 37–45.

Hay, Thomas R. "Charles Williamson and the Burr Conspiracy." *Journal of Southern History* 2 (1936): 183–96.

———. "Some Reflections on the Career of General James Wilkinson." *Mississippi Valley Historical Review* 21 (1935): 471–94.

Herbert, Jacob. "The Elusive Shadow of the Law." *Law and Society Review* 26 (1992): 565–90.

"History and Incidents of the Plague in New Orleans." *Harper's Magazine* 7 (1853): 797–806.

Hofstader, Beatrice. "Popular Culture and the Romantic Heroine." *American Scholar* 30 (1960–61): 98–116.

Hogeland, Ronald W. "The Female Appendage: Feminine Life-Styles in America, 1820–1860." *Civil War History* 17 (1971): 101–14.

Holden, Walter S. "Three Generations of Romance and Litigation: The Celebrated Gaines Will Cases." *Illinois Law Review* (1917): 464–88.

Holmes, Jack D. L. "Some Economic Problems of Spanish Governors of Louisiana." *Hispanic- American Historical Review* 42 (1962): 521–43.

Howe, Daniel Walker. "American Victorianism As a Culture." *American Quarterly* 27 (1975): 507–32.

Howe, William Wirt. "Memoir on François-Xavier Martin." Preface to François-Xavier Martin, *The History of Louisiana from the Earliest Period*. New Orleans: J. A. Gresham, 1882.

Ireland, Gordon. "Louisiana's Legal System Reappraised." *Tulane Law Review* 11 (1937): 585–98.

Jackson, Bernard. "Narrative Theories and Legal Discourse." In *Narrative in Culture: The Uses of Storytelling in the Sciences, Philosophy, and Literature*, ed. Christopher Nash. New York: Routledge, 1990.

Jameson, Fredric. "Ideology, Narrative Analysis, and Popular Culture." *Theory and Society* 4 (1977): 543–59.

———. "Magical Narratives: Romance As a Genre." *New Literary History* 7 (1975): 135–63.

Jenks, George C. "Dime Novel Makers." *Bookman* 20 (1904): 108–14.

Johnson, Jerah. "Colonial New Orleans: A Fragment of the Eighteenth-Century French Ethos." In *Creole New Orleans: Race and Americanization*, ed. Arnold R. Hirsch and Joseph Logsdon. Baton Rouge: Louisiana State University Press, 1992.

Jones, Betty H., and Alberta Arthurs. "The American Eve: A New Look at American Heroines and Their Critics." *International Journal of Women's Studies* 1 (1978): 1–12.

"Justice James Wayne." *Southern Quarterly Review* 16 (1850): 497–503.

Katz, Michael. "The Politics of Law in Colonial America: Controversies over Chancery Courts and Equity Law in the Eighteenth Century." *American Historical Review* 97 (1992): 257–84.

Keidel, George. "Catonsville Biographies." *Maryland Historical Magazine* 17 (1922): 74–89.

Kelley, Mary. "The Literary Domestics: Private Woman on a Public Stage." In *Ideas in America's Cultures*, ed. Hamilton Cravens. Ames: Iowa State University Press, 1982.

———. "The Sentimentalists: Promise and Betrayal in the Home." *Signs* 4 (1979): 434–46.

Kendall, John Smith. "According to the Code." *Louisiana Historical Quarterly* 23 (1940): 445–70.

———. "Early New Orleans Newspapers." *Louisiana Historical Quarterly* 10 (1927): 383–401.

———. "The Humors of the Duello." *Louisiana Historical Quarterly* 23 (1940): 443–70.

———. "The Strange Case of Myra Clark Gaines." *Louisiana Historical Quarterly* 20 (1937): 3–40.

Kerber, Linda. "Separate Spheres, Female Worlds, Woman's Place: The Rhetoric of Women's History." *Journal of American History* 75 (1988): 9–39.

Kiefer, Sister Monica. "Early American Childhood in the Middle Atlantic Area." *Pennsylvania Magazine of History and Biography* 68 (1944): 3–37.

Korobkin, Laura Hanft. "The Maintenance of Mutual Confidence: Sentimental Strategies at the Adultery Trial of Henry Ward Beecher." *Yale Journal of Law and the Humanities* 7 (1995): 1–48.

Lachance, Paul F. "Intermarriage and French Cultural Persistence in Late Spanish and Early American New Orleans." *Histoire-Sociale/Social History* 15 (1982): 47–81.

Laycock, Douglas. "The Triumph of Equity." *Law and Contemporary Problems* 56 (1993): 51–82.

Lears, T. Jackson. "The Concept of Cultural Hegemony: Possibilities and Problems." *American Historical Review* 90 (1985): 567–93.

LeBreton, Dagmar R. "Orestes Brownson's Visit to New Orleans in 1855." *American Literature* 16 (May 1944): 89–95.

Lerner, Gerda. "The Lady and the Mill Girl: Changes in the Status of Women in the Age of Jackson." *Midcontinent American Studies Journal* 10 (1969): 5–15.

Levi, Giovanni. "Microhistory." In *New Perspectives on Historical Writing,* ed. Peter Burke. University Park: Pennsylvania State University Press, 1992.

McLemore, Richard Aubrey. "Jeffersonian Diplomacy in the Purchase of Louisiana, 1803." *Louisiana Historical Quarterly* 18 (1935): 346–53.

Manthorne, Jane. "The Lachrymose Ladies." *Horn Book* 43 (June 1967): 375–84; (Aug. 1967): 501–13; (Oct. 1967): 622–30.

Marine, William B. "Bombardment of Lewes by the British, April 6 and 7, 1813." *Papers of the Historical Society of Delaware* 33 (1901): 3–41.

Meader, Louis J. "Dueling in Old Creole Days." *Century Magazine* 74 (1907): 15–21.

Megill, Alan. "Recounting the Past: 'Description,' Explanation, and Narrative in Historiography." *American Historical Review* 94 (1989): 627–53.

"Merrick, Edwin Thomas." *Dictionary of American Biography,* ed. Allen Johnson and Dumas Malone. Vol. 4. New York: Charles Scribner's Sons, 1960.

Merry, Sally Engle. "Courts As Performances: Domestic Violence Hearings in a Hawaii Family Court." In *Contested States: Law, Hegemony, and Resistance,* ed. Mindie Lazarus-Black and Susan Hirsch. New York: Routledge, 1994.

Minow, Martha. "'Forming Underneath Everything That Grows': Toward a History of Family Law." *Wisconsin Law Review* 4 (1985): 819–98.

Mitchell, Harry A. "Development of New Orleans As a Wholesale Trading Center." *Louisiana Historical Quarterly* 27 (1944): 933–63.

Mohl, Raymond. "The History of the American City." In *The Reinterpretation of American History and Culture,* ed. William H. Cartwright and Richard L. Watson. Washington, D.C.: National Council for the Social Studies, 1973.

"Mrs. Myra Clark Gaines." *Harper's Bazaar.* Feb. 7, 1885, 99.

"Myra Clark Gaines." *New Orleans Short Stories* 1 (1932): 22–7.

Nash, Gary B. "The Philadelphia Bench and Bar, 1800–1861." *Comparative Studies in Society and History* 7 (1965): 203–20.

"Noblesse Oblige: Report of Governor Esteban Miró and Intendant Martin Navarro on the Fire . . . March 21, 1788." *Louisiana Historical Quarterly* 8 (1914–15): 56–63.

Nye, Russell B. "The Novel As Dream and Weapon: Women's Popular Novels in the 19th Century." *Historical Society of Michigan Chronicle* 11 (1975): 2–16.

Packard, Joseph. "General Walter Jones." *Virginia Law Register* 8 (1901): 233–8.

Pessen, Edward. "The Distribution of Wealth in the Era of the Civil War." *Reviews in American History* 4 (1976): 222–9.

———. "The Egalitarian Myth and American Social Reality: Wealth, Mobility, and Quality in the 'Era of the Common Man.'" *American Historical Review* 76 (1971): 989–1034.

———. "The Lifestyle of the Antebellum Urban Elite." *Mid-America* 55 (1973): 163–83.

———. "Philip Hone's Set: The Social World of the New York City Elite in the 'Age of Egalitarianism.'" *New York Historical Society Quarterly* 56 (1972): 285–308.

Pierson, George W. "The M-Factor in American History." *American Quarterly* 14 (1962): 275–89.

Pritchard, Walter. "An Account of the Conflagration, 1788." *Louisiana Historical Quarterly* 20 (1937): 582–9.

———. "Selecting a Governor for the Territory of New Orleans." *Louisiana Historical Quarterly* 31 (1948): 269–393.

———. "Some Interesting Glimpses of Louisiana a Century Ago." *Louisiana Historical Quarterly* 24 (1941): 35–49.

Pusey, Pennock. "History of Lewes, Delaware." *Papers of the Historical Society of Delaware* 38 (1903): 3–37.

Rader, Perry Scott. "The Romance of the American Courts: Gaines vs. New Orleans." *Louisiana Historical Quarterly* 27 (1944): 5–322.

Ralph, Julian. "New Orleans, Our Southern Capital." *Harper's New Monthly Magazine* 86 (1892): 364–5.

Rhodes, Albert. "Louisiana Creoles." *Galaxy: An Illustrated Magazine of Entertaining Reading* 10 (1873): 254–60.

"The Romance of the Great Gaines Case: A Lifetime Lawsuit." *Putnam's Magazine: Original Papers on Literature, Science, Art, and National Interests*. New Series. 2 (1868): 201–11.

Rosaldo, Michelle. "The Use and Abuse of Anthropology: Reflections on Feminism and Cross-Cultural Understanding." *Signs*, supp. 5 (1980): 389–417.

———. "Women, Culture, and Society: A Theoretical Overview." In *Women, Culture, and Society*, ed. Michelle Rosaldo and Louise Lamphere. Stanford, Cal.: Stanford University Press, 1974.

Ruoff, John C. "Frivolity to Consumption; or, Southern Womanhood in Antebellum Literature." *Civil War History* 18 (1972): 212–29.

S. "The Gaines Case." *Southern Quarterly Review* 9 (Apr. 1854): 273–300.

Scott, Joan. "Women's History." In *New Perspectives on Historical Writing*, ed. Peter Burke. University Park: Pennsylvania State University Press, 1991.

Sewell, William H., Jr. "Narratives and Social Identities." *Social Science History* 16 (1992): 479–88.

Shepherd, William R. "Papers Bearing on James Wilkinson's Relations with Spain, 1787–1789." *American Historical Review* 9 (1904): 748–57.

———. "Wilkinson and the Beginnings of the Spanish Conspiracy." *American Historical Review* 9 (1904): 490–506.

———. "Wilkinson's Second Memorial, New Orleans, September 17, 1789." *American Historical Review* 9 (1904): 751–66.

Smith, Henry Nash. "The Scribbling Women and the Cosmic Success Story." *Critical Inquiry* 1 (1974): 47–70.

Smith, Leslie. "Through Rose-Colored Glasses: Some American Victorian Sentimental Novels." In *New Dimensions in Popular Culture*, ed. Russell B. Nye. Bowling Green, Ohio.: Bowling Green University Popular Press, 1972.

Smith-Rosenberg, Carroll. "Sex As Symbol in Victorian Purity: An Ethnohistorical Analysis of Jacksonian America." *American Journal of Sociology* 84 (1978): 212–47.

Snedaker, Kathryn Holmes. "Storytelling in Opening Statements: Framing the Argumentation of the Trial." *American Journal of Trial Advocacy* 10 (1986): 15–45.

Stanford, Ann. "Images of Women in Early American Literature." In *What Manner of Woman? Essays on English and American Life and Literature*, ed. Marlene Springer, 184–210. New York: New York University Press, 1977.

Stein, Stuart J. "Common-Law Marriage: Its History and Certain Contemporary Problems." *Journal of Family Law* 9 (1969): 271–99.

Stirling, A. M. W. "A Transatlantic Invasion of 1816." *The Nineteenth Century and Afterwards* 39 (1909): 1058–75.

Stone, Ferdinand. "The Law with a Difference and How It Came About." In *The Past As Prelude: New Orleans, 1718–1968,* ed. Hodding Carter. New Orleans: Tulane University, 1968.

Stone, Lawrence. "Revival of Narrative: Reflections on an Old New History." *Past and Present* 85 (1979): 3–24.

Taylor, Georgia Fairbanks. "The Early History of the Episcopal Church in New Orleans, 1805–1840." *Louisiana Historical Quarterly* 22 (1939): 432–59.

Teitelbaum, Lee. "Family History and Family Law." *Wisconsin Law Review* (1985): 1135–81.

Tregle, Joseph G., Jr. "Creoles and Americans." In *Creole New Orleans: Race and Americanization,* ed. Arnold R. Hirsch and Joseph Logsdon. Baton Rouge: Louisiana State University Press, 1992.

———. "Early New Orleans Society: A Reappraisal." *Journal of Southern History* 18 (1952): 21–36.

Tucker, John H., Jr. "Source Books of Louisiana Law." *Tulane Law Review* 8 (1934): 396–405.

T. W. "Our Millionaires." *Galaxy: An Illustrated Magazine of Entertaining Reading* 5 (1868): 529–35.

Veeder, Van Vetchen. "A Century of Federal Judicature." *Green Bag* 15 (1903): 136–45.

Voloshin, Beverly R. "The Limits of Domesticity: The Female *Bildungsroman* in America, 1820–1870." *Woman's Studies* 10 (1984): 283–302.

Walters, Ronald. "The Family and Antebellum Reform: An Interpretation." *Societies* 3 (1973): 87–104.

Wellborn, Alfred T. "The Relations between New Orleans and Latin America, 1810–1824." *Louisiana Historical Quarterly* 22 (1939): 710–94.

Welter, Barbara. "The Cult of True Womanhood: 1800–1860." *American Quarterly* 18 (1966): 151–74.

Whitaker, Arthur Preston. "James Wilkinson's First Descent to New Orleans in 1787." *Hispanic- American Historical Review* 8 (1928): 82–97.

———. "Reed and Forde: Merchant Adventurers of Philadelphia, Their Trade with Spanish New Orleans." *Pennsylvania Magazine of History and Biography* 61 (1937): 231–9.

White, G. Edward. "The Appellate Court Opinion As Historical Source Material." *Journal of Interdisciplinary History* 1 (1971): 491–509.

Wigmore, John H. "Louisiana: The Story of Its Legal System." *Southern Law Quarterly* 1 (1916): 1–15.

Winslow, Ola Elizabeth. "Books for the Lady Reader, 1820–1860." In *Romanticism in America: Papers Contributed to a Symposium Held at the Baltimore Museum of Art, May 13–15, 1940,* ed. George Boas. Baltimore: Johns Hopkins Press, 1940.

Winston, James E. "Notes on the Economic History of New Orleans, 1803–1836." *Mississippi Valley Historical Review* 2 (1924): 200–26.

Wohl, Michael. "Not Yet Saint nor Sinner: A Further Note on Daniel Clark." *Louisiana History* 24 (1983): 195–205.

"Women As Lawyers." *Lippincott's Magazine* 5 (Mar. 1879): 386–8.

Wood, Ann Douglas. "The 'Scribbling Women' and Fanny Fern: Why Women Wrote." *American Quarterly* 23 (1971): 5–13.

Wood, Minter. "Life in New Orleans in the Spanish Period." *Louisiana Historical Quarterly* 22 (1939): 642–709.

Young, A. D. "A Romance of the Courts." *Green Bag* 18 (1904): 91–4.

Zacharie, James E. "New Orleans, Its Old Streets and Places." *Louisiana Historical Quarterly* 2 (1900): 45–88.

Zaeske, Susan. "The 'Promiscuous Audience' Controversy and the Emergence of the Early Woman's Rights Movement." *Quarterly Journal of Speech* 81 (1995): 191–207.

Index

In this index, *Myra* refers to Myra Clark Gaines. *Zulime* refers to Zulime Carrière.

before U.S. Supreme Court, 142–4, 144n30; compared with sentimental novels, 144–9, 179, 182; fictionalized account of, 147–8, 198; Edmund Gaines's involvement in, 154, 155, 168–9; before U.S. Supreme Court in 1841 and 1844, 165, 169, 217–8; and Caroline DesGrange Barnes, 166, 175; *Barnes v. Gaines,* 167–9, 169n25; and Myra's presentation to Louisiana jury, 167–9; Myra as "universal heir" under Clark's 1813 will, 169, 217–9, 226; *Patterson v. Gaines,* 169–70, 172, 173, 175, 181–92, 204, 205, 207, 208, 211, 212, 218, 226; depositions for, in 1849, 193; *Gaines v. Relf, Chew, and Others* (1850) in U.S. Circuit Court, 198–207, 218, 225; Latin certificate in 1850 trial, 198, 200; mutilated record in 1850 trial, 198, 199–200, 203; *Gaines v. Relf, Chew, and Others* appeal (1852) in U.S. Supreme Court, 207–13, 214, 217, 218, 222, 225; Myra's petition of 1855 to, for probate of Clark's 1813 will in Second District Court of New Orleans, 218–20; involvement of City of New Orleans in, 219, 222, 232, 237–9, 241–2; Lea's impartiality in, 219; Myra's appeal in 1855 to Louisiana Supreme Court on probate of Clark's 1813 will, 220–2, 235; *Gaines v. Hennen* before U.S. Supreme Court (1861), 222, 224–7, 232, 235, 237–8; Myra's claims against all purchasers of Clark property in 1850s, 222, 226, 230–2; *Myra Clark Gaines v. John M. Brown* (1861), 230; *Gaines v. Fuentes,* 231n41; *Gaines v. Delacroix* (1865), 232; *Gaines v. The City of New Orleans* (1865) in U.S. Circuit Court, 232; *Gaines v. The City of New Orleans* (1867) in U.S. Supreme Court, 232, 233–5, 238–9; after Myra's death, 241–3. *See also* Gaines, Myra Clark

Gaines v. Delacroix (1865), 232

Gaines v. Fuentes, 231n41
Gaines v. Hennen (1861), 222, 224–7, 232, 235, 237–8
Gaines v. Relf, Chew, and Others: ecclesiastical record in, 90–2, 198–9, 203; Latin certificate in, 198, 200; mutilated record in, 198, 199–200, 203; witnesses in, 200–3; attorneys' arguments in, 203–5; in U.S. Circuit Court in 1850, 203–7, 218, 225; decision on, in U.S. Circuit Court, 205–7, 225; appeal of, to U.S. Supreme Court in 1852, 207–13, 214, 217, 222; in U.S. Supreme Court, 207–13, 214, 217, 218, 225; decision on, in U.S. Supreme Court, 208–13, 217, 225; dissents to opinion of U.S. Supreme Court, 212–3
Gaines v. The City of New Orleans: in U.S. Circuit Court in 1865, 232; in U.S. Supreme Court in 1867, 232, 233–5, 238–9
Gallatin, Albert, 93
Gálvez, Bernardo de, 66n6, 67n8
Gambling, 40, 41, 60
Gannett, Deborah Sampson, 159
Gardette, James (husband of Zulime), 85, 123–4, 183–4, 188, 193–4, 196–7, 204, 206–7, 234
Gardette, James (son of Zulime), 124, 194, 200, 219, 220
Gardette, Zulime. *See* Carrière, Zulime
Gardoqui, Diego, 67–8
Gayoso (de Lemos), Manuel, 75, 76
Gehman, Mary, 79n29
Georgia, 210, 228
Gibbs, George, 209
Gothic or melodramatic novels, 146–7
Graham, John, 109
Grant, Ulysses S., 235
Great Britain: and trade with New Orleans, 48, 66, 67, 95, 112; colonies of, 65n4, 86; and navigation of Mississippi River, 67n8; Spanish fear of, 69, 74n20; Spain's maritime war with, 75; and Peace of Amiens, 87; and Burr's schemes in Louisiana, 110; American women married to British